# Local and Urban Governance

**Series Editor**

Carlos Nunes Silva, LISBOA, Portugal

This series contains research studies with policy relevance in the field of sub-national territorial governance, at the micro, local and regional levels, as well as on its connections with national and supranational tiers. The series is multidisciplinary and brings together innovative research from different areas within the Social Sciences and Humanities. The series is open for theoretical, methodological and empirical ground breaking contributions. Books included in this series explore the new modes of territorial governance, new perspectives and new research methodologies. The aim is to present advances in Governance Studies to scholars and researchers in universities and research organizations, and to policy makers worldwide. The series includes monographs, edited volumes and textbooks. Book proposals and final manuscripts are peer-reviewed.

The areas covered in the series include but are not limited to the following subjects:

- Local and regional government
- Urban and metropolitan governance
- Multi-level territorial governance
- Post-colonial local governance
- Municipal merger reforms
- Inter-municipal cooperation
- Decentralized cooperation
- Governance of spatial planning
- Strategic spatial planning
- Citizen participation in local policies
- Local governance, spatial justice and the right to the city
- Local public services
- Local economic development policies
- Entrepreneurialism and municipal public enterprises
- Local government finance
- Local government and sustainable development
- Anthropocene and green local governance
- Climate change and local governance
- Smart local governance

The series is intended for geographers, planners, political scientists, sociologists, lawyers, historians, urban anthropologists and economists. **Local and Urban Governance—now indexed in Scopus**

Francisco Velasco Caballero
Martin Burgi • Karl Kössler
Editors

# Municipal Tasks and Financing

## An Urban-Rural Perspective

Springer

*Editors*
Francisco Velasco Caballero
Faculty of Law
Universidad Autónoma de Madrid
Madrid, Spain

Martin Burgi
Faculty of Law
LMU Munich
München, Germany

Karl Kössler
Institute for Comparative Federalism
Eurac Research
Bolzano, Italy

ISSN 2524-5449 ISSN 2524-5457 (electronic)
Local and Urban Governance
ISBN 978-3-031-99811-9 ISBN 978-3-031-99812-6 (eBook)
https://doi.org/10.1007/978-3-031-99812-6



This Springer imprint is published by the registered company Springer Nature Switzerland AG
The registered company address is: Gewerbestrasse 11, 6330 Cham, Switzerland

# Acknowledgement

This project has received funding from the European Union's Horizon 2020 research and innovation programme under grant agreement No 823961.

# Contents

# Chapter 1
# Tasks and Financing of Urban and Rural Local Governments: Four Issues in Focus

**Martin Burgi and Francisco Velasco Caballero**

**Abstract** The laws regulating local government powers and services, as well as their financing, tend to be uniform within each country, paying no particular attention to the size of municipalities or the urban or rural nature of local governments. However, beneath this legal uniformity lies a very diverse practical reality. Only large urban municipalities can provide certain services (such as public transit) that require extensive infrastructure, high technical capacity and substantial funding. In addition, rural municipalities face great difficulties in the indirect management of services (through contracts with companies) due to their limited capacity to define contractual relationships and monitor compliance. This technical difficulty is particularly evident in public private partnerships (PPPs), which are unaffordable for rural municipalities. Similarly, although local financing laws usually offer a uniform system for all municipalities, in practice the financial sources of urban and rural municipalities are very diverse. Urban municipalities can obtain significant revenue from their own taxes and fees, with regional or state financial transfers playing a complementary role. In contrast, rural municipalities are more dependent on transfers. This explains why, in some countries, supra-local financial transfers include levelling or equalization instruments for the benefit of rural municipalities.

**Keywords** Municipal tasks · municipal services · public private partnerships · local financing · equalization · local fees

The Horizon 2020 project on "Local Government and the Changing Urban-Rural Interplay – LoGov" brought together 18 partner institutions from six continents, combining expertise in public law, political science, public administration, and

M. Burgi
Public Law, Business Administrative Law, Environmental and Social Security Law, Ludwig-Maximilians-Universität München, Munich, Germany
e-mail: martin.burgi@jura.uni-muenchen.de

F. Velasco Caballero (✉)
Institute of Local Government Law, Autonomous University of Madrid, Madrid, Spain
e-mail: francisco.velasco@uam.es



F. Velasco Caballero et al. (eds.), *Municipal Tasks and Financing*, Local and Urban Governance, https://doi.org/10.1007/978-3-031-99812-6_1

economics. The aim is to provide solutions for local governments in order to address the changing urban-rural interplay and manage its impacts.

The chapters in this edited book focus on issues related to the tasks and financing of urban and rural local governments, i.e. the tasks that urban and rural local governments perform, their ways of public service provision, financial equalization between urban and rural local governments and the use of special fees and user charges as alternative sources of local revenue.

The case studies included in this volume, conducted across multiple countries, underscore the extensive geographical breadth of the LoGov project. While some of the core themes explored have been previously addressed in scholarly literature, the distinct contribution of this edited collection lies in its global comparative scope. To expand the analytical horizon, it includes lesser-known cases which have so far been understudied in relation to classical European cases. Anchored in a comparative framework, the volume adopts a multiple case study design (Yin, 2003, 56). This enables a systematic cross-case analysis while preserving the integrity of intra-case specificity. The aim is to identify convergences and divergences in how comparable governance challenges are addressed across different institutional, legal, and socio-political contexts, and to assess the potential for policy transfer and contextual adaptation.

Methodologically, the chapters enhance the credibility and robustness of their findings by using, to the extent possible in each case, multiple data sources (Patton, 2002, 38). Each case study endeavors to integrate multiple sources of evidence, contingent upon contextual feasibility and data accessibility. The interdisciplinary character of the volume—drawing upon the expertise of scholars specialized in public law, political science, and public administration—facilitates a methodologically pluralistic approach. Data sources include but are not limited to statutory and constitutional texts, judicial decisions, statistical data, reports issued by governmental and non-governmental organizations, and peer-reviewed publications from the three above-mentioned disciplinary fields.

While desk research has played a key role, our authors have, to varying degrees, also engaged in original field research. This includes, in particular, semi-structured interviews with local government stakeholders, conducted within the framework of the LoGov project's country reports,[1] which are referenced in the chapters where analytically pertinent. The synthesis of data from these diverse sources enables each case study to deliver a multidimensional analysis, enhancing descriptive richness, mitigating single-source bias, and producing robust, triangulated findings concerning the four salient issues identified above. These four overarching topics and their respective research questions structure the chapters assembled in this edited book.

[1] https://www.logov-rise.eu/country-map/

## 1.1 Tasks of Urban and Rural Local Governments

Local governments are facing complex issues. As institutions closest to citizens, they are, among other things, expected to respond to the consequences of rural exodus, agglomeration, and demographic change (Reschl, 2007, 295). Nevertheless, the changing conditions affect urban and rural local governments differently. For example, economically strong regions will be affected later and to a lesser extent by demographic change (Reschl, 2007, 297). After all, if employment prospects decline, many young workers will move out of rural local governments, leaving behind an aging population (Accordino, 2019, 218). In return, the availability of affordable housing or the preference of living close to nature are important factors leading people to move into suburban or rural areas (Gall-Roehrig et al., 2022, 159). In contrast, major cities are experiencing significant population growth and are expanding geographically. In a self-reinforcing pattern, more businesses offering innovative services are thus pushing into metropolitan areas to take advantage of this pooled influx of talented workers, thereby raising housing costs and leading to increased traffic (Accordino, 2019, 218). At the same time, as a result of rapid urbanization, the urban fringe or edge tends to move further outward into formerly rural areas. In larger functional city-regions, it is important to have a strategic metropolitan or city-regional governance structure to coordinate and ensure a coherent and effective approach to cross-border infrastructure, services, and policies among the individual local authorities (Simon, 2021, 1–2).

Overall, in terms of population and size of their territory, local governments are significantly diverse (Kuhlmann & Schwab, 2017, 29). At the same time, the capability of local governments to provide local services of general interest to their citizens and to take on new tasks are closely related to their territorial viability. In general, large (urban) local governments are more efficient, have more professional administrations, and tend to be in a better position to generate cost savings due to economies of scale (Kuhlmann et al., 2022, 4). This heterogeneity confronts the legislator with challenges in allocating tasks to local governments. It is important to ensure that only those tasks are transferred to local authorities for which the administrative power required to perform them can be guaranteed (Ruge & Ritge, 2021, 128–129). Therefore, the question arises as to which criteria should be applied when allocating responsibilities among local governments, taking into account the differences between urban and rural local governments. This issue will be addressed in the first chapter of this book.

Even if the *law* in many countries does not distinguish between urban and rural local governments when allocating tasks, the public services provided will likely differ in *fact* due to varying needs and demands. A striking example of the different challenges faced by rural and urban local governments in providing public services is public transport. Mobility demands are constantly growing which results in increasing individual traffic (Reschl, 2007, 295). Therefore, public transport plays an important role in shaping future living and working conditions, as well as in achieving climate protection goals (Dorsch, 2023, 91). In large cities and metropolitan areas, demand for public transportation can be expected to remain high in the future (Dorsch, 2023, 88). In contrast, many rural local governments are not properly connected to public transportation due to various economic and physical challenges in coordinating and providing rural transportation services (Babío et al., 2023, 5). The dependency on cars is higher in rural local governments. This has an effect on urban local governments since a large number of people commute to cities by car every day (Babío et al., 2023, 4). For the development of rural local governments located far from employment opportunities, a good connection to the city is crucial. However, a shift in traffic from cars to public transport can only be achieved through an overarching, systematic approach in which cities and rural municipalities, urban and rural regions work together (VDV, 2021, 19). Against this background, the further chapters of the first section of this book focus on public transport in functional urban regions (city regions) and rural areas in the case study countries Spain, Austria, and Canada.

To ensure coherence, the case studies address the following questions:

1. Is there a uniform scheme of responsibilities, or are they distributed according to the capabilities of particular local governments, taking into account differences between urban local governments (ULGs) and rural local governments (RLGs)?
2. What are the criteria for the allocation of responsibilities regarding the selected policy field, i.e. public transport, between local governments and other government levels?
3. Do local governments enjoy autonomy from higher levels of government in fulfilling their responsibilities?
4. Is there a gap between the scope of the autonomous functions of local governments and their actual role in performing them and, if so, why does this gap exist?
5. What is the role of both vertical and horizontal intergovernmental dialogue and coordination in the successful provision of public services that involve multi-level governance?
6. How do ULGs and RLGs adapt their provision of public services to changes in the demographic structure of their populations?

### 1.1.1 Ways of Public Service Provision by Urban and Rural Local Governments

The responsibilities of local governments are undergoing profound changes due to the growing urban-rural divide. This not only affects the type and scope of the tasks, but also the modality in which they are performed. There are variances in the way different countries provide public services. The way in which local governments provide services also depends on the service in question (Kuhlmann et al., 2022, 26–35). Local governments can provide services to their citizens not only directly through their own authorities. Rather, the organizational structure of local services is becoming increasingly diverse. Local governments use municipal enterprises to provide services, involve private partners in the provision of services, or outsource some or all of their services to private providers. In this respect, local governments today have considerable options when it comes to organizing their public services (Kuhlmann & Schwab, 2017, 101–103). This range of organizational options must be seen against the backdrop of a new guiding concept in the public sector called "New Public Management", according to which the state is no longer expected to provide all politically requested services itself. Instead, the state can concentrate on its safeguarding function by ensuring that the politically desired services are provided to the required quality standards (Kuhlmann & Schwab, 2017, 103).

Apart from that, the increase in the number and complexity of state functions and the poor budget situation are factors that encourage local governments to privatize public services (Burgi, 2019, 287). One of the main motives for corporatization and the outsourcing of public tasks and services to private actors is the expectation that the costs of public services can be reduced by enabling private actors to work more productively, especially due to higher efficiency, as well as by lowering the wage level (Friedländer et al., 2021, 297). Also, frequent changes and special challenges, for example in the technological field, may require the mobilization of considerable private resources for the performance of specific tasks. In such a case, institutional public-private-partnerships (PPP) allow local governments to access new funding without the need to borrow, while they may also benefit from private expertise (Pitschas & Schoppa, 2011, 121). Nevertheless, it should be mentioned that contracting out services to private providers has not always delivered the results expected by its promoters (Bel & Gradus, 2018, 11).

The reverse trend may also occur, where formerly privatized services are once again provided by the local government itself, for example, when local governments cancel concession contracts previously awarded to external private providers or even buy back utilities (Friedländer et al., 2021, 293). This phenomenon has become increasingly common, particularly in light of the international financial market crisis, which has visibly demonstrated the negative consequences of a de-regulated state system (Kuhlmann & Wollmann, 2013, 167–168).

While the different privatization arrangements may lead to budget improvements and an increase in the quality of services, they are also accompanied by negative effects such as problems of governance (Burgi, 2022, 431). For example, a greater distance between the authority and the institution providing the public service can lead to conflicting goals and information asymmetries. Mitigating these effects requires a broad range of capacities that are not naturally available in smaller communities (Voorn et al., 2017, 823–824). In some larger cities highly complex corporate structures with hundreds of municipal holdings have emerged. Even if these cities have the necessary capacities, such shareholding structures are hard to control and steer solely by the traditional bureaucratic concepts of hierarchy and planning (Friedländer et al., 2021, 295). Since different ways of providing public services come with different challenges, advantages, and disadvantages, they may therefore be more suitable for rural or urban local governments.

Therefore, if local governments want to make a decision about which organizational arrangements to use to fulfil a public task, various criteria should be considered, such as the relevance of performing the task for implementing political goals or the cost-effectiveness of the task performance by comparing the production costs and transaction costs (e.g., for contract initiation, coordination and monitoring) of different organizational forms (Friedländer et al., 2021, 293–294).

Against this backdrop, this book's second section aims to contribute to comparative research by exploring different privatization arrangements in the case study countries Germany, Spain, Australia, and Brazil.

To ensure coherence, the case studies address the following questions:

1. Do local governments provide services by themselves or through local enterprises?
2. If both forms of service provision exist, which services are covered by which form?
3. If local enterprises exist, are they owned and run by the local authority?
4. Are there differences between the use of public enterprises in urban and in rural areas?
5. To what extent do local governments involve the private sector in fulfilling their responsibilities?
6. What is the role of local governments in awarding concessions and entering into public contracts with private companies?
7. Are there differences between PPP in urban and in rural areas?

## 1.2 Equalization Of Financing Between Urban and Rural Local Governments

With very few exceptions, municipalities around the world have almost the same funding sources (Bird, 2011, 11; OECD/UCLG, 2016, 42). The major difference between different municipalities and among countries rather lies in the relative importance of each source of revenue. In general, all municipalities are financed through their own taxes, fees and other user charges for municipal services, transfers from higher levels of government, public or private credit and finally, other secondary or less relevant sources (fines, sales and leasing of own property, etc.). In almost all countries there are limits to municipal borrowing, which is mainly directed at capital investments (OECD/UCLG, 2016, 54; Ladner et al., 2019, 136). Also, fines or property transactions produce a very limited economic return. Some contemporary public-private cooperative instruments, such as public-private partnerships, have partially affected this system, insofar as the residents benefiting from works or services performed by concessionary companies pay the price for the services directly to these companies.

Consequently, the main sources of financing in almost all countries are: municipal taxes; supra-municipal transfers; and fees for municipal services (Hertzog,

2012, 223). There are countries with a long tradition of municipal self-financing (with the yield of own taxes or fees) and where transfers play a complementary or secondary role. But there are also countries where local financing is largely based on transfers (state or regional) and only to a more limited extent on own taxes and fees for municipal services.

The relative importance of each municipal source of revenue is frequently connected to the urban or rural character of the different municipalities. Generally, large cities tend to be more self-reliant in financial terms through their own taxes and fees (Slack, 2017, 5). This naturally responds to the greater economic capacity that large cities usually have: either because of the higher value of their real estate (which results in more lucrative municipal real estate taxes); or because the greater economic activity results in more revenue from direct municipal taxes (on businesses, vehicles registered in the municipality, business profits or income of individuals or legal entities) and indirect taxes (on trade or construction activity). They also tend to have more credit (due to their greater reliability in the credit markets and the greater importance of infrastructure spending). In contrast, rural municipalities tend to be financed to a greater extent by transfers. In this case, the relative weight of transfers is very diverse: it can greatly exceed revenues from own sources, or it can be a complementary (albeit qualified) source of own revenues.

Although transfers in favor of municipalities are more or less present in most countries, they can be differentiated based on two distinct functions: financial sufficiency and equalization (Slack, 2022, 233). In many cases, supramunicipal transfers are only intended to guarantee municipal financial sufficiency. That is, they are intended to ensure that all municipalities have sufficient economic resources to fulfill municipal tasks (whether these are legally mandatory or defined by each municipality). At other times, the transfers are not limited to ensuring the financial sufficiency of all municipalities but are intended to level or partially approximate the income of the different municipalities (especially between urban and rural municipalities).

The distinction between sufficiency transfers and equalization transfers makes particular sense in the member states of the Council of Europe that have signed the European Charter of Local Self-Government (Velasco Caballero, 2022). All these countries have assumed the international obligation to ensure not only the financial sufficiency of their municipalities, but in Article 9(5) also "[the] institution of financial equalization procedures or equivalent measures which are designed to correct the effects of the unequal distribution of potential sources of finance and of the financial burden they must support".

Having already established that transfers can be directed to a greater or lesser extent towards sufficiency or equalization between municipalities, the third section of this book pays special attention to transfers with an equalizing function. To this end, the reality of Canada, Italy, Austria, and several Eastern European countries is analyzed. As will be seen in these studies, income equalization can be achieved through vertical transfers (from the regional or central government) or horizontal transfers (between municipalities). Vertical transfers have a leveling function when, for their allocation, additional factors with respect to population are considered, or when they introduce weighting criteria that compensate for the lower demographics of rural or small municipalities (Bach, 2019, 184). In this sense, not every vertical transfer fulfills a leveling function because not every supra-municipal transfer improves the financial situation of the weakest municipalities with respect to the financially stronger ones. On the other hand, horizontal transfers always have a leveling function, insofar as they always involve the transfer of own resources (those coming from municipal taxes) from the richer municipalities to the municipalities with lower fiscal capacity.

For equalization purposes, each country may have a unique combination of vertical and horizontal transfers. There are also different criteria of expenditure needs when configuring the different types of transfers. Normally, the determining criteria for equalization transfers are based on the characteristic circumstances of rural municipalities, such as lower population density (which determines a higher cost of some services highly dependent on infrastructure, such as water supply), larger elderly population (which requires greater assistance from the municipalities) or the orography of the territory (which increases the costs of almost all municipal services). Paradoxically, some transfer criteria benefit municipalities with greater fiscal capacity. This is the case of the so-called centrality transfers, which compensate for the positive externalities (cultural services, leisure, and interurban transport) produced by large cities in relation to the smaller municipalities in their surroundings. This shows that a system of financial equalization articulated through various criteria or funds does not always/only act in favor of the fiscally weaker municipalities, but can also strengthen the financial position of municipalities with greater fiscal capacity.

To ensure coherence, the case studies address the following questions:

1. Do municipalities receive vertical financial transfers (from higher levels of government)? If so:
   (a) From whom do these transfers come: from the central government, regional governments, or the second level of local government?
   (b) What proportion of municipal income comes from transfers?
   (c) Are transfers, to a greater extent, earmarked or unconditional?
   (d) Are there different vertical transfers for urban and rural municipalities? If so, what criteria are considered for differentiation?
   (e) Are there specific funds for rural municipalities?
2. Is there any form of direct horizontal transfers between municipalities? If so:
   (a) Do governments of metropolitan areas play a role regarding these transfers?
   (b) Is there any direct equalizing mechanism between the large cities and the surrounding rural municipalities?

## 1.3 Special Fees and User Charges as Alternative Sources of Local Revenue

In local government finance, it is a common feature, in both developed and developing countries (United Nations, 2015, 18), that part, or all, of the costs of certain local services (such as water supply, sewerage, waste collection and disposal, public transport, and even certain social services) are financed through user charges. However, beyond this broad statement, it is more complex to determine and compare the scope of user charges between countries at the local level. The first reason is conceptual. The broad concept of user charges includes different types of payments, among them: fees for services consumed (the most important type from a quantitative perspective), fees of a proprietary nature such as rents for social housing, and fees that are regulatory in nature such as permits, licenses or development charges. Another factor that makes the comparison more complex is the diversity in the functions assigned to the local entities, since some are more easily financed through user fees than others. In addition, local and regional governments frequently have overlapping responsibilities, which, as a result, they co-finance. Despite the difficulty in drawing general conclusions, some empirical studies state that, since the 2000s, municipalities have increased their reliance on user fees. This is the case of the largest municipalities in Ontario (Tassonyi & Kitchen, 2021, 3) or the counties and municipalities in the United States (Pagano, 2009, 375).

Regarding the question of when user payments are applied, as a rule, what is now priced by local governments in most countries, and how it is priced, reflects historical accident and administrative convenience more than rational policy (Bird, 2001, 171). The principal strength of a user fee is its capacity to recover all costs of providing a service by linking charges for its use to those who use it (Bird & Slack, 2019). Therefore, they are ideal for funding services for which specific beneficiaries can be identified, non-users can be excluded, and the quantity of service consumed can be measured (Tassonyi & Kitchen, 2021, 3). Most local utility-type services meet these characteristics, hence their proliferation at the local level. Moreover, when user charges for services fully cover the marginal social cost of providing them, people buy such a service only up to the point at which the value they receive from the last unit they consume is just equal to the price they pay, improving the allocation of resources (Bird & Slack, 2017, 2). In addition to resource efficiency, user charges allow for greater accountability and transparency (Bird & Tsiopoulos, 1997, 48), as well as control over the provision of services.

As we have pointed out, user charges fulfill the classic benefits-received model of public finance, which contrasts with taxation based on the ability to pay. The lack of consideration of the ability-to-pay principle has been one of the main objections to the widespread introduction of user fees. However, the regressivity of user fees also needs to be considered in the broader context of the whole tax system (Duff, 2004, 403–405). At the same time, the design of user fees (especially for services consumed) has been increasingly adjusted to consider personal circumstances. In this regard, to be equitable, discounts should be based only on income level, avoiding subsidies based on other criteria such as the user's age because people of all age cohorts may have a high income or not (Kitchen, 2015).

This last factor connects to another key aspect of user charges: the determination of their amount. Existing fees often suffer from technical deficiencies. For instance, water rates have been frequently applied as fixed charges, or even when metering of water consumption has been applied, the use of declining block rates have favored large water consumers. Furthermore, sewer chargers were usually pro-rated on the amount of the water bills, which only exacerbated the pricing errors. (Bird, 2001, 179 and Kitchen, 2017, 15–16). However, these shortcomings have been systematically improved.

To price local service more effectively, the full cost of providing each service should be determined which can be complex, especially when overhead costs must be allocated. This should be done regardless of whether the objective is to recover the cost fully or only partially. If the intention is the latter, this information will make transparent the degree of subsidy involved in providing the service (OECD, 1998, 8). For user fees and regulatory charges based on costs, it is crucial to have complete cost information because it usually represents the maximum legal revenue that a fee can generate. In contrast, as a rule, there is no requirement for the revenue from the user fee to fully offset costs. However, potential overruns will have to be financed from the general budget (Tedds, 2020, 186). Legal restrictions on the amount of the user fee are a controversial issue when the provider is a private operator. The solution, in some cases, such as Spain, has been to link the nature of the user fee and, consequently, its regulation, to the management formula of the service (Ortiz, 2018, 24, and Martínez, 2020, 79).

The implementation of user fees is a multi-step process that, usually, begins with the legal authorization from the central or regional government to the local government to charge a fee for certain services or the granting of certain licenses. The establishment of a user fee frequently does not have to meet the constitutional and legal requirements and restrictions concerning taxes (Zielke, 1991, 439), or the conditions are more flexible. Also, it offers the advantage of not directly competing for any tax base with central or regional governments, and therefore central authorities tend to be much more generous in granting autonomy to subnational governments to set user fees (United Nations, 2015, 18). The legal constraints associated with user fees are related, normally, to restrain their employment as a general revenue tool or to cross-subsidize publicly other provided goods (Tedds, 2020, 186–187).

In this context, the chapters in this book section seek to analyze from a comparative perspective to what extent user charges are becoming a growing type of own-source revenue that allows local authorities to mitigate the constraints of limited local budgets and what kind of restrictions their more widespread use face.

To ensure coherence, the case studies address the following questions:

1. To what extent do municipalities have the power to decide the financing of their services through a direct payment by the citizens/users (fees), or is this decision made exclusively by the national and/or subnational government levels?

2. To what degree is financing through fees relevant? If so, regarding which municipal activities or services, is it most important?
3. How are territorial development actions (such as the transformation of rural land into urban areas or the establishment of new services/public works) financed?
4. To what extent does the management formula of the service (whether it is directly managed by the local government or through a public-private partnership) impact the nature and characteristics of user fees?
5. Are principles such as the ability to pay or the personal and family circumstances of the user taken into account when determining the amount of user fees?

## References


Accordino, J. (2019). Introduction to bridging the "urban–rural divide". *State and Local Government Review, 51*(4), 217–222. https://doi.org/10.1177/0160323X20932624

Babío, L., Duxfield, I., Milne, J., & Pickup, L. (2023). *Just Transition Webinar Report—Addressing urban-rural transport divisions, putting the periphery at the core*. Retrieved September 22, 2023, from https://www.polisnetwork.eu/wp-content/uploads/2023/03/Just-Transition-Webinar-Regions-Report.pdf

Bach, M. (2019). *Der kommunale Finanzausgleich als Existenzsicherung der Selbstverwaltungsgarantie. Eine dogmatische und rechtstheoretische Analyse des Gemeindefinanzsystems*. Mohr Siebeck.

Bel, G., & Gradus, R. (2018). Privatization, contracting-out and inter-municipal cooperation: New developments in local public service delivery. *Local Government Studies, 44*(1), 11–21. https://doi.org/10.1080/03003930.2017.1403904

Bird, R. M. (2001). User charges in local government finance. In M. Freire & R. Stren (Eds.), *Challenge of urban government: Policies and practices* (pp. 171–182). World Bank Publications.

Bird, R. M. (2011). Are there trends in local finance? A cautionary note on comparative studies and normative models of local government finance. *IMFG Papers on Municipal Finance and Governance*, 1. https://hdl.handle.net/1807/81272

Bird, R. M., & Slack, E. (2017). Financing infrastructure: Who should pay? In *Proceedings. Annual Conference on Taxation and Minutes of the Annual Meeting of the National Tax Association* (Vol. 110, pp. 1–18). McGill-Queen's University Press.

Bird, R. M., & Slack, E. (2019). Municipal taxation in a federal system: Linking taxes and expenditures. In E. Slack, L. Phillips, L. M. Tedds, & H. L. Evans (Eds.), *Funding the Canadian City* (pp. 22–43). Canadian Tax Foundation and Institute on Municipal Finance and Governance.

Bird, R. M., & Tsiopoulos, T. (1997). User charges for public services: Potentials and problems. *Canadian Tax Journal, 45*(1), 25–86.

Burgi, M. (2019). *Kommunalrecht*. C.H. Beck.

Burgi, M. (2022). Entwicklungslinien. In D. Ehlers & P. Hermann (Eds.), *Allgemeines Verwaltungsrecht* (pp. 416–441). C.F.Müller.

Dorsch, M. (2023). *Öffentlicher Personennahverkehr*. utb Uni-Taschenbücher.

Duff, D. G. (2004). Benefit taxes and user fees in theory and practice. *University of Toronto Law Journal, 54*, 391–447.

Friedländer, B., Röber, M., & Schaefer, C. (2021). Institutional differentiation of public service provision in Germany: Corporatization, privatization and re-municipalization. In S. Kuhlmann, I. Proeller, D. Schimanke, & J. Ziekow (Eds.), *Public Administration in Germany* (pp. 291–309). Palgrave Macmillan.

Gall-Roehrig, S., Rosier, S., Riss, K., & Greiving, S. (2022). Service of General Interest in the Rhenish coal-mining area in context of structural change. In S. Bartke & S. Kabisch (Eds.),

*Urban-rural-partnerships: Sustainable and resilient* (pp. 149–165). https://doi.org/10.3390/land11070956

Hertzog, R. (2012). Local government in France. In M. Molina & A. Manuel (Eds.), *Local government in the member states of the European Union: A comparative legal perspective* (pp. 203–232). Instituto Nacional de Administración Pública. https://www.researchgate.net/profile/Juraj-Nemec/publication/304680758_Slovakia/links/5a02c595a6fdcc55a1605fca/Slovakia.pdf

Kitchen, H. (2015). *No seniors' specials: Financing municipal services in aging communities*. IRPP Study, IRPP. Retrieved from https://irpp.org/wp-content/uploads/2015/02/study-no51.pdf

Kitchen, H. (2017). Paying for water in Ontario's cities: Past, present, and future. *IMFG Papers on Municipal Finance and Governance*, 35. University of Toronto. https://tspace.library.utoronto.ca/bitstream/1807/80200/1/Kitchen_Harry_2017%20IMFG%20Paper%2035%20Online.pdf

Kuhlmann, S., & Schwab, O. (2017). *Starke Kommunen—wirksame Verwaltung, Fortschritte und Fallstricke der internationalen Verwaltungs- und Kommunalforschung*. Springer VS.

Kuhlmann, S., & Wollmann, H. (2013). *Verwaltung und Verwaltungsreformen in Europa, Einführung in die vergleichende Verwaltungswissenschaft*. Springer VS.

Kuhlmann, S., Dumas, B. P., & Heuberger, M. (2022). *The capacity of local governments in Europe—Autonomy, responsibilities and reforms*. Palgrave Macmillan.

Ladner, A., Keuffer, N., Baldersheim, H., Hlepas, N., Swianiewicz, P., Steyvers, K., & Navarro, C. (2019). In A. Ladner, N. Keuffer, H. Baldersheim, N. Hlepas, P. Swianiewicz, K. Steyvers, & C. Navarro (Eds.), *Patterns of local autonomy in Europe* (pp. 125–150). Palgrave Macmillan.

Martínez, C. (2020). Las prestaciones patrimoniales de carácter público no tributario en el ámbito local: origen y regulación actual. *Anuario de Derecho Municipal, 13*, 57–83. Retrieved from https://www.revistasmarcialpons.es/anuarioderechomunicipal/article/view/prestaciones-patrimoniales-de-caracter-publico-no-tributario-en-

OECD/UCLG. (1998). *User charging for government services. Best practice guidelines and case studies, 22*. https://www.oecd.org/gov/budgeting/41213602.pdf

OECD/UCLG. (2016). *Subnational governments around the world: Structure and finance*. https://www.oecd.org/regional/regional-policy/Subnational-Governments-Around-the-World-%20Part-I.pdf

Ortiz, E. (2018). Las fronteras del derecho tributario. A propósito de las prestaciones patrimoniales de carácter público no tributario. *Quincena Fiscal, 19*, 1–24.

Pagano, M. A. (2009). United States of America. In N. Steytler & J. Kincaid (Eds.), *Local government and metropolitan regions in federal systems* (pp. 364–391). Queen's University.

Patton, M. Q. (2002). *Qualitative evaluation and research methods*. SAGE.

Pitschas, R., & Schoppa, K. (2011). Kriterien für die Wahl der Rechtsform. In T. Mann & G. Püttner (Eds.), *Handbuch der kommunalen Wissenschaft und Praxis* (Vol. 2, pp. 105–147). Springer.

Reschl, R. (2007). Vom Leben in der Stadt—Gemeinden und Kreise als soziale Gebilde. In M. Thomas & P. Günther (Eds.), *Handbuch der kommunalen Wissenschaft und Praxis* (Vol. 1, pp. 291–306). Springer.

Ruge, K., & Ritge, K. (2021). Local self-government and administration. In S. Kuhlmann, I. Proeller, D. Schimanke, & J. Ziekow (Eds.), *Public Administration in Germany* (pp. 123–141). Palgrave Macmillan.

Simon, D. (2021). Co-productive tools for transcending the divide: Building urban–rural partnerships in the spirit of the New Leipzig Charter. In S. Bartke & S. Kabisch (Eds.), *Urban-rural-partnerships: Sustainable and resilient* (pp. 1–16). MDPI. https://doi.org/10.3390/land10090894

Slack, E. (2017). How much local fiscal autonomy do cities have? A comparison of eight cities around the world. *IMFG Perspectives, 19*, 1–18. https://tspace.library.utoronto.ca/bitstream/1807/82864/1/imfg_perspectives_no19_localfiscalautonomy_slack_2017.pdf

Slack, E. (2022). Local fiscal autonomy in Toronto. *Anuario de Derecho Municipal, 16*, 223–244. https://doi.org/10.37417/ADM/16-2022_2.07

Tassonyi, A., & Kitchen, H. (2021). Addressing the fairness of municipal user fee policy. *IMFG Papers on Municipal Finance and Governance*, 54. https://tspace.library.utoronto.ca/bitstream/1807/106601/1/imfgpaper_no54_userfee_almostassonyiharrykitchen_july_8_2021.pdf

Tedds, L. M. (2020). Who pays for municipal governments? Pursuing the user tax model. In E. A. Heaman & D. Tough (Eds.), *Who pays for Canada? Taxes and fairness* (pp. 1–20). McGill-Queen's University Press.

United Nations. (2015). *The challenge of local government financing in developing countries*. https://sdgs.un.org/sites/default/files/publications/1732The%20Challenge%20of%20Local%20Government%20Financing%20in%20Developing%20Countries%20_3.pdf

Velasco Caballero, F. (2022). Despoblación y nivelación financiera municipal en el marco de la Carta Europea de Autonomía Local. *Revista de Estudios de la Administración Local y Autonómica, 18*, 6–31. https://doi.org/10.24965/reala.11092

Verband Deutscher Verkehrsunternehmen e.V. (2021). *Positionspapier/Oktober 2021, Handlungsoffensiven für die Mobilitätswende*. Retrieved September 22, 2023, from https://www.vdv.de/pospap-handlungsoffensiven-mobilitaetswende.pdfx. Accessed 22 September 2023

Voorn, B., van Genugten, M. L., & van Thiel, S. (2017). The efficiency and effectiveness of municipally owned corporations: A systematic review. *Local Government Studies, 43*(5), 820–841. https://doi.org/10.1080/03003930.2017.1319360

Yin, R. K. (2003). *Case study research: Design and methods*. SAGE.

Zielke, L. J. (1991). User fees in lieu of taxes: Avoiding constitutional limitations. *The Urban Lawyer, 23*(3), 439–447.

# Part I
# Tasks of Urban and Rural Local Governments

# Chapter 2
# Does One Size Fit All? Assigning Responsibilities to Local Governments

**Laura Mähle and Daniel Wolff**

**Abstract** The mismatch between the responsibilities and capacities of local governments ("mismatch problem") is a global problem that needs to be addressed. This chapter sketches out the status quo of responsibility allocation in different countries, with a focus on the differentiation of rural and urban areas, and analyzes the criteria used for assigning responsibilities. With the help of these insights, a new allocation framework based on the criteria of "balance", "complexity", and "flexibility" is introduced. By adding balance through criteria considering the challenges and the capabilities of municipalities, adding complexity by having a four-tier municipality system and adding flexibility by allowing the municipalities to make certain choices regarding responsibility allocation themselves, mismatch problems can be reduced in the future.

**Keywords** Local government responsibility allocation · Rural and urban local governments · Relational criteria · Mismatch problem · Responsibility overload · Responsibility underload

## 2.1 Introduction: Tackling the Mismatch Problem

The functioning of hierarchically structured organizations and institutions like companies, militaries and governments depends on a careful definition and allocation of competences and responsibilities. It is not surprising that researchers have intensely analyzed the factors contributing to these organizations. In the case of governments, this would include research in fields like law and political sciences on the basic structures of governments, the relationships between the different governmental

L. Mähle (✉)
Faculty of Law, University of Augsburg, Augsburg, Germany
e-mail: laura.maehle@jura.uni-augsburg.de

D. Wolff
Faculty of Law and Economics, University of Greifswald, Greifswald, Germany
e-mail: daniel.wolff@uni-greifswald.de



F. Velasco Caballero et al. (eds.), *Municipal Tasks and Financing*, Local and Urban Governance, https://doi.org/10.1007/978-3-031-99812-6_2

levels and the legal framework accompanying these issues. However, the consequences and practical effects of responsibility[1] allocation[2] have not yet received the scholarly attention they deserve, particularly with respect to the responsibilities of local governments (Burgi, 2022, 115–123). This research deficit is as much unfortunate as it is surprising, considering the consequences of misallocating responsibilities can ultimately result in a (completely) dysfunctional municipality.[3]

Looking at the existing research regarding responsibility allocation in local governments across different countries, there seems to be a common problem: More often than not there is a mismatch between the responsibilities assigned to local government actors and the necessary capacities to fulfill them. The problem is not solely the responsibilities assigned nor the capabilities of the municipality, but the relation between these two factors.[4] Accordingly, in this chapter we refer to this problem as the *responsibility capability problem* or the *mismatch problem*. It cannot be solved by solely adapting one of the two factors. Rather, it is necessary to analyze the relation between these two factors in order to assess the particular issues in the country in question.

Smaller and more rural municipalities especially seem to struggle with an overload of responsibilities. Many factors contribute to this inability to fulfill the assigned tasks, particularly financial limitations[5] and limitations regarding access to enough and sufficiently qualified employees.[6] Although the mismatch problem mostly concerns the aforementioned overload (too many responsibilities, not enough capabilities), an underload of responsibilities is also imaginable. A municipality has an underload of responsibilities when it aspires and has the capabilities to take on more tasks, that could then be fulfilled in a more efficient way but is missing the regulatory competences to do so.

---

[1] A responsibility is defined as a task the competent municipality is responsible for fulfilling. In some countries the term responsibility refers only to the competence to administrate and implement laws a higher entity or level of government has previously enacted (administrative competence), whereas in other jurisdictions, the term also covers the municipality's competence to enact legislation (legislative competence).

[2] In some countries the allocation of responsibilities between the different governmental levels is exclusive, whereas responsibilities of municipalities in other jurisdictions overlap with those of higher governmental levels. This is due to various country-specific concepts like autonomy and subsidiarity and the possibility of higher entities (voluntarily) delegating certain tasks (Allain-Dupré, 2018, 21–23). When used is this chapter, the term "allocation" is intended to be understood in a broad sense.

[3] The term "municipality" can be used for various, differently structured legal entities. For this chapter the term municipality refers to the lowest entity of local government, not yet distinguishing between population sizes, rural and urban settings, or any other criterion. For more information on the second-tier of local government in Europe, see Heinelt and Bertrana (2011).

[4] In Germany the current crisis of local governments is due to exactly these two factors: diminishing financial resources face growing responsibilities. These developments have an amplifying effect on each other (Grohs et al., 2012).

[5] This can mean a lack of resources, but also a lack of fiscal autonomy (Allain-Dupré, 2018, p. 35).

[6] For more details see below Sect. 2.2.2.

The country reports published within the EU H2020 project LoGov[7] mention a variety of problems concerning the responsibilities of local governments, some more general than others. The report for Albania, for example, explicitly mentions that their facilities for early childhood education are underutilized, understaffed, and underfinanced, especially in rural areas (Stafa, 2021a, 10). In Canada, the more rural areas struggle with staff and financial capacity, whereas the urban areas don't only strain under fiscal but also jurisdictional limits for providing the services they were assigned (Horak & van den Brink, 2021, 6; Horak, 2021b, 11–12). India and Switzerland have problems regarding the capacities of their municipalities in general, but the respective country reports both specifically mention problems with finding appropriate staff or even any staff (Sarangi & Ravichandran, 2021a, 37; Felder, 2021, 5). The reports for Germany and Ethiopia show a general overburden of their municipalities (Krönke, 2021a, 6; Lieb, 2021, 57; Ayalew Workneh, 2021, 59), while in Argentina, Australia, Croatia, Moldova, and South Africa the municipalities in rural areas struggle to fulfill their assigned tasks (González, 2021, 5; Mills, 2021, 8; Pichler, 2021a, 60; Wirth & Schantl, 2021, 63; Mitterer & Pichler, 2021, 70; Runtic, 2021a, 16; Runtic, 2021b, 44; Girbu, 2021a, 6; Fessha, 2021, 72). As the various examples from the country reports verify, the problem of municipalities not being able to handle their burden of responsibilities in the way intended is common to all countries, regardless of their development or economic strength.[8]

Three (main) approaches for mitigating or suspending these consequences have emerged: The most complete but also the most costly and time-consuming option is a (partial) territorial reform. Much quicker to implement is inter-municipal cooperation, whereas the third option—which is the focus of this chapter—entails analyzing and adjusting the allocation of responsibilities.

Although the term territorial reform is not clearly defined and can encompass several approaches, what we mean by territorial reform is amalgamation (Swianiewicz & Gendźwiłł, 2017). As the overload problem results from a lack of capabilities on the part of the municipalities, the municipalities might simply be too small to deal with their assigned tasks. By way of a territorial reform, two or more smaller municipalities could be merged into one bigger one that would be more capable of fulfilling the respective responsibilities. Concerning the potential of territorial reforms, the country reports show vastly different situations in the respective countries. Following the Territorial and Administrative Reform of 2014 in Albania, the smallest unit of local government in the Albanian legal system can only be established in territories with more than 20,000 residents (Stafa, 2021b, 1). In contrast, in Germany, 93,5% of all municipalities have a population under 20,000 inhabitants (Statistisches Bundesamt, 2023). However, as territorial reforms are rather unpopular within the citizenry and among politicians, this option to mitigate

[7] As this chapter is embedded in the EU H2020 project LoGov, the analysis is primarily based on the country reports compiled in the course of this project. Even though only 16 countries have been examined, these reports yield valuable information to conduct comparative research.

[8] The OECD Territorial Reviews and Economic Surveys and studies by the IMF and World Bank came to the same conclusion. Also, Allain-Dupré (2018, 35–37).

the mismatch problem is rather hard to accomplish. Most municipalities fight against losing their status as self-governing entities and against being amalgamated with other municipalities, as this also means a loss of autonomy, power, and money.[9] Furthermore, the effectiveness of territorial reforms is at least debatable (Callanan, 2011; Ebinger et al., 2019; Swianiewicz, 2020, 31–33). Although the assumption that larger municipalities are more capable of fulfilling their responsibilities seems straightforward (Newton, 1982), according to international studies there is no optimal size for local governments, and in a significant number of cases, population size does not have any significant impact on the quality of the services provided by the municipality (Andrews et al., 2006).

Apart from costly and time-consuming reforms of the entire local government system, many jurisdictions already provide the possibility of inter-municipal cooperation (Teles & Swianiewicz, 2018). Inter-municipal cooperation refers to "when two or more municipalities agree to work together on any of the tasks assigned to them in order to gain mutual benefits and to enhance the effective provision of services to citizens" (Council of Europe, 2023; Giacomini, 2022). Municipalities struggling with an overload of responsibilities can therefore opt for inter-municipal cooperation, especially if the overload problem stems from the lack of financial resources or staff.[10] However, as inter-municipal cooperation faces its own problems—and is its own research field in the LoGov project—it is not further analyzed in this chapter.

While the two aforementioned options could help mitigate an overload or underload of responsibilities for the respective municipalities, in this chapter we will focus on the last of the three options laid out before: modifying the allocation of responsibilities. We will do so by first looking at the status quo of responsibility allocation in the different countries, paying special attention to differences between rural and urban municipalities (Sect. 2.2.1), as well as analyzing the criteria used for assigning responsibilities (Sect. 2.2.2). Then, we will outline an allocation framework that can help reduce mismatch problems in the future (Sect. 2.3). The chapter ends with a short conclusion (Sect. 2.4.).

---

[9] In Albania, for example, there is only a single case of a voluntary amalgamation (Stafa, 2021c, 31). Also, many municipalities have a rich history and with this a cultural value to their residents, resulting in them being even more opposed to merging with any other municipality.

[10] The impact of also taking the latter into account is often underestimated—and therefore all the more important to consider (Allain-Dupré, 2018, 38).

## 2.2 Assigning Responsibilities: The Status Quo

### 2.2.1 *Differentiation Between Rural and Urban Local Governments*

As the general circumstances of the different jurisdictions differ widely, for example the average population density,[11] it is not possible to establish generally applicable criteria for when a municipality is rural or urban. However, it is possible to evaluate whether the respective jurisdiction differentiates at all. If no such distinction is provided, every municipality has the same responsibilities. A respective legal arrangement risks smaller municipalities being overwhelmed by the tasks assigned to them, as they are then supposed to complete the same tasks as larger municipalities, who regularly have far more capacities at their disposal than their smaller counterparts.

When drafting a legal regime for the allocation of responsibilities to local governments, it is necessary to consider the reality of local governments. However, legal arrangements cannot provide case-specific rules but need to be based on a generalization of the situation to be regulated. In order to draft allocation rules, the competent entity will have to define a typical, generalized municipality. If that typical municipality is determined by creating an average without taking into account the differences between rural and urban local governments, the legal framework based on this average municipality will most likely fit neither urban nor rural local governments and will lead to mismatch problems for both of them.

Surprisingly, almost no country currently distinguishes rural and urban local governments on the same tier, even though the respective municipalities often face vastly different problems.[12] The only exception within the countries included in the LoGov project is India,[13] where different base structures for rural and urban local governments exist (Sarangi & Ravichandran, 2021b, 1–3). In 1992 India passed two constitutional amendments, the 73rd and 74th amendment, which established the current system for the different levels of rural and urban local government (Sarangi & Ravichandran, 2021b). These amendments provide a three-tier system for rural areas (exceeding a population of two million), as well as a (different) three-tier system for urban areas. Even within the category of urban areas there is a distinction between small and large urban areas. Depending on their classification, which is based on economic growth, population increase, and administrative functions, the

[11] An area that is considered rural in India might well be considered urban in other countries with a generally much lower population density.

[12] The need for more differentiation has been apparent for quite some time. In recent years it has led inter alia to more asymmetrical (differentiated) decentralization (Allain-Dupré, 2018, 9–11 and 23–26).

[13] In many countries the structure of local governments is different in each state, canton, province or region. These differences are beyond the scope of the country reports, as well as beyond the scope of this chapter.

municipalities will then have different types of local bodies (Sarangi & Ravichandran, 2021b, 2–3).

The Indian approach not only recognizes the importance of taking the different realities of rural and urban areas into account, but also that urban areas need to be further differentiated to create a legal structure that is sufficiently tailored to the different needs of smaller and larger urban municipalities. With the ongoing urbanization, agglomeration, and the rise of megacities that can be observed in many countries, the challenges different types and sizes of urban municipalities face will increasingly drift apart. According to the United Nation's World Urbanization Prospects, as of 2018 55% of the world's population lived in urban areas (United Nations, 2019, 56). These urban areas include everything from urban settlements with fewer than 300,000 inhabitants up to megacities with a population of ten million or more. This development shows that working with only two categories of local governments—rural and urban—is not sufficient to capture the vastly disparate realities urban municipalities face. To consider these disparities, responsibility allocation schemes should (at least) recognize a third category: the metropolitan area.

The importance of a more detailed differentiation of urban local governments has already led a handful of countries to consider the differences between mere urban and metropolitan areas in their legal framework for responsibility allocation. In Canada the so-called Charter Cities have the authority to enact their own legislation by which they are governed instead of being subjected to the (generalized) province-wide legislation that applies to other municipalities. This way they can adjust the legislation to best accommodate the reality of their municipality and provide efficient services by granting themselves additional powers or revenue sources where necessary (Horak & van den Brink, 2021, 2 and 5). Similarly, in some provinces, individual municipalities can apply to their provincial government to request private statutes as a remedy for a particular local problem if there is no other legal recourse (Horak & van den Brink, 2021, 6).

In South Africa, metropolitan municipalities have exclusive executive and legislative authority in their areas of jurisdiction (Chigwata, 2021, 1). However, there is no legal framework for them to adapt their provision of public services to changes, something the authors of the respective country report recognize as a problem (Chonco & Kaywood, 2021, 11). In Italy, metropolitan cities have additional tasks mostly linked to specific urban challenges. These are, among others, metropolitan strategic planning, general spatial planning including infrastructure and communication networks, the structuring and coordination of metropolitan public services, as well as mobility and roads (Kress & Alber, 2021, 5). These additional responsibilities are intended to help metropolitan cities with the challenges arising from urbanization and metropolitan growth (Kress, 2021, 18). Similarly, the Spanish legal system provides for general metropolitan government structures for managing specific municipal services (Velasco Caballero, 2021, 3).

As these examples demonstrate, several countries have already taken steps to address the growing need for greater legislative and administrative autonomy for large urban municipalities. After all, the ability to quickly respond to new or emerging challenges leads to a more efficient local government.

### 2.2.2 *Allocation Criteria in Use Today*

The currently used allocation criteria vary depending on the jurisdiction.[14] Mostly, there is not one criterion used but rather a combination of several. The criteria mentioned in the country reports include size-dependent criteria, financial criteria, and efficiency/effectiveness criteria. Size-dependent criteria are, e.g., the number of inhabitants (Runtic, 2021c, 1; Ayalew Workneh, 2021, 58; Sarangi & Ravichandran, 2021c, 7; Díez Sastre, 2021, 6) and the geographical size (Ayalew Workneh, 2021, 58; Sarangi & Ravichandran, 2021c, 7) of the municipality. Financial criteria focus on the financial capability (Krönke, 2021b, 1; Chigwata, 2021, 3) of the respective municipality, whereas criteria regarding efficiency and effectivity (González, 2021, 5; Pichler, 2021b, 1; Runtic, 2021c, 2; Krönke, 2021b, 1; Kress & Alber, 2021, 5; Chigwata, 2021, 3) stipulate that the tasks affecting the citizens more directly should be allocated to the entity which is the closest to the citizens. Similar to the general criterion of efficiency/effectiveness, social and economic activity or development are in use in Moldova, as well as in Ethiopia and India (Sarangi & Ravichandran, 2021c, 7; Girbu, 2021b, 3).

## 2.3 The Way Forward: Elements of a New Allocation Framework to Tackle the Mismatch Problem

The country reports underline the fact that—concerning responsibility allocation—one size does not fit all. As capabilities and challenges on the municipal level vary significantly, an effective legal framework for responsibility allocation needs to be as flexible as possible while still being as specific as required to give the necessary guidance. The following proposal aims to address the main problems the country reports illustrate by way of three main principles.

Firstly, most jurisdictions lack *balance* concerning allocation criteria. Currently, most of them focus one-sidedly on the challenges the local government face without also taking the capability side into account (Sect. 2.3.1). Secondly, more *complexity* must be included in the legal regimes regulating responsibility allocation. What is necessary are legal structures that acknowledge and reflect the heterogeneity of the challenges municipalities face (Sect. 2.3.2). Finally, as general and strict legal rules

[14] In federal jurisdictions with varying structures of local governments, the allocation criteria often differ even within the country. Also, due to specific historical circumstances some municipalities have a special legal status that is separate from and therefore not affected by the general allocation criteria.

cannot comprehensively address the dynamic complexities on the ground, including the vastly different and quickly changing sizes, challenges, and capabilities of municipalities, *flexibility* needs to be added to the legal rules. This can be done by providing options for municipalities to choose from when they reach a certain, legally defined threshold (Sect. 2.3.3).[15]

### 2.3.1 Adding Balance: Relational Criteria

The current criteria for allocating responsibilities are rather unilateral, as they almost exclusively focus on the challenges a municipality typically faces. For example, if a municipality exceeds a certain population threshold, it is assumed that certain challenges emerge, like a higher demand for high-speed internet services or access to healthcare. To be able to face these challenges, the respective competences are granted to the municipality. This by itself is already a problem as strict criteria often miss their target. However, against the backdrop of the mismatch problem, the challenges are only one part of the equation. The reason why certain municipalities cannot fulfill their duties is usually because they lack the necessary capabilities, be it regarding finances, employees, or other factors.

For determining the allocation of responsibilities, a jurisdiction should follow a two-step procedure: First, the criteria by which the scale of expected challenges can be measured need to be identified. Ideally, differences of rural, urban, and metropolitan areas would already be considered at this stage. In general, more people and a higher population density lead to more challenges, which is why these two factors are arguably the best baseline criteria to assert the scale of challenges. After having defined and ranked the criteria for evaluating the extent of the challenges, additional criteria should be established to assess the capabilities needed for managing the challenges on hand. Following the country reports, we suggest considering two inter-related criteria for this task: the financial strength and the number and qualifications of the staff employed by the municipality. These seem to be the factors mentioned the most as limiting the capacities of municipalities.

By identifying the challenges of municipalities and considering the necessary capabilities, the allocation of responsibilities to individual municipalities will be far more balanced compared to an allocation system based solely on strict criteria. Subsequently, cases in which a municipality is overwhelmed and can no longer fulfill its duties can be reduced significantly. A similar approach can already be observed in the Moldavian legal system, which classifies urban localities on four ranks according to a predefined catalogue of indicators evaluating their level of social and economic development (Girbu, 2021c, 23). Depending on the fulfilment

[15] Any legal regime allocating responsibilities can only be functional, as long as the municipalities are equipped with sufficient financial resources to fulfill the tasks assigned to them. Thus, in the following, when we refer to a municipality taking on further responsibilities, we assume this is accompanied by an appropriate (financial) compensation.

of the established requirements, the municipality is assigned a certain status and, according to the assigned status, the respective responsibilities.

### *2.3.2 Adding Complexity: Four-Tier Municipality System*

As mentioned above, at least some jurisdictions differentiate concerning responsibility allocation between rural and urban local governments. However, operating only with this binary distinction is not enough for an efficient allocation regime, as this dichotomy is too simplistic to appropriately represent the needs and structures of todays municipalities. Thus, it is necessary to establish the municipality type "metropolitan municipality" and expand the two-tier municipality system by (at least) one more tier.

Jurisdictions around the world should implement a four-tier municipality system (see Fig. 2.1) to accommodate all the different challenges and prerequisites inherent to municipalities in a much more tailored way. The lowest level in this system is the "minimal responsibility municipality", followed by the "default municipality", the "urban municipality" and, on the highest level, the "metropolitan municipality".[16] As soon as a municipality within this four-tier municipality system reaches one of the three country-specific thresholds,[17] it will be able to move up or down one of the levels.

The placement of a municipality within this system does not start at the lowest municipality tier, which brings with it the shortest catalogue of responsibilities, but rather at the second lowest municipality tier, which we call the default municipality.[18] Thus, municipalities have the responsibilities assigned to this tier by default. If they want to take on more or less responsibilities, they must meet the corresponding threshold and opt for the new set of responsibilities.

With the default municipality not being the lowest level in the four-tier system, it is important to have a catalogue of responsibilities that a municipality has to fulfill and cannot opt out of. This set of responsibilities is what we define as the minimal responsibility municipality. It includes tasks for which a delegation to a higher municipality level within this four-tier system or—depending on the responsibility in question—to a higher level of local government would be dysfunctional. These

[16] Although this system is organized hierarchically, the entire system and therefore all four tiers are located on the municipal level. Hence, even when a municipality moves up or down these four levels, it always remains on the lowest government level of the respective jurisdiction.

[17] As our proposal offers some structural ideas for legal allocation regimes that are applicable to more or less any jurisdiction, it is outlined on a rather high level of abstraction, without going into details concerning the allocation of specific responsibilities or the precise definition of a certain threshold.

[18] Entities in this tier are equipped with responsibilities that would under many current systems be allocated to rural municipalities. Thus, the set of tasks assigned to municipalities on this tier need to be within the scope of what can be expected the municipality is able to deal with.

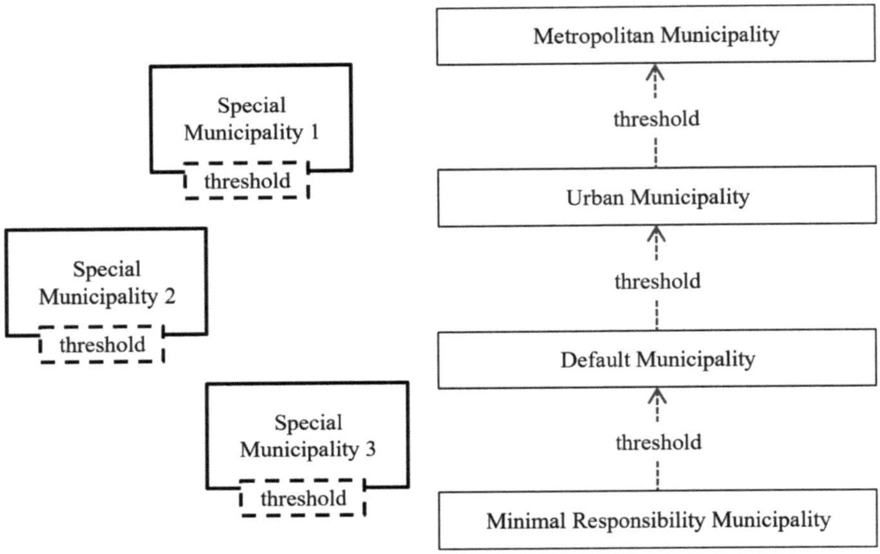


**Fig. 2.1** The Four-Tier Municipality System including special municipalities

could include responsibilities like waste management, water and sewage management, maintaining basic infrastructure, construction permits, and local police.

The urban municipality is one tier above the default municipality. Municipalities on this level are assigned additional responsibilities typical for urban areas. What exactly these responsibilities are will vary from country to country, but could include, inter alia, infrastructure (especially transit), affordable housing, education, and health services.

However, having only one municipal tier for urban municipalities would mean that the same legal structure would apply to mega cities with millions of inhabitants as well as to county towns with inhabitants in the (mere) tens of thousands. Thus, and as established above, a further distinction between urban and metropolitan is necessary to assign responsibilities accordingly. The highest level within the proposed four-tier system is the metropolitan municipality tier. The tasks assigned to municipalities on this level will include the most resource-consuming tasks that still make sense to be fulfilled on the lowest level of government.

As can be seen above, the proposed four-tier municipality system has three thresholds between the respective municipality tiers (see Fig. 2.1). These thresholds are the instruments to classify a municipality within the system by checking certain predefined criteria. As discussed above, the criteria used here should be relational criteria, meaning that they will take both the challenges and the capabilities of the municipality into account. For optimal applicability, the criteria should be defined as ranges. If a municipality falls within the range, other significant factors should also be considered to establish a comprehensive picture of what the municipality can efficiently handle before changing the allocated set of responsibilities.

Next to these four tiers the legal regime for allocating responsibilities should include specific arrangements for classes of municipalities that face extraordinary challenges. These so-called special municipalities are situated not within but parallel to the four-tier system (see Fig. 2.1). The number and kind of special municipalities depend on the particularities of a given country.[19]

For example, a "special" situation with a specific set of responsibilities worth addressing might be that of municipalities with relatively few inhabitants and a low population density that are located in very sparsely populated areas without any larger municipalities in close proximity. Such municipalities, which under normal circumstances would not reach the threshold for the urban municipality tier, regularly have to provide certain services, like education, hospitals, etc., that would usually fall within the tasks of an urban and not of a rural municipality. In Australia, for example, several small (rural) municipalities in sparsely populated areas have to provide services that would normally be offered by other actors, like the market or state government (Mills, 2021, 8). One of the key problems in Australia's rural areas is access to primary health care. Given this, rural local governments have created their own solutions. Brewarrina Shire Council, for example, is working together with the Charles Sturt University to provide free dental services to its residents (Mills, 2021, 8; Brewarrina Shire Council, 2023). In Western Australia's Sandstone Council, residents have access to doctors via the Royal Flying Doctor Service (Mills, 2021, 8), a charity that brings the "hospital emergency room, GP clinic, dentist chair, pharmacy and [their] dedicated professionals to patients" via helicopter (Royal Flying Doctor Service, 2023).

In Italy, the law already recognizes a structure similar to the one proposed by us, as the Italian legal system provides additional legal structures for so-called island and mountain communities (Klotz & Kössler, 2021, 2). The latter are established for the development of mountainous zones and unions of smaller towns, which can provide their services more efficiently when they join forces (Vesperini, 2009, 2).

### 2.3.3 Adding Flexibility: Responsibility Allocation by Choice

For the proposed allocation system to work as efficiently as possible, the system must not be too static but needs instruments to make it flexible enough to react to certain changes concerning the capabilities of the respective municipality as well as concerning the challenges the municipality faces. Thus, the allocation regime should provide options for the municipalities to choose their assigned set of responsibilities but also, at least to a certain extent, their municipal tier according to the four-tier system. By doing so, an overload of responsibilities can be avoided. As the world we live in continuously changes, the law has to change with it. For local

[19] This element of the proposed allocation regime should not be used for problems of individual municipalities. It is rather an instrument to be able to react to special situations that typically affect several municipalities.

governments, this means that they can be faced with new or changing tasks and, in some cases, will have neither the responsibilities nor resources needed for fulfilling them. But even if the tasks themselves might not be subject to change, modifications of the existing legal framework—that generally make the law more complex, difficult, and time-consuming to understand and apply—might pose a challenge for municipalities if they do not have appropriately qualified staff.

Finally, flexibility in the system is needed because the factors that are part of the (relational) criteria used to allocate responsibilities naturally change over time, with the most demonstrative factor being population and population density. For several reasons, including demographic changes in society but also unexpected incidents like the COVID-19-pandemic,[20] people change their lifestyle, which subsequently affects the extent to which certain services are needed in certain areas. If a vast number of families suddenly move to one part of a city, it is very likely that more teachers will be needed in this area and less in the areas the families lived in before. It will not only affect the demand for schools, but also for daycare options, playgrounds, pediatricians and much more.

Another key element of adding flexibility is allowing for choices regarding the assigned responsibilities. For example, if municipalities have the necessary capabilities and want to take on further responsibilities that would normally not be assigned to them according to the structure of the four-tier system (underload), they should have the option to "opt in". Using the opt-in mechanism can have two different consequences: Either the municipality takes on a specific responsibility (or a customized set of responsibilities) or it opts for a pre-defined municipality type with its respective responsibilities. For example, the before mentioned default municipality in a sparsely populated area may opt to be an urban municipality instead. Then it would have to fulfill all the tasks assigned to urban municipalities and would consequently also be granted the corresponding financial support.[21] This option will frequently apply to metropolitan areas, as they tend to have significant capacities. In Canada, for example, metropolitan areas struggle with communication and administration for certain responsibilities that are usually allocated to the next higher level of government (Horak, 2021a, 34). By using this option, they would be able to take on the respective responsibilities themselves which could otherwise compromise them in providing the necessary service in the most efficient way.

Depending on the responsibility in question and the underlying legal structure of the respective country, opting in to a responsibility could either mean the next higher municipality—following the four-tier system—will not have to fulfill the task in the area of the municipality taking on the additional task, or it could mean a relief for the next higher governmental level which would normally have dealt with the respective responsibility. In most cases, if a metropolitan municipality requests to

[20] Since the start of the pandemic, Canada has been experiencing new urban out-migration leading to all sorts of problems in the rural areas affected (Horak & van den Brink, 2021, 7–9).

[21] For more on (European) cities that already assume additional responsibilities in comparison to rural areas, see Kössler and Kress (2021).

take on additional tasks, these tasks will have been allocated to a higher level of local government, as the metropolitan municipality is already the highest tier within the four-tier system that in itself constitutes the lowest level of government. On the contrary, if the municipality opting in is one of the other three municipalities of the four-tier system, the task in question will most likely have been fulfilled by a higher municipality prior to the opt-in.

Much more relevant for the problems laid out in the country reports is the option to opt out, as this concerns cases of overload. Mirroring the opt-in mechanism, a municipality cannot opt out at will, but only if specific, predefined criteria are met. These could be, for example, insufficient financial resources, not enough employees or even an insufficient administrative organization. Opting out can mean opting out of specific responsibilities or downgrading to a lower municipality type. The ultimate limit to opting out is defined by the minimal responsibility municipality. The responsibilities assigned to these municipalities are those a municipality cannot opt out of.

For this system to stay flexible and adapt to possible changes over the course of a certain period of time, any of the criteria used—be it the relational criteria for opting in or opting out, or the definition of the thresholds—need to be reviewed on a regular basis and changed if necessary.

## 2.4 Conclusions

Given the mismatch problem is common to almost all countries and, therefore, needs to be addressed, in this chapter we have offered three instruments that, taken together, constitute a model system for tackling the causes and consequences of this problem.

The unilateral criteria-based allocation of responsibilities overlooking the capability part of the equation is (silently) contributing to the overload of responsibilities that can currently be observed in various countries. Hence, the criteria used should be relational, considering not only the challenges but also the capabilities of the municipality in question and weighing them up against each other. Distinguishing solely between rural and urban is not enough, as it does not sufficiently integrate the diversity of today's municipalities. Therefore, the four-tier system consisting of the minimal, the default, the urban and the metropolitan municipality adds complexity to the system of local governments. Next to these four municipality types, the possibility of establishing special municipalities offers the chance to consider the specific struggles and challenges certain types of municipalities face. As clear-cut thresholds cannot account for the challenges individual municipalities have to deal with, adding an opt-in and opt-out mechanism for municipalities adds a necessary amount of flexibility.

This responsibility allocation scheme is meant as a basic structure to be adjusted by lawmakers, i.e., to fit the requirements and necessities of the respective jurisdiction. Country-specific adjustments will always be necessary as the local government's systems and structures around the world vary greatly.[22]

Leaving the comprehensive structure of the proposal aside, it provides at least some generally applicable insights: For one, strict and inflexible criteria will always miss their target in one case or the other. The more considerate and flexible the process of responsibility allocation is, the more tailored the result will be. Giving municipalities the possibility to make their own choices in certain aspects of the allocation process will result in a better distribution of tasks and a better functioning municipality.

With the three main recommendations of adding balance, complexity, and flexibility, it is possible to assess and improve the current local government systems in an easier and more structured way.

## References

Allain-Dupré, D. (2018). Assigning responsibilities across levels of government. *OECD Working Papers on Fiscal Federalism*. Retrieved November 11, 2023, from https://www.oecd-ilibrary.org/taxation/assigning-responsibilities-across-levels-of-government_f0944eae-en

Ayalew Workneh, Y. (2021). The practice of local government creation (splitting). In Z. Ayele (Ed.), *Local government in Ethiopia: Responses to urban-rural challenges* (pp. 57–60). Zenodo. https://doi.org/10.5281/zenodo.5718733

Andrews, R., Boyne, G., Chen, A., & Martin, S. (2006). *Population size and local authority performance*. Department for Communities and Local Government. Retrieved November 11, 2023, from https://data.parliament.uk/DepositedPapers/Files/DEP2025-0199/Population_Size_and_LA_Performance_Final_Research_Report_2006.pdf

Brewarrina Shire Council. (2023). *Dental*. Retrieved November 10, 2023, from https://www.brewarrina.nsw.gov.au/community/medical-emergency-services/health/dental.aspx

Burgi, M. (2022). Was ist und zu welchem Ende studiert man Kommunalrecht? In M. Burgi & C. Waldhoff (Eds.), *Kommunale Selbstverwaltung im Bundes- und Finanzstaat: Festschrift für Hans-Günter Henneke zum 65* (pp. 115–131). Carl Heymanns Verlag.

Callanan, M. (2011). *Review of international local government efficiency reforms*. Retrieved November 11, 2023, from https://www.ipa.ie/_fileUpload/Documents/ReviewLocalGovEffeciencyReforms.pdf

Chigwata, T. C. (2021). The system of local government in South Africa. In M. R. Maziwisa & J. de Visser (Eds.), *Local government in South Africa: Responses to urban-rural challenges* (pp. 1–5). Zenodo. https://doi.org/10.5281/zenodo.5284157

Chonco, T., & Kaywood, L. (2021). Local responsibilities and public services in South Africa: An introduction. In M. R. Maziwisa & J. de Visser (Eds.), *Local government in South Africa: Responses to urban-rural challenges* (pp. 7–14). Zenodo. https://doi.org/10.5281/zenodo.5284181

Council of Europe. (2023). *Intermunicipal cooperation*. Retrieved November 10, 2023, from https://www.coe.int/en/web/good-governance/imc-eap

[22] Also, local governments structures often have deep roots in the history and the culture of the country in question, which makes reform difficult to accomplish, despite the oftentimes highly dysfunctional status quo.

Díez Sastre, S. (2021). Local responsibilities and public services in Spain: An introduction. In F. V. Caballero, S. D. Sastre, E. M. Peñas, M. D. Martín, A. Egea, & C. N. Gómez (Eds.), *Local government in Spain: Responses to urban-rural challenges* (pp. 6–7). Zenodo. https://doi.org/10.5281/zenodo.5733491

Ebinger, F., Kuhlmann, S., & Bogumil, J. (2019). Territorial reforms in Europe: Effects on administrative performance and democratic participation. *Local Government Studies, 45*(1), 1–23. https://doi.org/10.1080/03003930.2018.1530660

Felder, F. (2021). The system of local government in Switzerland. In F. Felder, E.-M. Belser, E. Schläppi, & K. Bishop (Eds.), *Local government in Switzerland: Responses to urban-rural challenges* (pp. 1–5). Zenodo. https://doi.org/10.5281/zenodo.5734454

Fessha, Y. (2021). A district coordinated development model. In M. R. Maziwisa & J. de Visser (Eds.), *Local government in South Africa: Responses to urban-rural challenges* (pp. 71–74). Zenodo. https://doi.org/10.5281/zenodo.5733436

Giacomini, D. (2022). Intermunicipal cooperation. In A. Farazmand (Ed.), *Global encyclopedia of public administration, public policy, and governance* (pp. 6917–6921). Springer International Publishing.

Girbu, V. (2021a). Local responsibilities and public services in Moldova: An introduction. In V. Girbu (Ed.), *Local government in Moldova: Responses to urban-rural challenges* (pp. 6–8). Zenodo. https://doi.org/10.5281/zenodo.5728386

Girbu, V. (2021b). The structure of local government in Moldova: An introduction. In V. Girbu (Ed.), *Local government in Moldova: Responses to urban-rural challenges* (pp. 22–26). Zenodo. https://doi.org/10.5281/zenodo.5728395

Girbu, V. (2021c). The system of local government in Moldova. In V. Girbu (Ed.), *Local government in Moldova: Responses to urban-rural challenges* (pp. 1–4). Zenodo. https://doi.org/10.5281/zenodo.5728384

González, L. (2021). Local responsibilities and public services in Argentina: An introduction. In L. González & R. Del Tredici (Eds.), *Local government in Argentina: Responses to urban-rural challenges* (pp. 5–7). Zenodo. https://doi.org/10.5281/zenodo.5708945

Grohs, S., Bogumil, J., & Kuhlmann, S. (2012). Überforderung, Erosion oder Aufwertung der Kommunen in Europa? Eine Leistungsbilanz im westeuropäischen Vergleich. dms—der moderne staat. *Zeitschrift für Public Policy, Recht und Management, 5*(1), 125–148.

Heinelt, H., & Bertrana, X. (2011). *The second tier of local government in Europe. Provinces, counties, départments and landkreise in comparison*. Routledge.

Horak, M. (2021a). Intergovernmental relations of local governments in Canada: An introduction. In M. Horak (Ed.), *Local government in Canada: Responses to urban-rural challenges* (pp. 34–35). Zenodo. https://doi.org/10.5281/zenodo.5725882

Horak, M. (2021b). Local responsibilities and public services in Canada: An introduction. In M. Horak (Ed.), *Local government in Canada: Responses to urban-rural challenges* (pp. 11–14). Zenodo. https://doi.org/10.5281/zenodo.5725853

Horak, M., & van den Brink, B. (2021). The system of local government in Canada: An introduction. In M. Horak (Ed.), *Local government in Canada: Responses to urban-rural challenges* (pp. 1–9). Zenodo. https://doi.org/10.5281/zenodo.5725850

Klotz, G., & Kössler, K. (2021). The system of local government in Italy. In K. Kössler & T. Morandell (Eds.), *Local government in Italy: Responses to urban-rural challenges* (pp. 1–3). Zenodo. https://doi.org/10.5281/zenodo.5254705

Kössler, K., & Kress, A. (2021). European cities between self-government and subordination: Their role as policy-takers and policy-makers. In E. H. Ballin, G. van der Schyff, M. Stremler, & M. de Visser (Eds.), *European yearbook of constitutional law 2020: The city in constitutional law* (Vol. 2, pp. 273–302). European Yearbook of Constitutional Law. Asser Press.

Kress, A. (2021). Strategic planning in geographically heterogeneous metropolises. In K. Kössler & T. Morandell (Eds.), *Local government in Italy: Responses to urban-rural challenges* (pp. 18–22). Zenodo. https://doi.org/10.5281/zenodo.5733362

Kress, A., & Alber, E. (2021). Local responsibilities and public services in Italy: An introduction. In K. Kössler & T. Morandell (Eds.), *Local government in Italy: Responses to urban-rural challenges* (pp. 5–6). Zenodo. https://doi.org/10.5281/zenodo.5254761

Krönke, C. (2021a). Local responsibilities and public services in Germany: An introduction. In M. Burgi, L. Hagen, & N. Lieb (Eds.), *Local government in Germany: Responses to urban-rural challenges* (pp. 6–7). Zenodo. https://doi.org/10.5281/zenodo.5206040

Krönke, C. (2021b). The system of local government in Germany. In M. Burgi, L. Hagen, & N. Lieb (Eds.), *Local government in Germany: Responses to urban-rural challenges* (pp. 1–4). Zenodo. https://doi.org/10.5281/zenodo.5205578

Lieb, N. (2021). Intergovernmental relations of local governments in Germany: An introduction. In M. Burgi, L. Hagen, & N. Lieb (Eds.), *Local government in Germany: Responses to urban-rural challenges* (pp. 57–60). Zenodo. https://doi.org/10.5281/zenodo.5235230

Mills, C. (2021). Provision of services in regional and rural areas. In C. Mills (Ed.), *Local government in Australia: Responses to urban-rural challenges* (pp. 8–9). Zenodo. https://doi.org/10.5281/zenodo.5725424

Mitterer, K., & Pichler, D. (2021). Management by objectives in the field of compulsory schooling. In A. Schantl, D. Pichler, & T. Prorok (Eds.), *Local government in Austria: Responses to urban-rural challenges* (pp. 70–74). Zenodo. https://doi.org/10.5281/zenodo.5711400

Newton, K. (1982). Is small really so beautiful? Is big really so ugly? Size, effectiveness, and democracy in local government. *Political Studies, 30*(2), 190–206. https://doi.org/10.1111/j.1467-9248.1982.tb00532.x

Pichler, D. (2021a). Administrative association in building law: Region Vorderland. In A. Schantl, D. Pichler, & T. Prorok (Eds.), *Local government in Austria: Responses to urban-rural challenges* (pp. 60–62). Zenodo. https://doi.org/10.5281/zenodo.5711382

Pichler, D. (2021b). The system of local government in Austria. In A. Schantl, D. Pichler, & T. Prorok (Eds.), *Local government in Austria: Responses to urban-rural challenges* (pp. 1–4). Zenodo. https://doi.org/10.5281/zenodo.5711074

Royal Flying Doctor Service. (2023). *The RFDS in WA: Responding to need across WA*. Retrieved November 10, 2023, from https://www.flyingdoctor.org.au/wa/

Runtic, D. (2021a). The fiscal equalization fund. In D. Runtic (Ed.), *Local government in Croatia: Responses to urban-rural challenges* (pp. 16–19). Zenodo. https://doi.org/10.5281/zenodo.5269004

Runtic, D. (2021b). Participatory budgeting in the City of Pazin: Pazi(n)! Proracun (Watch out! Budget). In D. Runtic (Ed.), *Local government in Croatia: Responses to urban-rural challenges* (pp. 40–44). Zenodo. https://doi.org/10.5281/zenodo.5269085

Runtic, D. (2021c). The system of local government in Croatia. In D. Runtic (Ed.), *Local government in Croatia: Responses to urban-rural challenges* (pp. 1–3). Zenodo. https://doi.org/10.5281/zenodo.5268767

Sarangi, A., & Ravichandran, L. (2021a). Local governments and their functioning. In A. Sarangi & L. Ravichandran (Eds.), *Local government in India: Responses to urban-rural challenges* (pp. 33–38). Zenodo. https://doi.org/10.5281/zenodo.5722539

Sarangi, A., & Ravichandran, L. (2021b). Local responsibilities and public services in India: An introduction. In A. Sarangi & L. Ravichandran (Eds.), *Local government in India: Responses to urban-rural challenges* (pp. 7–9). Zenodo. https://doi.org/10.5281/zenodo.5722512

Sarangi, A., & Ravichandran, L. (2021c). The system of local government in India. In A. Sarangi & L. Ravichandran (Eds.), *Local government in India: Responses to urban-rural challenges* (pp. 1–5). Zenodo. https://doi.org/10.5281/zenodo.5722507

Stafa, E. (2021a). Decentralized early childhood education. In E. Stafa (Ed.), *Local government in Albania: Responses to urban-rural challenges* (pp. 9–14). Zenodo. https://doi.org/10.5281/zenodo.5707224

Stafa, E. (2021b). The system of local government in Albania. In E. Stafa (Ed.), *Local government in Albania: Responses to urban-rural challenges* (pp. 1–4). Zenodo. https://doi.org/10.5281/zenodo.5707203

Stafa, E. (2021c). The Territorial and Administrative Reform. In E. Stafa (Ed.), *Local government in Albania: Responses to urban-rural challenges* (pp. 29–34). Zenodo. https://doi.org/10.5281/zenodo.5707253

Statistisches Bundesamt. (2023). *Anzahl Der Gemeinden In Deutschland Nach Gemeindegrößenklassen (Stand 31.12.2022)*. Retrieved November 10, 2023, from www.de.statista.com/statistik/daten/studie/1254/umfrage/anzahl-der-gemeinden-in-deutschland-nach-gemeindegroessenklassen/

Swianiewicz, P. (2020). Recent and contemporary trends in European studies of local government and local politics. In C. N. Silva (Ed.), *Contemporary trends in local governance: Reform, cooperation and citizen participation* (pp. 21–43). Springer International Publishing.

Swianiewicz, P., & Gendźwiłł, A. (2017). *Territorial reforms in Europe: Does size matter? Territorial Amalgamation Toolkit*. Retrieved November 11, 2023, from https://rm.coe.int/territorial-reforms-in-europe-does-size-matter-territorial-amalgamatio/168076cf16

Teles, F., & Swianiewicz, P. (2018). *Inter-municipal cooperation in Europe*. Springer International Publishing.

United Nations. (2019). *World urbanization prospects: The 2018 revision*. United Nations. Retrieved November 11, 2023, from https://www.un.org/development/desa/pd/sites/www.un.org.development.desa.pd/files/files/documents/2020/Jan/un_2018_wup_report.pdf

Velasco Caballero, F. (2021). The system of local government in Spain. In F. V. Caballero, S. D. Sastre, E. M. Peñas, M. D. Martín, A. Egea de Haro, & C. Navarro (Eds.), *Local government in Spain: Responses to urban-rural challenges* (pp. 1–4). Zenodo. https://doi.org/10.5281/zenodo.5733489

Vesperini, G. (2009). Regional and local government in Italy: An overview. *SSRN*. https://doi.org/10.2139/ssrn.1332762.

Wirth, K., & Schantl, A. (2021). Post-merger evaluation: Future-oriented organizational development in the City of Fehring/Styria. In A. Schantl, D. Pichler, & T. Prorok (Eds.), *Local government in Austria: Responses to urban-rural challenges* (pp. 63–65). Zenodo. https://doi.org/10.5281/zenodo.5711386

# Chapter 3
# Urban Pulse, Rural Resonance: Austrian Public Transport from a City-Regional Perspective

**Alexandra Schantl**

**Abstract** Public transport in Austria is a service of basic general interest (*Daseinsvorsorge*) and is therefore provided and guaranteed by the state. Beyond its basic necessity, public transport plays a pivotal role in curbing greenhouse gas emissions, making it indispensable not only for meeting climate targets but also for broader climate protection efforts. Nevertheless, the intricate organization and funding of public transport pose significant challenges. This complexity is exacerbated by Austria's federal system. Moreover, the availability and effectiveness of public transport vary widely between urban and rural areas with specific conditions for urban or rural local governments. This chapter examines the status quo of public transport in Austria, emphasizing the challenges and opportunities for bridging the urban-rural divide, with a territorial focus on Austria's city regions.

**Keywords** Austrian city regions · Climate protection · Functional urban areas · Local public service delivery · Public transport · Public transport financing · Rural areas · Rural local governments · Urban local governments

## 3.1 Introduction

Similar to fundamental aspects of life such as living arrangements, work, education, and leisure activities, mobility stands as a basic societal requirement. In particular, for rural areas to maintain their allure in the future, it is imperative that residents can navigate their surroundings effortlessly and independently, even without personal vehicles. The cornerstone of this endeavor lies in robust public transportation systems, encompassing flexible services like shared cabs and on-call buses. In Austria, approximately 60% of traffic-related emissions stem from cars, with a significant portion originating from outlying regions. Insufficient public transport options and an inconsistent network of pedestrian and cycling paths exacerbate the prevalent

A. Schantl (✉)
KDZ Centre for Public Administration Research, Vienna, Austria
e-mail: schantl@kdz.or.at



F. Velasco Caballero et al. (eds.), *Municipal Tasks and Financing*, Local and Urban Governance, https://doi.org/10.1007/978-3-031-99812-6_3

reliance on cars due to urban expansion. This reliance manifests in heightened car ownership rates, a larger share of daily commutes made by car, and increased travel distances.

The Austrian Climate Council of Citizens[1] has advocated for an Austria-wide mobility guarantee, accessible 24/7 within a 15-min walking distance, requiring a public transport system operating at least hourly and incorporating demand-responsive services and ride-sharing solutions. Regional mobility plans should be devised based on supra-regional public transport to determine the most effective combination of measures (*Arge Klimarat*, 2022). Moreover, many destinations, even in rural local governments, are reachable on foot. According to the Upper Austrian Mobility Survey (Land Oberösterreich, 2023), a significant portion of the population can access essential amenities such as grocery stores, kindergartens, schools, banks, and medical facilities within a 15-min walk.

This chapter zooms in on public transport in Austrian functional urban regions and rural areas, recognizing the significant potential and challenges in connecting core municipalities that are in general urban local governments with their surrounding municipalities that are typically more rural local governments. Addressing these challenges effectively not only benefits citizens but also contributes to achieving climate targets and thus combating climate change.

To gain insight into the role of Austrian local governments in public transport, it is essential to examine their position within the broader Austrian governance system, explore their competencies, and consider the multifaceted challenges they face nowadays.

## 3.2 Local Public Service Delivery in Austria

Local governments in Austria have distinct responsibilities within their autonomous functions (*eigener Wirkungsbereich*)[2] and tasks delegated (*übertragener Wirkungsbereich*) by the federation and the respective state (*Land*). According to Article 116 of the Austrian Constitution, all municipalities adhere to the principle of *Einheitsgemeinde*, granting them equal rights and duties, with exceptions for

---

[1] From January to July 2022, 100 randomly selected citizens from all regions and parts of Austrian society tackled the question: "What do we have to do today to live in a climate-healthy future tomorrow?" Together they formed the Climate Council. As a kind of "mini-Austria," they developed measures to actively help shape the climate future of Austria. https://klimarat.org/. Accessed December 9, 2023.

[2] Tasks under local responsibility are local police, markets, traffic facilities, land use planning, social services, water, sanitation and waste management, sports, and leisure facilities. Despite their self-governing status, the municipalities must adhere to state and federal laws in these areas and are monitored for legal and efficiency compliance. The states oversee the budgets of municipalities regarding economy, profitability, and expediency. The standards of supervision vary considerably between the states.

"statutory cities" (*Statutarstädte*) and Vienna, which serve as both a municipality and a state.

Both urban (ULGs) and rural (RLGs) local governments, acting as independent economic entities per Article 116(2) of the Austrian Constitution,[3] play a crucial role in providing diverse public services such as infrastructure (waste, water, sewage, public housing, etc.), kindergartens, primary schools, and retirement homes. They contribute to the broader economy by managing their own industrial and commercial enterprises.[4] In the area of public transport, local governments are particularly important as providers of local transport and in their role in transport networks and associations.

Despite this autonomy, the way Austrian local governments deliver public services varies depending on the nature of the service. The spectrum ranges from self-operated municipal companies to engaging in public-private partnerships.

Over the past two decades, Austrian municipalities have shifted from being purely administrative authorities to increasingly serving as providers of services for citizens. The Federal Constitutional Law makes no distinctions based on the size or population of municipalities, posing challenges for smaller ones in fulfilling their local responsibilities. Consequently, inter-municipal cooperation has emerged as a crucial aspect of local government in Austria, addressing the need for economies of scale and expertise that individual municipalities may lack. Municipal associations (*Gemeindeverbände*, Article 116(a)) play a vital role in managing public services such as water supply or waste management.

Similar to their counterparts in most Western European countries, both urban and rural municipalities in Austria face various challenges in delivering public services. The primary obstacles include a decline in public resources coupled with an increase in public tasks, driven by demographic changes (an aging population, migration from rural to urban areas), climate change, societal shifts (Generation Z dynamics, migration, and segregation), land use changes and limitations, energy transition, and digitalization (Schantl et al., 2021).

The migration of people from rural to urban areas is placing increasing pressure on the provision of public services, becoming a pivotal element for ensuring

[3]All municipalities are corporations and have the right to own property, run businesses, levy municipal taxes, and generally manage their own financial affairs.

[4]The instruments of public service delivery include the following: 1) Communal self-supply through enterprises owned and operated by the municipality itself. The *Stadtwerke*, as an organizational part of the municipal administration, form the economic foundation of municipal autonomy. 2) Communal enterprises as independent companies organized under private law. These "outsourced" communal enterprises do not only deliver public utilities' services but also increasingly operate cultural or social infrastructures. 3) Communal ordering of services by commissioning private companies. In recent years, the ordering of services has received a decisive boost and has replaced communal enterprises as a means of providing public services in some areas. 4) Public procurement has become a central instrument for securing public utilities. With a public service concession, the municipality grants a third party the right to provide full or partial public services. These public-private partnerships are used particularly in areas of the public utility sector that entail high infrastructure costs (e.g., school campuses, etc.).

favorable living conditions. Austria is experiencing overall population growth, yet significant regional variations exist, with many rural areas facing population declines. The primary drivers of population growth in Austria are cities and their surrounding regions. According to the population forecast by the Austrian Conference on Spatial Planning in 2021 (ÖROK, 2022), the projected population is expected to reach 9.22 million by 2030, reflecting a 3.2% increase from 2021 (based on January 1 of each respective year). The forecast further anticipates a population of 9.63 million by 2050, representing a 7.8% growth. The projections suggest that substantial population growth until 2050 will be concentrated mainly in larger cities and their environs. Notably, regions such as the Vienna metropolitan area (extending to Weinviertel and northern Burgenland), as well as areas around state capitals including Graz, Salzburg, Klagenfurt, Innsbruck, and Bregenz, along with the central Upper Austrian region of Linz-Wels, are expected to exhibit above-average dynamics. These regions are anticipated to experience a population increase of 10% or more by 2050. The growth in these areas will result from a combination of significant external immigration, positive internal migration balances, and birth surpluses. Additionally, besides the proximity to urban agglomeration areas, notable growth is observed along the east-west axis along major transportation corridors.

Conversely, the areas experiencing the most pronounced population declines primarily encompass the Waldviertel in Lower Austria, Upper Styria, and the peripheral regions of Carinthia outside the central area of Klagenfurt-Villach. These regions typically feature weaker economic foundations and grapple with substantial emigration and low birth rates. Across nine districts, population projections indicate declines of 10% or more by 2050, notably in Wolfsberg/Carinthia (10%), Spittal an der Drau/Carinthia, Murtal/Styria, and Jennersdorf/Burgenland (11% each), Hermagor/Carinthia (12%), Gmünd and Zwettl/Lower Austria (13% each), Waidhofen an der Thaya/Lower Austria (14%), and Murau/Styria (16%). Particularly in the more peripheral regions expected to see significant population decreases, there is a marked decline in the number of native-born Austrians. A total of 22 forecasted regions anticipate a decline of 10% to 18% in this demographic by 2050, including districts in Lower Austria, Upper Styria, and Carinthia. The factors prompting individuals to move away from rural regions are multifaceted, ranging from the waning influence of traditional industries and limited training opportunities to a dearth of employment prospects for highly skilled individuals. Challenges such as inadequate housing and infrastructure, including limited childcare facilities, further contribute to this trend. The departure of young adults and the continuous growth in older population segments initiates a vicious cycle for RLGs finding themselves doubly affected in the orchestration and funding of essential services and infrastructure as the diminishing resident count translates to reduced funding. This twofold impact entails managing both overcapacity and capacity bottlenecks, ultimately resulting in escalating costs and making it increasingly challenging to uphold the necessary infrastructure.

ULGs and thriving agglomerations in Austria have reaped the rewards of immigration, both from other regions within Austria and from abroad, resulting in sustained growth (see Fig. 3.1). However, this growth presents its own set of challenges, including a housing shortage and the strain on public infrastructure, which is consistently pushing the boundaries of its capacity and resilience. The influx of commuters, coupled with an unfavorable modal split and the cohabitation of individuals with diverse ethnic and cultural backgrounds, adds further layers of complexity to the expansion of ULGs in Austria.

To address challenges in both rural and urban local government, fostering collaboration between municipalities for the provision of public services has become a key focus on the political agenda in Austria. However, the approaches diverge between RLGs and ULGs. Acknowledging the significance of functional areas, ULGs are progressively working toward formulating comprehensive strategies and initiatives for territorial cooperation together with their often (more) rural neighboring municipalities (termed "city regions") and implementing them. In contrast, RLGs primarily engage in bilateral project-based cooperation (referred to as "inter-municipal cooperation"). Sometimes, these inter-municipal cooperations can be embedded in regional strategies within a certain geographical territory (e.g., LEADER regions for rural development) and/or thematically determined (e.g., KLAR! regions for climate change adaptation).

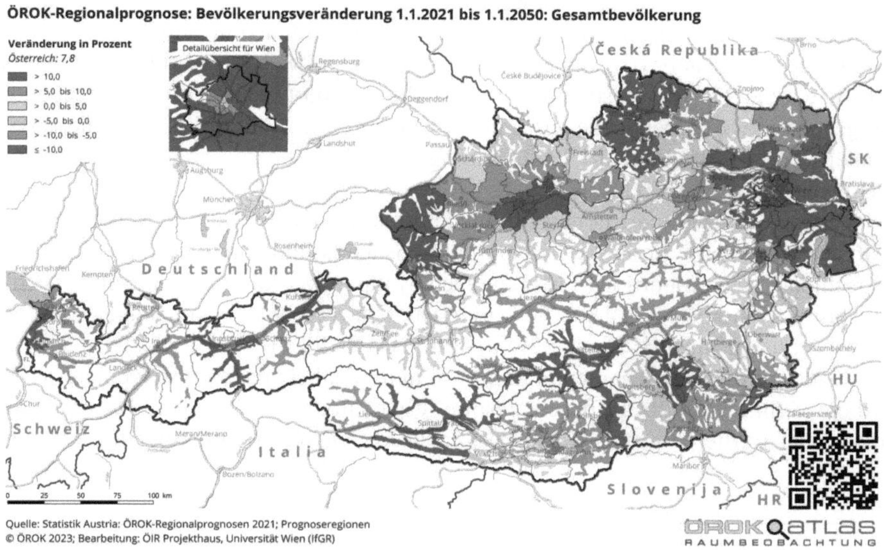


**Fig. 3.1** Population forecast 2050. (Source: Österreichische Raumordnungskonferenz (ÖROK), "ÖROK-Bevölkerungsprognosen 2021–2050", Vienna 2021, licensed under CC-BY 4.0)

## 3.3 Public Transport in Functional Urban Regions and Rural Areas

In general, Austria has a well-developed and effective public transport system, offering a wide array of options for both local commutes and long-distance travel. The system encompasses diverse modes of transport such as buses, trams, trains, and subways. Integration of multiple transport modes and streamlined ticketing systems aim at enhancing the overall convenience and usability of the network. The overarching aim is to ensure that Austria's public transport is dependable, punctual, and accessible across urban and rural regions alike to substantially reduce motorized individual traffic (MIT).

Recent calculations by the Environment Agency Austria reveal that Austria experienced a noteworthy 6.4% reduction in greenhouse gas (GHG) emissions in 2022 compared to the previous year, despite a concurrent increase in gross domestic product. This translates to a decrease of five million tons of $CO_2$ equivalents. Remarkably, this decline occurred across all sectors—namely, buildings, transport, agriculture, and industry—marking the first time such a comprehensive reduction has taken place alongside significant economic growth. Preliminary data indicates a 4.5% decrease (equivalent to 1.0 million tons of $CO_2$) in emissions from the transport sector compared to 2021, returning to the levels observed in the initial COVID-19 pandemic year of 2020. This reduction is primarily attributed to elevated fuel prices during the summer months of 2022. Additionally, advancements in technology and the growing adoption of e-mobility in individual transportation, accounting for approximately 16% of new car registrations in 2022, have contributed to this positive trend. Despite these improvements, the transport sector remains the second-largest emitter of greenhouse gases in Austria, emitting 20.6 million tons (approximately 28% of the total) in 2022, trailing behind the energy and industry sector (Umweltbundesamt, 2023).[5]

To achieve the climate targets outlined in Austria's 2030 Mobility Master Plan, a substantial increase in public transportation usage is imperative by the year 2040. Specifically, the proportion of MIT, gauged by passenger kilometers traveled, needs to shrink from 70% in 2018 to 54% by 2040. Conversely, the percentage of public transport usage must rise from 27% to 40% (BMK, 2021).

Aside from the environmental impact of individual car use, private vehicles contribute significantly to traffic congestion, especially in urban areas. By reducing individual traffic, congestion can be alleviated, leading to smoother traffic flow,

---

[5] The "NowCast 2023" provides preliminary data and trends on greenhouse gas emissions for 2022. The calculations for this near-term forecast were carried out using a simplified methodology and reflect the current state of knowledge of July 2023. In particular, the near-term forecast is based on the current Austrian Air Pollutant Inventory (OLI), the preliminary energy balance, the current data from emissions trading facilities as well as current surveys and statistics from the agricultural, waste management, and F-gas sectors. There is also a near-term forecast with detailed results for the transport sector.

shorter travel times, and lower stress levels for commuters. In addition, cars consume valuable resources such as fossil fuels and land for roads and parking.

However, the initial circumstances required for the essential shift in mobility vary greatly between RLGs and rural areas compared to ULGs and urban areas. Rural areas exhibit a diverse landscape, characterized by varying settlement structures, natural features, and infrastructure, each presenting its own set of functions and challenges. Climate-friendly mobility solutions tailored for urban and large city settings often prove impractical or inadequately funded when applied to rural and regional contexts. Moreover, the prevalence of car usage tends to increase with lower settlement densities in rural and regional areas.

The nationwide mobility survey *Österreich unterwegs* uncovers significant variations in the mobility patterns of Austrian citizens, contingent on the size of the municipality. Public transport emerges as a pivotal factor in ULGs with over 25,000 inhabitants. Conversely, in smaller ULGs and RLGs, both public transport and cycling constitute approximately 7% of the overall mobility share. In areas with low population density, individual car usage dominates mobility behavior (BMVIT, 2016).

Hence, rural areas in Austria are characterized by particularly high rates of MIT. Public transportation primarily serves purposes such as school commutes, work travel, shopping, and recreational outings. Typically, bus services in these areas operate under contractual agreements either between the respective municipalities and transport companies or between the respective Transport Association Organizations (*Verkehrsverbundorganisationsgesellschaften—VVOGs*, see also Sect. 3.4.1) and transport companies. In regions lacking train connections, commuter buses are often deployed. Accessibility to public transit is typically contingent upon proximity to central hubs and a correspondingly dense settlement pattern. Nevertheless, approximately one-fifth of the rural populace (those without personal vehicles) rely on external assistance to fulfill their transportation needs, notably through ride-sharing arrangements. In this context, publicly funded microtransit systems play a crucial role both in bridging the gap between public transport stops or central public transport hubs and the place of residence (keyword: "last mile") and enabling mobility for people without private vehicles. Hence, call-based systems are commonly implemented. These services entail (mini) buses with designated routes and stops, which either operate on demand or adhere to fixed schedules and routes. Upon receiving a request, these on-call buses may diverge from their regular routes to accommodate passengers before returning to their original course. Additionally, hailed shared taxis operate on prearranged schedules and fixed pricing within specified service areas, with vehicles and stops labeled as such (VCO, 2023).

Transitioning from private car usage to public transportation requires an enhancement of public transportation services, also in Austria's rural areas. However, economically speaking, expanding "traditional" public transport in RLGs with low population density poses challenges due to the difficulty in justifying the investment based on low-cost recovery rates. Conversely, a recent survey of KDZ—Centre for Public Administration Research (Hochholdinger et al., 2023) revealed that the subsidy demand for public transportation in cities with populations exceeding 30,000 (excluding Vienna) surged from 41% in 2016 to 44% in 2021. Projections indicate that by 2023 to 2025, this subsidy demand is anticipated to escalate further to 48 to 50%. This implies that expenditures are projected to increase approximately twice as much as revenues, significantly augmenting the subsidy requirement. The primary driver behind the escalating expenditure are the rising investments. Nonetheless, there are also notable increases in ongoing operational costs, attributed to factors such as expanded services, burgeoning passenger numbers, escalating energy prices, and higher operational expenses related to "clean" buses. Another survey on additional investment expenses shows that only the cities of Vienna, Graz, Linz, Salzburg, Klagenfurt, and Innsbruck incurred additional investment costs totaling EUR 1.9 billion for expanding supply and conducting capacity assessments. Another significant area of investment is the decarbonization of bus transportation. The Austrian Road Vehicle Procurement Act *(Straßenfahrzeug-Beschaffungsgesetz—SFBG*[6]*)* implementing the Clean Vehicles Directive of the European Commission[7] mandates a gradual transition to clean, emission-free buses for new purchases and ordering of transport services to avoid hefty fines. The investment costs for bus procurement in the aforementioned cities ranged from EUR 78–106 million between 2022 and 2025, increasing to EUR 2.0–2.2 billion by 2026. Additionally, there are supplementary expenses for infrastructure investments in depots required to facilitate the transition to alternative propulsion systems. Excluding Vienna, the costs are projected to total EUR 190 million from 2022 to 2025, and without Vienna and Linz, they are expected to amount to EUR 320 million from 2026 to 2030. By 2050 an additional investment requirement of approximately EUR 16 billion is estimated, along with an annual expenditure of EUR 530 million, in addition to the existing plans. This translates to an annual increase in scheduled kilometers of around 135 million for "electrified" bus kilometers and approximately 25.5 million kilometers annually for trams and metros (KCW, 2023).

Ensuring access to public transport in both ULGs and RLGs extends beyond mere affordability considerations. The efficiency of delivering public transport services at the local level faces challenges due to shared competencies and financial interconnections within the Austrian public transport sector. This challenge is particularly pronounced in functional urban regions, where there is a need for seamless connectivity between urban and regional transport services.

[6] Bundesgesetz über die Beschaffung und den Einsatz sauberer Straßenfahrzeuge (Straßenfahrzeug-Beschaffungsgesetz) https://www.ris.bka.gv.at/GeltendeFassung.wxe?Abfrage=Bundesnormen&Gesetzesnummer=20011618. Accessed December 2, 2023.

[7] See https://eur-lex.europa.eu/legal-content/EN/TXT/PDF/?uri=CELEX:32019L1161. Accessed December 2, 2023.

## 3.4 Public Transport in City Regions

To grasp the challenges concerning public transportation in city regions, it is worth briefly examining the historical, political, and administrative context of city regions in Austria. City regions have emerged as an increasingly crucial arena for political and planning interventions over the last decades, despite not typically holding sovereign authority. Whether addressing challenges arising from global economic competition or addressing the everyday needs of residents, the city region serves as the de facto spatial framework. Situated between and across formal administrative boundaries, the city region stands out spatially and conceptually. Consequently, cooperation and planning within city regions can be fostered through various approaches. The political and planning context outlines the range of intervention possibilities. City regions in Austria represent "soft spaces" lacking an ideal governance and planning approach. Instead, city-regional cooperation is best understood as a multifaceted, multilayered process requiring diverse political actions.

At the national level in Austria, there is a widely accepted definition of city regions determined by statistical characteristics, namely functional logic, which includes factors such as population density, employment density, and commuter patterns. This classification is supported by entities like Statistics Austria, the Austrian Conference on Spatial Planning (ÖROK), and the Austrian Association of Cities and Towns (AACT), identifying a total of 42 city regions with a designated core zone and surrounding outer zone. However, for collaborative purposes, the composition of active city regions may deviate from this statistical delineation, such as when individual local governments opt out or additional local governments wish to participate—a practice conducive to the overarching goals (Humer & Purkharthofer, 2020) (Fig. 3.2).

Given Austria's federal structure, support for city regions in spatial planning comes from both the regional planning authorities of the respective states and the local planning bodies of municipalities. In practice, it is left to the states to decide

**Fig. 3.2** City regions in Austria 2024. (Source: www.stadtregionen.at)

whether and how they incorporate the national concept of city regions into their planning frameworks. In the 2017 Upper Austrian Regional Spatial Planning Program (LAROP) for example, city regions were delineated for the first time, independent of regional development, with specific objectives tied to them in the program. Among these objectives is the voluntary establishment of shared (spatial) development perspectives. The aim is to design funding and implementation programs more strategically and utilize them more effectively. Assisted by *Regionalmanagement OÖ GmbH* (RMOÖ), Upper Austria saw the establishment of 16 city regions, each comprising a district town or regional center along with multiple surrounding municipalities. Supported by funding from the European Regional Development Fund under the Austrian Investments in Growth and Employment (IWB) program, as well as contributions from the state of Upper Austria, these city regions successfully executed approximately 70 projects focusing on "sustainable mobility" and "enhancement of settlement structures." These initiatives have significantly improved the overall quality of life and sustainability within their respective city regions.

At the national level, regional cooperation is primarily fostered through softer, dialogue-driven mechanisms, such as collaborative strategy documents like the *Agenda Stadtregionen* (ÖROK, 2015), platforms for discussion, and exchanges of best practices like the website www.stadtregionen.at or the (bi)annual Austrian City Region Day (*Österreichische Stadtregionstag*), both provided by the Austrian Association of Cities and Towns.

The 42 Austrian city regions represent interconnected living spaces comprising multiple cities (ULGs) and municipalities (mostly RLGs) where economic, cultural, and social activities transcend administrative boundaries. All residents benefit from the economic opportunities, educational institutions, and cultural amenities found within the core city areas. Similarly, outer zones offer ample residential space, recreational amenities, and green areas accessible to all. This interconnectedness has significant implications in the areas of settlement and location development, public infrastructure and services as well as transport, requiring a collaborative effort involving cities, municipalities, and stakeholders to achieve a high quality of life.

### 3.4.1 Organization and Financing of Public Transport in City Regions

Austrian public transport services operating within regions (*Öffentlicher Personennah- und Regionalverkehr—ÖPNRV*) defined and regulated by the Local and Regional Public Transport Act of 1999[8] include, on one hand, local passenger

[8] The Austrian Federal Law on the organization of local and regional public transport (ÖPNRV-G) regulates the organizational and financial basis for the operation of local and regional public transport in Austria. The scope of application of this federal law extends to operations, but not to infrastructure.

transport within an urban area, either within the city or connecting municipalities, and, on the other hand, regional passenger transport covering entire regions, especially rural areas. As a result, a variety of transport services coexist within this framework:

1. Rail transport in regional operations, encompassing options like high-speed rail.
2. Urban public transport, with a focus on urban operation, including city buses, trams, and metros.
3. Regional bus transport catering to areas outside cities and/or ULGs and the peripheral zones of urban areas.
4. Additionally, public micro-transit systems offering flexible and on-demand services to passengers within a specific area supplement the aforementioned modes of transportation.

Consequently, distinct responsibilities, stakeholders, and funding obligations emerge. Coordinating these systems and harmonizing services at transition points between different modes of transport and administrative areas present a multifaceted challenge. This applies in particular to the Austrian city regions.

The organization of ÖPNRV services involves various stakeholders. As mentioned before, in rural areas, the primary actors are the *Länder* (states) or the Transport Association Organizations (*VVOGs*), while in urban areas, there is a need to coordinate regional transport (*Länder/VVOGs*) and urban local transport. Consequently, the seven VVOGs (with VOR[9] encompassing three *Länder*) are established through private law contracts between federal, state, and local authorities, on the one hand, and the VVOGs, on the other hand, covering basic and financing agreements. Conversely, private law transport service contracts between local governments or the VVOGs and transport companies regulate the provision of transport services.

The strategic management and planning of regional and urban transport primarily fall under the responsibility of the *Länder*. However, in some city regions, the VVOGs also assume significant roles, while in other city regions, the VVOGs, and even cities and municipalities, are involved in strategic planning to varying degrees. Core cities, either independently or in close collaboration with urban transport operators, perform the task of strategic planning. The federal government's role in ÖPNRV is limited to managing basic rail services and cofinancing.

Regional rail transport, operational planning, and implementation, including the concrete design of services and timetables, are largely carried out by railway undertakings in coordination with the *Länder*. In regional bus transport, the VVOGs primarily handle operational planning. In urban public transport, core cities and/or urban enterprises essentially independently plan and design services. For urban cross-border traffic, responsibilities have largely evolved historically, and for new projects, responsibilities are clarified bilaterally or on a project basis. As the

[9] *Verkehrsverbund Ost-Region*—the transport association for Vienna, Lower Austria, and Burgenland. https://www.vor.at/en/. Accessed November 11, 2023.

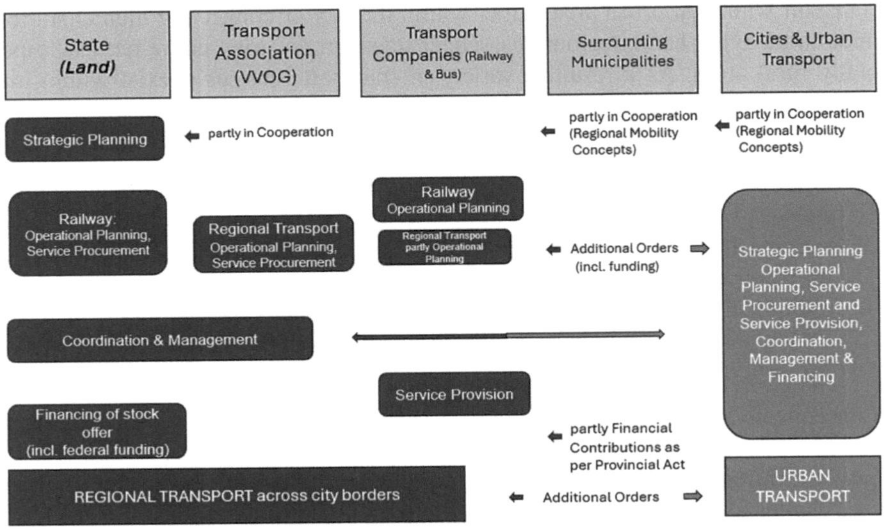


**Fig. 3.3** Actors and responsibilities in the city-regional ÖPNRV. (Sources: Mitterer et al. (2017, 6))

transition to gross contracts[10] progresses, transport companies take on fewer planning tasks.

The ordering of transport services from providers is conducted directly by the politically responsible body or entity in urban and rail transport. In regional bus transport, the VVOGs mainly negotiate transport service contracts with companies on behalf of the *Länder* as purchasers and clients. In specific cases, for cross-city traffic, the respective countries and cities jointly act as purchasers (Fig. 3.3).

The current financing structure of ÖPNRV services is intricate, owing to the involvement of various actors and funders in regional and local transport, resulting in a multitude of historically evolved management and financing mechanisms. The financing of regional transport primarily relies on support from the federal and state governments, with some local governments in certain *Länder* contributing small funding amounts through levies. Urban transport, on the other hand, is primarily funded by cities, with additional orders typically requiring self-financing by the local governments themselves. Nevertheless, in several *Länder*, additional orders from local governments are cofinanced by the *Länder*. Cross-city transport financing is predominantly project-based and varies across different city regions.

A KDZ study conducted in 2017 (Mitterer et al., 2017) on behalf of the Sub-Working Group on City-Regional Public Transport, comprising representatives of

[10] This type of contract arrangement means that the transport company is paid a fixed amount by the contracting authority (such as a city or municipality) to provide a specified level of service, regardless of the actual fare revenue collected from passengers. The contracting authority retains the fare revenue and bears the financial risk associated with passenger numbers and fare collection.

the Austrian Ministry of Transport, Infrastructure, and Technology (now Ministry for Climate Action, Environment, Energy, Mobility, Innovation, and Technology), the states, and the Austrian Association of Cities and Towns, comprehensively documented all financing flows for ÖPNRV services for the first time. The study encompassed revenue and expenditure data from the federal level (excluding long-distance transport), the states, the VVOGs, as well as cities such as Bregenz, Graz, Innsbruck, Klagenfurt, Linz, and Salzburg, and the municipal association Unteres Rheintal. However, no survey was conducted for all municipalities, and the data has not been updated, necessitating the utilization of 2014 survey data for the below-mentioned numbers.

In 2014, federal government spending amounted to EUR 587 million for the Austrian Federal Railways (*Österreichische Bundesbahnen—ÖBB*) and private railway companies for short-distance traffic and EUR 599 million for regional and local authorities and the VVOGs. This included funding to the states for basic rail-bound short-distance traffic services, student and apprentice free travel, basic and financing contracts, as well as funds for ordering services. Additionally, subsidies were provided to local governments under the Financial Compensation Act. State transfer spending totaled EUR 495 million, encompassing substantial financial contributions to the respective VVOGs for ordering transport services and covering the deficit for regional transport. Additionally, payments were made for transport service orders and infrastructure to ÖBB or private railway companies. Grants from the states or VVOGs to core cities and individual local governments for public transport were also included. The cash flows from the cities of Bregenz, Graz, Innsbruck, Klagenfurt, Linz, and Salzburg, excluding Vienna, to their urban transport companies amounted to EUR 113 million in 2014, utilized for basic financing and plugging the deficit. Additionally, basic financing from the City of Vienna totaled EUR 912 million. Occasionally, surrounding municipalities also made payments to urban transport companies for ordered transport services. However, the majority of transport services ordered by the surrounding municipalities were provided by the VVOGs.

Looking at the net burden (expenditure minus revenue) across territorial authorities, the federal government's financing share was 47% of all net expenditures in 2014. The states accounted for 19%, the city of Vienna for 27%, and the cities of Bregenz, Graz, Innsbruck, Klagenfurt, Linz, and Salzburg for 6%.

### *3.4.2 Public Transport in the City Region of Klagenfurt in Carinthia*

To exemplify the intricate nature of the aforementioned organization of public transport services, we will take the city region of Klagenfurt as a case in point with three main actors providing public transport: the City of Klagenfurt, together with its municipal utility company *KMG Klagenfurt Mobil GmbH*,[11] Klagenfurt's surrounding municipality Ebenthal, and the Carinthian VVOG (Mitterer et al., 2017). With approximately 158,000 residents, the city region encompasses 21 local governments, including two within the core zone (Klagenfurt, the capital city of Carinthia, and the municipality of Maria Rain), and 19 in the outer zone.

While Carinthia's overall population is declining, there is a slight increase in the Klagenfurt agglomeration, particularly noticeable in the surrounding areas known as the "bacon belt." Carinthia's transportation preferences lean heavily toward motorized individual transport (MIT), despite the presence of viable public transport alternatives that are not fully utilized (with the notable exception of the well-received Klagenfurt-Villach railway). This pattern endures largely due to the absence of significant traffic congestion in Carinthia's urban areas. Moving forward, a significant challenge looms in enacting effective measures to alter transportation patterns and foster a more diverse modal split.

The organization of public transport in the city region of Klagenfurt is divided between the state of Carinthia, overseeing regional bus and rail transport, the city of Klagenfurt, which handles urban public transport services, and Ebenthal, the municipality surrounding Klagenfurt which assumes responsibility for local transport in its territory.

At the regional level, the state of Carinthia takes charge of overall strategic planning for public transport, guided by the MOMAK 2025 (Mobility Master Plan Carinthia)[12] and the Carinthian Regional Transport Plan[13] as key mobility concepts. Meanwhile, within the city of Klagenfurt, strategic planning falls under the jurisdiction of the municipal government, with support from *KMG Klagenfurt Mobil GmbH* as a consultant. Key planning initiatives include the Urban Development Concept 2020+[14] (currently undergoing revision), the Smart City Climate Strategy,[15] and the Mobility Concept Klagenfurt 2035.[16]

For the operational planning and design of ÖPNRV services, the state of Carinthia holds responsibility, particularly in regional rail transport. Tariff planning and

---

[11] *KMG Klagenfurt Mobil GmbH* (formerly *STW Mobilität*) is a subsidiary of the City of Klagenfurt and *Stadtwerke Klagenfurt*, the public utility company of the City of Klagenfurt. It provides public transport mobility with more than 65 buses transporting around 20 million passengers every year, covering more than three million kilometers. See https://www.stw.at/privat/mobilitaet/. Accessed November 8, 2023.

[12] See https://portal.ktn.gv.at/Forms/Download/VT122. Accessed November 8, 2023.

[13] See https://www.kaerntner-linien.at/wp-content/uploads/2021/08/regionalverkehrsplan-2014.pdf. Accessed November 8, 2023.

[14] See https://www.klagenfurt.at/fileadmin/user_upload/Stadt_Klagenfurt/03-StadtINFOS/Leitbild/STEK_2020.pdf. Accessed November 8, 2023.

[15] See https://www.klagenfurt.at/fileadmin/user_upload/Stadt_Klagenfurt/01-StadtSERVICE/Klima-Umwelt/Smart_City_Strategie/Smart_City_Klimastrategie_Version_7.1.pdf . Accessed November 8, 2023.

[16] See https://www.klagenfurt.at/fileadmin/user_upload/Stadt_Klagenfurt/01-StadtSERVICE/Mobilitaet/Mobilitaetskonzept_Klagenfurt_2035/Mobilitaetskonzept_Klagenfurt_2035_OEPNV_190327.pdf. Accessed November 8, 2023.

coordination for regional bus transport are managed by the Carinthian VVOG (*Verkehrsverbund Kärnten GmbH—VKG*[17]). However, the majority of services planning within Carinthia is carried out by transport companies, which are also tasked with executing measures in regional bus transport.

In Klagenfurt's urban public transport domain, coordination of the planning process falls to both the city of Klagenfurt and *KMG Klagenfurt Mobil GmbH*. The latter also oversees the implementation of urban public transport services and collaborates with the municipality of Ebenthal, where they operate two bus lines that both connect Klagenfurt with Ebenthal and serve as an inner bus line for the municipality.

The ordering of services for regional bus and rail transport is managed by the Carinthian VVOG (*Verkehrsverbund Kärnten GmbH*), with revenue distribution between VKG and transport companies established through transport service contracts. Conversely, public transport services within Klagenfurt city are governed by a specific contract with *KMG Klagenfurt Mobil GmbH*. The Ebenthal municipality also procures public transport services from *KMG Klagenfurt Mobil GmbH*.

Public transport services in the city region of Klagenfurt encompass a diverse network, with rail transport operated by the Austrian Federal Railways (ÖBB) and regional bus services managed by a range of transport companies. Within the urban confines of Klagenfurt, *KMG Klagenfurt Mobil GmbH* assumes responsibility for service provision. As mentioned above, these services extend beyond city limits, including bus services in the municipality of Ebenthal and a branch bus line to the municipality of Krumpendorf.

The primary responsibility for financing the public transport network in Carinthia lies with the state government, along with partial contributions from the federal government through joint financing and basic services financing. This encompasses funding the Carinthian Transport Association (*VKG*), as well as additional services and, to some extent, local rail transport. Moreover, municipalities are obligated to contribute financially as per the Provincial Act (*Verbundbeiträge)*, with the amount contingent upon such factors as their financial capacity, traffic volume, and number of stops. This financing system also applies to regional public transport in the city region of Klagenfurt.

Urban public transport financing in Klagenfurt is primarily overseen by either the City of Klagenfurt or *KMG Klagenfurt Mobil GmbH*, except for rail lines within the city limits. The municipality of Ebenthal independently finances the bus transport services within its municipal area.

Given the complexity of the organization and financing of public transport in the city region of Klagenfurt, the lack of institutionalized cooperation and coordination between the individual ÖPNRV stakeholders (still) hinders effective public transport delivery. Coordination between the Carinthian Transport Association (VKG) and the *KMG Klagenfurt Mobil GmbH* is usually carried out informally and on

[17] See https://www.kaerntner-linien.at/die-karntner-linien/verkehrsverbundkaernten/. Accessed November 8, 2023.

demand. However, the introduction of mobility nodes contributes to enhancing both cooperation and coordination.[18] Anticipated effects on urban public transport within the urban area of Klagenfurt will be communicated to the public administration of the City of Klagenfurt by the municipal utility enterprise *KMG Klagenfurt Mobil GmbH*. ÖPNV topics between the city of Klagenfurt and the municipality of Ebenthal are handled through intermunicipal cooperation. The adopted inter-municipal cooperation model provides for joint planning and implementation in the field of public transport. This non-profit performance and cooperation agreement was concluded in 2015 between the municipality of Ebenthal and *Stadtwerke Mobilität* at the time.

To conclude, in the city region of Klagenfurt, two organizing authorities oversee the provision of public transport services: the regional transport association VKG and the City of Klagenfurt. Furthermore, Klagenfurt operates public transportation (bus) services through its municipal utility company *KMG Klagenfurt Mobil GmbH*, which also provides public transportation to the surrounding municipality Ebenthal with two bus lines. The regional transport association oversees regional rail traffic within the city region (S-Bahn) and provides public (bus) transport in the other municipalities within the city region. In addition, the regional transport association in Carinthia handles the setting of tariffs, procurement, and support planning. This multitude of actors together with complex funding structures and financial interlinkages, also applies in general to the other Austrian city regions in the area of regional public transport, particularly concerning city regions where the state capitals are the core cities. Hence, given these framework conditions, it is virtually impossible to guarantee both needs-based public transport for the residents of the city region and the necessary mobility transition to achieve the climate targets. Responsibilities must therefore be clarified, processes and mechanisms for improved coordination and cooperation established, and financial planning security guaranteed to effectively manage the high commuter flows between the municipalities in the city regions.

## 3.5 Conclusions

Local governments in Austria, both ULGs and RLGs, play a pivotal role in the provision of public transportation services, serving as key providers within their respective regions and contributing significantly to the functionality of transport networks and associations. Their involvement encompasses various aspects, including the establishment and maintenance of transport infrastructure, the operation of transit services, and the facilitation of transportation planning and coordination efforts. Within their jurisdictions, local governments are responsible for ensuring the

[18] In each Carinthian municipality, at least one mobility node is to be created, which spatially integrates the existing transport services of public transport and individual transport.

accessibility and efficiency of transportation options, catering to the diverse needs of residents and visitors alike. This can involve the deployment of buses, trams, metros, and other modes of transport to connect workplaces, educational institutions, and recreational areas. Moreover, local authorities collaborate with regional and national entities to optimize intermodal connectivity and promote seamless travel across different transport modes. Depending on the size and territorial context of local governments, thus either being a small RLG or a large ULG, local governments in Austria engage in or contribute to policymaking and regulatory initiatives aimed at enhancing the safety, affordability, and sustainability of public transportation systems. They may implement measures such as service frequency adjustments and infrastructure upgrades to address evolving mobility demands and environmental concerns. Furthermore, through partnerships with public and private stakeholders, local authorities strive to foster innovation in transportation technologies and promote the adoption of eco-friendly practices. Overall, the active involvement of local governments is indispensable for the development and operation of efficient, reliable, and inclusive public transport networks, thereby contributing to the livability and prosperity of urban and rural areas alike.

Nevertheless, the aforementioned complexity of the Austrian public transport system and the financial constraints for Austrian ULGs and RLGs hinder the provision of reliable regional and local public transport both in urban and rural areas. For RLGs, public transport accessibility is a precondition for the sustainable development of rural areas as living and working places. To achieve the mobility turnaround, a comprehensive range of mobility options needs to be provided, including in rural areas. This requires the expansion of public transport, new needs-based services, and a dense network of infrastructure for walking and cycling, thus fostering accessibility and promoting the shift of environmentally friendly modes of transportation toward "active mobility."

Austria will need to allocate significant funds to this endeavor over the coming years. Nevertheless, the potential costs of not taking action in the transport sector, one of Austria's major greenhouse gas emitters, would likely far exceed this investment, not to mention the impact on individual quality of life and society as a whole.

## References

ARGE Klimarat (ÖGUT—Österreichische Gesellschaft für Umwelt und Technik, pulswerk GmbH, PlanSinn GmbH). (2022). *Klimaneutralität bis 2040: Die Empfehlungen*. https://klimarat.org/wp-content/uploads/Klimarat-Endbericht-WEB.pdf

BMK—Federal Ministry of Climate Action, Environment, Energy, Mobility, Innovation and Technology. (2021). *Austria's 2030 Mobility Master Plan*. https://www.bmk.gv.at/en/topics/mobility/mobilitymasterplan2030.html

BMVIT—Bundesministerium für Verkehr, Innovation und Technologie. (2016). *Ergebnisbericht zur österreichweiten Mobilitätserhebung "Österreich unterwegs 2013/2014."* https://www.bmk.gv.at/dam/jcr:fbe20298-a4cf-46d9-bbee-01ad771a7fda/oeu_2013-2014_Ergebnisbericht.pdf

Hochholdinger, N., Mitterer, K., & Yildirim-Metz, K. (2023). *Finanzierung des ÖPNV in österreichischen Städten mit Ergebnissen der ÖPNV-Erhebung 2022*. KDZ.

Humer, A., & Purkharthofer, E. (2020). Stadtregionen als funktionale Handlungsräume. Kontexte des föderalen Österreichs und unitarischen Finnlands im Vergleich. In *IRS Bulletin 8/2020.* Österreichische Akademie der Wissenschaften. https://doi.org/10.1553/isr-bulletin20-08

KCW. (2023). *Finanzierungsmehrbedarf ÖPNRV durch Dekarbonisierung und Mobilitätswende—Ergebnisse der Datenabfrage*. KCW.

Land Oberösterreich. (2023). *Kurs halten & Zukunft gestalten. Erste Ergebnisse der Mobilitätserhebung 2022*.

Mitterer, K., Haindl, A., Hochholdinger, N., Schantl, A., & Valenta, A. (2017). *Stadtregionaler öffentlicher Verkehr. Organisation, Steuerung und Finanzierung. Kurzbericht. February 15, 2017*. KDZ.

ÖROK. (2015). *Für eine österreichische Stadtregionspolitik: Agenda Stadtregionen in Österreich. Empfehlungen der ÖREK Partnerschaft "Kooperationsplattform Stadtregionen."* https://www.oerok.gv.at/fileadmin/user_upload/Bilder/2.Reiter-Raum_u._Region/1.OEREK/OEREK_2011/1._Stadtregionstag_Wien/Agenda_Stadtregion_final.pdf

Österreichische Raumordnungskonferenz (ÖROK). (2022). *ÖROK-Regionalprognosen 2021 bis 2050: Bevölkerung; Schriftenreihe Nr. 212*. https://www.statistik.at/fileadmin/pages/415/OEROK_212_OEROK-BevPrognose_2021-2050.pdf

Schantl, A., Pichler, D., & Prorok, T. (2021). *Local government in Austria: Responses to urban-rural challenges*. Zenodo. https://doi.org/10.5281/zenodo.5711026

Umweltbundesamt. (2023). *Nahzeitprognose der österreichischen Treibhausgasemissionen für das Jahr 2022*. NowCast 2023. https://www.umweltbundesamt.at/fileadmin/site/publikationen/rep0869.pdf

VCO. (2023). *Bessere Mobilität für die Regionen*. Mobilität mit Zukunft 2/2023.

# Chapter 4
# Governing Public Transit in Canada

**Martin Horak**

**Abstract** This chapter provides a broad overview of the governance of public transit systems in Canada. Transit plays a relatively minor role in the overall Canadian transportation system, due to a combination of geographical and policy factors. Nonetheless, public transit is an important mode of transport in large Canadian cities. In legal terms, public transit is a responsibility of Canada's provinces, but all provinces except for one in turn delegate this responsibility to municipal governments. This jurisdictional decentralization, together with the lack of general-purpose transit legislation in most provinces, means that the structure and governance of transit systems varies widely across cities. Transit operations depend heavily on fare box revenues, and the steep decline in ridership during the Covid-19 pandemic has produced a lingering operating revenue crisis. The capital funding situation is more positive, since all three levels of government have recently invested significant funds in expanding urban transit infrastructure. However, the vertical and horizontal fragmentation of transit governance in some city-regions has politicized, complicated and delayed the construction of new high-capacity transit lines. The chapter examines these issues and challenges with a specific focus on the three largest city-regions in Canada: Vancouver, Montreal and Toronto.

**Keywords** Canada · Public transit · Governance · Toronto · Montreal · Vancouver

---

The author gratefully acknowledges the assistance of the Canadian Urban Transit Association, which provided current data on revenues and ridership across Canadian urban transit systems that underpin some of the analyses in this chapter.

---

M. Horak (✉)
Department of Political Science, Western University, London, Canada
e-mail: mhorak@uwo.ca



F. Velasco Caballero et al. (eds.), *Municipal Tasks and Financing*, Local and Urban Governance, https://doi.org/10.1007/978-3-031-99812-6_4

## 4.1 Introduction

Canada is a large country, in which long distances and low population densities create a challenging environment for the development of public transit systems. Transit use in Canada is highly concentrated in the largest urban centres. However, the decentralized character of Canadian federalism means that there is no one model or set of principles that structures transit governance. In order to provide a concise overview of transit governance in Canada, this chapter focuses on the three largest Canadian provinces by population—Ontario, Québec, and British Columbia—and, within them, on the three largest urban areas—Toronto, Montréal, and Vancouver. It discusses the governance and financing of transit operations, noting that local transit systems are at once operationally autonomous and fiscally constrained. It reviews efforts to develop integrated regional transit governance in Canada's largest cities, a process that had very different outcomes in different urban areas. Finally, the chapter examines the recent boom in rapid transit construction, focusing on how the politicization of transit infrastructure has created challenges for the development of new transit lines in urban Canada.

## 4.2 The Role of Public Transit in the Canadian Transportation System

Canada's passenger transport system is based largely around private vehicles. Public transit does play an important role, especially in large urban areas, but its prevalence is low in comparative perspective. In 2021, 7.7% of commuting trips in Canada were made by transit, compared with 83.9% by car (Statistics Canada, 2022a). While these figures in part reflect the effects of the Covid-19 pandemic, which led to a major drop in public transport use across many countries starting in 2020 (Qi et al., 2023), the share of Canadians who get around by public transit has long been lower than in most other wealthy industrialized countries, with the exception of the United States and Australia (Perl, Hern and Kenworthy 2020, 59–61). This limited role is the product of two interacting factors: low population density, and decades of automobile-centered transportation and land use planning policies.

Canada is a highly urbanized country. 72% of the population lives in urban centres with more than 100,000 residents (Statistics Canada, 2022b). But population density within urban centres is low by global standards (Xu et al., 2020). The product of a "land-rich" environment (Xu et al., 2020) and urban planning practices that have prioritized single family housing development and automobile-based urban transportation systems since the 1950s (Perl et al., 2020), low urban population densities make the provision of public transit more challenging and expensive on a per capita basis. However, there is a direct relationship between population and density in Canada—the larger a city-region is, the denser it tends to be. This in turn correlates strongly with transit use. While all Canadian urban areas with more than 50,000 people have some form of public transit service, the largest urban areas in Canada are the most densely populated and have the highest rates of public transit use, as Fig. 4.1 shows. As a result, actual transit use is highly concentrated in the largest city-regions. In 2022, the public transit agencies serving the Vancouver, Montréal and Toronto urban areas—which together house about 29% of Canada's population—accounted for 83% of all public transit trips taken in the country (calculated from Canadian Urban Transit Association, 2024a).

Public transit plays little to no role in inter-city and rural transportation in Canada. While numerous private operators provide inter-city bus services, with a few exceptions (notably, in some areas of British Columbia), there are no *public* inter-city bus services. Inter-city passenger trains were quite extensive several decades ago, but they have been repeatedly scaled back and are now limited to the heavily populated corridor between Windsor, Ontario and Québec City, and service frequencies are low. The vast majority of inter-city passenger trips occur by private

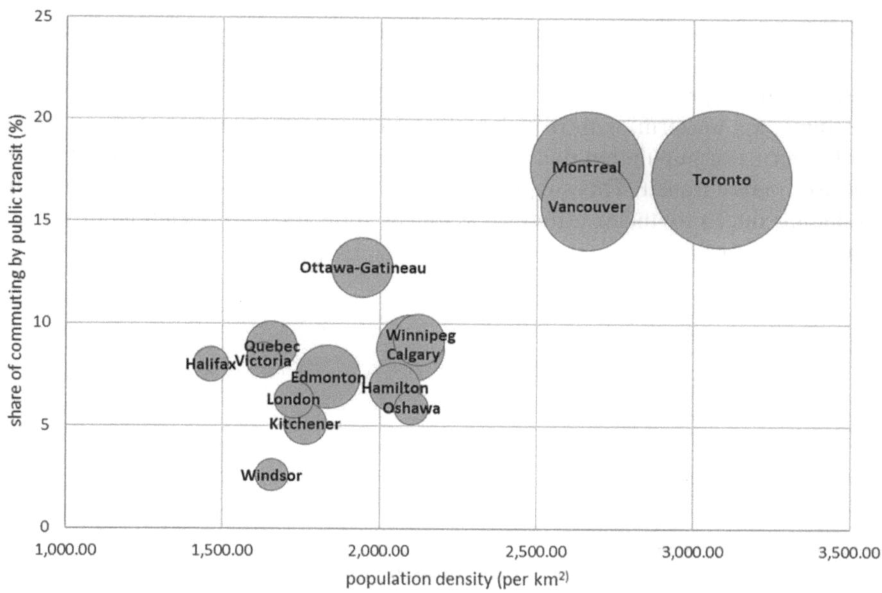


**Fig. 4.1** Population density and commuting by transit in Canada's 15 largest urban areas. (*Notes:* The size of each circle represents the population of the urban area. All data are for 2021. *Source:* Calculated by the author from Statistics Canada (2022a). Population density data are for "population centres", which reflect contiguous built-up areas, rather than municipal boundaries)

vehicle, and even air travel dwarfs train use. In 2022, for instance, Canada's nationally owned passenger train service, VIA Rail, carried 3.3 million passengers, whereas domestic air travel accounted for 74.1 million passengers (VIA Rail, 2023; Statistics Canada, 2023a).

Some smaller urban centres in Canada have modest public transit systems, but many do not. Outside British Columbia, there appears to be no local transit service in any municipality with less than 10,000 inhabitants.[1] A combination of highly dispersed settlement patterns, weak public demand, and lack of support by supra-local governments has, to date, presented insurmountable obstacles to the development of rural public transit in most of the country (Sutherland & Breen, 2022). This may be beginning to change. Among other things, in 2021 the Federal government launched a $250 million, five-year funding program aimed at supporting local authorities who want to build rural transit infrastructure (Infrastructure Canada, 2023). For the moment, however, public transit in Canada remains an overwhelmingly urban service. Indeed, Canada's only national association of transit authorities is called the Canadian *Urban* Transit Association (CUTA—see https://cutaactu.ca/).

As we will see in the next section, the governance of public transit in Canada is highly decentralized. Together with varied geographical patterns of settlement, this decentralization produces great inter-provincial variation in the prevalence of transit, seen in Table 4.1. In general, public transit is used much more heavily in more populous provinces, which contain larger urban areas. However, the relationship is not uniform, with British Columbia being an obvious outlier—it ranks third in terms of population, but first in terms of the proportion of the population that uses public transit. This suggests that provincial policies might play a role in producing inter-provincial differences. Let us turn, then, to questions of governance and policy.

[1] There is no comprehensive database of public transport systems in Canada, so this observation is based on the author's scan of a variety of partial and non-authoritative lists.

**Table 4.1** Proportion of public transit commuters by Canadian province, 2023

| | Newfoundland | Prince Edward Island | Nova Scotia | New Brunswick | Québec | Ontario | Manitoba | Saskatchewan | Alberta | British Columbia |
|---|---|---|---|---|---|---|---|---|---|---|
| Population (millions) | 0.5 | 0.2 | 1.1 | 0.8 | 8.9 | 15.8 | 1.4 | 1.2 | 4.8 | 5.6 |
| Commuting by transit (%) | 2.0* | 1.4* | 6.0 | 2.4 | 10.1 | 11.7 | 7.4 | 3.4 | 6.4 | 14.5 |

*Note:* * = 2021 data (latest available)
*Source:* Statistics Canada, 2023b

## 4.3 Canadian Public Transit: Decentralized and Politicized Governance

The governance of transit in Canada is shaped by the distinctive territorial and legal characteristics of the Canadian state. Transportation is a shared area of federal-provincial jurisdiction, but public transit systems are generally considered to be within provincial jurisdiction (Transport Canada, 2023). As a result, federal activity in the field is limited. Canada's inter-city passenger rail service, VIA Rail, is the only public transportation service operated by the federal government. As we will see later, the federal government has in recent years introduced significant funding programs to build new urban transit infrastructure, so its main involvement is in the realm of capital funding, not transit operations.

The constitutional assignment of jurisdiction over transit to provinces does not come with any stipulation on how provinces are to exercise their authority in the field. For the most part, provinces have chosen to delegate responsibility for transit to municipalities, but in concrete terms the governance of transit takes many different forms across the country. All Canadian provinces except for Québec operate under a common law system, in which governance arrangements are primarily the product of accumulated political decisions, rather than flowing from a codified set of legal-administrative principles. There are thus no generalizable written criteria or principles that structure the assignment of responsibilities and the design of governance arrangements for public transit in Canada. Instead, the governance of transit varies significantly both across and within individual provinces, having developed in different ways in response to locally differing sets of political and policy pressures. As Wood notes, "Canada's transportation governance structures and practices are uneven [and] inconsistent" (Wood, 2023, 11).

At a very basic level there is some inter-provincial congruence. All ten provinces have passed general-purpose municipal legislation, and nine of them use it to delegate responsibility over transit to municipalities—either as a "sphere of responsibility", or as a list of specified powers (Wood, 2023; Taylor & Dobson, 2020). The exception is British Columbia, where primary responsibility for public transit rests at the provincial level. In addition, Québec and British Columbia have legislation that lays out standardized principles for the organization of public transit authorities. Most provinces, however, do not have such legislation, instead leaving it up to municipal authorities to decide how transit systems are to be governed. And even in Québec and British Columbia, as we will see, the largest public transit systems—in the Montréal and Vancouver regions—are governed by special legislation.

The governance of public transit in Canada is thus highly decentralized and varied. Indeed, it is not even clear how many public transit operators there are in the country since no federal body gathers this information. The Canadian Urban Transit Association currently has 135 member agencies, of which more than half (72) are in Ontario (CUTA, 2024a); but quite a few smaller transit operators, especially in British Columbia and Québec, are not CUTA members. According to Statistics Canada, in 2020 a total of 218 municipalities across the country owned public transit assets (Statistics Canada, 2022c). Regardless, as we saw earlier, transit use is highly concentrated in the largest urban areas, and the ten largest transit agencies in Canada account for more than 90% of all transit trips (calculated from CUTA, 2024a).

## 4.4 Governing and Financing Transit Operations

The decentralization and politicization of transit governance in Canada means that we cannot identify a generally applicable set of principles and practices that structure the governance of transit. Given this, our discussion of how transit operations are governed and financed will focus on Canada's three largest provinces by population—Ontario, Québec and British Columbia—and within these three provinces, on the largest urban areas—Toronto, Montréal and Vancouver.

The legal foundations for transit governance are different in Ontario, Québec and British Columbia. In Ontario, transit is delegated to municipalities in the Municipal Act, but there is no provincial legislation that specifies how municipalities should govern transit, which is left to local discretion. Local transit systems are operated either directly or indirectly by individual municipalities, with budgets, fares, schedules and levels of service all determined locally. Many larger systems, including those in Ottawa, Hamilton and Mississauga, are run directly as administrative departments or divisions of the municipality. However, in other instances, transit is run by an arm's length agency overseen by the municipality. This is the case in Toronto, where the Toronto Transit Commission (TTC)—by far the largest transit agency in the province—is directed by a governing board made up of local politicians and citizen representatives, appointed by Toronto's city council (Toronto Transit Commission, 2024).

In Québec, transit governance is somewhat more standardized than in Ontario. A provincial law passed in 2001, the *Act respecting public transit authorities* (Government of Québec, 2023), creates nine local transit authorities in the province's largest urban areas. Most of these authorities existed prior to the adoption of the Act, but the Act standardized their governance arrangements. All nine are constituted as arm's length agencies, and the municipalities that they serve appoint a mix of local politicians and citizen representatives to their governing boards. As in Ontario, budgets, fares, schedules and levels of service are under local control. There are, however, also transit agencies in smaller urban centers that are not subject to the Act and are governed in varying ways. Furthermore, as we will see, in the Montréal area there is a complex web of transit agencies; some are constituted by the Act, others by special legislation.

British Columbia (BC) is the only province in Canada where public transit is largely managed by the provincial government. Provincial involvement with transit in BC dates back more than 100 years, and for several decades, transit delivery was a responsibility of BC Hydro, the provincial power generation company. In 1983 the province created BC Transit, a crown corporation (that is, specialized government agency) that coordinates and manages transit delivery across most of BC. BC Transit oversees the planning, financial and operating practices of 60 local transit agencies throughout the province. Services are usually provided through "a partnership between BC Transit, local government, and a contracted transit operating company" (BC Transit, 2024), with local Councils setting budgets and fares, subject to provincial regulations and standards. However, as we will see later, the largest transit system in BC by far—the one in the Vancouver area—is governed by separate legislation and is not part of the BC Transit network.

Across Canada, levels of service, fares and schedules are set locally. Canadian local governments thus have significant operational autonomy over transit delivery. However, they also depend largely on local revenue sources (as opposed to dedicated intergovernmental transfers) to fund transit operations, and the structure of these local revenue sources often results in unpredictable and/or constrained operating funds, limiting service delivery choices in practice. Comprehensive data on transit revenues at the provincial or federal level are not collected, unfortunately, but we can get a sense of the structure of operating revenues by examining recent data for Canada's three largest transit agencies.

Revenues from transit operations—that is, fare revenues—are among the main local source of operating funds for Canadian transit systems. Figure 4.2 shows the share of fare revenues vs. other sources of revenue for transit agencies in Toronto, Montréal and Vancouver. The proportions are not fully comparable across agencies due to differences in accounting—in Toronto, the figures represent operating funds only, whereas in Montréal and Vancouver, operating and capital funds are combined, so the figures underestimate the importance of fare revenues for operations, especially in the case of TransLink, which has managed several major transit

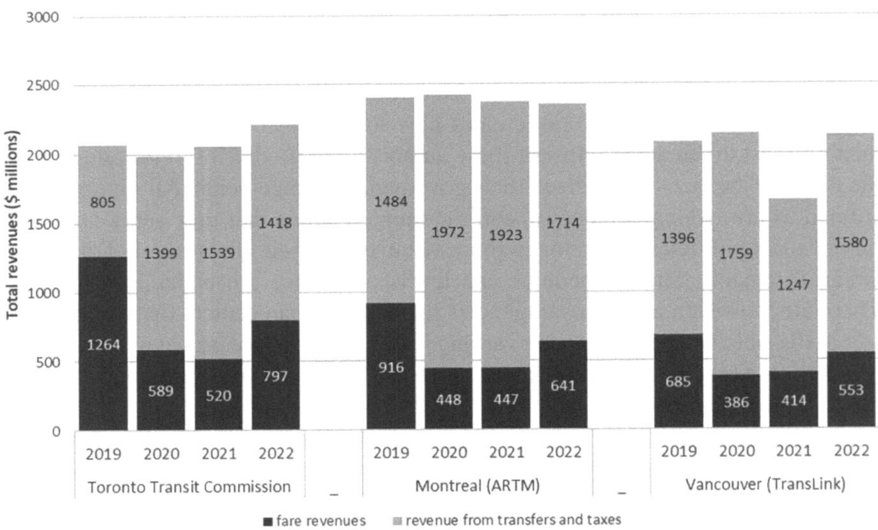


**Fig. 4.2** Fare revenues vs. other revenues, "big three" transit agencies. (*Source:* Calculated from annual reports and financial statements of the respective transit agencies)

infrastructure projects in recent years.[2] Notwithstanding, it is clear that until the Covid-19 pandemic undermined transit use, all three agencies relied heavily on fare revenues.

Subsidies from municipal budgets are another common source of local transit revenue (Eidelman et al., 2023). In 2019, for example, municipal subsidies made up 31 percent of the operating funds of the Autorité régionale de transport métropolitain (ARTM) in Montréal (ARTM, 2021, 14), and 17 percent of the TTC's operating funds (Toronto Transit Commission, 2020, 18). Heavy reliance on municipal subsidies makes transit funding vulnerable to changing political priorities, making long-range operational planning more difficult. However, not all Canadian transit agencies depend on the fickle largesse of municipal councils. Vancouver's TransLink did not receive any general municipal subsidies in 2019. This is because, unlike most other Canadian transit agencies, TransLink has the power to levy a range of local taxes, including a fuel tax, a property tax, a parking tax and a levy on electricity use (TransLink, 2013a, 4).

Intergovernmental subsidies for transit operations vary by province and locality, but always account for a minority of revenues. In 2019, intergovernmental transfers accounted for 16 percent of operating funds in Vancouver (TransLink, 2020, 21), 14 percent in Montréal (ARTM, 2021, 14), and less than 4 percent in the case of the TTC (Toronto Transit Commission, 2020, 40). Historically, the federal government has not been involved in providing operating subsidies, leaving this task to the provinces. However, this shifted in 2020 with the onset of the Covid-19 pandemic. As Fig. 4.3 shows, ridership on large urban transit systems plummeted after the start of the pandemic and did not come close to recovering to pre-pandemic levels in 2022. Statistics Canada data based on a sample of large transit providers indicates that ridership averaged 61.5% of pre-pandemic levels in 2022 and 77.4% in 2023, suggesting a slow and difficult recovery in transit modal share (calculated from Statistics Canada, 2024).

Given the operational dependence of transit agencies on fare revenues, the sudden drop in ridership resulted in a fiscal crisis for transit operators across Canada. The federal government rolled out pandemic relief funding in October 2020, which included $4.3 billion in emergency operating subsidies for transit. The relief funding was renewed in early 2022, but by early 2023 it had run out. As we will see later, the federal government has in recent years become heavily involved in supporting the construction of new transit infrastructure, but it has thus far resisted calls to provide longer-term funding support for transit *operations* (CBC News, 2024a; CUTA, 2024b). In 2023, as ridership stubbornly remained below pre-pandemic levels, Canadian transit systems "collectively faced unfunded operational shortfalls estimated at over three quarters of a billion dollars" (CUTA, 2024b). As of 2024, major transit systems have been kept running with ad-hoc annual provincial handouts to cover revenue shortfalls, but service levels have also been reduced in a

[2] The significant decrease in TransLink's revenues in 2021 is related to this, since construction on major capital projects slowed significantly that year, so fewer provincial funds were transferred for capital purposes.

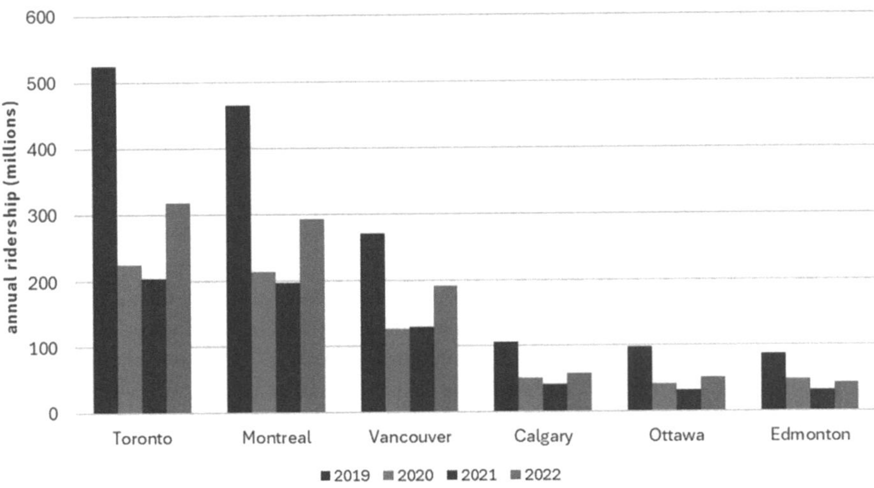


**Fig. 4.3** Annual ridership, 2019–2022, six largest Canadian transit agencies. (*Source:* Calculated from CUTA, 2024a)

number of major cities, raising fears that transit may enter a negative spiral of worsening service and decreasing ridership unless the broader operational funding model is shifted away from reliance on fare revenues (Davis, 2023).

## 4.5 Regional Transit Governance

As Wood notes, in many large city-regions around the world, transit and transportation is governed by "an arm's-length regional authority that coordinates the planning, funding, and operations of multiple modes of transportation for several municipalities with the involvement of several levels of government". In Canada, however, such a model is "neither common nor well developed" (2023, 11). Instead, the decentralized and politicized character of transit governance has led to different regional governance models emerging over time out of the distinct historical interplay of politics and policy in specific cities.

Regional transit governance systems can be designed to address two common kinds of coordination challenges: Horizontal and vertical. Horizontal coordination challenges typically emerge when there are multiple municipalities in one urban area, which necessitates the coordination of transit planning, development, and operations across municipal boundaries. In some Canadian cities—including Calgary, Edmonton, Ottawa, Halifax, London (Ontario), and others—the horizonal challenge is minimized because one municipality contains all or most of the urban population. However, the Toronto, Montréal and Vancouver urban areas are all polycentric, containing dozens of local municipalities. Vertical coordination challenges emerge when multiple levels of government are involved with transit systems. In

Canada capital funding for new transit infrastructure comes mostly from the provincial and federal governments, so vertical coordination challenges are particularly evident with respect to the planning and construction of new transit infrastructure, which we will discuss in the next section.

Table 4.2 presents a comparative overview of transit governance in Canada's three largest city-regions. The contrast between regionally consolidated governance in the Vancouver area and more fragmented governance models in Toronto and Montréal is clearly apparent. These differing arrangements have emerged over time out of a distinct interplay of transit needs and local and provincial political interests. In each case, there has been a complex and dynamic but clearly discernible relationship between the evolution of governance arrangements in the city-region as a whole, and the evolution of transit governance specifically.

Vancouver has a long history of regional planning and governance (Taylor, 2019). The urban area is governed by 21 local municipalities and an upper-tier regional government—Metro Vancouver—that is responsible for planning, water, waste, sewage, and affordable housing. Metro, which was originally established as the Greater Vancouver Regional District (GVRD) in 1967, is run by a board of politicians appointed by and from the councils of local municipalities. Transit is also regionally integrated, but it is managed by a separate, special purpose agency, TransLink. TransLink was founded in 1999 when the provincial government, which had controlled regional transit in Vancouver for several decades through a series of special-purpose authorities, was looking to divest itself of funding responsibility for the expansion of Vancouver's transit infrastructure (TransLink, 2013a).

TransLink operates all forms of public transit across the Vancouver area, and it also plans and develops new capital infrastructure, such as rapid transit lines. As we noted earlier, TransLink has the power to levy a range of local taxes, which support both operating and capital expenses. It is governed by a board of nine non-politicians. Seven of them are appointed by the TransLink Mayors' Council, and the other two by the BC provincial government. The Council, which sets long-range plans and financing strategies, includes the mayors of all 21 lower-tier municipalities, with voting weighted by population (TransLink, 2024). TransLink is thus primarily responsible to local politicians in the Vancouver area. While it is sometimes criticized for its complex internal governance arrangements and it has faced revenue shortfalls for its capital plans (see next section), TransLink is by far the strongest regional transit authority in Canada.

In the Greater Toronto Area (GTA), by contrast, there is no multipurpose regional government. Instead, there are 25 local municipalities. At the core of the urban area is the huge central City of Toronto, with about three million inhabitants. The remaining 24 local municipalities, which are located in the newer suburbs that surround the core city, are grouped into four "regions"—York, Durham, Peel and Halton—each of which has its own upper-tier government. Unlike in Vancouver, there is no history of planning and governing institutions that span the whole GTA, and no institutional connection between the City of Toronto and the suburbs that surround it.

As Table 4.2 shows, there are five transit agencies in the GTA that operate only within one municipality. They include the Toronto Transit Commission (TTC),

**Table 4.2** Transit Agencies in the Vancouver, Toronto and Montréal Urban Regions

| | Agency | Ridership (2022, M) | Scale | Who appoints governing board? | Infrastructure development? | Operational responsibilities |
|---|---|---|---|---|---|---|
| Metro Vancouver | TransLink | 192 | Regional | TransLink Mayors' Council (7) and Province of British Columbia (2) | Yes (including major road infrastructure) | All transit modes—"SkyTrain" urban rail, bus, SeaBus |
| Greater Toronto Area | Metrolinx | 38 | Regional | Province of Ontario | Yes | Commuter rail and airport rail link |
| | Toronto Transit Commission (TTC) | 319 | Municipal | Toronto City Council | Yes (until 2019) | Subway, bus, streetcar |
| | Mississauga Transit | 36 | Municipal | No board—Run directly by the city | No | Bus |
| | Brampton Transit | 31 | Municipal | No board—Run directly by the city | No | Bus |
| | York Region Transit | 16 | Sub-regional | No board—Run directly by the city | No | Bus |
| | Durham Region Transit | 7 | Sub-regional | No board—Run directly by the city | No | Bus |
| | Burlington Transit | 3 | Municipal | No board—Run directly by the city | No | Bus |
| | Oakville Transit | 2 | Municipal | No board—Run directly by the city | No | Bus |

| | Agency | Ridership (2022, M) | Scale | Who appoints governing board? | Infrastructure development? | Operational responsibilities |
|---|---|---|---|---|---|---|
| Montréal Metropolitan Community | Autorité régionale de transport métropolitain (ARTM) | n/a | Regional | Montréal Metropolitan Community (8) and Province of Québec (7) | Yes (including major road infrastructure) | None—Coordinates the activity of other transit agencies |
| | Société de Transport de Montréal (STM) | 294 | Sub-regional | Montréal Agglomeration Council | No | Subway, bus |
| | Société de transport de Laval | 16 | Municipal | Laval City Council | No | Bus |
| | Société de Transport de Longueuil | 14 | Sub-regional | Longueuil Agglomeration Council | No | Bus |
| | EXO | 37 | Sub-regional | Multiple municipalities | No | Bus |
| | REM (operating from 2023) | n/a | Sub-regional | CDPQ (3) and Province of Québec (2) | Yes | Commuter rail |

*Sources:* Ridership data are from CUTA, 2024a and (for smaller agencies) from individual agency websites; all other data are from Horak & Taylor, 2023 and individual transit agency websites

Canada's largest agency in terms of ridership, which operates in the City of Toronto.[3] There are also two *sub-regional* transit agencies, which are operated by two of the four upper-tier governments in the suburbs, and which each cover several local municipalities. Of the seven local and sub-regional agencies, only the TTC is run as an arm's-length body with a governing board.

There was no regional transit authority in the GTA until 2006, when the provincial government established Metrolinx with a mandate to run the provincially-owner commuter rail system and to "plan, finance and develop an integrated regional transportation network" (Horak, 2021). Although Metrolinx now operates both the commuter rail system and an airport rail link, most transit operations remain under the control of the seven local agencies, as Table 4.2 shows. Metrolinx has little power to influence these operations, since operating funds do not flow through it, and local agencies retain the authority to determine schedules, levels of service, and—until February 2024—fares as well (CBC News, 2024b).

For most of its existence, Metrolinx has been provincially controlled. It was initially governed by a board dominated by municipal appointees. However, the Toronto region has little history of interaction between the City of Toronto and the outer suburbs, and the board was plagued by infighting over priorities. In 2009 the province restructured it, replacing local appointees with provincial ones (Horak, 2021, 252). There is thus no institutional connection between Metrolinx and the city councils that manage municipal and sub-regional transit agencies.

In addition, and in contrast to TransLink, Metrolinx has no autonomous taxing authority, so it depends largely on provincial capital grants for its multi-billion-dollar annual budget. Metrolinx manages all major rapid transit infrastructure projects in the GTA suburbs. Until 2019, some transit projects in the City of Toronto were managed by Metrolinx and others by the TTC; but in 2019, the province "uploaded" all responsibility for rapid transit construction in the city to Metrolinx. As of 2020, Metrolinx had spent about $27 billion building new transit infrastructure (Horak 2021, 251). As we will see in the next section, however, the institutional disconnect between Metrolinx and local city councils has often made this process messy and difficult.

The Montréal region has a complex governance system. There are 82 municipalities in the region, of which the City of Montréal (population 1.8 million) is by far the largest. The City is in turn subdivided into 19 Boroughs, each with its own elected council. At a broader scale, the Urban Agglomeration of Montréal, which covers the Island of Montréal, includes the City of Montréal and 14 other smaller municipalities. Beyond the Island there are several dozen suburban municipalities, large and small, on the north and south shores of the St. Lawrence River. Finally, the Montréal Metropolitan Community (MMC), a weak regional planning authority established by the provincial government in 2001, covers the whole urban region (Taylor, 2020). Governing tasks are thus divided among multiple tiers, but primary political authority lies with local municipalities, since the governing councils of the

[3] To be precise, some of these agencies run service just beyond their boundaries to facilitate transfer connections to local services in neighbouring municipalities.

Montréal Urban Agglomeration and the Montréal Metropolitan Community are both made up of mayors and councilors from local municipalities, with representation weighted by population.

Transit governance in Montréal reflects the multi-layered structure of metropolitan governance, and has been subject to many rounds of restructuring over the decades. During the second half of the twentieth century, public transit on the Island of Montréal was consolidated under one locally-run agency, while numerous agencies served the off-island suburbs. In 1996, the Québec provincial government created the Agence Metropolitaine de Transport (AMT), a provincially controlled regional transportation agency with a mandate to coordinate transit delivery among local providers, and to plan and develop new transit infrastructure and major roads. The AMT was given access to dedicated taxes, including a fuel tax for transit operations and a share of local property taxes for capital works, which it collected and redistributed to local transit agencies, which continued to run all transit operations (TransLink, 2013b).

In 2016, the province replaced AMT with the Autorité régionale de transport métropolitain (ARTM). Control was shifted towards local government, with the MMC Council appointing 8 of the 15 positions on the ARTM's Board of Directors, and the province appointing 7. At the same time, the provincial government consolidated seven small suburban transit operators and the commuter rail system into one new operating agency, EXO (ARTM , 2024). This left four transit operators in the Montréal region, one serving a single municipality, and three others serving multiple municipalities. By far the largest operator in terms of ridership is the Société de Transport de Montréal (STM), which serves the Island of Montréal.

The ARTM is thus designed as a relatively strong upper-tier authority in an integrated two-tier transit governance system. However, in 2015, just before the government established the ARTM, it also launched the construction of an electrified suburban rail system, the Réseau électrique métropolitain (REM). The REM is being built as a "public-public" partnership between the Government of Québec and the province's pension fund manager, the Caisse de dépôt et placement du Québec (CDPQ). The ARTM has no control over the project, despite its nominal role as the regional transportation planning body. As Roy notes, "by entrusting the CDPQ with the mandate to design, build and operate … the REM, the Québec government is bypassing the ARTM by imposing on it a major public transit project that it had not chosen" (Roy, 2022, 12). The development of the REM, by far the largest transit project tin Montréal in recent years, has undermined the ARTM's ability to act as a regional transportation planner and given rise to new coordination challenges and inter-agency conflicts at the very time when an integrated system of regional transit governance appeared to be on the verge of consolidation (Roy, 2022).

All three of Canada's largest city-regions have thus seen initiatives to develop regional transportation authorities in recent years. The results have arguably been strongest in Vancouver, with its long history of regional collaboration, and weakest in Toronto, where Metrolinx has become a dependent arm of the provincial government, rather than a mechanism for intermunicipal coordination and cooperation. One reason why progress towards regionally integrated transit governance has been halting and uneven is that provincial governments, who have both a financial and a political stake in big city transit, are reluctant to cede control, and periodically intervene to protect or advance their own political interests. Nowhere is this phenomenon more evident than in the dynamics of transit infrastructure construction.

## 4.6 Governing the Development of Rapid Transit

While transit operating costs are largely locally funded, local governments rely mostly on intergovernmental grants for capital projects. In the 1980s and 90 s such grants were scarce, and little new transit infrastructure was built. Canadian cities continued to grow, however, and along with them their traffic problems. Responding to a growing infrastructure deficit, provincial and federal governments got back into the business of infrastructure grants in the new millennium, and over the past 15 years there has been something of a boom in the construction of new rapid transit infrastructure in Canadian cities. However, in many instances this process has been messy and contentious, with rapid transit initiatives subject to delays and reversals.

Several factors make the implementation of new rapid transit initiatives challenging in many Canadian cities. First, provincial and federal political parties do not operate in local politics, which either is non-partisan, or has distinct local political parties. This makes it more difficult to sustain intergovernmental agreement on infrastructure priorities. Second, administrative communication and coordination across levels of government is weakly institutionalized (Horak, Forthcoming), further accentuating vertical coordination challenges. Third, intergovernmental infrastructure funding is generally distributed on a project basis, rather than as formula-based transfers, which gives non-local governments the chance to use infrastructure grants to pursue their own short-term political interests. Finally, the weak development of metropolitan transit authorities further enhances opportunities for politicians—both provincial and local—to prioritize immediate political goals over longer-term policy considerations in making choices about rapid transit infrastructure (Horak, 2021, 248).

Nowhere has this triumph of politics over policy been more evident than in the City of Toronto. In 2007 the City, under mayor David Miller, responded to the availability of new provincial infrastructure funding by proposing a plan to build six new light rail lines. The plan was well received by transit experts, and the provincial government pledged to fund it, but before construction had started, a new mayor—Rob Ford—was elected on a promise to scrap the plan, and instead build one subway to avoid taking road space away from cars (Silver et al., 2020). Ford's plan made little sense from a transit perspective, but the provincial government deferred to local politics and five of the six light rail lines in the Miller light rail plan were shelved. In 2014, yet another mayor—John Tory—was elected with a promise to build yet another, different rapid transit line, while Ford's subway remained on the drawing board, and construction of one light rail line from the Miller era continued at a snail's pace, hobbled by disputes over details between Metrolinx and the TTC (Horak 2021, 251).

The saga of successive and largely unrealized rapid transit plans in Toronto continued until 2019, when a new Conservative provincial government suddenly produced its own proposal for yet another new subway line. The province then reached an agreement with the city, whereby Metrolinx would manage all rapid transit construction, and the provincial government promised to fully fund four rapid transit lines, comprising a mix of old and new subway and light rail proposals (StrategyCorp, 2019). For now, this arrangement seems to have held, and there is some progress on construction, but after nearly 20 years of effort, not a single new rapid transit line is yet in operation in Toronto. Lacking its own revenue base and autonomous planning powers, Metrolinx remains an instrument of the provincial government, and transit construction in Toronto remains vulnerable to political reversals and uncertain funding commitments.

In Montréal, the provincial government has created an ironic circumstance in which the ARTM, regional transit planning and construction body that it created in 2016, does not manage the largest rapid transit expansion project in the city, the REM. The REM is a 67-kilometre light rail system connecting the airport, the city centre, and the southern and western suburbs of Montréal. The first segment opened in 2023 and has attracted international attention for being built quickly and at a relatively low cost (English, 2023). The governance of the project has been centralized in one entity—an infrastructure subsidiary of the CDPQ, which the province exempted from local planning consultation requirements—and it has had strong political support from both the premier of Québec and the mayor of Montréal. Together, these factors have enabled rapid and relatively cost-effective construction so far (English, 2023).

However, a planned eastern extension of the REM ran into major public opposition, ultimately leading the CDPQ to withdraw from the project in 2022. The ARTM, which had criticized the CDPQ's plans for the eastern extension, was put in charge of producing a revised version. In 2023, it unveiled a plan that addressed resident concerns by putting the whole project underground but tripled its price tag to $36 billion (Ouellette-Vezina, 2023). The provincial government promptly rejected the plan as unrealistic, effectively killing the project. In short, insulating the REM project from the broader transit governance system may have expedited its realization thus far, but it is unclear if this model is sustainable, and it has come at the cost of undermining the overall coordination of rapid transit development in the region.

Among Canada's three largest cities, Vancouver has the strongest record in terms of systematic rapid transit construction. Underpinning this is the area's long tradition of regional planning, which has produced a relatively broad and stable consensus about where rapid transit lines should be built (Horak, 2021). Vancouver's first two rapid transit lines, the Expo and Millennium lines, were built and funded by the provincial government. Since the creation of TransLink in 1999, two more rapid lines have been built, largely on time and on budget, and a major extension to an existing line is now under construction.[4]

[4] See https://www.broadwaysubway.ca

However, TransLink has not been the undisputed lead agency for these projects as might be expected. The main problem is that TransLink's dedicated revenue streams are insufficient to fund such projects, and repeated attempts to increase them have run up against electoral considerations at the provincial level. In 2000, for example, the TransLink Mayors' Council proposed a vehicle registration levy, but the provincial government rejected it ahead of an election (Horak, 2021, 254); in 2013 a new provincial government promised a referendum on any new transportation taxes in the Vancouver area, after which voters defeated a ten-year investment plan by the Mayors' Council that would have been funded by a 0.5% sales tax increase (Taylor, 2022, 151). In the absence of sufficient revenues, TransLink has depended heavily on funding from other levels of government—especially the province—to realize rapid transit projects. The province, in turn, has insisted on having a hand in project governance, so in practice, rapid transit projects in Vancouver are significantly shaped by provincial interests.

## 4.7 Conclusions: Facing the Challenges of Transit Governance in Canada

The governance of public transit in Canada is highly decentralized and politicized. As a result, specific governance arrangements and transit system performance vary widely. Nonetheless, our review has identified some widely occurring challenges. Since transit operations tend to depend heavily on fare box revenues and municipal subsidies, their fiscal health is vulnerable to shifts in local politics and in ridership. This vulnerability is highlighted by the current fiscal crisis that many transit operators face in the wake of the Covid-19 pandemic, which has sparked discussion about the need to diversify sources of operating revenue.

Building rapid transit infrastructure, by contrast, depends heavily on intergovernmental grants. These grants are generally distributed on a project basis, rather than as formula-based transfers, and in a context where both vertical and horizontal coordination tends to be weakly institutionalized, this gives federal and provincial governments opportunities to insert short-term political considerations into their decisions about which projects to support. This politicization of intergovernmental grants also has another pernicious consequence: provincial and federal governments tend to find it more politically attractive to promise new transit lines, rather than allocating funds to maintain existing infrastructure; as a result, state-of-good-repair concerns are chronically underfunded, decreasing the quality of transit service (Davis, 2023).

Finally, with few exceptions, regional transit governance institutions in Canadian cities tend to be weak and unstable. In a context where provincial governments have full control over local affairs, these institutions are largely a product of provincial decision-making. The three cases that we have reviewed in this chapter suggest that provincial action in this regard is structured by a fundamental tension between the logics of policy and politics. From a policy perspective, provincial governments recognize the need for regional transit coordination, and they have made concerted efforts to establish regional transit authorities that can coordinate transit operations and plan and deliver infrastructure. But from a political perspective, provincial governments have been reluctant to give such regional authorities *too* much power and autonomy, since doing so would limit provincial opportunities to strategically intervene in transit governance. As a result, provincial approaches to regional transit governance—and indeed, to transit governance in general—have been inconsistent and unstable.

It is tempting to conclude that, given the fundamental challenges facing transit governance in Canada, policymakers have much to learn from practices in other countries. To some extent, this is no doubt true. However, as we have seen, the challenges facing transit governance in Canada are strongly influenced by underlying factors that are specific to the country, including low population densities, provincial dominance over local affairs, and low levels of horizontal and vertical coordination in the broader governance system. As Canadian urban centres continue to grow and environmental and social imperatives to encourage transit use intensify, new solutions to the challenges of transit governance must be grounded in a systematic understanding of the ways in which institutions, politics and policies at multiple levels of government have interacted over time to shape the current realities of transit governance in Canada.

## References

Autorité régionale de transport métropolitain [ARTM]. (2021). *Budget 2021*. Retrieved March 20, 2024, from https://www.artm.Québec/wp-content/uploads/2021/02/2082_ARTM_BUDGET_2021_web_150dpi_Final.pdf

Autorité régionale de transport métropolitain [ARTM]. (2024). *Gouvernance*. Retrieved March 15, 2024, from https://www.artm.Québec/a-propos-de-l-artm/gouvernance/

BC Transit. (2024). *Funding and governance*. Retrieved March 25, 2024, from https://www.bctransit.com/about/funding-and-governance/

Canadian Urban Transit Association [CUTA]. (2024a). *Selected transit ridership and revenue data*. Data provided to Martin Horak upon request.

Canadian Urban Transit Association [CUTA]. (2024b). *CUTA calls for urgently needed transit funding in 2024 federal budget*. Press release. Retrieved March 26, 2024, from https://cutaactu.ca/cuta-calls-for-urgently-needed-transit-funding-in-2024-federal-budget/#:~:text=The%20federal%20government%20plans%20to,good%20repair%20for%20existing%20infrastructure

CBC News. (2024a). TTC, 2 other major transit operators ask for feds to release approved funds in upcoming budget. *CBC News*. Retrieved March 26, 2024, from https://www.cbc.ca/news/Canada/toronto/ttc-ask-federal-funds-1.7150199

CBC News. (2024b). Ontario rolling out GTA-wide transit fare integration on Feb. 26. *CBC News*, February 5. Retrieved April 1, 2024, from https://www.cbc.ca/news/canada/toronto/fare-integration-gta-ttc-go-1.7105022

Davis, S. S. (2023). Who broke the TTC? *Toronto Life*, July 6. Retrieved March 13, 2024, from https://torontolife.com/deep-dives/who-broke-the-ttc-inside-torontos-public-transit-disaster/

Eidelman, G., Forman, K., Neufeld, S., & Riaz, K. (2023). Backgrounder: Transportation policy. In *The municipal role in transportation* (pp. 1–6). Institute on Municipal Finance and Governance.

English, J. (2023). *How Montréal built a blueprint for bargain rapid transit*. Retrieved April 2, 2024, from https://www.bloomberg.com/news/articles/2023-10-30/how-Montréal-s-new-rapid-transit-line-saved-millions-per-mile?embedded-checkout=true
Government of Québec. (2023). *Act respecting public transit authorities*. Retrieved February 22, 2024, from https://www.legisQuébec.gouv.qc.ca/en/document/cs/s-30.01
Horak, M. (2021). Building rapid transit in Canada: The problem of governance. In F. V. Caballero (Ed.), *Anuario de Derecho Municipal 2020* (pp. 243–258). Universidad Autonoma de Madrid.
Horak, M. (Forthcoming). Multilevel urban governance in Canada. In K. Good & J. Nelles (Eds.), *Canadian urban governance in comparative perspective*. University of Toronto Press.
Horak, M., & Taylor, Z. (2023). *Canadian Municipal Attributes Portal*. Retrieved April 1, 2024, from https://westernurban.shinyapps.io/CMAP/
Infrastructure Canada. (2023). *Backgrounder: Canada opens intake for the Rural Transit Solutions Fund's Capital Project stream*. Retrieved February 20, 2024, from https://www.canada.ca/en/office-infrastructure/news/2023/01/backgrounder-canada-opens-intake-for-the-rural-transit-solutions-funds-capital-project-stream.html
Ouellette-Vezina, H. (2023). 100% souterrain pour 36 milliards. *La Presse*, July 1. Retrieved April 2, 2024, from https://www.lapresse.ca/actualites/grand-Montréal/2023-07-01/rapport-final-sur-le-rem-de-l-est/100-souterrain-pour-36-milliards.php
Perl, A., Hern, M., & Kenworthy, J. (2020). *Big moves: Global agendas, local aspirations, and urban mobility in Canada*. McGill-Queen's University Press.
Qi, Y., Liu, J., Tao, T., & Zhao, Q. (2023). Impacts of COVID-19 on public transit ridership. *International Journal of Transportation Science and Technology, 12*(1), 34–45. https://doi.org/10.1016/j.ijtst.2021.11.003
Roy, J. (2022). *La gouvernance du transport collectif au Québec: Enjeux et pistes de solution*. Centre sure la productivite et la prosperite. Retrieved March 10, 2024, from https://cpp.hec.ca/wp-content/uploads/2022/12/PP-2022-03.pdf
Silver, D., Taylor, Z., & Calderón-Figueroa, F. (2020). Populism in the city: The case of ford nation. *International Journal of Politics, Culture, and Society, 33*, 1–21. https://doi.org/10.1007/s10767-018-9310-1
Statistics Canada. (2022a). *Census profile, census of population 2021*. Retrieved February 23, 2024, from https://www12.statcan.gc.ca/census-recensement/2021/dp-pd/prof/details/page.cfm
Statistics Canada. (2022b). *Annual demographic estimates: Subprovincial areas: July 1, 2022*. Retrieved March 12, 2024, from https://www150.statcan.gc.ca/n1/pub/91-214-x/91-214-x2022001-eng.htm
Statistics Canada. (2022c). *Canada's core public infrastructure survey: Public transit assets, 2020*. Retrieved March 12, 2024, from https://www150.statcan.gc.ca/n1/daily-quotidien/220421/dq220421b-eng.htm
Statistics Canada. (2023a). *Air passenger traffic at Canadian airports, annual*. Retrieved March 18, 2024, from https://www150.statcan.gc.ca/t1/tbl1/en/tv.action?pid=2310025301
Statistics Canada. (2023b). *Number and proportion of public transit commuters by province, 2016 to 2023*. Retrieved March 19, 2024, from https://www150.statcan.gc.ca/n1/daily-quotidien/230822/t002b-eng.htm
Statistics Canada. (2024). *Passenger bus and urban transit statistics, by the North American Industry Classification System (NAICS)*. Retrieved April 1, 2024, from https://www150.statcan.gc.ca/t1/tbl1/en/tv.action?pid=2310025101
StrategyCorp. (2019). *Toronto has a transit deal. What's next?* Retrieved April 2, 2024, from https://strategycorp.com/2019/10/we-appear-to-have-a-transit-deal-what-happens-next/
Sutherland, C., & Breen, S.-P. (2022). Not in service: A typology of barriers facing rural transit systems. *Canadian Planning and Policy/Aménagement et politique au Canada, 2022*, 172–190. https://doi.org/10.24908/cpp-apc.v2022i1.15783
Taylor, Z. (2019). *Shaping the metropolis: Institutions and urbanization in the United States and Canada*. McGill-Queen's Press.
Taylor, Z. (2020). *Theme and variations: Metropolitan governance in Canada*. Institute on Municipal Finance and Governance. https://hdl.handle.net/1807/101763

Taylor, Z. (2022). Regionalism from above: Intergovernmental relations in Canadian metropolitan governance. *Commonwealth Journal of Local Governance, 26*, 139–159. https://doi.org/10.5130/cjlg.vi26.8141

Taylor, Z., & Dobson, A. (2020). *Power and purpose: Canadian municipal law in transition*. Institute on Municipal Finance and Governance.

Toronto Transit Commission. (2020). *2019 Annual Report*. Retrieved March 3, 2024, from https://www.ttc.ca/transparency-and-accountability/Annual-Reports

Toronto Transit Commission. (2024). *About the Board*. Retrieved March 3, 2024, from https://www.ttc.ca/about-the-ttc/the-board

TransLink. (2013a). *TransLink governance review: Appendix 1—TransLink governance history*. Retrieved February 2, 2024, from https://www.translink.ca/-/media/translink/documents/about-translink/governance-and-board/board-of-directors/board-minutes-and-reports/translink_governance_review_appendix_1.pdf

TransLink. (2013b). *TransLink governance review: Appendix 3—Results of International Urban Transport Governance Review*. Retrieved March 20, 2024, from https://www.translink.ca/-/media/translink/documents/about-translink/governance-and-board/board-of-directors/board-minutes-and-reports/translink_governance_review_appendix_3.pdf

TransLink. (2020). *2019 Year-End Financial and Performance Report*. Retrieved February 2, 2024, from https://www.translink.ca/-/media/translink/documents/about-translink/corporate-reports/quarterly_reports/2019/2019_year_end_financial_and_performance_report_final_with_appendix-1.pdf

TransLink. (2024). *About TransLink*. Retrieved April 1, 2024, from https://www.translink.ca/about-us/about-translink

Transport Canada. (2023). *Federal Authorities and Levers*. Retrieved March 4, 2024, from https://tc.canada.ca/en/corporate-services/transparency/briefing-documents-transport-canada/2023-dm/transport-canada-overview/federal-authorities-levers

VIA Rail. (2023). *Annual Report 2022*. Retrieved March 18, 2024, from https://media.viarail.ca/sites/default/files/publications/VIA%20Rail_2022%20Annual%20Report_0.pdf

Wood, P. B. (2023). The municipal role in transportation governance. In *The municipal role in transportation* (pp. 11–15). Institute on Municipal Finance and Governance.

Xu, G., Zhou, Z., Jiao, L., & Zhao, R. (2020). Compact urban form and expansion pattern slow down the decline in urban densities: A global perspective. *Land Use Policy, 94*, 104563. https://doi.org/10.1016/j.landusepol.2020.104563

# Chapter 5
# Public Transport in Functional Urban Areas and Rural Areas of Spain

**Jorge Castillo Abella**

**Abstract** Rural and urban areas face very different challenges in regard to public transport services. This chapter explores those challenges in the Spanish context against the backdrop of a fragmented local government map and a variety of governmental levels. The analysis sets out with the responsibilities allocated to these levels of government, with special attention to local governments, and their performance in carrying them out. Local autonomy and administrative collaboration are analysed, as well as more recent issues, developments or initiatives both in urban and in rural mobility. The contribution shows that rural and urban transport services face fundamentally different challenges and discusses the different trends to solve them.

**Keywords** Urban mobility · Rural mobility · Public transport · Local autonomy · Low emission areas · On-demand mobility

## 5.1 Introduction

It is difficult to understate the importance of mobility policies as one of the branches of public (administrative) activity which directly impacts citizens' lives. It influences on a daily basis how or even whether citizens can travel from their homes to wherever they may need or want to go, be it for work, pleasure, family or any other reason. Transport policies are, therefore, clearly related to the *freedom of movement* guaranteed in Articles 21 of the Treaty on the Functioning of the European Union and 45 of the Charter of Fundamental Rights of the European Union. On a national level, they are also directly connected to the freedom of movement granted by Article 19 of the Spanish Constitution (Hernando Rydings, 2009, 249; Belintxon Martín, 2016, 20).

---

J. Castillo Abella (✉)
Institute of Local Government Law, Autonomous University of Madrid, Madrid, Spain
e-mail: jorge.castillo@uam.es



F. Velasco Caballero et al. (eds.), *Municipal Tasks and Financing*, Local and Urban Governance, https://doi.org/10.1007/978-3-031-99812-6_5

This chapter focuses on one side of transport policies: those related to *collective public transportation.* It analyses public transport services provided (directly or indirectly) by different levels of government. Private transportation regulations or policies will therefore not be addressed. Private road transports and, notably, cars are not a part of this analysis, unless they have a direct connection to the issues discussed. Taxi services also fall outside the scope of this chapter due to two factors. On the one hand, it is arguable whether taxi service is a "public" service, as it is exclusively provided by private persons who hold authorization. On the other hand, taxi services face their own challenges, mainly the coexistence with other individual transports (Uber, Cabify, Bolt, etc.).

The social and demographic reality in Spain is one of contrasts. As the second largest country in the European Union, it is home to the fourth largest population of a member state and two of the most populated cities in the Union (Madrid and Barcelona). However, vast swathes of land are sparsely populated and there is a very high concentration of inhabitants in or around large cities. This has led to a phenomenon dubbed the "emptied Spain" *(España vaciada)*, in reference to the demographic challenge it represents and the very real risk of many local communities disappearing through rural exodus or sheer demographic decline. The relevance of this issue is reflected even in the national government's structure, which since the Royal Decree 2/2020 has a department dedicated to ecological transition and the demographic challenge (Fig. 5.1).

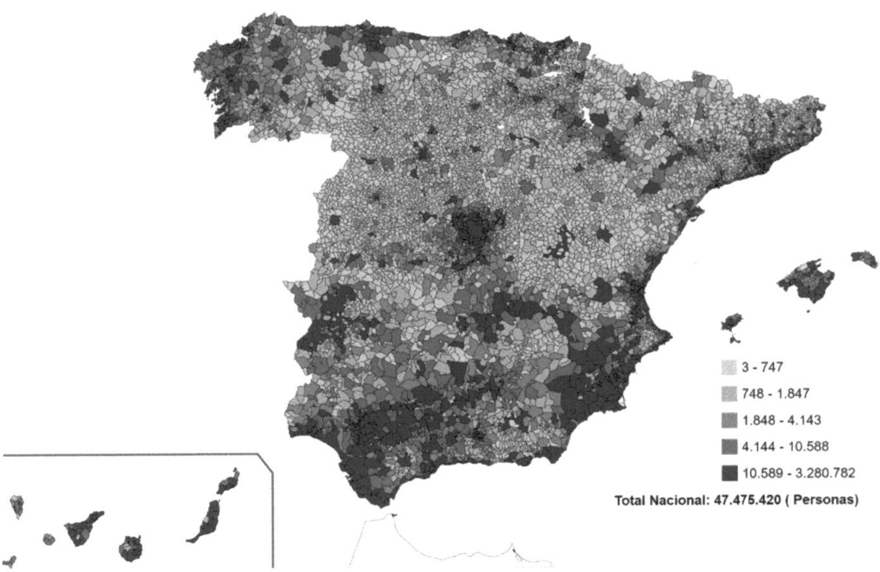


**Fig. 5.1** De jure population by municipality in Spain in 2022. (Source: Instituto Nacional de Estadística, licensed under CC-BY 4.0)

Another trait of the Spanish geographical landscape is its remarkable fragmentation at the lowest level of local government: Spain has 8124 municipalities, 72% of which have less than 2000 inhabitants (European Commission and OECD, 2018, 6). This naturally leads to two very different realities: while cities and metropolitan areas, in general, enjoy strong administrative (and political) apparatuses, small municipalities struggle to provide basic services through their small administrative organizations. One such service is public transport. This can be partially attributed to the *one-size-fits-all design of local governments* set out in Law 7/1985, of 2nd April, on the Basic Regulation of Local Governments (LBRL). Although later amended by Law 57/2003 to include specific regulations regarding cities, this law effectively prevents a different organization of municipalities which may, nevertheless, differ greatly in demographic, urban or economic terms. This has led to some criticism and proposals for a specific regulation of small municipalities (Velasco Caballero, 2020; Velasco Caballero, 2022; Almeida Cerreda, 2023a).

If this is true, how have small municipalities been able to function (however satisfactorily), if their situation is so precarious? Enter here the second-tier level of Spanish local government: the *province*. All municipalities are integrated into one of the 50 provinces that make up the Spanish territory. In turn, provinces are the traditional division of the regional level of government, the autonomous communities.[1] Their main task is to assist municipalities in the provision of those public services for which they are responsible (Article 36 LBRL). While this is roughly the structure set out in the Constitution and the LBRL, there are nevertheless other local governments peculiar to certain autonomous communities or islands which are usually lodged between municipality and province and have their own powers and responsibilities.

In such a landscape, public transport is a basic service that must be provided and in whose provision local governments take a large part. What exactly that entails, however, is a question that requires a nuanced answer that considers the stark contrast between urban and rural areas, demographic fluxes, financial aspects and, above all, what the citizens need (i.e. demand) in each case.

## 5.2 Responsibilities of Local Governments Regarding Public Transport: Even Allocation, Uneven Execution

When talking about public transport, a basic distinction is necessary: intra- and inter-urban transport. This, of course, distinguishes between transport *within* the municipal limits and transport *between* municipalities. Responsibility over each may be allocated to different bodies, citizen demand is diverse, and so are the issues or problems peculiar to each of them. While intra-urban transport typically refers to

[1] To avoid administrative duplication, the provincial administration is fused with that of the autonomous community if the latter is made up of only one province.

buses and trams, inter-urban (or metropolitan) transport includes metro, inter-urban buses and, in some instances, short-distance trains (Matas Prat & Perdiguero García, 2022, 117).

*Intra-urban collective transport* in Spain is the responsibility of municipalities (Article 25(2)(g) LBRL). Public transport is hence at the core of responsibilities allotted to municipalities (Carbonell Porras & Cano Campos, 2006, 119). If a given municipality has a *de jure* population of over 50,000 inhabitants, it has an obligation to provide a collective public transport service for intra-urban trips (Article 26(1)(d) LBRL). Under that threshold, municipalities are free to provide that service, but are under no obligation to do so. As autonomous communities pass more detailed regulations on local governments, concrete responsibilities may vary slightly from one to another. Traditionally, intra-urban public transport has been provided directly by municipalities, with little involvement of private actors, especially in larger cities (Fernández Farreres, 2009, 32; Cano Campos, 2009, 430).

Conversely, *inter-urban transports* normally fall under the purview of autonomous communities, provided they take place within their respective limits but in more than one municipality's territory (for instance, Articles 26(1)(6) of the Statute of Autonomy for the Community of Madrid and 70.1.8° of the Statute of Autonomy for Castile and León).[2] Short-distance trains are the exception, as they generally are the national government's responsibility. Here, concessionaires have played a more important role, as they are the main providers of public transport service of persons by road (buses).

This already highlights a few facts. The first one is that, from a legal point of view, *territory* determines which level of government is responsible for transport (territoriality principle). Each level is competent for transport that does not exceed its territorial limits (Carbonell Porras & Cano Campos, 2006, 122). Using territory to allocate responsibility implies that the competent level of government should be the one which meets two requirements: it represents all interests involved and is "spatially" closest to them. That is particularly evident in the case of municipalities and intra-urban transport, as expressly acknowledged by Spanish legislation[3] (Cano Campos, 2009, 394–395). This also helps uphold the principle of subsidiarity granted in Article 4(3) of the European Charter of Local Self-Government (ECLSG) which Spain has ratified. Notwithstanding, territory and its peculiar interests in distributing responsibilities may lead to dysfunctions in terms of inter-administrative collaboration.[4]

[2] Transports that take place in the territory of more than one autonomous community are responsibility of the national government (Article 149(1)(21)(a) of the Spanish Constitution). They are, however, less relevant to this investigation.

[3] Apart from numerous regional laws, Article 25(1) LBRL sets out that "[t]he municipality, for the management of its interests and within the scope of its powers, may promote activities and provide public services that contribute to *satisfying the needs and aspirations of the local community* under the terms provided for in this article" (emphasis added).

[4] See Sect. 5.4 below.

Also interesting is a further realization: population is the only criterion for allocating an *obligation* to provide (intra-urban) public transport to municipalities. As mentioned above, all municipalities have responsibility for intra-urban public transport services. Only when its population is over 50,000 inhabitants is a municipality obligated to provide this service. This, however, *hinders in no way* those municipalities under 50,000 inhabitants which freely decide to provide it.

Population size is, above all, a clear and easy to apply criterium. It also has the virtue of correlating with where public transport is needed: larger populations usually mean larger settlements and longer distances.

While this is positive in terms of local self-government, it is also true that population size is not always an adequate proxy for public transport *needs*. This is clear in the case of those (generally coastal) municipalities with a small *de jure* population, which triplicates or quadruplicates during the summer months. There is a contrast between the municipality's lack of express obligation to provide this service and the evident need for it during the summer. Alongside problems inherent to these circumstances (what to do with the infrastructure or how to compensate private partners during low seasons), these municipalities tend to have smaller administrative structures that are ill-equipped to manage large or complex services such as these. Responsibility to provide public transport services is therefore not always distributed according to the capabilities of each municipality.

It must be said, however, that taking population size as the key criterium *does tend to align with the urban-rural divide*. This is due to the strong correlation between the rural character of municipalities and their small (and often dwindling) population. Consequently, rural municipalities are not obligated to provide this service, as they are systematically under the 50,000 inhabitants threshold. Of course, this also correlates with smaller distances for daily movements and a lower need for public intra-urban transport (De los Mozos Touya, 2000, 143).

Regarding inter-urban transportation services, autonomous communities are responsible for planning and provision (Barrero Rodríguez, 2009, 189). There are here at least two clearly distinguished kinds of inter-urban transport. The first refers to transport between municipalities whose urban networks are integrated in a *metropolitan area* and which share intense economic and social connections (Cano Campos, 2009, 395). The main challenges here are providing a satisfactory public transport system between these municipalities and achieving the proper coordination with their respective intra-urban transport networks (Carbonell Porras, 2007, 314).

This is extremely difficult to achieve while preserving local autonomy (Velasco Caballero, 2009). All the while, metropolitan inter-urban transport faces similar challenges to intra-urban transport in densely populated areas: contamination and environmental preservation, proliferation of traffic jams, distribution of public space (roads) among numerous different means of transport or the transition to newer (greener and/or healthier) transports, to name but a few (Marco Dols & Soriano Martí, 2020, 38; Matas Prat & Perdiguero García, 2022, 112). All of these can be summed up with the expression "sustainable mobility".

**Table 5.1** Responsibilities over public collective transport by scope and environment

| | | SCOPE OF TRANSPORT | |
|---|---|---|---|
| | | Intra-urban | Inter-urban |
| **ENVIRONMENT** | **Rural** | **Transport within small rural municipalities**<br>Municipalities have responsibility but low need<br>No obligation to provide the service under 50,000 inhabitants | **Transport between small rural municipalities, separated metropolitan areas or both**<br>Responsibility belongs to autonomous community when transport takes place within its limits |
| | **Urban** | **Transport within urban municipalities**<br>Municipalities have responsibility and high need<br>Obligation to provide the service over 50,000 inhabitants<br>Often, necessary coordination with interurban urban transport (see right) | **Transport in cities or large metropolitan areas (urban amalgamations)**<br>Responsibility belongs to autonomous community (transport between municipalities)<br>Intertwined with intraurban urban transport (see left) |

The second kind of inter-urban transport takes place in *rural areas*. In these settings, priorities are different and include designing a network that covers the most territory with minimal inefficiency, while making waiting and travel times still attractive for potential users. While public transport in urban areas competes directly against private transport (cars) and aims to substitute it, rural inter-urban public transport *mainly complements private means of transport* and caters to those population sectors which cannot drive (elderly, disabled, children) (Marco Dols & Soriano Martí, 2020, 40) (Table 5.1).

## 5.3 Autonomy Vs. Coordination with Other Government Levels: A Necessary Paradox

The attribution of responsibilities to different levels of government and the diverse scenarios in which transport services must be provided inevitably lead to many situations in which different governmental levels need to collaborate. Collaboration may, therefore, arise in mainly two sets of circumstances:

1. When a lower level of government (i.e. municipality) is not able to fully carry out its public transport provision responsibilities, a higher level of government *provides assistance* to the former, generally of an administrative nature. In the institutional structure described above, provinces (or autonomous communities, where applicable) would aid municipalities in the provision of intra-urban transports (Carbonell Porras & Cano Campos, 2006, 175). It is worth noting that inter-urban transport is not a municipal responsibility and, therefore, would not

fall within this category. All in all, however, higher governmental level assistance is not a relevant factor in the public transport sector and has not led to any specific good practices (Carbonell Porras, 2021, 6).
2. More important here are those frequent cases in which different transport networks require an *integration or interconnection* with others. Each network is usually the responsibility of a different level of government or of different units of the same level (as in metropolitan areas). This naturally leads to a necessary collaboration between different administrations.

The latter is where most intergovernmental dialogue takes place regarding public transport, especially where local governments are concerned. Here, most instances of administrative collaboration are cases of *coordination*. According to Spanish legal tradition, coordination normally occurs when different government levels have concurring or shared responsibilities over an issue and they must act together to provide a unified solution, as diverging actions by each administration may cancel each other out or lead to undesirable results. This is usually achieved through the attribution to the higher administration of a faculty to, eventually, impose a single course of action to all coordinated administrations (Almeida Cerreda, 2023b, 327).

Hence, regulations typically lay down mechanisms to coordinate inter- and intra-urban public transport, especially in metropolitan areas. As well as through general regulations passed by the higher level of government (autonomous community), coordination tends to be articulated through *institutional structures which integrate representatives of all administrations involved*. Good examples are Barcelona,[5] Valencia,[6] or Seville,[7] to name a few. In other cases, the same body integrates all transport in an autonomous community, thus combining transport in metropolitan and rural areas. Such is the case of Madrid[8] or Asturias.[9] These structures are traditionally known as consortia, although their actual legal nature does not always match that denomination (Carbonell Porras & Cano Campos, 2006, 262–273; Barrero Rodríguez, 2009, 205–209).

However, some cases of administrative collaboration do not consist of coordination and rely instead on the free will of all administrations involved. This is

[5] Metropolitan Area of Barcelona, a body that integrates different municipalities of the Barcelona metropolitan area for the common provision of public services, one of which is public transport (Article 14 of Catalan Law 31/2010, of 3rd August, on the Metropolitan Area of Barcelona; Spanish Official Gazette no. 231, of 23rd September 2010).

[6] Metropolitan Transport Authority of Valencia (Article 90 of Valencian Law 13/2016, of 29th December, on fiscal, administrative, financial and organizational measures; Spanish Official Gazette no. 34, of 9th December 2017).

[7] Consortium for the Metropolitan Transport of Seville.

[8] Consortium for Regional Transport of Madrid (Article 1 of Madrid Law 5/1985, of 16th May, on the creation of the Consortium for Regional Transport of Madrid; Spanish Official Gazette no. 250, of 18th October 1985).

[9] Consortium for Transport of Asturias (Article 1 of Asturian Law 1/2002, of 11th March, on the Consortium for Transport of Asturias; Spanish Official Gazette Number 98, of 24th April 2002).

conventionally known as cooperation and can be articulated through *ad hoc* agreements or more stable institutional structures.

There is nothing unusual or surprising in the need for different administrations to collaborate when such collaboration is necessary to fulfil their shared responsibilities, as is the case with public transport. This is true even if we consider that all Spanish local governments enjoy a relatively high level of autonomy thanks to a clear constitutional (and international) guarantee of local self-government (Articles 137 of the Spanish Constitution and 3 ECLSG). However, collaboration with other levels of government *necessarily entails a certain sacrifice of autonomy* in order to accommodate all positions.

This circumstance is further exacerbated by two factors. On the one hand, coordination powers may increase that sacrifice as, along the way, the latter becomes *less voluntary* and more compulsory. On the other hand, collaboration with "stronger" (larger, better financed) administrations tends to mean that "weaker" administrations do not have the leverage to push their preferred solutions (Velasco Caballero, 2009, 140). This is the case with autonomous communities and their respective municipalities, with the exception of large cities (mainly, Madrid and Barcelona).

As a result, local governments and, especially, municipalities, exercise a lower level of autonomy in regard to their public transport responsibilities. At a more fundamental level, this circumstance arises because the same instance (autonomous community) decides which specific responsibilities are attributed to municipalities, what aspects of public transport are of supra-municipal interest and what coordination mechanisms exist. It has been suggested that, in practice, this means that the role of local governments is rather that of *carrying out the autonomic programs and decisions* within the framework that the autonomous community sets (Velasco Caballero, 2009, 144–145).

A good example of this is the interplay between intra- and inter-urban transport. There are instances in which a municipality, exercising its own powers, decides to set up or expand its intra-urban public transport service. And, when it does, there already exists an inter-urban transport network managed (directly or indirectly) by the autonomous community, also making use of its own powers. There is a clear *friction point* between: the number and the location of stops and stations for the inter-urban road transport service. The municipality will tend to limit their number and favor their location in places that do not hinder traffic. The autonomous community will prefer the opposite to ensure the network's efficacy (and, often, the protection of the inter-urban transport concessionaire).

When solving this problem, the *scales have frequently tipped in favour of the autonomous community*, as it only needs to pass regulations which set out its preferred solution and is binding for municipalities. This can be seen as an unjustified restriction of local autonomy (Carbonell Porras, 2007, 316–317). However, there have also been attempts at a more nuanced approach. Such is the case in Galicia, where Law 6/1996 established new proceedings for the coordination of inter- and intra-urban transport services. The main intention behind this regulation was to achieve an optimum between the responsibilities and preferences of both municipality and autonomous community. This mechanism consisted of a complete procedure whose inputs were preferences, needs and technical information. The aim was therefore to reduce tensions and reach a consensus on the best solution for each problem, somewhat similar to the German *Planfeststellungsverfahren*. However well-intentioned this regulation was, it seems that, in practice, administrations prefer to resort to other, more flexible mechanisms (singularly, collaboration agreements) (Míguez Macho, 2009, 227).

Finally, another relevant aspect that concerns local governments' autonomy is financial: how municipalities pay for their intra-urban public transport services. Although this is an issue that well merits its own analysis, two essential factors may be mentioned. The first one is that the relatively low income of many municipalities renders them partially incapable of financing all their services independently, and so they must turn to specific (and often earmarked) subsidies from the state or autonomous community (Ministerio de Transportes, Movilidad y Agenda Urbana, 2022, 82). This dependency is also related to the fact that user fees typically cover only a fraction of the actual service cost (Matas Prat & Perdiguero García, 2022, 118). Since financial autonomy is a fundamental aspect of local self-government, a lack of the former entails a restriction of the latter. The second relevant factor is that fees and tariffs for the use of public transport are frequently not established by the responsible municipality, but rather by the consortium to which it belongs. Even where consortium membership is voluntary, this necessarily means a reduction in autonomy for each member.

All in all, standard municipal autonomy is significantly affected in this sector of public activity, given the considerable powers autonomous communities wield and their often colliding interests.

## 5.4 Changes in Urban Mobility: New Perspectives in the Face of Social and Climate Challenges

If rural and urban transportation realities are so different, it naturally follows that their respective evolutions greatly vary as well. This is evident not only in the current needs and problems peculiar to transport "in the city" or "in the countryside", but also in their upcoming challenges. This section will discuss those new trends and analyze how they may affect urban local governments, as well as their role in carrying them out.

New developments in mobility in urban areas equally involve *intra- and interurban (metropolitan) transport*. The main challenges address the need to rationalize and distribute the use of urban roads, the promotion of active mobility and more climate-friendly means of transport and the interaction between private cars, taxis, and other individual private transports such as Uber or Cabify.

A specific feature of transport of persons in cities is that movements are extremely dense and heavily interwoven, as likely departure and destination points for each present a high spatial concentration. Such movement density creates traffic, which may generate longer waiting and travel times, contamination and a general dysfunction of public transport (and, indeed, of transport in general). Traditional urban transports are now *insufficient* to cover citizens' needs while preventing or solving these problems. Hence, besides buses, trams, metro, and short-distance trains, other means of transport are being promoted by authorities.

The clearest example is the *bicycle* and, to a lesser extent, the electric scooter. Bicycles are fast means of transport that do not contaminate the environment and actively promote healthier habits in users. It is therefore no surprise that authorities are making strong efforts to integrate cycling into their transport systems. However, it is important that policy implementation draws new users from discouraged means of transport (cars), and not from other desirable forms of public transport (Matas Prat & Perdiguero García, 2022, 112). Bicycles are not a substitute for public transport, but rather its complement, especially in the case of multi-modal trips (OECD, 2018, 19). And so, public transport systems should facilitate this integration.

The high concentration of vehicles on urban roads has led many municipalities to reserve or design specific spaces or lanes for public buses or bicycles. This has proved to be an effective solution for reducing travel times while increasing efficiency and avoiding traffic. Given its success, further proposals aim to implement intelligent transport systems (ITS). These are dynamic mechanisms that regulate the use of specific lanes on a real-time basis, adapting to traffic or prioritizing public or high-occupancy vehicles. The benefit of Intelligent Transport Systems (ITS) would ultimately be a more efficient and sustainable urban mobility (Ministerio de Transportes, Movilidad y Agenda Urbana, 2022, 24).

Accessibility is another field in which urban public transport is making progress. Now that user demands are met (however satisfactorily), authorities are taking steps to ensure that public transport environments and features do not prevent vulnerable users from making use of it. Some initiatives aim to make all spaces free of stairs and wheelchair-friendly, either through the elimination of physical barriers or the installation of lifts. Others are directed to guaranteeing that there are no usability barriers for blind persons (Transports Metropolitanos de Barcelona, 2010; Metro de Madrid, 2021).

Urban local governments have an *important role* to play in all this. They are the level of government mainly responsible for urban mobility, with the exception of metropolitan transport and short-distance trains discussed above. In addition, not only are they competent in this area, but they also have responsibilities in adjacent fields that contribute to strengthening their position. These include urban planning, traffic, parks and urban environment, contamination prevention, and vehicle parking. While urban local governments are still bound by general regulations passed by the state or autonomous community, they have broad room for action.

For instance, if a municipality wants to promote the use of public transport while reducing car usage, they may implement measures that boost alternative means of transport (public or private, individual or collective), increase the cost of using a vehicle (through taxes, paid parking or access fees) or limit the number of vehicles allowed to travel (Matas Prat & Perdiguero García, 2022, 114). This last option, known as Low Emission Area *(Zona de Bajas Emisiones)* has received special attention from authorities and has been implemented in several cities, among which are

Madrid, Barcelona, Valencia, and Seville (Ministerio de Transportes, Movilidad y Agenda Urbana, 2022, 105). These measures have been complemented by other initiatives, such as dissuasive parking, which provides incoming cars with parking places outside the city and close to public transport options heading to the city center.

Low Emission Areas have been met with mixed opinions. They undoubtedly help achieve better environmental conditions in cities, better air quality and citizens' increased awareness of contamination, all of which may find a legal basis in Article 45 of the Spanish Constitution. However, restrictions on access to cities raise questions in terms of equality, as people with lower incomes tend to have their vehicles now prevented from entering cities while people with higher incomes own more modern and less contaminating vehicles.

## 5.5 Changes in Rural Mobility: New Perspectives in the Face of Financial and Demographic Challenges

Rural mobility is another field in which creative changes are taking place. In this context, more climate-friendly transport, healthier habits, traffic rationalization or regulation of private means of transport do not play a significant role. These are worries peculiar to modern urban transport, where satisfaction of transportation needs is sufficiently covered and concerns turn to sustainable mobility. *Rural (interurban) transport trends* focus instead on achieving a minimum level of economic efficiency in the provision of public transport services (as distances, waiting times and low usage rates threaten their existence) while guaranteeing sufficient territorial coverage and the satisfaction of rural inhabitants' transport needs. This is connected to the realization that a good rural transport system is essential for fighting against depopulation (Carbonell Porras, 2021, 4) and that rural public transport cannot replace private transport and should therefore complement it (OECD, 2015, 13).

From a general perspective, transport in rural areas has evolved unevenly. This is due not only to the fact that different administrations may have acted without coordination, but also because there are *different kinds of transport taking place simultaneously*. This is notably the case of general and school transport. While both are regular transports (i.e. subject to a fixed itinerary, calendar and timetable), they differ in the users to which they cater: general transport may be used by any person, but school transport is dedicated to students coming or going from their respective schools. In this regard, school transport is a type of special transport, as it is reserved for a specific group of users with homogeneous characteristics (school students, disabled persons, etc.) (Carbonell Porras & Cano Campos, 2006, 146).

Having dedicated transport subnetworks for some specific groups can be a relevant cause for inefficiency in contexts of very low usage, as all subnetworks may end up falling into deficit. Therefore, some recent proposals have included the fusion of both general and school transports, in order to minimize costs and concentrate network usage (Badía Lázaro, 2016, 3). This is possible because, in rural settings, *public transport scarcity makes such divisions irrelevant* (Carbonell Porras,

2021, 8). In order to achieve this, plans usually opt for one of the subnetworks and allow other users to use it or reserve seats for the other subnetwork's users. At the same time, this solution prevents potential redundancies that may exist between different networks. However, a relevant drawback is the subordination of transport timetables to school hours, as it sometimes leads to user dissatisfaction (Badía Lázaro & Climent López, 2019, 130).

Further developments in rural transport focus on adapting current systems to *actual user demands*. Traditional rural transport prioritized territorial coverage over other factors, such as trip duration. However, a useful transport system must consider other aspects and analyze the various reasons people move and the resulting movements. There is an important difference between daily pendular trips from home into the city to work and a weekly trip to a mid-size town for grocery shopping or leisure purposes. Very low bus frequency or hours-long trips will discourage the former, while itineraries that only connect rural settlements with large cities prevent the latter. It is therefore important to measure user accessibility to work and leisure in both, as well as the trip durations and frequencies (Gutiérrez Puebla, 1991, 210–213).

To achieve this, it is essential to study the population settlement structure in a given territory, as it will influence public transport user demand. This analysis must consider, at least, population density and density of settlements. Additionally, transport routes must be classified according to their function in the system. Thus, there may be *structuring routes* which connect large population hubs between themselves. These hubs provide basic and specialized public services (health, education, administration) and a wide-ranging offer of other services (commerce, leisure). Besides these there may also exist *centrality routes*, which connect these large hubs with smaller (rural) settlements (Badía Lázaro & Climent López, 2019, 129).

Another recent shift regarding rural transport concerns the role of private service providers who are integrated into the public system. Historically, private concessionaires of inter-urban bus transport services were granted the exploitation of specific bus lines for a certain period of time (Cano Campos, 2009, 401). This creates two sets of difficulties in the current context of rural transport. Firstly, any changes in transport planning must consider pre-existing concessions, thus limiting or conditioning solutions to previous or new problems. Secondly, some linear concessions with very low user demand may be *anti-economic* (Delgado Urrecho & Martínez Fernández, 2016, 543).

To address both issues, there are suggestions to replace linear concessions with *zonal concessions* for the provision of inter-urban transport by road. If concessionaires provide service in a previously defined area, profitable lines may compensate for the losses of unprofitable lines (Carbonell Porras, 2021, 8). This should also lead to more flexibility in the design and amendment of itineraries, as this will not impact other concessionaires with adjacent lines. A successful implementation of these zonal concessions requires correctly identifying structural and centrality itineraries and delimiting zones based on these (Badía Lázaro & Climent López, 2019, 132).

The last major developments in rural transport are related to *on-demand mobility*. Scientific and technical progress and the proliferation of private initiatives for individual transport have significantly driven advances in this field in recent years. The clearest examples are private platforms for discretionary individual urban transport, such as Uber or Cabify, which compete directly with taxi services. The advantages of demand-responsive transport in rural areas are directly related to its flexibility, adaptability, and relative cost-effectiveness. Itineraries and frequencies can be adjusted to factor in temporary low demand, unpopular (or popular) travel times or changing likely destinations such as weekly markets (OECD, 2015, 11; Delgado Urrecho & Martínez Fernández, 2016, 544).

This facilitates a *better match* between transport needs and supply, which, in turn, significantly contributes to higher cost efficiency, user satisfaction and usage rates. On-demand transport also promotes better penetration of public transport in those areas where regular transport would not be feasible. Although regulations applicable to this form of transport are somewhat restrictive, they do not prevent its implementation and allow it to be included in linear or zonal concessions (Carbonell Porras, 2021, 9). In fact, there is already some experience of demand-responsive mobility in rural areas of Castile and León. In this region, the implementation started with the design of on-demand transport areas based on the demographic structure. Each area includes a service hub (city or large town) and considers where health and social services branches are located. They were also conceived with the intention of avoiding excessive travel distances to the hub from rural areas. So far, they have only been partially implemented, but results are very positive in terms of coverage, usage, reception, satisfaction, and cost-effectiveness (Delgado Urrecho & Martínez Fernández, 2016, 544).

The *involvement of rural local governments* in the design and implementation of these policies is low. The main obstacle for them is that they hold no responsibility over inter-urban transport, and so it is the autonomous community who will normally take up the mantle. However, nothing would impede the autonomous community from involving the affected local governments to receive their input, be it through a hearing process, the production of reports or any other adequate mechanism.

## 5.6 Conclusions

The demographic and territorial differences in Spain cause a stark contrast between rural and urban areas. In the context of public transport, these differences have given rise to specific challenges in both areas. More recent developments confirm this trend. While metropolitan transport is engaged with more climate-friendly goals, rural mobility faces a rural demographic exodus, a declining (user) population and the fatal threat of deficit.

The institutional design of local government in Spain is not well suited for these challenges. Attribution of responsibilities over transport does not consider the rural or metropolitan character of municipalities, although needs and capabilities are significantly different in each context. This calls for a renewed perspective on the legal configuration of municipalities and for a new regulation which better matches their responsibilities and obligations with their needs and capabilities.

Furthermore, in both instances municipalities must collaborate with higher levels of government; a collaboration which tends to restrict their local autonomy. While this is, to a certain extent, unavoidable in collaborative contexts, new mechanisms should be explored to minimize loss of municipal autonomy while achieving a satisfactory level of service quality regarding public transport. Since formal and complex procedures seem to be shunned due to their lack of flexibility, there may be room for action for voluntary instruments such as collaboration agreements. Consensual or qualified majority decisions could play a role here as well, instead of simple majority rules.

Nevertheless, mobility in both rural and urban areas has proved to be highly responsive to new challenges. Cities are concerned with greener mobility and have implemented measures to discourage the use of cars that, at the same time, enhance active mobility and alternative transports. The integration of cycling within the system or the limitation of private cars in city centers are good examples. Conversely, rural transport is now focused on renovating inter-urban network designs to eliminate redundancies and unnecessary costs while preserving its usefulness for users and satisfying their demands. This is increasingly the case with demand-responsive transport systems that cater to specific needs, as well as the experimental integration of general and school transport networks.

Substantial legal issues arise from these new developments. Changes in rural transport affect relevant rights of concessionaires and raise interesting questions from an organisational (legal) perspective, such as the position of private providers and the role of public procurement law in this. In urban settings there is an expansion or optimisation of the rights of disabled citizens, which is connected with universal design and reasonable accommodation concerns. No less relevant are those trends related to air quality and a right to a healthy environment, as opposed to cities as contamination hubs. In this regard, for instance, Low Emissions Areas pose challenges for people who do not own less contaminating (modern) cars or live in the city centre. A balance must be reached between a desirably healthy environment and the restriction of rights of those people who tend to have lower incomes and, therefore, cannot afford to live in the city centre or to own newer and less contaminating vehicles. Good living conditions in cities should not be attained at the expense of poorer people's rights. The complexity of the matter allows only for case-specific solutions and requires a careful consideration of all interests involved. Throughout all this, local governments play an uneven but no less relevant role.

## References

Almeida Cerreda, M. (2023a). Un posible régimen especial para los pequeños municipios: Justificación, naturaleza, contenido y articulación. *Revista de Estudios de la Administración Local y Autonómica, 19*, 59–81.

Almeida Cerreda, M. (2023b). Las relaciones entre Administraciones públicas. In F. V. Caballero & M. M. D. Gardella (Eds.), *Manual de Derecho administrativo* (pp. 318–343). Marcial Pons.

Badía Lázaro, R. (2016). Las posiblidades de integración del transporte escolar y regular en Aragón. *Geographicalia, 68*, 1–24.

Badía Lázaro, R., & Climent López, E. (2019). De concesiones lineales a contratos de gestión zonales: Una propuesta para el transporte público interurbano de viajeros por carretera en Aragón. *Revista de Estudios Andaluces, 38*, 121–143. https://doi.org/10.12795/rea.2019.i38.07

Barrero Rodríguez, C. (2009). El papel de las entidades locales supramunicipales en la prestación del servicio público de transporte en los espacios metropolitanos. In E. C. Porras & T. C. Campos (Eds.), *Derecho público del transporte en la ciudad: Renovación y nuevas perspectivas de la movilidad urbana* (pp. 183–213). Servicio de Publicaciones de la Facultad de Derecho de la Universidad Complutense de Madrid.

Belintxon Martín, U. (2016). Derecho internacional privado y transporte de viajeros por carretera: Algunas cuestiones sobre jurisdicción y ley aplicable. *Cuadernos de Derecho Transnacional, 8*, 17–35.

Cano Campos, T. (2009). El transporte público urbano y su regulación jurídica. In E. C. Porras & T. C. Campos (Eds.), *Derecho público del transporte en la ciudad: Renovación y nuevas perspectivas de la movilidad urbana* (pp. 391–447). Servicio de Publicaciones de la Facultad de Derecho de la Universidad Complutense de Madrid.

Carbonell Porras, E. (2007). El transporte público de viajeros. In *Las competencias locales* (pp. 283–317). Marcial Pons.

Carbonell Porras, E. (2021). El transporte de personas en el medio rural. In D. S. Iglesias, L. M. Macho, A. J. F. Fernández, A. De Nuccio, & B. A. Costa (Eds.), *Instrumentos jurídicos para la lucha contra la despoblación*. Thomson Reuters-Aranzadi.

Carbonell Porras, E., & Cano Campos, T. (2006). *Los transportes urbanos*. Iustel.

De los Mozos Touya, I. (2000). Obligaciones especiales de servicio público en el transporte rural. *Revista de Estudios de la Administración Local y Autonómica, 282*, 119–156.

Delgado Urrecho, J. M., & Martínez Fernández, L. C. (2016). On-demand transport as alternative mobility system in low density areas: The case of Castilla and Leon. *Boletín de la Asociación de Geógrafos Españoles, 72*, 541–546.

European Commission and OECD. (2018). *Key data on local and regional governments in the European Union*. Retrieved January 8, 2024, from https://www.oecd.org/regional/EU-Local-government-key-data.pdf

Fernández Farreres, G. (2009). El sistema concesional de transporte de viajeros por carretera ante el nuevo Reglamento CE 1370/2007, de 23 de octubre, y el Informe de la Comisión Nacional de la Competencia de 2008 "Sobre la competencia en el transporte interurbano de viajeros en autobús en España.". In E. C. Porras & T. C. Campos (Eds.), *Derecho público del transporte en la ciudad: Renovación y nuevas perspectivas de la movilidad urbana* (pp. 21–55). Servicio de Publicaciones de la Facultad de Derecho de la Universidad Complutense de Madrid.

Gutiérrez Puebla, J. (1991). Indicadores de accesibilidad en transporte público en el medio rural: Una propuesta metodológica. *Estudios Geográficos, 52*, 205–221.

Hernando Rydings, M. (2009). El Libro Verde "Hacia una red transeuropea de transporte mejor integrada al servicio de la Política Común de Transportes": Algunas reflexiones generales. In E. C. Porras & T. C. Campos (Eds.), *Derecho público del transporte en la ciudad: Renovación y nuevas perspectivas de la movilidad urbana* (pp. 247–262). Servicio de Publicaciones de la Facultad de Derecho de la Universidad Complutense de Madrid.

Marco Dols, P., & Soriano Martí, J. (2020). Transporte público y despoblación en el mundo rural: El caso del interior castellonense. *Cuadernos de Geografía, 105*, 29–50.

Matas Prat, A., & Perdiguero García, J. (2022). El transporte público urbano: Financiación y uso. *Papeles de Economía Española, 171*, 109–124.

Metro de Madrid. (2021). *Plan de accesibilidad e inclusión 2021–2028*. Retrieved January 8, 2024, from https://www.metromadrid.es/sites/default/files/documentos/planaccesibilidad2021-2028.pdf

Míguez Macho, L. (2009). El transporte metropolitano en Galicia. In E. C. Porras & T. C. Campos (Eds.), *Derecho público del transporte en la ciudad: Renovación y nuevas perspectivas de la*

*movilidad urbana* (pp. 215–233). Servicio de Publicaciones de la Facultad de Derecho de la Universidad Complutense de Madrid.
Ministerio de Transportes, Movilidad y Agenda Urbana. (2022). *El transporte urbano y metropolitano en España*. Retrieved January 8, 2024, from https://cvp.mitma.gob.es/el-transporte-urbano-y-metropolitano-en-espana%2D%2Ddiciembre-2022
OECD. (2015). *International experiences on public transport provision in rural areas*. Retrieved January 8, 2024, from https://www.itf-oecd.org/sites/default/files/docs/15cspa_ruralareas.pdf
OECD. (2018). *Integrating urban public transport systems and cycling*. Retrieved January 8, 2024, from https://www.itf-oecd.org/integrating-urban-public-transport-systems-cycling
Transports Metropolitanos de Barcelona. (2010). *Pla Director d'Accessibilitat Universal*. Retrieved January 8, 2024, from https://www.tmb.cat/documents/20182/111197/Pla+director+d%27accessibilitat+universal.pdf/74bc3ba8-4f3e-4a93-8827-5e3f535a0b24?t=1468937343000
Velasco Caballero, F. (2009). Transporte urbano por carretera y competencias municipales. In E. C. Porras & T. C. Campos (Eds.), *Derecho público del transporte en la ciudad: Renovación y nuevas perspectivas de la movilidad urbana* (pp. 139–149). Servicio de Publicaciones de la Facultad de Derecho de la Universidad Complutense de Madrid.
Velasco Caballero, F. (2020). Municipios urbanos versus municipios rurales: Homogeneidad y diversidad en el régimen local. *Anuario de Derecho Municipal, 2019*(13), 21–53.
Velasco Caballero, F. (2022). Reformas en el régimen local general: El inicio de un nuevo ciclo. *Anuario de Derecho Municipal, 2021*(15), 23–48.

# Part II
# Ways of Public Service Provision by Urban and Rural Local Governments

# Chapter 6
# Methods of Funding Service Provision by Australian Local Government

**Carol Mills and D'Arcy Blaxell**

**Abstract** This chapter examines the intricate landscape of local government funding and service provision in Australia. Despite serving similar functions, local governments operate under distinct governance systems across the country, determined by their local state or territory jurisdiction. They also confront major resourcing variations—resulting from differences in population size, geography and economic capacity between councils. The sector has undergone significant change over the last 30 years, affected by factors such as forced amalgamations, broadening responsibilities and changing community expectations. Australian local government has progressively moved away from a traditional focus on "rates, roads, and rubbish" to offer more diverse services such as services in recreation, childcare, and community building. For many councils, however, this shift presents fundamental challenges. Financially, their capacity to generate revenue is often limited, commercial partnerships are difficult to secure, and many remain financially dependent on grants from federal and state governments.

**Keywords** Local government · Local council · Government funding · Australian government · Service provision

## 6.1 Introduction: Overview of Local Government

Local government in Australia is largely shaped by the country's federated administrative model. Australia is a federation with three levels of government: the Commonwealth (federal /national), states and territories, and local government. Unlike the other layers of government, local government is currently not formally recognized in the Australian Constitution, and although there have been attempts to

C. Mills (✉) · D. Blaxell
Institute for Public Policy and Governance, University of Technology Sydney, Sydney, NSW, Australia
e-mail: Carol.Mills@uts.edu.au; DArcy.Blaxell@uts.edu.au



F. Velasco Caballero et al. (eds.), *Municipal Tasks and Financing*, Local and Urban Governance, https://doi.org/10.1007/978-3-031-99812-6_6

amend this (including two referendums), its legal status remains dependent on state legislation.

Established through the separate constitutions of each state and one territory, many of the powers and responsibilities of local government are subordinate to state and national governments. Therefore, although councils perform similar functions, there are effectively seven different governance systems across the country. Further, while traditionally local government's role was largely complementary to the other levels of government, in recent decades there have been shifts, and an increase in the overlap of many policies and programs.

As the third-tier of government, local government has traditionally been responsible for services such as planning, building approvals, libraries, waste management, local roads, footpaths, parks, and other infrastructure such as sports facilities.

The size, scope, influence, and budget of local governments in Australia varies dramatically, which can make generalizations and direct comparisons problematic. The largest local government area (LGA) by population is Brisbane City Council in Queensland, which serves a community of over a million people and has an operating budget of more than $4 billion AU (Brisbane City Council, 2023). In contrast, Sandstone Shire Council, in Western Australia, has a population of just 109, and an annual expenditure of only $5.7 million AU (Shire of Sandstone, 2023). By total land area, the East Pilbara Council in Western Australia is the country's largest LGA, covering nearly 380 thousand square kilometers—slightly more than the whole country of Germany (Western Australian Local Government Association, 2016a). Compare this to Peppermint Grove council, in the Western Australian city of Perth, which covers a mere 1.4 square kilometers, and the incredible diversity of scale in Australian local government is evident (Western Australian Local Government Association, 2016b). This, in turn, impacts the nature of services provided and the capacity of local governments to fund these services.

Reflecting the country's British administrative heritage, local governments across Australia are variously referred to as a 'council', 'city', 'municipality', 'shire', or 'town' depending on factors such as their size, location, or history. 'County councils' also exist as incorporations of, and controlled by, two or more local governments. These were established to deliver services such as water and sewerage, usually across rural areas. There are currently 537 local governments in Australia (Australian Local Government Association, 2023b), which reflects a reduction from a peak of 1000 due to ongoing structural reform. These reforms have largely been driven at the state and territory government level, and have been aimed primarily at improving efficiency and effectiveness—though not necessarily succeeding in achieving this goal. Over the last thirty years, this reduction has mostly been obtained through the process of amalgamation.

Of the 537 current local governments, approximately 20% cover only urban areas; 25% cover urban and urban fringe; and 55% are classified as rural, regional, or remote (Australian Local Government Association, 2023b). In total, Australian local governments employ nearly 200,000 staff—about 10% of the total public sector. Despite their reach and influence, Australian local governments remain somewhat unexamined in academia, perhaps owing to their relative lack of power compared to their state and federal counterparts (de Vries, 2021).

## 6.2 Trends in Australian Local Government

### *6.2.1 Amalgamation*

Over the last 30 years, the most significant change in Australian local government has come from a wave of forced or 'semi-voluntary' amalgamations that have occurred in every jurisdiction except Western Australia (though not for lack of trying by the state government) (Sansom, 2020, 23). In the Northern Territory, for example, 53 local governments were merged into just eight regional shires covering vast tracts of land (Michel & Taylor, 2012). The largest program occurred in 1994 in the State of Victoria, when 210 councils were dissolved by the state government and replaced by 78 councils created through amalgamations.

Despite often facing strong resistance from local communities and councils, amalgamations were pursued as a means to increase efficiency, build economies of scale, and pool resources and capabilities (Drew et al., 2014). Fierce opposition to amalgamations focused on concerns about loss of local government identity and connectedness, skepticism about purported efficiency gains, a perceived lack of information about the trade-offs of amalgamation, and mixed or inadequate evidence about the success of amalgamations in achieving their aims (Commonwealth of Australia Productivity Commission, 2017). Smaller communities and those in regional areas railed against the loss of local government services, institutions and employment opportunities, and many local governments—themselves effective and self-concerned political actors—became strong opponents of the amalgamation process (Hyslop et al., 2022).

State governments, concerned about the political risks of pursuing fraught policy, gradually lost their appetite for reform. The Western Australian and Queensland governments abandoned their amalgamation policies in the early 2010s (with Queensland allowing amalgamated councils to de-amalgamate), with NSW following in 2017, and since then, forced amalgamations have slipped off the public policy agenda (Hyslop et al., 2022). However, the legacy of amalgamations is still being played out in local governments across the country, with several new, larger councils still coming to grips with their expanded size and scope, and communities grappling with the reality—both positive and negative—of their new governance arrangements.

### *6.2.2 State and Federal Authority*

The top-down push for amalgamations reflected the legal status and power imbalance between local government, and state and federal governments. As noted, local government is currently not formally recognized in the Australian Constitution and many of its powers and responsibilities are subordinate to state and national governments. Despite attempts to amend this, the legal status of local government remains governed through state legislation and its structure and funding remains deeply dependent on the decisions of scrutineering (Sansom, 2020), and often interventionist, state governments (Wilkinson et al., 2021).

The largely residual power of local government was demonstrated in the early days of the Covid-19 pandemic, when changes were made to national decision-making arrangements. A new intergovernmental model, called the National Cabinet, was established in March 2020 to collaboratively address issues of national significance. Although originally announced as an interim measure, it quickly replaced the Council of Australian Governments (COAG), which had operated for two decades as the country's peak intergovernmental decision-making body and on which local government was formally represented. However, the new arrangement excluded local government. This change came despite local governments providing nearly a quarter of government services across the country (Mills, 2021), and has been largely identified as reflecting a lack of recognition of the potential of local government as a strategic partner through and after the Covid-19 crisis period (Sansom, 2020).

Under its Terms of Reference, the National Cabinet is required to meet at least four times a year and be "underpinned by a commitment to genuine partnerships between the Commonwealth and States and Territories on issues of national significance" (Federation, 2020, 1).

Following intense lobbying, in 2022, the incoming Australian Government committed to giving local government a 'seat' at the National Cabinet. In practice this took the form of an invitation for the Australian Local Government Association (ALGA)—the sector's peak body—to attend one meeting of the National Cabinet each year. The ALGA has continued to argue that this arrangement fell short of the government's pre-election commitment to "give local government a genuine voice on National Cabinet" (Skatssoon, 2023).

Historically, the other major engagement link between local government and the Commonwealth was the Australian Council of Local Government (ACLG). It was established in 2008 as an annual meeting involving senior representatives of both layers of government but was abolished by the national Coalition Government in 2013. It was re-instated in 2023 by the Labor Government, which described it as an arrangement that "showcases the important partnership the Australian Government has with local governments across Australia" (Department of Infrastructure, Transport, Regional Development, Communications and the Arts, 2023a).

In discussing the 2023 ACLG meeting, the government stated that local governments "are a trusted partner and fundamental to the development and delivery of policies and programs for all Australians" and that "the re-establishment of the ACLG builds on the Australian Government's commitment to work with local governments to build liveable and socially equitable communities in Australia's cities and regions" (Department of Infrastructure, Transport, Regional Development, Communications and the Arts, 2023a).

## 6.3 Pressures on Traditional Revenue Sources

There are three main categories of local government revenue in Australia—property taxes (known in Australia as 'rates') and annual charges; user fees and services (such as parking, building services, childcare, aged services, or for the use of facilities like swimming pools); and grants and development contributions (Australian Local Government Association, 2023a).

Overall, the single main source of revenue for local government is property rates, accounting for about 40% of the total $17 billion AU revenue collected by councils nationally in 2018.

In Australia, the national government collects the majority of tax revenue (over 70%) through mechanisms such as Income Tax and a Goods and Service Tax (GST), despite being responsible for less than half (about 40%) of all public sector expenditure on service delivery. This is a relatively new model of tax collection, as prior to the introduction of GST in July 2000, states also collected a number of taxes and duties. These were largely replaced by the GST, and a redistributive process was established to allocate national revenue to the other layers of government and across jurisdictions. For local government, this redistribution is determined through the Financial Assistance Grants (FAG) system. There are many critics of this model at the state and local government levels.

Nationally, local government collects about 3% of all tax revenues and is responsible for about 6% of total public sector expenditure on service delivery. Compared to their OECD counterparts, Australian local governments' reliance on rates and fees for services means that they generate a relatively high proportion of their own income (Hyslop et al., 2022).

While the rhetoric of partnering that underpinned the re-establishment of ACLG was welcomed by local government representatives, in reality the relationship is complex and much of local government funding is dependent on the Commonwealth, through the ongoing Financial Assistance Grants system (FAG), or on non-recurrent grants from either the Commonwealth or state governments. While the use of FAG income is at the discretion of a council, the latter form of grants are often tied to capital funding for infrastructure such as roads or community facilities.

In recent decades local government has exhibited a growing financial dependence on grants, though the pattern is not uniform. The extent of reliance on grants is impacted by individual state government regulatory policies and the profile of each council. For example, high-density urban councils are able to self-generate more revenue due to factors such as higher land values, population numbers and user charges, compared to those in rural and regional areas. In the best cases, total own-source revenue (such as rates and services charges) can still comprise over 80% of an urban local government's revenue. However, own-source revenue contributes less than 20% towards the expenditure of many rural and regional councils. For example, in the state of New South Wales (NSW), councils raise an average of one-third of their revenue through rates. However, this disguises the fact that in 2021–22, own-source revenue ratios in individual councils ranged from 9.8% to 87.3% (Yourcouncil, 2022).

Access to rates revenue has been impacted in several jurisdictions by legislated limits on property taxes imposed through a practice known as 'rate-capping' or 'rate-pegging', by which states limit a council's ability to raise rates year on year, despite growth in population, development, or land value in that period. This policy has been in place since 1977 in NSW, 2008 in the Northern Territory and 2016 in Victoria.

The mechanism of rate-capping means that councils in affected states must justify to their state's pricing authority any increases in property taxes above a state-wide level in the context of their strategic and financial plans (Sansom, 2020). The Australian Local Government Association (ALGA) argues that rate capping deprives councils of much-needed income, limits their ability to invest in services and infrastructure (Australian Local Government Association, 2023a), and reflects an inherent lack of trust in local government. A 2020 study on development contributions by the Australian Government's Productivity Commission found that rate capping can act as a disincentive for councils to accommodate growth in response to population growth (Australian Local Government Association, 2022).

As an example of its operation, since 2010, an Independent Pricing and Regulatory Tribunal (IPART) has been responsible for rate peg calculations in NSW. In 2021–22 the maximum rate increase was set at 2%, and in 2023–24 IPART set the rate cap at a baseline of 3.7% at a time when the annual inflation rate was sitting at just over 6% (Independent Pricing and Regulatory Tribunal NSW, 2023b). The baseline is the maximum pricing increase a council can apply. An individual council can increase some rates above this level so long as others are less than the baseline, to ensure that the overall increase in total rate revenue does not exceed the rate peg. As in other states, NSW councils have the right to apply to IPART for exemptions from the rate peg, but the majority argue that the process is too expensive, complex and arduous, and may not result in change.

However, a successful challenge to the rate cap can be significant. For instance, Woollahra Council, situated in a high socio-economic area in central Sydney, received approval from IPART to increase rates by 22.2% over 2 years from 2023–24 in order to improve its financial sustainability and to fund a series of identified priorities, including climate change adaption measures, footpath upgrades and online service improvements (Woollahra Council, 2023). With 53,500 residents, and a population density of 4364 persons per square kilometre, the council estimated that this would result in a rate increase of, on average, \$212 AU per annum for residential properties and \$462 AU for businesses (Woollahra Council, 2023).

While councils in impacted states have been operating on the assumption that there is little prospect of rate-caps being removed in the near future (Commonwealth of Australia Productivity Commission, 2017), some limited change is underway. Following a review in 2023, in NSW, IPART will trial a 'simplified' system from 2024–25 that will use "forward looking measures of councils' base costs" in an attempt to better accommodate changes in the costs of services delivered by councils. This change will also seek to reflect the diversity of the 128 councils in the state by creating three geographic groups—metropolitan, regional, and rural—instead of applying a single state-wide measurement (Independent Pricing and Regulatory

Tribunal NSW, 2023a). The new Base Cost Charge (BCC) will also have three categories—employee costs, asset costs, and all other costs to more realistically represent councils' operations.

This methodological change was introduced following extensive analysis and consultation and was accompanied by a recommendation to the NSW Government that it review councils' financial model to improve equity, efficiency and trust in the sector. In part, this proposal was driven by IPART's finding that NSW councils' financial positions had worsened between 2016–17 and 2020–21, and that adjustments to rate pegging would only partially alleviate the problem.

### *6.3.1 Financial Assistance Grants*

The fact that changes to rate pegging will not necessarily improve a council's financial viability is also demonstrated by the levels of financial pressure many councils are under, even in states where the capping model does not apply. Part of this is due to a lack of growth in FAG funding, which has served to highlight the intrinsic importance of the program to the local government system.

These grants have long been a significant source of funding for councils with less revenue-raising capacity, but the level of dependence is increasing. The Commonwealth has provided over $67 billion dollars AU to local governments through the FAG program since 1974 (Department of Infrastructure, Transport, Regional Development, Communications and the Arts, 2023b). However, the value of these grants relative to Australian GDP has declined significantly since their peak in the 1960s (Australian Local Government Association, 2023a).

A range of criteria is used to determine the value of Financial Assistance Grants, and the formula is often the subject of intergovernmental disagreement. Councils and their stakeholders have repeatedly argued that the needs of regional and remote local governments are inadequately reflected in these formulas. They have also expressed frustration at their limited capacity to advocate for change due to the structure of federal arrangements, particularly since the creation of the National Cabinet.

The ALGA has long lobbied for changes to the FAG arrangements to assist councils to meet the increasing costs of services. It argues that while between 1994–95 to 2018–19 there was a fourfold increase in local government spending in nominal terms, this has not been reflected in the distribution of tax revenue. The ALGA's official policy position is that local government's share of taxes should be restored to 1% of GDP, the level it was in 1996 when FAGs were introduced, and far higher than the current level of just over 0.5%. It has also called for the restoration of funding 'lost' since an indexation freeze was introduced in 2014–15.

As noted, in parallel with this downward trend in FAG funding, there has been an increase in councils' reliance on other forms of grants. While these make up only around 10% of local government's total revenue, they have become particularly important for small, low rate-base councils, especially those in rural and regional areas. A growing reliance on such grants has been identified as a barrier to the effective functioning of local government. It has been argued that a dependence on short-term grants can make governance unpredictable and volatile and undermine the potential for long-term planning (Michel & Taylor, 2012).

## 6.4 The Evolving Role of Local Government

As Australian local governments are established by statute and not recognized in the constitution, their responsibilities are enshrined in state legislation and have tended to be far narrower in scope than their European counterparts (Hyslop et al., 2022). However, there has been a broadening of scope in recent years. Traditionally, local governments focused primarily on the collection of property taxes; the provision and maintenance of roads; and waste disposal—(derisively) referred to as the 3Rs: rates, roads, and rubbish (Bejracharya & Khan, 2020).

Roads remain a significant portion of the local government portfolio, with councils responsible for around 75% of Australia's roads by length (over 650 thousand kilometers in total). According to the Australian Bureau of Statistics [Government Statistics Department], the primary areas of local government expenditure in Australia are transport and communications (including roads), general public services (including waste management), and recreation, culture, and religion (Local Government Information Unit, 2023). Core social services like education, social welfare, and health generally remain the remit of state and federal governments, meaning that local government expenditure in these areas is far lower than the OECD average (Hyslop et al., 2022). According to a report by the University of Tasmania, within the OECD, the function of Australian local governments is most comparable to those in Spain (apart from New Zealand, our Tasman neighbour) (Hyslop et al., 2022).

The ability of local governments to raise their own revenue or explore commercial partnerships was hampered significantly through the latter part of the twentieth century with the rise of new managerialism and the associated neoliberal privatization of public services under the guise of efficiency (Van Gramberg & Teicher, 2000). Areas of local government that could operate profitably—for example, swimming schools run at local government managed pools—were often sold to the private sector, leaving local governments primarily in charge of unprofitable or loss-making services. Simultaneously, even as councils were left with fewer profit-making enterprises, council staff were expected to behave more like their private sector counterparts, focusing on immediate narrow outputs rather than broader long-term outcomes and treating residents as customers rather than as community stakeholders (Novak, 2019).

This started to shift as a wider move towards a people-focused service delivery model began gathering pace both in Australia (de Vries, 2021) and overseas (Hyslop et al., 2022). In recent decades, Australian local governments have taken increasingly prominent roles in the provision of community facilities like child care, and as well as place-making, urban renewal, and the creation of circular economies (Khan & Bejracharya, 2020; Bolger & Doyon, 2019). This expanded remit is reflected in ALGA's 2020–23 strategic plan, which highlights the significance of local government's emerging role in community resilience and climate change alongside the traditional focus on waste, roads and infrastructure, and financial sustainability (Australian Local Government Association, 2020).[1]

A financial and capacity challenge for local government in assuming these additional functions is that the new managerialist legacy of ceding the most commercially viable services is still in place. Further, decisions to take on many of the newer roles have often been reactive or ad hoc, meaning that long-term viability planning is often not in place. For example, there are multiple examples of councils assuming a service in response to decisions made by other levels of government to transfer responsibility without the allocation of commensurate funding streams.

Compounding these pressures has been the fact that despite being the level of government closest to the people, until very recently, a long-term community perception of councils having a narrow remit (the 3Rs) has remained. Without structural influence at the national and state levels, the absence of community and business advocacy further weakened local government's bargaining powers, impacting its ability to lobby for funding arrangements that better reflected both its long-term and broadening roles.

Recently, however, there has been renewed community interest in the issue of federalism and a greater recognition of the diversifying role of local government. A catalyst for this change has been the prominent role councils played in responding to Covid-19 and natural disasters, as well as a growing awareness of the transfer of numerous policy and program functions from states to local government, and concerns about reductions in local services from traditional providers such as banks, community services, health, and aged care. In regional and rural areas, in particular, residents recognize their local council as the sole source of an array of social and health services, as the area's major employer, and as a force for long-term sustainable development. This has amplified support for the shift towards 'maximalist' local government (Hastings et al., 2016).

While the scope and speed of these service delivery changes varies between jurisdictions and councils, several common functions may be distinguished.

### 6.4.1 'Core' Local Government Functions

There is an expectation that local governments provide core services to a minimum standard before others are considered. Examples of these include building approvals and certification, waste collection and management, and cultural and recreation services.

[1] Interestingly, ALGA's recently released 2024–2026 strategic plan focuses only on governance, partnerships, and collaborations, and does not set any priorities related to service provision.

### 6.4.2 "Market Gap" and "Thin Market" Services

Particularly in rural areas, local governments often face pressure to provide services that are not economically viable. This viability, or lack thereof, is commonly due to small population numbers, large and/or remote service areas, a lack of alternative providers, and uncoordinated policy from the state and federal governments. Local governments thus become 'providers of last resort', fulfilling needs that the market cannot or will not offer.

Examples of functions that local councils have assumed following the withdrawal by other providers include medical clinics, aged care services, and social housing. In New South Wales, for instance, Brewarrina Shire Council formed a partnership with a university to offer free dental services to its underserved residents (Brewarrina Shire Council, 2023).

Councils have also assumed a leadership role in the absence of other parties to tackle emerging policy priorities such as climate change mitigation, disaster preparedness, community resilience, and advocacy for affordable housing.

### 6.4.3 Services Delivered in Competition with Other Providers

For a range of reasons, local governments have also sometimes chosen to deliver services in competition with other providers. Examples include childcare and commercial car parks. These activities can often generate new revenue sources.

It is useful to demonstrate the challenges associated with performing these functions and the cost of service delivery through two case studies: childcare services and aquatic facilities.

The evolving—and at times uncertain—role of local government in Australia can be illustrated by councils' involvement in the provision of childcare and early education. Although the exact number of local government-run childcare centres is difficult to ascertain, figures show that between 7% and 11% of all childcare facilities in Australia are run by councils or state government (Commonwealth of Australia Productivity Commission, 2023; Bray, 2023), and there is an understanding that "local government is making a significant contribution to ECEC [Early Childhood Education and Care] in Australia" (Bray, 2023, 15). Some local governments—particularly those in rural areas—step in to fill a market gap, where the small populations and large distances involved make childcare an unattractive commercial proposition. Other local governments compete directly with commercial and not-for-profit centres, with ALGA claiming that council-run services "consistently outperform other for-profit services in quality and standards" (Australian Local Government Association, 2022, 47).

However, as with most aspects of local government governance, the provision of childcare is subject to vagaries of funding, with significant disparities across jurisdictions (Bray, 2023). In 2023, several councils in the state of Victoria cut back or completely withdrew childcare offerings, while at the same time neighbouring councils were investing heavily in ambitious new projects (Payne, 2023).

For instance, Knox City Council, located in the east of Melbourne, Victoria, announced the cessation of childcare services in 26 of its 28 centres from the end of 2024 (Waters, 2023), while programs run by the regional Mornington Peninsula Shire were reported to be in 'jeopardy' due to inadequate funding (Mornington Peninsula Shire, 2023). In addition, the mayor of south-eastern Melbourne's Glen Eira council, Jim Magee, noted that his council-run early learning centres were unable to compete with their far larger and newer commercial counterparts and had been running at an annual loss of some $570,000 AU. Although not quite proposing a closure of services, the mayor flagged a reassessment of priorities and a need to weigh up costs to the community against the benefits to the relatively small group of residents who make use of childcare facilities.

In contrast to the issues facing Knox, Mornington Shire and Glen Eira, Yarra City Council, in Melbourne's inner east, recently opened a new $two million AU childcare facility capable of accommodating 132 children per week (far greater than the previous centre's capacity of 56) (Lucas, 2023).

As well as illustrating differences in funding, the divergent trajectories of the councils' childcare offerings perhaps reveal a deeper dilemma about the contemporary core role of local government. Claudia Nguyen, mayor of Yarra City Council, expounded a version of the maximalist vision at the new centre's opening, stating that "[c]ouncils are the closest form of government to the community", and the "spaces in which we deliver services like early childhood education need to reflect the growing needs of the community" (Payne, 2023). For councils like Yarra City, local government's core role is no longer just about the 3Rs but about responding to the growing and diverse needs of residents.

In this context, the pressure of relying on a traditional and largely static funding model while expanding services is challenging. Few councils have had the capacity, capability, or scale of projects to allow them to adopt innovative funding arrangements such as Public Private Partnerships (PPPs), meaning that government funding is crucially important.

A second case study concerns aquatic facilities. Across Australia, local councils have traditionally played a prime role in the provision of community sport and recreation facilities—from open space to high-cost infrastructure such as swimming pools. In 2022 there were 1306 government-owned public pools (primarily local government) and 807 private sector accessible pools across Australia. Revenue from these facilities is principally derived from swimming school fees and around three-quarters of the private facilities were in the highest Socio-Economic Indexes for Areas (SEIFA) decile, while 80% of pools in areas of the lowest SEIFA decile were publicly owned (Summers & Houston, 2022).

A 2022 report by Royal Life Saving Australia, the State of Aquatic Facility Infrastructure in Australia, found that "many [c]ouncils struggle to afford to maintain or replace swimming pools and increasingly councils are considering closing their pools" (Summers & Houston, 2022, 4). This was in the context of a finding that by 2032 up to 40% of local government pools will need to be replaced at an estimated cost of $8 billion AU (Summers & Houston, 2022, 4). The report calculated that the closure of 10% of existing aquatic facilities would "result in a net loss of $910 million AU annually in social, health and economic benefits" (Summers & Houston, 2022, 13).

While councils regularly rely on state or Commonwealth government grants to contribute to the construction or upgrade of such facilities, those funds rarely exceed 30% of the cost of the project. This means that councils will need to find over $5 billion AU over the next decade, simply to maintain existing service levels in this area.

That expense is unlikely to be evenly borne by councils, as grants vary significantly across jurisdictions. In NSW, funds of up to $300,000 AU are available for swimming pools, while in Victoria grants for the same purpose offer up to $three million AU. For context, the cost of a basic outdoor swimming pool is approximately $ten million AU (Summers & Houston, 2022, 13).

Royal Life Saving found that rural and regional councils, who own almost 60% of pools, were most at risk of being unable to fund such a renewal program and made several recommendations that are illustrative of both the reality and perceptions of local government funding arrangements. The report identified that "[a]dditional *funding from state and federal governments is clearly the default remedy* [my emphasis], however, there are several other approaches … that warrant further examination" (Summers & Houston, 2022, 7).

Those other approaches were not tested, but suggestions included exploring options for collaboration between councils, offering subsidies to private providers for non-commercial services such as lap swimming, and exploring PPPs as a new way of funding swimming pool infrastructure.

The fact that these options were considered new or innovative in 2022 highlights councils' continued dependence on traditional self-funded approaches and grants as the way to deliver infrastructure.

This example also illustrates another funding challenge for councils. The grants available for swimming pools from both Commonwealth and state governments are structured similarly to other government grant programs. That is, funds are invariably available only for capital purposes—one-off funding towards construction or upgrades. The cost of maintaining the asset and delivering services rests with the local council.

Further, the state of aquatic centre infrastructure—with an estimated 40% of pools reaching the end of their lifespan between 2022 and 2032—is reflective of general infrastructure management challenges facing local councils.

In 2021, the ALGA reported that 10% of all local government assets nationally were in poor condition, and a further 26% had defects "requiring regular and/or significant maintenance to reinstate the service" (Australian Local Government Association, 2021, 5). The ALGA estimated that the cost of replacing all poor and very poor assets would be $51 billion AU and the cost of replacing assets in fair condition would be up to $138 billion AU (Australian Local Government Association, 2021, 2). Its position on securing funding for this program of asset maintenance and renewal was, as previously noted, to call for an increase in the

FAG program back to at least 1% of federal taxation revenue and for the maintenance and expansion of targeted grants programs. Without a change of this nature, it is difficult to see how many councils can strategically manage their assets, and there is a major risk of delayed maintenance and upgrades shortening an asset's economic life.

## 6.5 Innovating Through Cooperation

As outlined above, for many years state governments pursued a top-down program of forced council amalgamations as a means of driving efficiency in the local government sector. The results of that policy have been mixed at best, and in the face of often hostile community and council opposition and with limited measurable financial benefits, states are currently no longer pursuing this model.

While amalgamations did not provide a solution to the local government sector's ongoing reliance on grants programs, many councils have looked to other forms of innovation to drive efficiency.

Given that Australian local governments are often small and distributed across large areas, and despite growing community expectations and demands from other layers of government, many have been unable to secure the funding needed to sustainably provide a full suite of services.

To counter these difficulties (and to allow the fulfilment of a more maximalist vision of local government), there has been a recent rise in cooperation between councils in an attempt to create economies of scale and overcome some of the structural funding constraints they face.

These arrangements vary from issue-specific to wider, more formal models, such as collaborations of several neighbouring local councils to form 'Joint Organizations' (JOs) and 'Regional Organizations of Councils' (ROCs) across the country. Some have focused on core services, while others have included emerging areas of responsibility, such as climate change management.

These arrangements operate in a range of environments, from small rural councils to well-resourced local governments in large cities. Councils commonly report that the key benefit of JO and ROC membership is the ability to leverage economies of scale to engage private providers and enter into partnerships with industry and communities that would not be available to, or feasible for, individual councils.

In Sydney, for example, five local government councils joined forces on a push to transition away from fossil fuels by creating a regional energy master plan involving the mass uptake of solar and other renewable energy (Cheung et al., 2019, 220). Taking a combined approach allowed the councils to negotiate from a position of strength, securing favourable energy deals that would not have been available to them individually.

The largest ROC by population and revenue also operates in Sydney. The Southern Sydney Regional Organization of Councils (SSROC) incorporates nearly 1.9 million residents across 12 councils in metropolitan Sydney—nearly a third of the city's total population. SSROC includes the City of Sydney, home of Sydney's central business district and the nation's financial capital. As well as the traditional focus on waste, transport, and planning, SSROC also prioritizes environmental, biodiversity, and sustainability issues, reflecting the broadening scope of the local government sector and the additional opportunities available to larger metropolitan councils.

In Perth, the largest city in Western Australia, six councils joined together to form the Eastern Metropolitan Regional Council (EMRC), with a focus on creating an economy of scale to deal with waste and resource management issues. Since its foundation in 1993, the EMRC's scope has broadened to incorporate sustainability, tourism, training, planning, and natural and built environment services (Khan & Bejracharya, 2020).

Using a different model, in 2018 three regional councils in western NSW worked with local tourism-focused businesses to jointly form a destination marketing organization—Orange 360—and adopt a shared brand identity to promote the region as a year-round tourist destination. Orange 360 operates with a board comprising local councillors and business representatives and is supported by a mix of employees and council tourism managers. In mid-2022, it had 360 registered members (Orange 360, 2022).

The number, models and focus of these collaborations continues to grow. Given that many councils still self-generate a significant proportion of their revenue, this is unsurprising. Some collaborations are sufficiently established to demonstrate tangible benefits, while others are still nascent. They can, however, be seen as representing innovation in the way councils procure, market, and deliver services.

At the same time, however, the majority of Australian councils remain heavily dependent on traditional sources of revenue generation to deliver services and are often too small or financially insecure to enter into commercial partnerships such as PPPs.

## 6.6 Conclusions

While councils across Australia are facing shared challenges as they adapt to the shifting requirements of federal and state governments and increasing community expectations, their ability to respond is highly varied.

Although metropolitan councils tend to have a greater capacity to generate income than their rural and regional counterparts, and funding arrangements differ between states, financial sustainability remains precarious for many councils. Further, while policies such as rate capping impact even a large councils' revenue, regional councils, with small populations dispersed over areas the size of European countries, have fewer own-source revenue options and can struggle to fund their core operations.

As the role of local government continues to evolve to meet community expectations, these existing challenges will be amplified by emergent issues such as aging infrastructure, climate change, technology and cyber security, affordable housing and community resilience.

In this context it is vital that the nature and conditions of government funding be reviewed to provide greater certainty, autonomy, and recurrent support to councils where it is needed. In rural areas, where communities are both small and highly dependent on their local councils as the sole provider of a range of essential services the need for such reform is even greater.

To support government-led reforms, in parallel, Australian councils need to develop—either individually or, more commonly, through collective arrangements—an enhanced capacity to self-generate revenue and diversify income sources. This will require a further evolution in all councils' capacity to adapt, however, the variations in capacity and capability that already exist, particularly between urban, regional and rural councils, means that targeted solutions are required.

## References


Australian Local Government Association. (2020). *Strategic Plan 2020–2023.*

Australian Local Government Association. (2021). *National state of the assets report.*

Australian Local Government Association. (2022). *Research for submission to local government productivity inquiry.*

Australian Local Government Association. (2023a). *Background on local government funding.*

Australian Local Government Association. (2023b). *Local government key facts and figures.*

Bejracharya, B., & Khan, S. (2020). Urban governance in Australia: A case study of Brisbane City. In B. Dahiya & A. Das (Eds.), *New Urban Agenda in Asia-Pacific: Governance for sustainable and inclusive cities* (pp. 225–250). Springer.

Bolger, K., & Doyon, A. (2019). Circular cities: Exploring local government strategies to facilitate a circular economy. *European Planning Studies, 27*(11), 2184–2205. https://doi.org/10.1080/09654313.2019.1642854

Bray, R. (2023). *Childcare in Australia: Historical trends in provision and Australian Government funding. A statistical compendium 1969–2022.* Australian National University Center for Social Research and Methods.

Brewarrina Shire Council. (2023). *Medical Emergency Services.*

Brisbane City Council. (2023). *Annual Plan and Budget 2023–24.*

Cheung, G., Davies, P., & Truck, S. (2019). Transforming urban energy systems: The role of local governments' regional energy master plan. *Journal of Cleaner Production, 220*, 655–667. https://doi.org/10.1016/j.jclepro.2019.01.179

Commonwealth of Australia Productivity Commission. (2017). *Productivity Review Supplementary Paper No. 16—Local government.*

Commonwealth of Australia Productivity Commission. (2023). *A path to universal early childhood education and care. Draft report.*

de Vries, S. (2021). The power of procedural policy tools at the local government level: Australian local governments contributing to policy change for major projects. *Policy and Society, 40*(3), 414–430. https://doi.org/10.1080/14494035.2021.1955471

Department of Infrastructure, Transport, Regional Development, Communications and the Arts. (2023a). *Australian Council of Local Government.*

Department of Infrastructure, Transport, Regional Development, Communications and the Arts. (2023b). *Financial Assistant Grant to local government.*

Drew, J., Kortt, M., & Dollery, B. (2014). Economies of scale and local government expenditure: Evidence from Australia. *Administration and Society, 46*(6), 632–653. https://doi.org/10.1177/0095399712469191

Federation. (2020). *National Cabinet terms of reference*.

Hastings, C., Wortley, L., Ryan, R., & Grant, B. (2016). Community expectations for the role of local government in regional Australia: Meeting the challenges of 'slow burn'. *Australasian Journal of Regional Studies, 22*(1), 158–180.

Hyslop, S., Eccleston, R., Johnson, L., Langridge, M., & Moran, F. (2022). National and international trends in local government and their relevance to Tasmania. In *Future of Local government Review Background Research Paper 2*. Retrieved February 13, 2024, from https://figshare.utas.edu.au/articles/report/National_and_International_Trends_in_Local_Governance_and_their_Relevance_to_Tasmania_Future_of_Local_Government_Review_Background_Research_Paper_No_2/24227803

Independent Pricing and Regulatory Tribunal NSW. (2023a). *Review of the rate peg methodology: Final report*.

Independent Pricing and Regulatory Tribunal NSW. (2023b). *The rate peg*.

Khan, S., & Bejracharya, B. (2020). The changing role of regional organization of councils in Australia: Case studies from Perth metropolitan region. In B. Dahiya & A. Das (Eds.), *New Urban Agenda in Asia-Pacific: Governance for sustainable and inclusive cities* (pp. 93–116). Springer.

Local Government Information Unit. (2023). *Facts and figures: Australia*.

Lucas, F. (2023). Yarra City Council officially opens Richmond Kindergarten. *The Sector*. Retrieved February 13, 2024, from https://thesector.com.au/2023/10/10/yarra-city-council-officially-opens-richmond-kindergarten/

Michel, T., & Taylor, A. (2012). Death by a thousand grants? The challenge of grant funding reliance for local government councils in the Northern Territory of Australia. *Local Government Studies, 38*(4), 1–16. https://doi.org/10.1080/03003930.2012.666212

Mills, C. (2021). The key trends shaping local government in 2021 and beyond. *Council Magazine*. Retrieved February 13, 2024, from https://councilmagazine.com.au/the-key-trends-shaping-local-government-in-2021-and-beyond/.

Mornington Peninsula Shire. (2023). *More investment needed to deliver kindergarten reform*.

Novak, S. (2019). Reinventing government starts at the local government level. *The Mandarin*. Retrieved February 13, 2024, from https://www.themandarin.com.au/106121-reinventing-government-starts-at-the-local-level/

Orange 360. (2022). *Annual Report: 2021/2022 Financial Year*.

Payne, S. (2023). Melbourne councils leaving childcare to the private sector gives families fewer options. *ABC News*. Retrieved February 13, 2024, from https://www.abc.net.au/news/2023-10-13/victorian-councils-closing-childcare-centres/102966894

Sansom, G. (2020). Recent trends in Australian local government reform. *Commonwealth Journal of Local Government Governance, 23*. https://doi.org/10.5130/cjlg.vi23.7546

Shire of Sandstone. (2023). *Annual Budget for the year ended 30 June 2024*.

Skatssoon, J. (2023). PM&C accused of breaking commitment to local government. *Government News*. Retrieved February 13, 2024, from https://www.governmentnews.com.au/pmc-accused-of-breaking-commitment-to-local-government/

Summers, J., & Houston, R. J. (2022). *The state of aquatic facility infrastructure in Australia—Rebuilding our aging public swimming pools*. Royal Life Saving Society.

Van Gramberg, B., & Teicher, J. (2000). Managerialism in local government—Victoria, Australia. *International Journal of Public Sector Management, 13*(5), 476–492. https://doi.org/10.1108/09513550010350869

Waters, C. (2023). Kinder surprise: 1100 kids in limbo as council pulls plug on kinder services. *The Age*. Retrieved February 13, 2024, from https://www.theage.com.au/national/victoria/kinder-surprise-1000-kids-in-limbo-as-council-pulls-plug-on-kinder-services-20230815-p5dwok.html

Western Australian Local Government Association. (2016a). *Shire of East Pilbara.*
Western Australian Local Government Association. (2016b). *Shire of Peppermint Grove.*
Wilkinson, G., McKenzia, F., & Bolleter, J. (2021). Federalism and urban primacy: Political dimensions that influence the city-country divide in Australia. *International Journal of Urban Sciences, 26*(3), 438–462. https://doi.org/10.1080/12265934.2021.1997631
Woollahra Council. (2023). *Special rate variation update.*
Yourcouncil. (2022). *2021/22 NSW Overview: Finances.*

# Chapter 7
# Ways of Public Service Provision by Urban and Rural Local Governments: Brazilian Experience and Challenges

**Thiago Marrara**

**Abstract** After introducing the main aspects of the Brazilian federation, this chapter describes the evolution of the country's municipalities and presents their competences regarding public services provision according to the 1988 Constitution. It also analyses if rural and urban divisions of the local territory through perimeter laws play any role when it comes to the competences of local governments. Based on that, the chapter presents three basic models for public services provision, i.e. standalone provision by each local government, associated provision involving inter-municipal cooperation and regionalized provision. Additionally, it describes the types of contractual partnerships used in Brazil and their limits with regard to different types of services (divisible and individiable). In conclusion, it points out how regionalization policies and the recognition of asymmetries between local governments are important to help them overcome problems related to public service provision.

**Keywords** Brazilian municipalities · Public service provision · Local partnerships

## 7.1 Introduction

Cities are spaces of interaction and exchange. Human beings gather in urban areas to satisfy their needs through the exchange of goods, services, affection, culture, knowledge, etc. In addition, the increase of people in urban areas raises the risks of resource depletion, hinders mobility, increases tensions as well as the value of land and properties. Ultimately, it generates risks of compromising the original cities' functions or makes them unfeasible in the worst cases.

Under these circumstances, public services and infrastructure play a dual role. On the one hand, in the urban zones, its provision allows citizens to enjoy an adequate standard of dignity and, at the same time, contributes to the efficiency of the city as a complex system. Services and infrastructure, planned well in advance and

T. Marrara (✉)
Department of Public Law, FDRP, University of São Paulo (USP), Ribeirão Preto, Brazil
e-mail: marrara@usp.br



F. Velasco Caballero et al. (eds.), *Municipal Tasks and Financing*, Local and Urban Governance, https://doi.org/10.1007/978-3-031-99812-6_7

offered in adequate quantities, ensure that the city continues to function as an exchange space.

On the other hand, in rural zones, the provision of public services and infrastructure serves to prevent the "rural exodus", or the "scape to the city", to maintain a balance between rural and urban activities, as well as to foster population spread. This occurs because poor conditions of the rural population, not only in economic terms, but also due to the absence or the low quality of services and basic amenities of life, is one of the factors that stimulates the rural exodus and contributes to the overload of cities.

In many countries, the escape from rural spaces means the "search for the state" itself. In other words, people tend to flee from rural areas when the State cannot reach them and provide them with adequate public services. Under such conditions, citizens move to access services and facilities that are concentrated in urban areas. It is primarily for this reason that, in recent decades, poor or less developed countries have formed metropolises and megacities much more quickly and intensely than European countries. Such a trend leads to the importance of discussing not only how to organize and provide public services and infrastructure in urban areas, but how to reach the urban expansion and the rural zones beyond the urban zones themselves.

In Brazil, such discussion is deeply related to the institutional and operational capacities of local governments, since they are competent for many important public services. However, the provision of such services is not an easy task due to: (1) the large number of small municipalities, i.e., those with a population of fewer than 20,000 inhabitants; (2) the operational fragilities of the local public administration; (3) the lack of sufficient financial resources to sustain basic administrative functions; and (4) the shortage of qualified teams to perform complex functions as those related to public services provision and infrastructure.

The main objective of this chapter is to demonstrate how Brazilian local governments seek to overcome such difficulties in organizing the provision of public services in both urban and rural areas. However, before examining the forms of service provision, it is indispensable to clarify how municipalities are positioned in the Brazilian federation, which public services fall under their competence, and if the division between rural and urban zones affects their competences.

## 7.2 Local Governments in the Brazilian Federation

The legal status of Brazilian municipalities has undergone significant changes over the last 200 years. From 1500 to 1822, Brazil functioned as a colony linked to the Kingdom of Portugal, whose interests were primarily focused on the economical exploitation of the territory and its natural resources, supplying the metropolis and friendly nations. Portugal had no interest in establishing a new country in the South American territory; the objective was purely to extract financial resources through natural wealth exploitation or tax collection.

During the nearly three centuries of the colonial period, Brazilian cities were founded and developed in accordance with economic cycles (Ribeiro, 2023). Initially, they concentrated on the coast, where large-scale sugarcane cultivation for export and the establishment of forts and territorial equipment took place. As mineral resources, especially gold, were discovered, the population gradually moved inland, forming towns and cities in areas that now encompass the states of Goiás, Mato Grosso, and Minas Gerais. Later, during the rubber exploration cycle, cities in the northern region experienced significant expansion, especially Manaus and Belém.

Besides that, in 1808, circumstances which determined the conditions and status of Brazil as a colony began to change due to Portugal's invasion by Napoleon, culminating in the transfer of the Portuguese Empire's headquarters to Rio de Janeiro (Gomes, 2007, 29). This led to the strengthening of the national public administration (Marrara, 2020), with the emergence of banks, libraries, medical schools, and other institutions (Fausto, 2002, 121). Simultaneously, movements led to the declaration of independence in 1822 and the granting of the Imperial Constitution of 1824.

During the Empire (1822 to 1889), Brazil operated as a unitary state without political decentralization. The national government, divided into four powers (legislative, executive, judiciary and the moderating power exercised by the emperor), heavily centralized the budget, public policies, and services. Despite that, the roots of local government autonomy were already noticed at that time. Article 167 of the Imperial Constitution stipulated that in all cities and towns, the *Câmara de Vereadores*, a local council, had the competence to exercise "economic government". These councils, formed by councilors through elections, were responsible for establishing rules regarding, for example, police conduct and resource allocation, and for exercising other attributions defined by the Empire's Constitution (Article 169). They were not politically autonomous, but could enact rules, especially using their police power.

In 1889, Brazil abandoned the imperial state model and became a republic. Subsequently, inspired by the United States, the congress promulgated the 1891 Republican Constitution. It reduced the powers from four to three due to the extinction of moderate power; replaced the imperial, monarchic and hereditary system by a presidential model based on democratic elections; and turned the unitary state into a two-level federation, divided into the union and provinces (Articles 1 and 2).

This first Republican Constitution also foresaw the provinces as the subnational level of the federation and formally created municipalities (Dias & Lopes, 2021, 47751), but not as a third federative level. Instead, municipalities were part of the state's indirect administration and the Constitution prescribed that the states should be organized in a way to ensure the autonomy of municipalities concerning matters of their "particular interest". Besides that, there were no specific norms about local functions or the role of the city councils. This meant that the provinces had wide legislative discretion to enact rules on municipal law and to organize municipalities and local governments.

Throughout the period from the 1891 First Republican Constitution to the current Constitution, promulgated in 1988, Brazilian federalism has tremendously changed. Provinces became states of the federation and their number increased due to the division of large states (like Mato Grosso and Goiás), as well as the transformation of federal territories into new states (like Acre). Municipalities also multiplied and got a new constitutional status.

In fact, Brazil kept its two-level federalism through the Constitutions of 1891, 1934, 1937, 1946, 1967 and 1969. Since 1988, though, the new Constitution characterizes municipalities as a federative sphere, alongside states and the union. As a result, Brazil now adopts a tripartite federalism, which is divergent from the traditional dual federal structure that typifies Germany (Marrara, 2008, 33) and the United States.

Despite its innovative character, in my point of view, the formal recognition of municipalities as the third level of the federation by the 1988 Constitution (Articles 1 and 18) can be criticized and deemed as artificial for many reasons:

1. While the union and states have three powers, municipalities have only two powers, as there is no local judiciary;
2. Municipalities do not count on their own Audit Courts, apart from a few exceptions (São Paulo and Rio de Janeiro). Therefore, local public management is under the control of the states' Audit Courts;
3. Municipalities do not have military agents, only civilian agents with limited powers, including civil guards, whose main function is to protect the local public domain, such as parks and streets;
4. Municipalities are not represented in the state legislative power. If the states of the federation are represented in the senate within the unions' bicameral legislature, by symmetry, the municipalities should be represented in the state legislature, but this does not happen, since it is unicameral;
5. Municipalities have scarce financial resources, that are often insufficient to maintain their own teams of public agents, which makes it impossible for them to invest in expensive infrastructure networks and basic public services without aid and assistance from states and the union.

Despite these several problems and challenges, formally, the 1988 Constitution recognizes municipalities as an autonomous federative sphere. Consequently, it allocates them numerous public services and guarantees the power to organize themselves, manage their services, their public agents and local assets, collect taxes, prepare their own budgets, and to edit and enforce laws.

## 7.3 Municipalities, Demographic Growth and Urbanization

Over the last century, Brazil's population and its number of municipalities have increased significantly, especially since the 1960s, due to industrialization and the pursuit of jobs in the service sector. At the same time, urbanization accelerated, and by the 1970s, more than half of the Brazilian population had moved to cities.

Some basic data can prove this rapid demographic and urban growth. According to the 1872 census, Brazil had ten million inhabitants. The 2022 census, finished by the Brazilian Institute of Geography and Statistics (IBGE), indicates a population of 203 million inhabitants. Today's population is, therefore, 20 times larger than that of 150 years ago. According to Stamm et al. (2013, 254), specifically from 1940 to 2010, the urban population grew by 1049%, while the rural population increased by a low rate of 5.2%. It is also noteworthy that from 1980 until 2020, the Brazilian population increased by about 100 million people.

Currently, more than 85% of the Brazilian population resides in urban areas, with 124.1 million people living in "urban concentrations", namely municipalities with over 100,000 inhabitants. Official data of IBGE shows that, out of the 5570 municipalities in 2022, 44.8% had up to 10,000 inhabitants and 70.6% (i.e., 3935) had up to 20,000 inhabitants (Poder 360, 2023). On the other hand, no more than 15 municipalities contained populations exceeding one million inhabitants. Nowadays, the country's 319 largest municipalities account for 57% of the population, while the 20 most populous municipalities absorb 22.1% of the population (IBGE, 2023).

The IBGE official research also indicates that the group of municipalities with up to 20,000 inhabitants has suffered the greatest population reduction in recent years, while the group between 100,000 and one million inhabitants is the one that proportionally grew the most. Municipalities with more than one million inhabitants showed a halfway demographic growth between 0 and 1% per year.

This data reveals a double urban phenomenon in Brazil: the smallest municipalities tend to disappear or become even smaller. This means that their revenue generation also tends to decrease. As a result, low financial resources hinder the ability of these municipalities to invest in infrastructure and, above all, to serve the urban and rural population with quality and suitable public services. At the same time, the diminutive population does not make public bidding procedures for public service privatization sufficiently attractive to the market and private investors, since the need for investment is high, the economies of scale are small, and profits are doubtful. Under such circumstances, these municipalities will certainly become increasingly dependent on financial aid and assistance from states and the union.

At the same time, Brazil is experiencing the phenomenon of "demetropolization", that is, the gradual reduction of population in large metropolises, like Sao Paulo, Salvador, Rio de Janeiro, and many others. Demographic shrinkage occurs due to numerous factors, such as urban violence, high costs of housing, and mobility difficulties. In a certain way, it may also be explained by the "deterritorialization", i.e., the possibility for some professionals to sell their workforce in huge cities without the need to live or be present in their territories thanks to new communication technologies and incremented home office facilities. Technological advances have enabled intellectual service professionals to leave metropolises and move to small or midsized cities in search for better quality of life.

In the Brazilian context, the simultaneous shrinkage of small and large cities is therefore evident. Municipalities with medium populations are the only ones that progress in demographic terms and, as a consequence, they will tend to suffer more pressures for the improvement and expansion of public services and infrastructures, in urban or rural areas.

## 7.4 Competences Regarding Public Services Provision in Brazil

In addition to establishing a tripartite federative state where municipalities were disconnected from states to form their own political sphere, following a strongly standardized model, the 1988 Federal Constitution specifies a series of public services of economic and social nature, allocating many of them to local governments.

"Economic public services" are distributed among the three federative spheres: federal, state, and local. According to Article 21 of the Constitution, the union (federal government) is responsible for providing postal services; public telecommunications; broadcasting services; electricity production, transmission and distribution; air and aerospace navigation services, as well as railway, waterway, interstate and international passenger road transportation services. Additionally, managing airports and seaports, rivers, and lakes falls under the federal government's jurisdiction.

On the other hand, states take charge of local piped gas services (Article 26), while municipalities (or local governments) handle local-interest services (Article 30), such as urban public transportation, public lighting and basic sanitation. Nevertheless, the 1988 Constitution is not precise when it comes to the competences of the municipalities. For example, since it does not mention in a clear way the local competence for basic sanitation or funerary services, the Supreme Court, sectoral laws or the "Organic Laws" (i.e. the "local constitution") must clarify many of these attributions.

Particularly in the field of local public transportation, municipalities decide how they will offer the services and if they will charge for them. In 2012, the National Congress enacted the National Mobility Law and determined many principles and directives for municipalities in this field. The same happened with public sanitation. Considering that the 1988 Constitution grants to the National Congress the competence to enact directives in this sector, it approved the National Basic Sanitation Law in 2007, establishing detailed rules regarding basic sanitation provision, planning, regulation, and monitoring, as well as rules on regionalization, concessions, and other types of partnerships with the private sector.

In addition to the economic services, the 1988 Constitution indicates a significant number of "social public services" like healthcare, education, leisure, and culture. The competencies of the federative levels in these areas are not isolated but shared. All governments in the three spheres of the Brazilian federation must operate simultaneously and, in certain cases, within the framework of public policy systems, such as the Unified Health System (SUS). Activities labeled as social public services can, at the same time, be offered by market players as pure economic activities under state regulation. This means that, parallel to the public education and the public health systems as public services, the market offers remunerated private education and health services under administrative licensing and regulatory control, reaching a huge part of the population.

The problem with the market's performance in these activities not monopolized by the state is its selectivity, i.e., its concentration in areas with the highest incomes and consumption capacities. As most municipalities have a small population and short income, the market tends to concentrate service provision on wealthy medium and large municipalities, especially in search of higher-income populations, with the exception of private university education services, which reach a significant part of low-income citizens due to federal government aids and incentive measures.

In this context, considering that small municipalities often do not have resources for their most basic public services, nor can attract sufficient market investment, it is a natural consequence that: (1) they depend heavily on state and federal aid and assistance to provide public services and (2) their populations seek better opportunities and service provisions in larger Brazilian municipalities, especially regional cities, explaining their above-average demographic growth in the last decades.

## 7.5 Rural or Urban Areas: Implications to Service Provision

Characterized as the third federative level by the 1988 Constitution, the 5570 local spheres are equivalent to municipalities, as legal entities governed by internal public law, divided into the executive branch and the legislative branch, and their respective indirect administrations, formed by specialized local autarchies, state enterprises and foundations. These different entities operate within the municipal territory in the exercise of restrictive administrative functions and services provision, extending their competences across two large areas: rural and urban.

The "urban zone" is mainly subject to the instruments of the City Statute (i.e., the National Urban Policy Law) and urban development policies, in particular the so-called Master Plan (*Plano Diretor*). On the other hand, although they are subject to the Land Statute (*Estatuto da Terra*) and the union's agricultural policies, the "*rural zone*" is also part of the municipality's territory. Therefore, this area must also be considered in its development policies and served by its public administration. In some municipalities, local legislation still provides for "urban expansion zones". These areas are originally rural, but reserved for the future expansion of urban centers. When defined in territorial planning, they signal to the market and local population the direction of urban growth in order to avoid uncontrolled and random urbanization.

From a legal point of view, in each municipality, the precise distinction between rural zone and urban zone as parts of the municipal territory is given by the Urban Perimeter Law (*Lei de Perímetro Urbano*), approved by the Chamber of Councilors (municipal Legislative Branch) and subject to change at any time. Until 2012, there were no national rules on how municipalities should elaborate this law regarding the perimeter definition. In many cases, therefore, the separation between rural and urban zones was established without prior studies, without planning and, in the worst situations, to exclusively serve private interests, opening space for practices of "urban corruption".

From 2012 onwards, a series of urban disasters led to the revision of the City Statute, as the most important national act of the Brazilian urban law. As a consequence, Article 42(b) was introduced in the City Statute, requiring that the expansion of the urban perimeter be preceded by a specific technical study. Before changing the limits between urban and rural zones, municipalities must nowadays enact a specific law with urbanization restrictions, identification of vulnerability areas to disasters, guidelines for infrastructure, road system and public facilities, parameters for land subdivision, use and occupation, separation of land for social housing, guidelines for environmental protection, among other elements.

Once the urban perimeter has been defined by local law, that is, the border between the rural zone and the urban zone is legally determined, municipalities may begin to shape their development and occupation policies, prepare infrastructure and the provision of local public services. The most important municipal law in this matter is the so-called Master Plan (*Plano Diretor*). Necessarily based on the rules and directives of the City Statute, it contains the urban policy instruments to organize local development, to control the exploration of real estate properties and to manage areas of public domain, where public service equipment and infrastructure networks are installed. The City Statute clearly prescribes that the Master Plan must encompass urban and urban expansion zones, as well as rural zones. The problem is that, except in special cases, such local plan is not compulsory for municipalities with up to 20,000 inhabitants. As such, still today, a significant number of municipalities have not approved it.

In the urban area, municipalities are also responsible for taking care of land management (Article 30(VIII) of the 1988 Constitution). To fulfill this task, city councils generally enact laws on the use, occupation and division of urban land, which must align with the requirements of the municipal Master Plan and the general rules of the National Land Division Law and the City Statute. Local laws on land use, occupation and division provide rules on the parceling of urban land, the size of properties, the characteristics of buildings, the rules for using properties, and the installation of public service infrastructure in neighborhoods, among other elements. However, primarily, these local laws are not mandatory, nor can they deal with the subdivision or occupation of rural land, as it is subject to federal rules enacted by the National Congress.

Despite these different competencies in relation to land use, occupation and division, the fact that a local property or land is included in the rural or the urban zone does not generate significant implications for the responsibilities related to the provision of public services and the installation of infrastructure. While outlining the federative distribution of competences for public services, the Brazilian Constitution does not differentiate between urban and rural zones. Hence, the municipality's jurisdiction over basic sanitation, public transportation, and public lighting, among other local services reaches, in principle, covers its entire territory, not merely urban areas.

Nonetheless, the challenges faced by local governments are huge. When extending public services to rural zones or urban expansion zones they must count on heavy investments, which depend either on their own budget, or on private investments. However, as stated before, most municipalities are very small and lack financial, material, and human resources. At the same time, their diminutive population, demographic shrinkage, and low payment capacities tend to make public procurement unattractive for market investors.

Federal and state governments are aware of this situation. Therefore, in many cases, the union creates financial aid policies or executes specific tasks in rural areas, which should, in principle, be part of the municipality's responsibility. An example of such initiative is evident in the basic sanitation policy, where, according to law, the federal government must address the needs of indigenous land and "quilombos", that is, traditional communities founded by former slaves during the nineteenth century within the rural zone.

## 7.6 Public Services Provision Models in Brazil

Basically, there are three general models for providing public services in Brazil, which apply equally to federal, state, and local governments. It is important to differentiate between (1) standalone provision; (2) associated provision; and (3) regionalized provision (Marrara, 2023, 14). Regardless of the model chosen by the government, public service provision can be direct or indirect. These two execution arrangements also apply to all public services at the three federal levels, since they were authorized by the 1988 Constitution (Article 175).

In the "standalone provision model", each local government delivers the services within its entire territory, encompassing urban, urban expansion and rural zones, unless specific sector rules dictate otherwise. However, standalone provision often struggles at the local level since, as stated before, many municipalities are relatively small in terms of population and budget. This means that they often lack sufficient resources to sustain high-quality services to expand infrastructure networks and maintain specialized staff.

In the "associated provision model", local governments cooperate in two ways. Firstly, they can create intergovernmental associations, either public or private entities, known as "consortia" (Law 11,107/2005). Consortia established by local laws of the participating municipality become part of its indirect public administration. This is the institutional solution, placing public service in the hands of an inter-federal entity. Secondly, municipalities can combine efforts through contractual instruments known as *convênios*. This contractual method does not give birth to any intergovernmental legal entity of internal public law. Each local government operates through its own organs and entities, which cooperate at the inter-municipal level.

In the "regionalized model", municipalities, along with the state in which they are located, join metropolitan regions, urban agglomerations, or micro-regions. These three types of regional units are created by state law, defining "common public functions", which can include public services that transition to the regional level. As a consequence, the decision-making and organization of these public services will depend on shared decisions between municipalities and the state. Nevertheless, this does not mean that the service provider will serve all the regional states and municipalities. The regionalization of the service responsibility does not imply the regionalization of the service provision itself. Therefore, municipalities and the state involved in the metropolitan area or other regional unit may choose between selecting one provider for all or keeping the provision under the standalone model, so that different providers work simultaneously in the same regional unit.

In both standalone, associated, or regionalized models, local governments can adopt either direct or indirect service provision systems. In "direct provision" (*prestação direta*), the service is delivered to the population by entities of the direct administration or entities of the indirect administration, including autarchies, foundations, or state-owned companies. This is the most common situation in Brazil. Since many municipalities are small and generate limited financial resources, they often establish autarchies (as public legal entities) or state-owned enterprises (private legal entities) to execute services such as public lighting, public security, education, health, and basic sanitation.

When it comes to the direct provision, but through the indirect administration, it is important to highlight that municipalities may choose which type of entity they will create. There is no mandatory rule for them to create state enterprises in any sector. For example, per the National Statute of State Enterprises (Law 13,303/2016), local governments decide if they prefer to follow a purely administrative legal regime, using autarchies, or to follow a hybrid legal regime, using local enterprises.

Such state enterprises comprehend two forms: (1) "public enterprises", whose capital is solely owned by the municipality, regardless of the enterprise type, and (2) "mixed-economy societies", i.e. companies, whose capital is under the control of municipalities, but accept minor private investors. However, up until 2016 their legal regime was unclear, since there was no national law to regulate them. Therefore, despite some local initiatives to create enterprises in the field of basic sanitation and lighting, they are not usually public service providers on the local level.

On the other hand, through "indirect provision", public service is transferred to a private company or business consortium that executes it based on limited-time administrative concession or permission contracts. These administrative contracts are formalized after a bidding procedure (public procurement) through the "competitive dialogue" or the "competition" models. Occasionally, the contract winner will establish a specific-purpose company to fulfill contractual obligations, but legislation does not allow municipalities to be shareholders in these companies.

Indirect provision of public services has become more usual in Brazil since 1995. However, it is still concentrated in larger municipalities, like state capitals, where public services reach a vast population and generate enough financial resources to make them attractive to private investors. In large cities, like São Paulo, government agencies have been created to offer technical assistance on structuring partnerships between local government and the market, such as "SP Parcerias". This has resulted in many privatization projects, including parks, cemeteries and funeral services, public transportation, basic sanitation, stadiums, public lighting and so on.

## 7.7 Local Partnerships with the Private Sector

In Brazil, the models of standalone, associated, or regionalized provision, as well as the forms of direct or indirect provision, are applicable to any type of public service, regardless of whether they are federal, state, or local, or whether they are provided in urban, urban expansion, or rural areas. In indirect provision, what changes is only the type of administrative contract that the public administration, including local governments, may celebrate.

There are three major types of concession contracts used for this purpose (Di Pietro, 2022, 77). In "ordinary concessions" (*concessões comuns*, under Law 8987/1995), public service provision is mainly supported through public prices paid by the users. Once these fees are compulsory, this kind of administrative contract is not suitable for "indivisible" public services (*uti universi*) or "divisible" unpaid public services (*uti singuli*). Indivisible services, such as public lighting or public security, do not allow the measurement of use by each citizen or resident, since that would be technically impossible. Therefore, they must be supported by the state budget instead of being covered by a usage-dependent fee. Divisible services, on the other hand, are suitable for a measurement of consumption, but sometimes are free due to legal or constitutional determinations, i.e., fees are forbidden by law. Hence, despite their divisibility, local services such as education and healthcare are incompatible with fees in Brazil and cannot be privatized through ordinary concession since the Constitution and legislation expressly prohibit fees in these fields. By contrast, it is lawful and quite common for local governments to use ordinary concessions when privatizing other divisible services such as urban public transportation, water supply and sewage).

Since 2004, there are also public-private partnerships ("PPPs", under Law 11,079/2004), which take the form of either sponsored concession (*concessão patrocinada*), or administrative concession (*concessão administrativa*). The sponsored modality demands the payment of user fees plus a government contribution to the private service provider, either monetary or non-monetary. On the other hand, the administrative concession modality is entirely supported by the public partner. Due to its financing arrangement, this type of PPP contract allows the privatization of free public services, such as public education, healthcare, penitentiaries and so on, as well as the privatization of indivisible services, such as public light and street cleaning.

It is relevant to highlight that, like ordinary concessions, PPPs in Brazil are only administrative contractual agreements subject to wide standardized national rules on administrative law. These partnerships are not companies with shared public and private capital, nor are they characterized as legal entities of any type. The winner enterprise or enterprise consortium of the public procurement signs the PPP contract and, after that, is required to create a company with the only purpose to execute the contract obligations. However, this is a non-state company, i.e., its share capital is private, and it is solely owned by the procurement winner.

In addition, the Federal Constitution requires the completion of a bidding process before the union, states and municipalities can sign any ordinary concession, permission, or public-private partnership contract. These bids are administrative processes conducted by the government that has jurisdiction over the public service to be privatized. As municipalities constitute an autonomous federative sphere, they are directly responsible for carrying out procurement procedures in order to privatize their respective public services. They must also manage and supervise the contract execution, resolve disputes, and impose administrative penalties for contractual violations.

In sum, both ordinary concessions and PPPs can be used in any sector, whether in urban or rural areas. Such contracts are only prohibited for state regulation, police power or other administrative functions excluded from privatization policies. Beyond these few restrictions, they have broad applicability.

However, PPPs are not usual in smaller municipalities. As stated before, such local governments do not have specialized public servants and, without external financing, can barely afford costly specialized consultants. Besides that, short budgets do not allow them to afford the public partner contributions, which are compulsory by law. Under these circumstances and because these administrative contracts are also very complex (demanding public procurement, many preparatory studies, etc.), it is no wonder that they are not frequently celebrated in smaller municipalities.

Besides that, regardless of whether local governments intend to use traditional ordinary concessions or PPPs, the success of privatization policies depends inexorably on the market interest for the public contract, which increases proportionally to the gain expectations and return rates. Based on this assumption, contracts offered by municipalities with smaller populations and with high demand for investments in infrastructure tend to be unattractive to the market and private investors.

Considering this, the ascertained proliferation of concessions and PPP contracts in Brazil in the last decades must be interpreted cautiously. Data shows that the number of initiatives to celebrate concessions and PPP increased from 88 in 2010 to 342 in October 2023. Of approximately 5000 ongoing privatization initiatives for public services and infrastructure, more than 67% are organized by local governments (Martins, 2023). However, this is mainly a result of the efforts taken by mid-sized and larger municipalities in order to privatize their public services.

Most of the Brazilian municipalities, i.e., those with a population of up to 20,000 inhabitants, still have substantial challenges to overcome. In my point of view, in the short term, they will not easily profit from such administrative contracts to achieve the desirable level of public service provision unless they strengthen regionalization strategies by which one provider becomes responsible for the service provision within a group of cities, generating scale economies and infrastructure sharing.

At the same time, given their population scarcity and demographic spread in such realities, even if administrative concessions take place, they will not make it easy for small municipalities to adequately reach their rural population. In this scenario, the recognition of decentralized and asymmetric techniques for service provision, as those seen in the basic sanitation policy, may be a better alternative than public contracts based on the traditional network expansion and on a rigid standardized provision model.

## 7.8 Conclusions

The evolution of Brazilian municipalities'legal status over the last two centuries reflects a dynamic journey. From an initial colonial focus on resource extraction to the establishment of a tripartite federal system, municipalities proliferated intensively and have experienced significant political and demographic transformations. While urbanization raised the Brazilian population by more than 100 million people within the last 40 years, concentrating citizens in urban zones, the constitutional recognition of a third federative level allocated to municipalities new competences and more responsibilities in terms of service provision.

In order to provide public services under their responsibilities, in urban or rural zones, local governments may consider the standalone provision, the associated provision or regionalization strategies. It may also consider indirect provision through private actors instead of providing services directly through direct or indirect administration.

Despite such wide possibilities, demographic concentration in a few urban Brazilian centers complicates resource allocation and the capacity, particularly of smaller municipalities, to provide adequate public services, since these local governments count on few service users and deal with financial resource constraints, staff fragilities and administrative limitations. Besides that, they have a higher percentage of rural population than midsized and larger municipalities.

Considering that the success of public procurements for concessions or PPPs, as well as the efficacy of indirect provision contracts depend on factors such as population size and distribution, user's payment capacities, the amount of investments needed for infrastructure, models of indirect provision for smaller municipalities acting by themselves do not seem to be an adequate approach.

Rather, the Brazilian experience suggests that local governments in smaller municipalities should consider regionalization policies (one contract and one provider for many cities) and alternative provision strategies to apply different provision techniques for rural and urban areas simultaneously. By preserving direct provision in a regional arrangement, they could reduce maintenance costs, increase scale economies, combine investments, and share infrastructure through the creation of either inter-federal state associations (consortia under Law 11,107/2005), or inter-federal state enterprises (Law 13,303/2016).

So that these initiatives can be successful, municipalities depend on a shift of political and legal culture. On the one hand, politicians must accept that regionalization implies power sharing among local governments, but this is compensated though better service provision capacities and financial relief. On the other hand, the National Congress must understand that Brazil is not Brasilia. Since it is competent to enact basic national rules regarding administrative contracts, state enterprises and associations, as well as regional units, congress must be aware that the administrative reality faced by smaller municipalities is very different to that faced by the union, states and large municipalities. Administrative laws must be elaborated by the congress under the premise of institutional and operational asymmetries, not based on the false idea that all Brazilian municipalities share similar financial, operational, and institutional conditions when it comes to service provision.

## References

Di Pietro, M. S. Z. (2022). *Parcerias na Administração Pública*. Forense.

Dias, M. O., & Lopes, R. O. A. (2021). A evolução dos Municípios no Brasil: Das origens à atualidade. *International Journal of Development Research, 11*(6), 47751–47755.

Fausto, B. (2002). *História do Brasil*. Edusp.

Gomes, L. (2007). *1808: Como uma rainha louca, um príncipe medroso e uma corte corrupta enganaram Napoleão e mudaram a história de Portugal e do Brasil*. Editora Planeta do Brasil.

IBGE. (2023). *De 2010 a 2022, população brasileira cresce 6,5% e chega a 203,1 milhões*. Agência IBGE Notícias. Retrieved November 15, 2023, from https://agenciadenoticias.ibge.gov.br/agencia-noticias/2012-agencia-de-noticias/noticias/37237-de-2010-a-2022-populacao-brasileira-cresce-6-5-e-chega-a-203-1-milhoes

Marrara, T. (2008). Do modelo municipal alemão aos problemas municipais brasileiros. *Revista Brasileira de Direito Municipal—RBDM, 9*(27), 33–52.

Marrara, T. (2020). De onde viemos e aonde vamos? O direito administrativo brasileiro da colônia ao século XXI. *Revista de la Facultad de Derecho de Mexico, 70*(278), 553–568.

Marrara, T. (2023). *Manual de direito administrativo* (Vol. 2). Foco.

Martins, A. (2023). *Em 2023, editais de concessões e PPPs chegam a maior número na história*. Exame. Retrieved December 20, 2023, from https://exame.com/brasil/em-2023-editais-de-concessoes-e-ppps-registram-maior-numero-na-historia/

Poder 360. (2023). *70.6% das cidades do Brasil têm até 20.000 habitantes*. PODER 360. Retrieved November 15, 2023, from https://www.poder360.com.br/brasil/706-das-cidades-do-brasil-tem-ate-20-000-habitantes/

Ribeiro, D. (2023). *O povo brasileiro: A formação e o sentido do Brasil*. Global.

Stamm, C., Staduto, J. A. R., Lima, J. F., & Wadi, Y. M. (2013). A população urbana e a difusão das cidades de porte médio no Brasil. *Interações, 14*(2), 251–265.

# Chapter 8
# PPP and Public Enterprises in Germany

**Christoph Krönke and Lisa Hagen**

**Abstract** The chapter addresses the provision of public services in Germany by the local government in cooperation with private individuals. After analyzing the legal framework for public enterprises on the federal, state and local level, it highlights the specific challenges this instrument faces in urban and especially in rural areas. Additionally, the importance of public private partnerships (PPPs) as well as administrative concessions and their respective legal challenges are being addressed. While the usage of PPPs seems to be preferred in urban areas, municipalities in rural areas predominantly refer to concession contracts which the authors attribute to their comparatively less complex legal structure.

**Keywords** German public-services · Public private partnerships · Public enterprises · Administrative concessions

## 8.1 Introduction

There are various ways for local governments to provide services for their citizens. They can provide public services through the departments of the public administration, in cooperation with other public entities, or by involving the private sector. Local governments are no longer expected to provide all politically desired services themselves. Instead, they can concentrate on their function as guarantors of public service provision (Grossi & Reichard, 2017, 102–103). In recent decades, the provision of public services has increasingly been shifted to institutions outside the core administration, involving external (non-profit and private) organizations (Friedländer et al., 2021, 291–292). The process of outsourcing requires new skills and strategies

C. Krönke (✉)
Public Law, Economic Administrative Law, Sustainability and Technology Law (Public Law I), University of Bayreuth, Bayreuth, Germany
e-mail: Christoph.Kroenke@uni-bayreuth.de

L. Hagen
Higher Regional Court München, Munich, Germany



F. Velasco Caballero et al. (eds.), *Municipal Tasks and Financing*, Local and Urban Governance, https://doi.org/10.1007/978-3-031-99812-6_8

from the respective local governments. By outsourcing the provision of local public services to third parties, local governments are losing the ability to be directly involved in the provision of these services. Nevertheless, they remain responsible for ensuring the reliable provision of services at a certain level of quality (Grossi & Reichard, 2008, 598). This results in a complex network of public and private actors (Friedländer et al., 2021, 292).

In the following, we would like to take a closer look at the provision of public services through public private partnerships (PPP) and public enterprises in Germany, both in urban and rural areas, from a legal perspective. To this end, we will first outline the role of local government within the German state structure (Sect. 8.2). We will then turn our attention to the activities of public enterprises in Germany (Sect. 8.3). Following a description of the relevant legal framework (Sect. 8.3.1), we will focus on the differences found in urban and rural areas respectively (Sect. 8.3.2). We then turn our attention to the provision of public services by PPPs and the awarding of concessions (Sect. 8.4). To this end, we will outline the practical relevance (Sect. 8.4.1) and the legal framework (Sect. 8.4.2) of these instruments and briefly examine the differences between urban and rural areas (Sect. 8.4.3). Finally, we take a brief look at the role that public enterprises and PPPs could play in bridging the gap between urban and rural areas with regard to the provision of public services (Sect. 8.5). The chapter concludes with a brief summary (Sect. 8.6).

## 8.2 Local Government's Position Within the German State Structure

While the federal government ("*Bund*") and the sixteen federal states ("*Länder*") enjoy state status under the Basic Law, the local governments are considered part of the state ("*Länder*") level. Therefore, they are not an independent third level of government. However, local governments in Germany enjoy a special status, as their right to self-government is guaranteed under constitutional law (Ruge & Ritgen, 2021, 131).

Article 28(2) sentence 1 of the German Basic Law (BL) states that municipalities must be guaranteed the right to regulate all local affairs on their own responsibility within the limits prescribed by the laws. Municipalities are therefore responsible for all matters that affect the local community and do not require any legal mandate to act in these matters (Ruge & Ritgen, 2021, 132). Given that local autonomy is only guaranteed "within the law", it can be restricted by federal (*Bund*) and state (*Land*) legislation. The legislative power for the organization of local governments lies with each of the sixteen states, which is why the specific structure of local self-government may vary from state to state (this is true both for the internal organization and for the precise scope of responsibilities and powers, see Burgi, 2009, 140). Alongside the municipalities, the German Basic Law also mentions municipal associations. Article 28(2) sentence 2 of the BL states that they shall also have the right of self-government in accordance with the laws, however only within the limits of their functions designated by a law. This refers to counties, which function as associations of municipalities and local authorities with the constitutionally guaranteed right to self-government (Ruge & Ritgen, 2021, 126–127). If the rights under Article 28 of the Basic Law are violated for instance by the state legislature, municipalities and municipal associations can take legal action before the state constitutional courts or the Federal Constitutional Court (Ruge & Ritgen, 2021, 132).

Local governments serve not only as self-governing units but also, depending on the respective task in question, as the lowest state administrative authority (Burgi, 2009, 137). Not only are they responsible for many original self-administration tasks, but also for the implementation of significant parts of federal and state laws, thereby providing most public services in direct contact with the citizens (Ruge & Ritgen, 2021, 124).

## 8.3 Public Enterprises in Germany

According to the definition of the so-called EU Transparency Directive (commission directive 2006/111/EC of November 16, 2006, OJ L 318/17), an enterprise is classified as a public enterprise if public authorities may exercise directly or indirectly a dominant influence over it by virtue of their ownership, their financial participation or the rules which govern it (see Article 2(b)). This applies regardless of whether they are organized under public or private law (Burgi, 2019, 258). Public enterprises play an important role in providing services of general interest in Germany (Warm et al., 2018, 548). The public funds, institutions and enterprises of municipalities and municipal associations accounted for the largest share (87.9%) of the 20,033 reporting units with commercial accounting that were included in the annual balance sheet statistics for 2021 (Statistisches Bundesamt, 2024). This shows that German local governments have a dense and diverse network of municipal enterprises, particularly in the area of supply and disposal, but also concerning other local government tasks (Grossi & Reichard, 2017, 105–106). The German Association of Local Public Utilities of municipally determined infrastructure undertakings and economic enterprises can already count more than 1500 member companies, which are primarily active in the fields of energy supply, water supply and sewage, waste management, municipal cleaning and telecommunication (Verband kommunaler Unternehmen e.V., 2023, 2–3). These numbers demonstrate the practical significance of local governments' commercial activities, which reflect a long tradition (Burgi, 2019, 258–259). There are many reasons why local governments choose to perform their tasks using a public enterprise. The difficult budgetary situation of local governments plays a major role in this. Without economic activity, many deficient facilities, e.g. in the social or cultural sector, would no longer be financially viable (Gaß & Popp, 2021, 4). Another factor promoting the outsourcing of municipal tasks is the economization of local authorities that has been introduced as part of the policy of administrative modernization (according to Burgi, 2019, 259 this is due to the fact that the entrepreneurial sector is experiencing an upswing when even public authorities are evaluated according to economic standards).

### 8.3.1 Regulatory Framework for Municipal Enterprises

Certain articles of the German Basic Law, e.g. Article 87(e)(3) with regard to the federal railroads, stipulate that the state may operate commercially. Apart from those provisions, the German Basic Law does not contain any prohibition or explicit requirements regarding the permissibility of public enterprises (Burgi, 2019, 264). Accordingly, the state is, in principle, free to decide whether and how the public sector engages in economic activity. Nevertheless, state and municipal economic activity must comply with the Basic Law (Wollenschläger, 2021, 37–38). Since the entrepreneurial activity of the state is merely a mode of fulfilling state tasks, public enterprises must serve a public purpose and may not be purely for profit (Burgi, 2019, 264–265). Furthermore, the principle of democracy demands that a local government must maintain sufficient rights of influence and control over its legally independent public enterprises (for example, reporting obligations, rights to information, and issuing instructions can contribute to this, Gaß, 2023, 491–492).

Regarding the entrepreneurial activities of local governments, the guarantee of Article 28(2) of the BL is of particular relevance: The guarantee of local self-government also includes the so-called organizational autonomy, which grants local governments the right to decide independently on their internal administrative organization (this is recognized in the case law of the Federal Constitutional Court 2014, paragraph 49). This includes the decision to involve a municipal enterprise in the performance of a public task. Against this background, the legal framework must leave municipalities sufficient scope for dealing with local matters, including by means of economic activity (Wollenschläger, 2021, 40).

Local governments could also operate economically through their own administrative bodies. In practice, however, the performance of the respective tasks is typically transferred to a public enterprise of the municipality (Burgi, 2019, 287).

More detailed are the local government regulations of the federal states, which provide general conditions regarding the permissibility of a local authority's economic activity. In general, the regulations of all federal states prescribe that a municipality may only establish or significantly expand an enterprise if it can be justified by a public purpose, the nature and scope of the enterprise is in reasonable proportion to the municipality's capacity as well as its anticipated needs and the purpose is not or cannot be fulfilled better and more economically by another party (Gaß & Popp, 2021, 11). In general, the county codes contain identical provisions on the economic activities of counties (Gaß, 2023, 488).

If a local government has decided to perform a task through a public company, in principle, it is free to choose between public-law and private-law forms of organization. When choosing a form of organization under private law, the municipality remains subject to its obligations under public law, while at the same time being subject to the relevant regulations under private (commercial) law (Burgi, 2019, 288). The municipal codes of the federal states stipulate special rules for the establishment of a company under private law or participation in such companies, which require, for example, that the fulfilment of the public purpose must be ensured in the company agreement (Gaß & Popp, 2021, 40–43). In 2021, more than 70% of all public enterprises were organized under private law (Statistisches Bundesamt, 2023). The most common legal form of public companies is the limited liability company (GmbH) (Warm et al., 2018, 549). Smaller municipalities have often chosen the organizational form of the so-called "*Eigenbetrieb*", especially in the water supply and wastewater disposal sectors. This legal form is not independent in legal terms, but largely independent from the municipal administration in organizational and financial terms (Cronauge, 2016, 157).

### 8.3.2 Differences Between the Use of Public Enterprises in Urban and in Rural Areas

The constitutional guarantee of self-government applies to all local governments regardless of their size or economic importance (Burgi, 2009, 143). Furthermore, the regulations on the entrepreneurial activities of local governments apply regardless of their size. However, since the entrepreneurial activity of local governments is regarded as a mode of fulfilling public tasks, local governments are not permitted to extend the scope of their responsibilities by setting up a company (Gaß, 2023, 490). In this context, the principle of general competence becomes relevant for municipalities, according to which they may deal with all matters of the local community that are not already assigned to another public authority by law (Gaß, 2023, 503).

In rural regions, public services are provided by individual (smaller) municipalities and counties (Burgi, 2009, 140). As mentioned above, self-administration is constitutionally guaranteed to the individual municipalities as well as the counties. However, unlike municipalities, counties do not enjoy general competence for all local matters. Therefore, the counties' right to self-administration depends on the allocation of tasks by the legislator (Wollenschläger, 2021, 40). The respective state laws define the exact distribution of tasks between counties and municipalities. As a rule, counties are responsible for tasks that exceed the capacity of the individual municipality (this is due to reasons of administrative efficiency, see Burgi, 2009, 140). For example, tasks such as the provision of local public transport in rural areas or running hospitals fall within the responsibility of the counties and may therefore be performed by a public enterprise owned by the respective county (Ruge & Ritgen, 2021, 129).

Apart from that, some cities do not belong to a county. Due to their size, the administrations of the so-called county-free cities have the capacity to provide all public services themselves (Burgi, 2009, 140). As a result, larger municipalities provide a broader range of services for their citizens and regularly have a larger number of outsourced tasks (Bremeier et al., 2006, 31). In large cities, the result is the formation of complex municipal groups with interwoven shareholding structures. Grossi and Reichard (Grossi & Reichard, 2017, 106) point out that the control of these corporations is not always unproblematic. For example, the City of Munich alone runs 248 associated companies to provide various services of general interest (Landeshauptstadt München, 2021, 2).

Irrespective of the legal framework, rural and urban local governments encounter different challenges. Especially smaller cities and municipalities often face the problem that the responsible municipal administrations do not have the necessary knowledge and experience to handle the legal, organizational, or business management challenges arising from the establishment of a municipal enterprise (Cronauge, 2016, 373). Nevertheless, participating in public enterprises is an important instrument for the provision of public services, even for smaller municipalities (Bremeier et al., 2006, 52–53).

## 8.4 Public Private Partnerships (PPP) and Concessions[1]

In addition to the activities of public enterprises, the provision of public services through private actors in Germany also comes in the form of public-private partnerships (PPP, in German: "*öffentlich-private Partnerschaften*" or "*ÖPP*") and (other) types of administrative concessions (Sect. 8.4.1). The complexity of the legal framework for PPPs and concessions largely depends on the volume of the respective construction and/or service contracts (Sect. 8.4.2). This is probably why PPP projects are mainly realized in urban contexts and/or at the state or federal level, while municipalities –particularly those in rural areas—seem to operate rather on the basis of concession agreements (Sect. 8.4.3).

### *8.4.1 PPP Projects and Concession Contracts in Germany*

Until about 20 years ago, *PPPs* had not been used frequently in Germany—in contrast to other EU member states, which had gained extensive positive experience with such projects in the 1990s. Even when the Federal Government of Germany drafted its "Law to accelerate the implementation of Public Private Partnerships and to improve the legal framework for Public Private Partnerships" ("PPP Acceleration Act", in German: *"Gesetz zur Beschleunigung der Umsetzung von Öffentlich Privaten Partnerschaften und zur Verbesserung gesetzlicher Rahmenbedingungen für Öffentlich Private Partnerschaften"—"ÖPP-Beschleunigungsgesetz"*) in 2005, the explanatory memorandum of the law still stated at BT-Drucks 15/5668, page 1: "Positive experiences [with PPP] are available in Europe—in Great Britain, the

[1] The following considerations are based on Krönke (2020, 71–88).

Netherlands, Denmark, Sweden, France, Portugal, and Greece. Savings potentials in the amount of 10–20% in relation to conventional public infrastructure projects are realizable. In Germany, however, methods of public-private partnerships have so far only been pursued occasionally." In the early 2000s, in the context of the general privatization efforts at that time, various initiatives were launched at the federal and state levels to promote and standardize PPP structures in Germany as well (Redlich & Unbehauen, 2017, 446). As a consequence, PPPs quickly became a well-recognized form of delivering public services in Germany, even compared to other EU member states. According to a special report of the European Court of Auditors (European Court of Auditors, 2018, 16), in the EU market for PPP between 1990 and 2016, Germany ranked 4th. The United Kingdom launched the most projects by far. In France and Spain, the PPP investment sums were still twice as high as in Germany. Accordingly, most of the fundamental scholarly (Ziekow & Windoffer, 2008; Burgi, 2008, D33–D41, D109–D113; Yu, 2009) and practical (Meyer-Hofmann et al., 2005; Weber et al., 2005) writings on PPP in Germany were made in the mid-2000s and shortly thereafter. Today, PPPs play a considerable role as an option to provide public services at all levels of administration in Germany—at the federal, state and municipal level. Bonhage and Roberts (2020) state that, despite the rather negative signal sent out by Article 90(2) of the German Basic Law, a reform of the German highway administration was passed by the German legislator in 2017 and that this reform "may lead to substantially more PPP projects with regard to the construction and operation of German motorways"; they argue that it "may well be an indication of a more active PPP market in Germany in the years to come". In relation to the investment sums, the most important areas in which PPP projects have been applied are certainly the construction and operation of transport infrastructure (above all: federal highways) and the construction and managements of public buildings (e.g. schools, cultural and sport facilities as well as administrative buildings).

Between 2002 and 2017, a total of 210 projects were launched nationwide in these areas alone, with investment volumes of 6.05 billion EUR in building construction (191 projects) and 3.84 billion EUR (19 projects) in road construction (PPP-Projektdatenbank, 2017).

Of course, the strength and performance of Germany's public enterprises (see above in Sect. 8.3) is likely to be a key factor in preventing PPPs from achieving a major breakthrough in Germany, similar to their relevance in other member states. In fact, many public-sector companies in Germany are actually mixed companies and could hence count as institutionalized PPPs. The airport of Frankfurt, for example, is operated by Fraport AG, a mixed company with two public (State of Hessen: 31.31%; Frankfurt's municipal public enterprise "*Stadtwerke Frankfurt GmbH*": 20%) and several private shareholders.

A legal instrument that is often used but not restricted to PPP projects is the award of *concessions*. Concession contracts are widely used in German administrative practice, including projects that are much simpler than PPPs. When it comes to practical applications of concession agreements in Germany, there are many areas in which concessions are being awarded, including but by no means limited to (more complex) PPP projects. There are no robust data concerning the actual number of concessions awarded in Germany, but concession contracts are generally regarded as a "booming" form of procurement in Germany (Burgi, 2005, 610; Opitz, 2014, 754). The countless examples of successful concessions involve, for instance,

1. services for sewage disposal and drinking water supply,
2. passenger transport services,
3. rescue services,
4. outdoor advertising and street furniture services,
5. collection and recycling of old textiles,
6. operation of bicycle stations,
7. maintenance and operation of public toilets,
8. operation of town halls, swimming pools and other leisure facilities,
9. operation of radiotherapy practices,
10. provision of broadband, radio and television services,
11. operation of cremation facilities,
12. management of car parks and parking spaces,
13. operation of casinos,
14. typesetting, printing and advertising for official gazettes,
15. provision of laundry for hospitals, nursing homes and senior citizens' facilities,
16. marketing of equipment,
17. the rental or leasing of sales outlets for the sale of motor vehicle signs,
18. social family assistance in accordance with the applicable laws on child and youth care,
19. operation of catering facilities in public buildings and
20. the provision of food for public facilities (e.g. school cafeterias) (Opitz, 2014, 754 note 16).

With regard to other important cases of licensing, it is controversial in German jurisprudence whether these fall under the concept of a concession within the meaning of the Directive. This applies in particular to contracts concluded by energy supply companies with municipalities for the use of public transport routes for the laying and operation of lines belonging to an energy supply network for the general supply in a certain municipal area. The German legislator took the view that those contracts were not to be classified as concessions within the meaning of Directive 2014/23/EU (*cf.* the reasoning in BR-Drucks 73/16, 9 and 10). There are specific rules governing these contracts set out in Section 46 of the German Energy Sector Act ("*Energiewirtschaftsgesetz*").

## 8.4.2 Legal Framework for PPPs and Concessions

As such, *PPPs* are only addressed by legal norms in exceptional cases, e.g. in Article 90(2) of the German Basic Law. Special codifications of PPP-related regulations exist, as far as can be seen, only in one of the 16 German federal states. PPPs are therefore predominantly governed by the general rules applicable to privatizations, which may include the general rules on public contracts as well as other, more specific rules such as the provisions of the Act on Private Financing of Federal Highways ("*Fernstraßenbauprivatfinanzierungsgesetz*") in the context of PPPs for the purpose of constructing and maintaining federal highways. Even though there are only a few formal rules specifically addressing PPPs, many local and national bodies have been issuing working instructions and guides on PPP since their emergence in the early 2000s (Fischer & Schubert, 2017, 362). One important example of these PPP soft laws is the 2007 Guide on "Public Private Partnership – Economic Viability Studies" created by the German Finance Ministers Conference ("FMC", in German: "*Finanzministerkonferenz*"—"*FMK*") (FMK, 2007). The guidelines contained therein were made legally binding for administrative bodies as the Federal Ministry of Finance ("MoF", German: "*Bundesministerium der Finanzen*"—"*BMF*") and the ministries of the *Länder* respectively issued the guide as a whole as "internal administrative rules" ("*Verwaltungsvorschriften*") for the purpose of interpreting and applying Section 7(2) of the German Federal Budget Code ("FBC", in German: "*Bundeshaushaltsordnung*"—"*BHO*"; the rules were formally published as "BMF-Rds. II A 3 H 1000/06/0003 *vom* 20. August 2007") and incorporated the guide's principles into the general administrative rules on economic viability studies.[2] *Internal* administrative rules are binding upon the administration but do not have *external* legal effects. This means that individual citizens or companies cannot invoke the provisions of internal administrative rules.

In contrast, there are specific laws in Germany with regard to the award of *concessions* within the meaning of and for the purpose of implementing Directive 2014/23/EU. The basic requirements are contained in the German Act against Restraints of Competition (ARC), together with the fundamental rules on public procurement. More detailed provisions are set out in the Procurement Regulation (PReg), i.e. a specific regulation issued by the Federal Government in order to implement Directive 2014/23/EU. Below the EU thresholds, however, the (autonomous) German rules on public contracting only apply to works concessions, as stated in Section 23(2) of the first section of part A of the Award and Contract Regulation for Construction Services ("*Vergabe- und Vertragsordnung für Bauleistungen*"—"*VOB/A*"). The first section of part A of the VOB/A rules apply by virtue of references in the budget and procurement laws of the *Länder*. The VOB/A rules are rules specifically designed for public procurement in the field of construction works and services, and they were drafted by the German Procurement and Contract Committee for Construction Services ("*Deutsche Vergabe- und Vertragsausschuss für Bauleistungen*"—"*DVA*"). The award of service concessions below the relevant threshold of around 5,400,000 EUR per concession are hence not subject to specific national public procurement rules. Issues other than the decision on the award of works and services concession contracts (e.g. on the substantive

[2] The rules were formally published as "BMF-Rds. II A 3 H 1012–10/08/10004 vom 12. January 2011, zuletzt geändert durch Rundschreiben vom 2. Oktober 2017", available on http://www.verwaltungsvorschriften-im-internet.de/bsvwvbund_20122013_IIA3H1012100810004.htm. The text of the rules is available on https://olev.de/w/BMF-Arbeitsanleitung.pdf

legality of the contract and on the contract performance) are covered, in principle, by the general rules applicable to public contracts.

In Germany the rules on *public contracts* need to be carefully distinguished from the *public procurement* rules. The latter rules only concern the award of the contract and are hence covered by the European procurement directives. The rules on public contracts (i.e. contracts concluded by an administrative body) concern the substance of the contract and the modalities of its performance. Public contracts in Germany are either governed by German civil law or by Sections 54–62 of the German Federal Act on Administrative Procedure ("*Verwaltungsverfahrensgesetz*"—"*VwVfG*") and the corresponding administrative procedure laws of the *Länder*.

This shows that the complexity of the legal framework largely depends on the *volume* of the respective contract. While smaller contracts up to a volume of 5.4 million EUR remain largely "unregulated", larger contracts require a formal procurement procedure and an EU-wide tendering process.

### *8.4.3 Differences Between Urban and Rural Areas*

Empirical data on differences in the use of PPPs and concessions in urban and rural areas in Germany does not yet exist, as far as can be seen. However, the legal differentiations suggest that municipalities in rural areas will predominantly fall back on (simple) concession contracts and try to avoid Europe-wide tenders for larger PPP projects. It is likely that players from urban areas will venture into much more complex projects.

## 8.5 (Prospective) Function of PPPs and Public Enterprises in Bridging the Urban-Rural Divide

PPPs and public enterprises can be instruments for bridging the gap between urban and rural areas by combining their respective strengths and weaknesses. The provision of public services and the relevant infrastructure by municipal enterprises plays an important role in enhancing rural areas as places to live and work and thus relieve cities of even greater influxes and the corresponding intensification of the problem regarding rents, etc. (Association of German Municipal Enterprises refers to this with regard to the question of how equal living conditions can be ensured in Germany, see Verband kommunaler Unternehmen e.V., 2019). Apart from that, the involvement of the private sector can be a useful tool for local governments to provide services of general interest despite the changing realities of life.

One example of the successful involvement of private parties is the Wolfsburg AG, a cooperation between the city of Wolfsburg and the Volkswagen AG, which arose from the main motivation of strengthening the region's economic position (Wolfsburg, 2023). The aim is to make the region more attractive for its residents in the long term, which benefits both the city of Wolfsburg as a potential tax recipient and Volkswagen AG as a potential employer (Bieker et al., 2004, 74–75). The cooperation covers a comprehensive range of tasks that is not limited to the former local government tasks in order to ensure the competitiveness of the Wolfsburg region (Bieker et al., 2004, 74–75).

To give another example, against the backdrop of drier and warmer summer months combined with a growing population, the water management tasks of cities are becoming increasingly important. To meet these challenges, there are projects to improve water management tasks and to secure the drinking water supply in the Stuttgart metropolitan region in cooperation with, among others, the distribution system operator Netze BW GmbH and the Bodensee-Wasserversorgung (Netze BW GmbH, 2023), which is an association of local governments that provides drinking water from Lake Constance (Bodensee-Wasserversorgung, 2024). A further initiative in this direction is a funding measure by the Federal Ministry of Education and Research, which supports numerous projects for a balanced, fair and sustainable development of urban, suburban and rural areas, whose aim is, among other things, to balance the interests of urban and rural areas (Stadt-Land-Plus, 2024).

## 8.6 Conclusions

In summary, our considerations have shown that the provision of public services in Germany is largely carried out by public companies and within the framework of PPPs and concessions. Based on an analysis of the practical and legal conditions for providing public services through these instruments, it became clear that complex and diverse structures are predominantly found in the cities. The range of public companies in the large conurbations, for example, is noticeably greater than in rural areas, and recourse to more complex PPP projects is also reserved for the resource-rich providers of local self-government in urban contexts. Nevertheless, the potential of public enterprises and public-private partnerships in rural areas should not be underestimated. At least on a large scale, the provision of public services would be inconceivable without recourse to public companies and the involvement of private service providers.

## References

Bieker, S., Knieling, J., Othengrafen, F., & Sinning, H. (2004). *Kooperative Stadt-Region 2030—Forschungsergebnisse*. Beiträge zu STADT+UM+LAND 2030 Region Braunschweig.

Bodensee-Wasserversorgung. (2024). *Eine Grosse Gemeinschaft*. Retrieved January 29, 2024, from https://www.bodensee-wasserversorgung.de/unternehmen/verband.html

Bonhage, J., & Roberts, M. (2020). Germany. In A. L. Freire, T. L. S. Sombra, & R. D. dos Santas Neto (Eds.), *The public-private partnerships law review* (pp. 78–90). Law Business Research Ltd.

Bremeier, W., Brinckmann, H., & Kilian, W. (2006). Kommunale Unternehmen in kleinen und mittelgroßen Kommunen sowie in Landkreisen. In W. Kilian, P. Richter, & J. H. Trapp (Eds.), *Ausgliederung und Privatisierung in Kommunen* (pp. 25–53). edition sigma.

Burgi, M. (2005). Die Vergabe von Dienstleistungskonzessionen: Verfahren, Vergabekriterien, Rechtsschutz. In *Neue Zeitschrift für Baurecht und Vergaberecht* (pp. 610–617).

Burgi, M. (2008). *Privatisierung öffentlicher Aufgaben—Gestaltungsmöglichkeiten, Grenzen, Regelungsbedarf: Gutachten D für den 67. Deutschen Juristentag*. C.H.Beck.

Burgi, M. (2009). Federal Republic of Germany. In N. Steytler (Ed.), *Local government and metropolitan regions in federal systems* (pp. 136–165). McGill-Queen's University Press.

Burgi, M. (2019). *Kommunalrecht*. C.H.Beck.

Cronauge, U. (2016). *Kommunale Unternehmen*. Erich Schmidt Verlag.

European Court of Auditors. (2018). *Public private partnerships in the EU: Widespread shortcomings and limited benefits*. Retrieved January 29, 2024, from https://www.eca.europa.eu/Lists/ECADocuments/SR18_09/SR_PPP_EN.pdf

Fischer, H., & Schubert, T. (2017). Wirtschaftlichkeitsuntersuchung. In M. Weber, M. Schäfer, & F. Hausmann (Eds.), *Praxishandbuch public private partnership* (pp. 361–394). C.H.Beck.

FMK. (2007). *Public private partnership—Wirtschaftlichkeitsuntersuchungen bei PPP-Projekten*. Retrieved January 29, 2024, from https://www.bmwsb.bund.de/SharedDocs/downloads/Webs/BMWSB/DE/publikationen/bauen/leitfaden-wirtschaftlichkeitsuntersuchungen-ppp.pdf;jsessionid=DC6B705A413E7FF4FC16DC51B7D854FE.live862?__blob=publicationFile&v=4

Friedländer, B., Röber, M., & Schaefer, C. (2021). Institutional differentiation of public service provision in Germany: Corporatization, privatization and re-municipalization. In S. Kuhlmann, I. Proeller, D. Schimanke, & J. Ziekow (Eds.), *Public Administration in Germany* (pp. 291–309). Palgrave Macmillan.

Gaß, A. (2023). Verwaltungsrechtliche Organisationsvorgaben betreffend das Öffentliche Unternehmen in kommunaler Trägerschaft. In M. Burgi & M. Habersack (Eds.), *Handbuch Öffentliches Recht des Unternehmens* (pp. 485–549). C.H.Beck.

Gaß, A., & Popp, J. (2021). *Die Gemeinde als Unternehmer*. Kommunal- und Schul-Verlag.

Grossi, G., & Reichard, C. (2008). Municipal corporatization in Germany and Italy. *Public Management Review, 10*(5), 597–617. https://doi.org/10.1080/14719030802264275

Grossi, G., & Reichard, C. (2017). Die Organisation kommunaler Dienstleistungen. Befunde aus einigen europäischen Ländern. In S. Kuhlmann & O. Schwab (Eds.), *Starke Kommunen—wirksame Verwaltung, Fortschritte und Fallstricke der internationalen Verwaltungs- und Kommunalforschung* (pp. 101–116). Springer VS.

Krönke, C. (2020). PPP and concessions in Germany. In P. Bogdanowicz, R. Caranta, & P. Telles (Eds.), *Public private partnerships and concessions in the EU* (pp. 71–88). Edward Elgar Publishing.

Meyer-Hofmann, B., Riemenschneider, F., & Weihrauch, O. (2005). *Public private partnership—Gestaltung von Leistungsbeschreibung, Finanzierung, Ausschreibung und Verträgen in der Praxis*. Heymann.

München, L. (2021). *Finanzdaten- und Beteiligungsbericht*. Retrieved January 29, 2024, from https://stadt.muenchen.de/dam/jcr:eabdb20b-6824-43dd-9b1f-da058e69ac84/FDB_2021_Internet.pdf

Netze BW GmbH. (2023). Pressemitteilung. *Klimawandel stellt Kommunen vor große Herausforderungen*. Retrieved January 29, 2024, from https://www.netze-bw.de/news/netze-bw-tag-des-wassers-2023

Opitz, M. (2014). Die Zukunft der Dienstleistungskonzession. In *Neue Zeitschrift für eVerwaltungsrecht* (pp. 753–760).

PPP-Projektdatenbank. (2017). *ÖPP-Projekte mit Vertragsabschluss im Hoch- und Straßenbau*. Retrieved January 29, 2024, from https://www.ppp-projektdatenbank.de/fileadmin/user_upload/170131_OEPP-Projekte_mit_Vertragsabschluss__im_Hoch-_und_Strassenbau_Investitionsvolumen_getrennt.gif

Redlich, M., & Unbehauen, R. (2017). Hilfestellung durch öffentliche ÖPP-Beratungseinrichtungen bei Projektvorbereitung und Projektrealisierung. In M. Weber, M. Schäfer, & F. Hausmann (Eds.), *Praxishandbuch public private partnership* (pp. 446–462). C.H.Beck.

Ruge, K., & Ritgen, K. (2021). Local self-government and administration. In S. Kuhlmann, I. Proeller, D. Schimanke, & J. Ziekow (Eds.), *Public Administration in Germany* (pp. 123–141). Palgrave Macmillan.

Stadt-Land-Plus. (2024). *Home*. Retrieved January 29, 2024, from https://Www.Zukunftsstadt-Stadtlandplus.De/

Statistisches Bundesamt. (2023). *Öffentliche Fonds, Einrichtungen und Unternehmen (FEU)*. Retrieved January 29, 2024, from https://www-genesis.destatis.de/genesis/online?sequenz=tabelleErgebnis&selectionname=71811-0003&leerzeilen=true#abreadcrumb

Statistisches Bundesamt. (2024). *Public funds, institutions, and enterprises*. Retrieved January 29, 2024, from https://www.destatis.de/EN/Themes/Government/Public-Finance/Public-Funds-Institutions-And-Enterprises/public-funds-institutions-enterprises.html

Verband kommunaler Unternehmen e.V. (2019). *Gleichwertige Lebensverhältnisse: Worauf es jetzt ankommt*. Retrieved January 29, 2024, from https://www.vku.de/themen/daseinsvorsorge/gleichwertige-lebensverhaeltnisse-worauf-es-jetzt-ankommt/

Verband kommunaler Unternehmen e.V. (2023). *Figures data facts 2023*. VKU Verlag GmbH. Retrieved January 29, 2024, from https://www.vku.de/en/

Warm, S., Schaefer, C., & Friedländer, B. (2018). Role and performance of public enterprises: A case study on the strategic relevance and specificity of enterprises at the German federal level. *Annals of Public and Cooperative Economics, 89*(3), 543–558. https://doi.org/10.1111/apce.12208

Weber, M., Schäfer, M., & Hausmann, F. L. (2005). *Praxishandbuch public private partnership*. C.H.Beck.

Wolfsburg AG. (2023). *About us*. Retrieved January 29, 2024, from https://wolfsburg-ag.com/ueber-wolfsburg-ag/ueber-uns

Wollenschläger, F. (2021). Europa- und verfassungsrechtliche Vorgaben. In G. Wurzel, A. Schraml, & A. Gaß (Eds.), *Rechtspraxis der kommunalen Unternehmen* (pp. 15–63). C.H.Beck.

Yu, W. (2009). *Praktische Erfahrungen und rechtliche Probleme mit Public Private Partnership in der Verkehrsinfrastruktur in Deutschland und China*. Peter Lang.

Ziekow, J., & Windoffer, A. (2008). *Public private partnership—Struktur und Erfolgsbedingungen von Kooperationsarenen*. Nomos.

# Chapter 9
# Legal Arrangements for the Provision of Local Public Services in Spain: Differences in Rural and Urban Environments

**Silvia Díez Sastre**

**Abstract** The geographic distribution of the Spanish population is highly uneven. The provision of public services by local governments thus poses multifaceted challenges in rural and urban environments. However, the legal regime governing the management of these services does not take these differences into account: services can be provided directly by the local authority, or indirectly through third parties. This chapter contextualizes the provision of local public services in Spain, considering the existing gap between local government in rural and urban areas. To this end, I outline the main features of the current legal regime and use empirical data to identify the forms of public service management preferred in practice by rural and urban municipalities.

**Keywords** Local public services · Direct management · Indirect management · Public procurement · Public undertakings · Rural and urban municipalities

## 9.1 Introduction

The 1978 Spanish Constitution structures the state into three levels of territorial government: central government, autonomous communities (17 autonomous communities and two autonomous cities), and local government (Article 137 of the Spanish Constitution). At the local level there are 8131 municipalities (Ministerio

This work is part of the LoGov project (Local Government and the Changing Urban-Rural Interplay) under the Horizon 2020 program, Marie Slodowska-Curie Action, grant agreement No 823961. It is also part of the activities of the R&D&I Project of the National Challenge Plan: "The public sector at the service of the strategic responsibility of the state" / "*El sector público al servicio de la responsabilidad estratégica del Estado*" (Ref.: PID 2020-115834RB-C31).

S. Díez Sastre (✉)
Institute of Local Government Law, Autonomous University of Madrid, Madrid, Spain
e-mail: silvia.diez@uam.es



F. Velasco Caballero et al. (eds.), *Municipal Tasks and Financing*, Local and Urban Governance, https://doi.org/10.1007/978-3-031-99812-6_9

de Política Territorial y Memoria Democrática 2023), 50 provinces and 11 islands (in the Canary and Balearic archipelagos), - prejudice to other local entities created in accordance with the regulations of each autonomous community. Among these, county districts (*comarcas*),[1] municipal associations (*mancomunidades*), and metropolitan areas stand out. Local Government Act 7/1985, of April 2, 1985 (*Ley reguladora de las Bases del Régimen Local* or LBRL)—a state law—lays down the basic rules for the organization and operation of local governments, as well as the services they must provide. The autonomous communities may adopt the relevant implementing regulations. Local authorities, for their part, may specify the regulatory framework in the exercise of their constitutionally guaranteed local autonomy (Articles 140–141 of the Spanish Constitution).

The geographic distribution of the population is highly uneven. The vast majority of the 48 million inhabitants residing in Spain are concentrated in Madrid, and the peripheries, especially in the eastern coast,[2] as can be seen in Fig. 9.1. Thus, 40% of the Spanish population is concentrated in less than 1% of the municipalities (large cities with more than 100,000 inhabitants), while 72% of the municipalities have only 6% of the population (municipalities with less than 1000 inhabitants) (Sevilla 2021, 12). Although there is no single criterion for determining the rural nature of the territory, European countries focus on population density (Díez Sastre 2020, 446). Eurostat considers an area to be rural when its population density does not reach 150 inhabitants/km$^2$, while the risk of depopulation is set below 12.5 inhabitants/km$^2$. In Spain, 3939 municipalities (48% of the total) face this risk, affecting 1.3 million inhabitants. These municipalities are mainly located in the interior (Sevilla 2021, 10–11).

The reinforcement of public—especially social—services in rural areas is considered a key measure to combat depopulation (FEMP 2017, 18–19), which since 2015 has aggravated the demographic-territorial imbalance (Santiago Iglesias 2020, 397). However, the provision of services in rural areas, which are in many cases depopulated, presents numerous challenges. The population is widely dispersed, which hinders service provision and accessibility (Alloza et al. 2021, 11), resulting in a greater abandonment of rural areas (Santiago Iglesias 2020, 401) both in small and medium municipalities (Velasco Caballero 2020, 40). On the other hand, the rural population is aging at a faster rate than the urban population. In 2019, the population over 65 years of age represented 28.5% of the total population in rural areas (municipalities with less than 2000 inhabitants), compared to 18.5% in urban areas (municipalities with more than 10,000 inhabitants) (Díez Sastre 2020, 447). Moreover, in 2020, those over 80 accounted for 11% of the population in rural regions, compared to 5% in urban areas (Instituto Nacional de Estadística 2021).

---

[1] There are 83 county districts in the autonomous communities of Aragón, Castilla y León, Catalonia, and the Basque Country. Despite the differences in their legal regime, their common purpose is to cooperate, advise, and coordinate their municipalities.

[2] The Spanish population, according to the Spanish National Statistics Institute (*Instituto Nacional de Estadística*—INE) as of November 7, 2023, is 48,446,594 inhabitants.

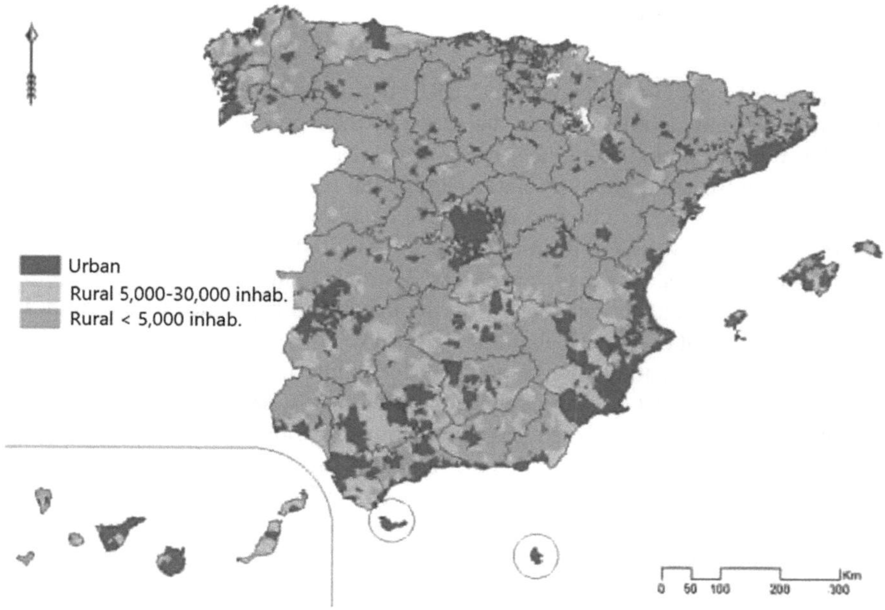


**Fig. 9.1** Map of urban and rural municipalities in Spain (2020). (*Source*: Ministry of Agriculture, Fisheries and Food 2021)

These particularities of the rural population require adapting the services provided by local governments. For instance, in the case of services for the elderly, in rural areas there is a tendency to create nursing homes compared to urban areas, where more services are provided directly at home (home care services, telecare, laundry, meals at home, etc.) (Díez Sastre 2020, 450). The differences are also reflected, albeit more subtly, in the form of provision: through private economic operators or organizational formulas within the municipality itself, usually in the form of publicly owned private companies.

The purpose of this chapter is to analyze the legal arrangements available to local governments in Spain for managing their public services—with special attention to the differences in rural and urban areas. As a starting point, the legal system does not set different rules for rural and urban municipalities. Nevertheless, in Sect. 9.2 I outline the mechanisms for direct management (by the local authority itself) and indirect management (in collaboration with third parties). In Sects. 9.3 and 9.4 I explore each of these management systems through the main legal problems that arise in practice. In order to identify the differences between rural and urban areas, this chapter draws on abundant empirical data showing the preferences for one or another form of management in relation to the different types of services. Finally, in Sect. 9.5 I make some concluding remarks and suggest reshuffling the traditional framework for the management of local public services, which should include a broad catalog for the diverse local, rural, and urban government bodies.

## 9.2 Conceptual Framework

The Spanish Local Government Act (LBRL) defines local public services as those provided by municipalities within the scope of their powers (Article 85(1) of the LBRL). Without prejudice to the services that local authorities may provide under the powers entrusted to them by state and regional legislation, the LBRL requires a specific list of services to be provided at the local level. These obligations depend on the population, which in practice implies a certain distinction between rural and urban municipalities. However, it would be desirable to introduce a provision specifying the powers and services based on the needs and capacities of the rural and urban environment (Velasco Caballero 2020, 11).

Thus, all municipalities are responsible for public lighting, cemetery services, waste collection, street cleaning, domestic water supply, sewerage, access to population centers, and public road paving. In municipalities with less than 20,000 inhabitants, the relevant supra-municipal authority—usually the province—coordinates the provision of most of these services (Article 26(1)(a) and (2) of the LBRL), which is a key element to assist smaller municipalities (Santiago Iglesias 2020, 406). This basic catalog of mandatory services is complemented according to the municipality's population, as shown in Table 9.1. In addition, the cities of Madrid and Barcelona have special powers and specificities in the provision of their services due to their special legal regime.[3]

The central state legislature entrusts the exclusive management of the following mandatory services to local authorities: domestic water supply and purification; waste collection, treatment and use; and public passenger transportation (Article 86(2) of the LBRL). State or regional laws may entrust further services. Service

**Table 9.1** Mandatory municipal services according to their population (Article 26(1) of the LBRL)

| All | >5000 | >20,000 | >50,000 |
|---|---|---|---|
| Public lighting<br>Cemetery<br>Waste collection<br>Street cleaning<br>Household drinking water supply<br>Sewerage<br>Access to population centers<br>Public road paving | Public parks<br>Public library<br>**Waste treatment** | Civil protection<br>Assessment and information of situations of social need<br>Immediate attention to people in situation or risk of social exclusion<br>Fire prevention and extinction<br>Public sports facilities | **Urban public passenger transportation**<br>Urban environment |

*Source*: own elaboration

[3] For Barcelona: Act 22/1998, of December 30, 1998, on the municipal charter of Barcelona (Catalonia); and Act 1/2006, of March 13, 2006, regulating the special regime for the municipality of Barcelona (central state). For Madrid: Act 22/2006, of July 4, 2006, on the capital status and special regime of Madrid (central state).

provision under monopoly requires the prior agreement of the plenary of the local government, approval by the competent regional body (Article (86(2) of the LBRL), and the favorable opinion of the competition authority (Montoya Martín 2023, 41–42). This is often the case for water supply (Villar Rojas 2016, 208). In the absence of a monopoly, private parties may participate in the provision of these services. Also, certain restrictions to competition are admissible, such as offering below-market prices (López de Castro and Ortega 2021, 483–484). This gives effect to the constitutional provision that allows restricting certain essential resources or services to the public sector—especially in the case of monopolies (Article 128(2) of the Spanish Constitution)—while striking a balance between public powers and service operators, whether public or private (Malaret García 2003, 607).

It is possible to set up supra-municipal bodies to manage local public services. The basic legislation provides for the creation of municipal associations or *mancomunidades* (in rural environments) and metropolitan areas (in urban environments). These local entities are considered public authorities for the purposes of determining their legal regime. So far, municipalities have voluntarily constituted 963 municipal associations in Spain (Ministry de Política Territorial y Memoria Democrática 2023). These supra-municipal entities jointly manage the provision of different services, mainly: water supply and purification, solid urban waste management, sports, slaughterhouses, libraries, tourism, and social services.[4] There are hardly any arrangements for supra-municipal associations in the urban sphere. Only three metropolitan areas exist: one in Barcelona, with powers over water, social and territorial cohesion, economic and social development, infrastructures of metropolitan interest, environment, waste, transport, and mobility and urban planning; and two in the Valencian Community, in charge of managing hydraulic services and waste treatment, respectively.

Cooperation between local governments can also take the form of joint personified instrumental entities, as described below (Fig. 9.5). It is also possible to create consortiums—with their own legal personality and subject to public law—to jointly manage certain services or to implement joint projects. Occasionally, they may also include private subjects. These entities will be considered institutional or instrumental bodies, so that their legal regime will be different from that of public authorities. Consortiums exist in Andalusia, the Canary Islands, Castilla y León, and Castilla-La Mancha for the management of the following services: water, fire prevention and extinction, civil protection and rescue, and waste management. In Catalonia, consortiums have been created to provide innovative services in the field of energy and energy transition.

Figure 9.2 shows the total number of these associative entities created in each autonomous community and their relationship with the number of municipalities. The greater the number of municipalities (which is usually accompanied by a greater territorial dispersion), the greater the resort to municipal associations and, to

[4] The complete list of local districts can be consulted in the inventory of state, autonomous and local public sector entities (INVENTE) (Ministerio de Hacienda 2023).

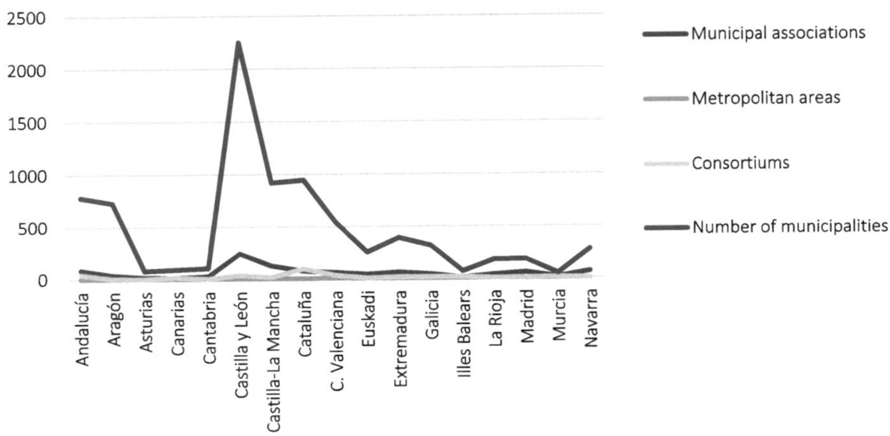


**Fig. 9.2** Number of municipalities and local associative entities for the management of public services by type, by autonomous community (2023). (Source: own elaboration based on data from the Ministerio de Hacienda (2023) and the Ministerio de Política Territorial y Memoria Democrática (2023))

a lesser extent, consortiums. This is mostly the case in Castilla y León, Castilla-La Mancha, and Catalonia. Catalonia is particularly noteworthy for its tendency to create numerous local and instrumental entities, as shown in this chapter.

The specific rules on the forms of management of local public services are similar to those that govern state and regional services (Villar Rojas 2018, 76). The LBRL draws a clear distinction between direct and indirect management (López de Castro and Ortega 2021, 491):

1. *Direct management* implies that the local government provides the service, either by itself (Article 85(2)(A)(a) of the LBRL) or through a personified instrumental entity, which may be subject to public law (autonomous bodies and public undertakings) (Article 85(2)(A)(b) and (c) of the LBRL) or to private law (publicly-owned local private companies) (Article 85(2)(A)(d) of the LBRL). In order to establish a public undertaking or a private-law company, it is necessary to prove that they are more sustainable and efficient than direct management by the local government itself or by an autonomous body. Moreover, private-law companies cannot carry out activities involving the exercise of public authority. Certain autonomous communities provide for other types of instrumental entities, such as local foundations or agencies (López de Castro and Ortega 2021, 492).[5]

[5] Regional legislation in Andalusia provides for the creation of local agencies. So far, two are registered in the INVENTE for the management of museums, and urban planning and housing, respectively.

2. *Indirect management* implies entrusting the management of the service to a third party. In this regard, the LBRL refers to public procurement legislation—and in particular to public service management contracts. However, the Spanish Public Procurement Act 9/2017, of November 8 (LCSP), eliminated this type of contract. Therefore, the reference must be understood to be made to the service contract or the service concession contract, depending on whether or not the contractor bears the operational risk. These management schemes are subject to a fundamental limit—i.e., the prohibition of carrying out activities involving the exercise of public authority.

The central state legislature has maintained this general management framework since the approval of the LBRL in the 1980s. However, there are other complementary forms of management, both direct and indirect. In the case of direct management, one or (jointly) several local governments may create an instrumental entity to manage the service. Moreover, the state, and/or the autonomous communities as well as local governments may participate in certain instrumental personifications, thus contributing to the management of local public services. In the case of indirect management, joint contracting by several governments is also possible, using the techniques provided for this purpose in public procurement legislation. In addition, some autonomous communities provide for the indirect management of social services through collaboration agreements or coordinated action (*acción concertada*) (Domínguez Martín 2020). This arrangement also involves entrusting the management of the service to a third party, but outside the scope of public procurement rules, since it is considered a non-contractual mechanism—on which the Court of Justice of the European Union (CJEU) has recently issued an interesting ruling (CJEU, judgment of 14 July 2022, *ASADE*, C-436/20, EU:C:2022:559).

The choice of public service management is subject to the criteria of greater sustainability and efficiency (Article 85 of the LBRL). In addition, according to an increasingly widespread interpretation, the criteria set forth in Act 40/2015, of October 1, on the Legal Regime of the Public Sector (Article 86(2)(a)), should also apply at the local level—even if they are addressed to the state public sector. Such interpretation makes it necessary to analyze whether the use of an instrumental entity is more efficient than public procurement, more sustainable and more effective under economic profitability criteria. This introduces a sort of subsidiarity principle and limits the use of personified entities. The empirical data below show the impact of this interpretation on the choice of direct or indirect management.

Finally, the provision of the abovementioned mandatory services, together with others that may be determined by the state and regional legislatures, does not prevent local governments from developing other services as part of their public economic initiative. In this case, they will normally use a local private-law company. The possibility for local governments to participate in the market is subject to guaranteeing budgetary and financial sustainability in the exercise of their powers (Article 86(1) of the LBRL), as well as to compliance with competition regulations.

## 9.3 Direct Management

As already explained, direct management allows the provision of services directly by the local government or through an instrumental personification under different legal forms. In practice, however, it is common to create instrumental entities, either individually by a single local government, jointly by several local governments, or even with higher territorial levels—i.e., central state and autonomous communities. Below, I analyze the characteristics of these types of entities and the practical problems posed by their legal regime, pointing out the differences between rural and urban areas.

### *9.3.1 Personified Entities*

According to basic state legislation, the direct management of public services by a personified entity must meet sustainability and efficiency criteria, which translates into certain procedural requirements—basically the issuance of certain reports (Article 85(2)(A)(d)(2) of the LBRL). The decision to create, modify and suppress these entities lies with the plenary of the local government, which approves their governing charter. In the case of autonomous bodies (ABs) and public undertakings (PUs), the legal regime is the same as that applicable to the state, with some particularities (Article 85(2) of the LBRL). ABs are governed by administrative law, while PUs are subject to a mixed public-private regime. Private law applies to (publicly owned) local private companies, except for the rules on budgetary, accounting, financial control, efficiency control and contracting matters (Article 85(3) of the LBRL); and a similar regime applies to public foundations.

In the specific case of publicly-owned local private companies, the capital stock is usually owned in its entirety by a single municipality—without prejudice to cases of joint ownership, as explained below. The main governing bodies of the company are the general meeting (in which all the municipal political groups are represented), the board of directors (which is usually made up of councilors and the mayor), and the management (which is usually assigned to a professional with public or private experience).

Figure 9.3 shows the number of personified entities normally created at the local level in the different autonomous communities for the management of public services. It can be inferred from the data that there is a greater number of these entities in autonomous communities with a larger urban population, such as Andalusia, Catalonia, Valencia, the Basque Country, Madrid, and the Canary Islands. In autonomous communities with predominant rural municipalities there are no entities of this type. Instead, we can find municipal associations (see Fig. 9.2) that either manage directly the services entrusted to them or opt for an indirect management arrangement. The reason for this difference lies in the complexity of integrating into the local organization an entity with its own legal personality and a legal regime different from that applicable to public authorities.

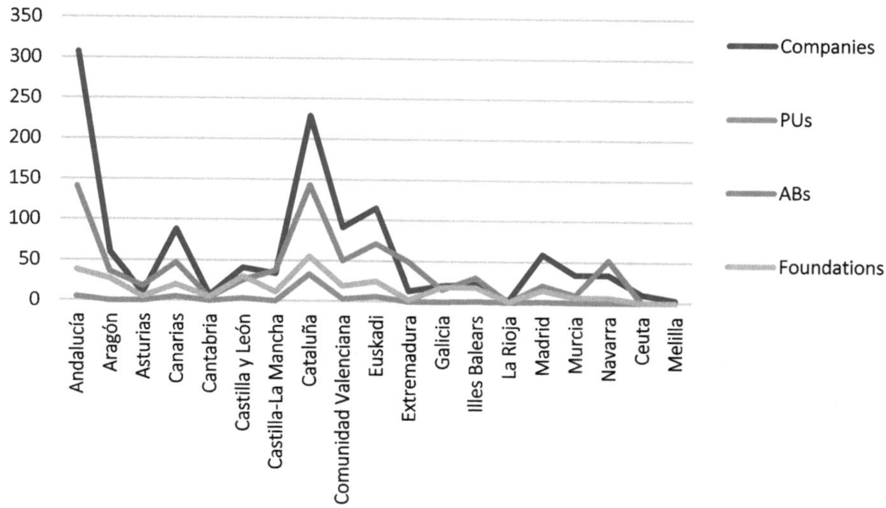


**Fig. 9.3** Number of local instrumental entities by type, by autonomous community (2023). (Source: own elaboration based on INVENTE data (Ministerio de Hacienda 2023))

With respect to the organizational forms, private-law companies clearly prevail, followed by ABs, foundations and, lastly, PUs. It is difficult to identify a pattern in the services entrusted to private-law companies, which are responsible for activities such as water management, waste and street cleaning, energy, social services, transport, and urban mobility. On the other hand, ABs tend to manage sports services or employment centers. Foundations are mainly dedicated to the management of cultural services (theaters, museums), as well as sports and welfare activities (see, for instance, the significant number of nursing homes managed by foundations in Castilla y León). As explained below, among the patrons of these foundations are usually several municipalities, supra-municipal entities and even the autonomous community. Finally, PUs are hardly the preferred form of instrumental personification for the management of local public services. Only Catalonia and the Canary and Balearic Islands use them to manage a wide range of services.

On the other hand, since data became available in 2015, there has been a clear standstill in the creation of personified instrumental entities in relation to other direct and indirect management alternatives. The strict rules introduced in 2013 at the local level in the context of the economic crisis[6] led to a drastic reduction of the instrumental public sector (as reflected in Fig. 9.4), driven by the need to comply with budgetary stability regulations. A significant number of private-law companies and ABs disappeared. Only the creation of public foundations seems to have increased, which compensates for the elimination of these types of entities.

[6] Specifically, Act 27/2013, of 27 December, on the rationalization and sustainability of local government (LRSAL) enacted an important reform of the LBRL. Among other purposes, it sought to resize the local public sector.

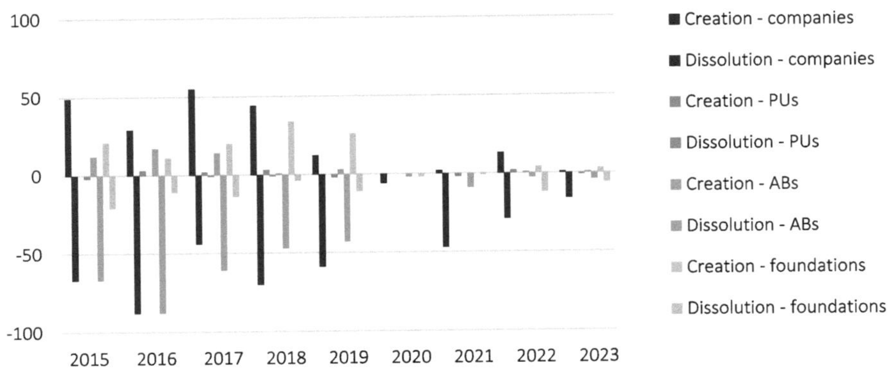


**Fig. 9.4** Number of local instrumental entities created and dissolved, by type (2015–2023). (Source: own elaboration based on INVENTE data (Ministerio de Hacienda 2023). There are no data prior to 2015)

The re-municipalization trend at the center of the political debate in the 2010s (Tornos Mas 2017; Alemany Garcías 2020) did not put an end to the dissolution of instrumental entities. The explanation probably lies in the loss of the advantages offered by their legal regime vis-à-vis public authorities. This, in turn, is due to the Europeanization of numerous sectors, such as public procurement, which has resulted in a brake on the flight to private law (Chinchilla Marín 2016; Martínez-Alonso Camps 2018, 85–86).

In 2020, due to the pandemic, there was a halt in both the creation and dissolution of new personified entities. From 2021 onwards, the elimination of companies has continued—generally linked to urban management, local development and housing.[7] Since 2020, the creation of private-law companies has been modest, with an upturn in 2022. They focus on the management of certain services such as home care, water management, and urban cleaning.[8] In some instances, indirect management may have not worked properly—leading to a change in management. However, this hypothesis requires a more in-depth study of the data, which is beyond the scope of this study.

The above regulation set forth in Articles 85 and 86 of the LBRL remains silent on the way in which local governments can relate to their instrumental entities,

[7] For instance: Suelo Ind. Santoña, S.L.; Remade Reciclaje, S.L.; Berriz Sociedad Urbanística, S.A.; Empresa Municipal de Suelo y Vivienda Algeciras, S.A.; Granada Desarrollo Innova, S.A.; Turismo Gaditano; Empresa Municipal de Manzanares, S.A.; Empresa del Suelo y Equipamiento de Valdepeñas, S.L.; Sociedad Urbanística Municipal de Paterna, S.A.; Sociedad Desarrollo Local Tocina-Los Rosales, S.L.; Empresa Municipal de la Vivienda Sanlúcar de Barrameda; Aguas Termales, S.A.; Gestión Insular de Aguas de Tenerife, S.A.; Empresa Municipal del Suelo y Vivienda de Algete, S.A.; Viladecans Renovación Urbana, S.L.

[8] The newly created companies are: Servizos Urbanos Municipais de Arteixo, S.A.; Servicio de Atención al Domicilio Pamplona, S.L.; Enargi Araba, S.A.U.; Lixura Baztan, S.L.; Aguas de Alcázar Empresa Municipal, S.A.U.; Empresa de Serveis de Villamajor, La Municipal, S.L.U.; Gesoca Servicios, S.L:; Gesoca Limpieza, S.L.; Serveis Urbans del Masnou, S.L.; Sastrako Kirol Zerbitzuak, S.L.; Aira Gestión Ambiental, S.A.U.; El Pilalaero, S.L.U.; Bressolgramenet, S.A.; AquaOleiros, S.A.; Ecoastúrica, S.L.; Cicle de L'aigua del Ter, S.A.

especially in the case of private-law companies. In practice, the main—if not exclusive—objective of these companies is to provide the services that constitute their corporate purpose. In addition, their control is exercised directly by the local government insofar as the councilors are members of their governing bodies. Finally, they are usually financed through current transfers or operating subsidies from the municipal budget, which are intended to cover the total cost of providing the service and operating the entity.

Against this backdrop, it is easy to deduce that these entities intended for the management of public services normally meet the requirements of the in-house exception under EU law, and specifically Article 12(1) of Directive 2014/24/EU, transposed domestically by Public Procurement Act 9/2017, of November 8 (*Ley de Contratos del Sector Público* or LCSP) (Articles 32 and 33): the contracting authority exercises over the legal person concerned a control which is similar to that which it exercises over its own departments; more than 80% of the activities of the controlled legal person are carried out in the performance of tasks entrusted to it by the controlling contracting authority or by other legal persons controlled by that contracting authority; and there is no private capital participation in the controlled legal person when it is a private-law personification.

Domestic law has added some requirements to the Directive's regulation: the bylaws of the instrumental entity must recognize its in-house status; the controlling authority must confirm that the instrumental entity has sufficient means to carry out the functions entrusted to it (Article 32(2)(d) of the LCSP); and the controlling authority must set the fees for the provision of the assigned services, which must cover only the actual cost borne (Article 32(2)(a) of the LCSP). In addition, the in-house entity cannot participate in tenders called by its controlling authority (Article 32(2)(d) of the LCSP), and there are restrictions for subcontracting the assigned services on the market (Article 32(7)(b) of the LCSP). Finally, the assignment must be formalized and published in the relevant Procurement Platform (Article 32(6)(b) of the LCSP), and it may be subject to the special procurement appeal in accordance with the Remedies Directives when its value exceeds 100,000 EUR (Article 44(2)(e) of the LCSP).

For the purposes of this chapter, the difficulty of interpreting the scope of the in-house exception in domestic law is resulting in a greater preference for indirect, over direct, management. As has been explained, these instrumental entities are created directly to provide one or more public services and their financing is assured in the municipal budgets. For this reason, some authors consider that the in-house exception is not necessary in these cases, since there would simply be a transfer of powers in the sense of Article 1(6) of Directive 2014/24/EU[9] and CJEU's case law[10] (Vilalta Reixach 2019, 288; Amoedo and Cutrín 2019, 423). In other words, this

[9] Article 1(6) of Directive 2014/24/UE: "Agreements, decisions or other legal instruments that organize the transfer of powers and responsibilities for the performance of public tasks between contracting authorities or groupings of contracting authorities and do not provide for remuneration to be given for contractual performance, are considered to be a matter of internal organization of the Member State concerned and, as such, are not affected in any way by this Directive."

[10] CJEU, judgment of 21 December 2016, *Remondis*, C-51/15, EU:C:2016:985; and CJEU, judgment of 18 June 2020, *Porin Kaupunki*, C-328/19, EU:C:2020:483.

would be a form of self-organization. However, to the extent that this provision of the Directive has not been transposed, there are others who find it difficult to classify these cases as transfers of powers. From this perspective, the in-house exception may apply if these instrumental entities are entrusted with specific assignments (Arigmany 2020). The result, in many cases, is the annual publication of the local services assigned to these entities in exchange for the established fees. Specifically, in 2022, the Independent Office for Regulation and Supervision of Public Procurement reports the publication of 658 assignments to in-house entities at the local level (OIReScon 2023).

## *9.3.2 Personified Joint Entities*

Some instrumental entities arise from the collaboration of several local—supra-municipal and municipal—governments, with the autonomous communities and the central state. These arrangements usually take the form of publicly-owned private companies and public foundations. Figure 9.5 shows the data on joint companies and foundations that are part of the local public sector. As in the case of consortiums (Fig. 9.2), these types of joint entities increase with the number of municipalities. Once again, Catalonia stands out for its tendency to create joint instrumental entities.

The participation of different public bodies in these entities is usually articulated through equity ownership (companies) or interests in the foundation's assets (foundations); and, in some cases, through the assignment of voting rights to certain partners or trustees. The governing bodies usually include representatives of all the

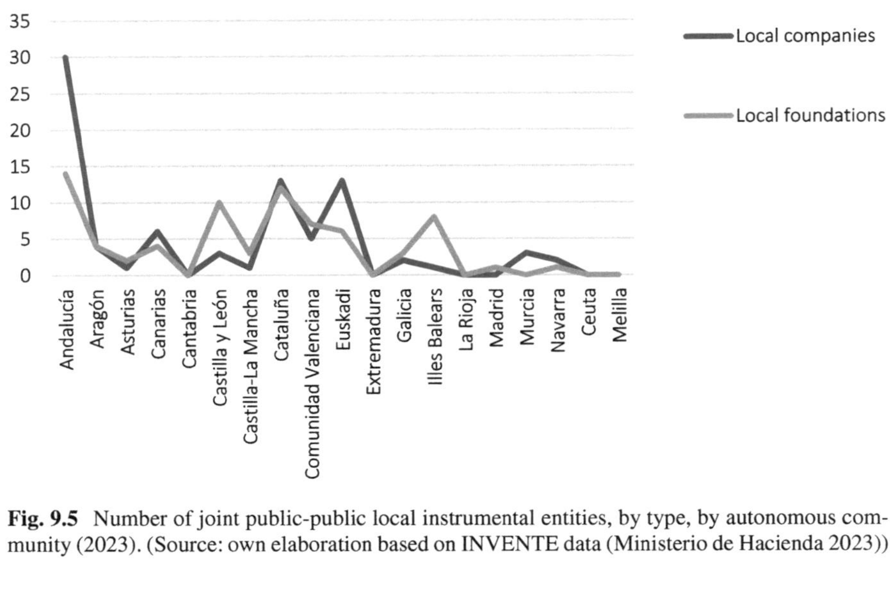


**Fig. 9.5** Number of joint public-public local instrumental entities, by type, by autonomous community (2023). (Source: own elaboration based on INVENTE data (Ministerio de Hacienda 2023))

participating entities. Among others, these entities manage cultural, sports, social, water and waste management services.

In practice, applying the in-house exception to these entities is particularly complex. The Spanish case law on administrative judicial review makes a restrictive interpretation of the joint control criteria set by the CJEU and under Directive 2014/24/EU (Article 12(3)). In this regard, domestic courts consider that a minority shareholder in a publicly-owned private company cannot exercise a similar control, despite having a representative in the decision-making bodies of the controlled entity and being able to jointly exercise decisive influence over its strategic objectives and significant decisions.[11] The reasoning focuses both on the ability of each partner to condition the activity of the instrumental entity and on the percentage shareholding—while EU case law has progressively relaxed this latter requirement (Hugas Garriga 2023).

In addition to the strictly local joint entities, the public sector of the central state and the autonomous communities allows for personified arrangements with the participation of local governments. Thus, different companies may manage central supply markets,[12] infrastructure,[13] water[14] or local development.[15] Among them, Empresa de Transformación Agraria, SA (TRAGSA) is part of the state public sector and comprises 39 provincial councils (0.13% shareholding), seven Canary Island councils (0.02% shareholding) and four Balearic Island councils (0.01% shareholding), as well as the 17 autonomous communities, Ceuta and Melilla (0.06% shareholding), and the central state (99.77% shareholding). The CJEU recognized the compatibility of this arrangement with EU law in its judgment of 19 April 2007, Asemfo, C-295/05. Since then, TRAGSA has been strengthened and is now legally recognized as an in-house entity of all the shareholding public bodies (Additional Provision 24 of the LCSP). It plays a special role in rural areas, given that its main functions include rural development, environmental conservation, animal health control, emergency assistance and the adaptation and maintenance of IT applications. In November 2023 alone, it received 21 assignments from local governments for a value of more than seven million euros, mainly for works in rural areas.[16]

---

[11] See, for instance, judgment of the High Court of Justice of Catalonia (judicial review chamber), case 5240/2020, December 17, ES:TSJCAT:2020:11276.

[12] In the state public sector: Mercados Centrales de Abastecimiento de Asturias, S.A., Mercados Centrales de Abastecimiento de Badajoz, S.A., Mercados Centrales de Abastecimiento de Las Palmas, S.A., Mercados Centrales de Abastecimiento de Málaga or Mercalgeciras, S.A.

[13] For example, at the state level: Puerto Seco de Madrid, SA; in the autonomous community of Valencia: Aeropuerto de Castellón, S.L.

[14] In the autonomous community of Madrid: Canal de Isabel II, SA.

[15] At the state level: Sociedad para el Desarrollo Industrial de Extremadura, SA.

[16] All its assignments can be seen at Tragsa Group (2024).

**Table 9.2** Local public procurement (2018–2022)

| Year | Base tender budget (VAT excl.) | % of all public procurement | Number of procurement files (contracts awarded after bidding) | % of all public procurement |
|---|---|---|---|---|
| 2018 | 18,74 billion EUR | 31.96% | 49,654 | 49.05% |
| 2019 | 17,39 billion EUR | 24.75% | 66,098 | 51.06% |
| 2020 | 20,33 billion EUR | 32.48% | 58,709 | 44.52% |
| 2021 | 30,73 billion EUR | 32.03% | 78,726 | 48.65% |
| 2022 | 33,38 billion EUR | 33.15% | 91,754 | 50.06% |

*Source*: Own elaboration based on data from OIReScon's annual supervision reports

## 9.4 Indirect Management

Indirect management appears as an alternative to direct management. Local governments usually resort to the market to provide the public services for which they are responsible. For this purpose, they normally use service contracts or service concessions. Table 9.2 shows an increasing trend in spending through contracts at the local level and their relevance in public procurement as a whole. Significantly enough, nearly half of the tenders are issued at the local level. Many of them concern the mandatory services to be provided by municipalities (water, waste, transport, public lighting, sports, etc.).

The significance of local public procurement contrasts with the legislature's scant sensitivity to local governments. The LCSP provides a dense regulation for all tendering, regardless of the economic threshold, whether for harmonized or non-harmonized contracts. This regulation covers all phases (including implementation) of the contracts entered by local governments (Book II of the LCSP). The legal-administrative regime for contract implementation is only relaxed to some extent in the case of instrumental entities, especially publicly owned private companies (Book III of the LCSP). The legal regime applicable to public contracts entered by local governments is practically identical to that provided for the central state and the autonomous communities—with only a few organizational particularities (Additional Provisions 2 and 3 of the LCSP). In practice, this often makes it difficult for local authorities to ensure compliance with public procurement regulations, since they do not have specialized personnel capable of adequately applying the complex regulatory framework in force. This, in turn, sometimes leads to the splitting of contracts to facilitate their direct award[17] or the provision of public services

[17] A direct award is provided for works contracts with an estimated value of less than 40,000 EUR and for service and supply contracts with an estimated value of less than 15,000 EUR (so-called "minor contracts"), provided that the subject of the contract is split up to avoid application of procedure and publicity rules (Article 118 of the LCSP).

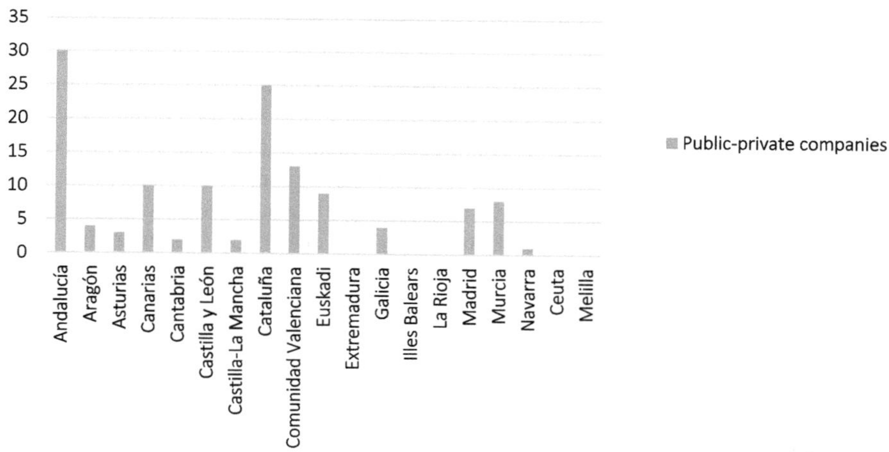


**Fig. 9.6** Number of local public-private companies by autonomous community (2023). (Source: own elaboration based on INVENTE data (Ministerio de Hacienda 2023))

without contractual coverage when, after the termination of a contract, the next one is not awarded in time (González Sanfiel 2023). In this sense, the Court of Auditors has recommended local councils to improve contract planning and to strengthen personal and material resources to monitor the provision of services through public contracts (Tribunal de Cuentas 2023, 96–97).

Central procurement offices—that normally tender framework contracts—are somewhat alleviating the public procurement challenges faced by municipalities. The provincial councils and the Spanish Federation of Municipalities and Provinces have created central procurement offices to facilitate the tender process, especially for smaller rural municipalities. Some of these contracts focus, for example, on energy supply. However, these techniques do not apply to public services: municipalities (with the assistance of the provinces, where appropriate) will be responsible for processing the relevant tenders.

Finally, public-private companies are also sometimes created to manage certain services. They are established after the tender process, normally for a service concession contract to be managed by the company with the selected private partner. The use of these types of entities is not particularly frequent, but it does occur in practically all the territory, as shown in Fig. 9.6. They are common in the management of water-related services.

## 9.5 Conclusions

The current legal regime shows a profound disregard for the particularities of local governments in the management of public services—and even more so for the different needs and capacities of rural and urban municipalities. In practice, there are more instrumental entities in urban areas, usually in the form of private-law companies.

However, since the economic crisis there has been a clear trend towards the suppression of these entities in favor of indirect management through public contracts. The difficulty in internalizing the scope and meaning of the in-house exception and the transfer of powers (both provided for under EU law) has reinforced this trend. All this has led to a scenario where it is not easy to identify the suitability of specific forms of management—direct or indirect—with specific public services. Also, indirect management is somehow assumed to be more efficient than direct management. The problem lies in the challenge of effectively and efficiently implementing complex procurement rules when the appropriate technical and personal means are not available. The creation of joint management arrangements and provincial support are essential to make up for these shortcomings, especially in rural areas.

## References

Alemany Garcías, J. (2020). Los modos de gestión del servicio público en el ámbito local. *Revista General de Derecho Administrativo, 53*, 1–39.

Alloza, M., González-Díez, V., Moral-Benito, E., & Tello-Casas, P. (2021). El acceso a servicios en la España rural. *Banco de España Documentos ocasionales, 2111.*

Amoedo-Souto, C.-A., & Cutrín Domínguez, M. (2019). El impacto de la Ley 9/2017, de Contratos del Sector Público, en la gestión directa de servicios públicos locales a través de medios propios. *Revista de Administración Pública, 210*, 393–432. https://doi.org/10.18042/cepc/rap.210.14

Arigmany Lamoglia, E. (2020). Gestión directa y descentralizada de servicios públicos locales: Encargo a medio propio o transferencia de competencias. *Revista de Administración Pública, 213*, 141–178. https://doi.org/10.18042/cepc/rap.213.07

Chinchilla Marín, C. (2016). El derecho de la Unión Europea como freno a la huida del Derecho administrativo. *Revista de Administración Pública, 200*, 361–383. https://doi.org/10.18042/cepc/rap.200.18

Díez Sastre, S. (2020). Los servicios municipales para mayores en el entorno rural y urbano. *Istituzioni del Federalismo, 2*, 441–460.

Domínguez Martín, M. (2020). La acción concertada de los servicios a las personas en la ley de contratos del sector público y en la legislación autonómica. ¿Instrumentos no contractuales para la prestación de servicios públicos destinados a satisfacer necesidades de carácter social? In L. T. Alas & M. C. Pérez (Eds.), *La prestación de servicios socio-sanitarios. Nuevo marco de contratación pública* (pp. 47–75). Tirant lo Blanch.

FEMP (Federación Española de Municipios y Provincias). (2017). Documento de acción. Comisión de despoblación. *Listado de medidas para luchar contra la despoblación en España.* Retrieved February 27, 2024, from https://www.femp.es/sites/default/files/doc_despob_definitivo_0_0.pdf

González Sanfiel, A. M. (2023). Enriquecimiento injusto ante las consecuencias de la contratación irregular. *Revista de Administración Pública, 222*, 99–137. https://doi.org/10.18042/cepc/rap.222.04

Hugas Garriga, H. (2023). *A vueltas con el control de los medios propios. De Teckal (1999) a Sambre & Biesme (2022).* Blog del Observatorio de Contratación Pública. Retrieved February 27, 2024, from https://www.obcp.es/opiniones/vueltas-con-el-control-de-los-medios-propios-de-teckal-1999-sambre-biesme-2022

Instituto Nacional de Estadística. (2021). *Zonas rurales y urbanas: Diferencias.* Retrieved November 20, 2023, from https://www.ine.es/prodyser/demografia_UE/bloc-3d.html?lang=es

López de Castro García-Morato, L., & Ortega Bernardo, J. (2021). Los servicios públicos locales. In F. V. Caballero (Ed.), *Tratado de Derecho Local* (pp. 471–505). Marcial Pons.

Malaret García, E. (2003). Servicio público, actividad económica y competencia. ¿Presenta especificidades la esfera local? *Revista de Estudios de la Administración Local, 291*, 567–608. https://doi.org/10.24965/reala.vi291.9190

Martínez-Alonso Camps, J. L. (2018). Los debates sobre los servicios públicos locales: Estado de la cuestión. *Revista catalana de dret públic, 57*, 72–96. https://doi.org/10.2436/rcdp.i57.2018.3228

Montoya Martín, E. (2023). Algunas reflexiones sobre los servicios públicos e iniciativa económica local: Balance tras diez años de aprobación de la LRSAL. *Revista de Estudios de la Administración Local y Autonómica, 19*, 29–58. https://doi.org/10.24965/reala.11204

Ministerio de Hacienda. (2023). *Inventory of public sector entities*. Retrieved November 20, 2023, from https://www.igae.pap.hacienda.gob.es/sitios/igae/es-ES/BasesDatos/invente/paginas/inicio.aspx

Ministry de Política Territorial y Memoria Democrática. (2023). *Registry of local entities*. Retrieved December 18, 2023, from https://ssweb.seap.minhap.es/REL/frontend/inicio/municipios/all/all

Ministry of Agriculture, Fisheries and Food. (2021). Demografía de la población rural en 2020. *AgrInfo, 31*, 1–7.

OIReScon. (2023). Informe anual de supervisión 2023. *Módulo VI. La publicidad de los encargos a medios propios*. Retrieved February 27, 2024, from https://www.hacienda.gob.es/RSC/OIReScon/informe-anual-supervision-2023/ias2023-modulo6.pdf

Santiago Iglesias, D. (2020). El papel de la provincia en España en la garantía del acceso a servicios e infraestructuras en zonas rurales despobladas. *Istituzioni del Federalismo, 2*, 395–418.

Sevilla, J. (2021). *Brecha entre el mundo rural y el mundo urbano*. El Observatorio Social. Fundación "la Caixa". Retrieved February 27, 2024, from https://elobservatoriosocial.fundacionlacaixa.org/es/-/brecha-entre-el-mundo-rural-y-el-mundo-urbano

Tornos Mas, J. (2017). La llamada remunicipalización de los servicios públicos locales: Algunas precisiones conceptuales. *Cuadernos de Derecho Local, 43*, 12–30.

Tragsa Group. (2024). *Orders*. Retrieved February 27, 2024, from https://www.tragsa.es/_layouts/15/GrupoTragsa/encargos.aspx

Tribunal de Cuentas. (2023). *Informe de la fiscalización del control municipal sobre la prestación de los servicios de limpieza viaria, recogida y tratamiento de residuos y mantenimiento de parques y jardines de los Ayuntamientos de municipios de población entre 50,.000 y 100,.000 habitantes de Comunidades Autónomas sin órgano de control externo propio, ejercicio 2021*. https://www.google.com/url?sa=t&rct=j&q=&esrc=s&source=web&cd=&ved=2ahUKEwjIsaP9lNCEAxWSVPEDHaLADUoQFnoECBIQAQ&url=https%3A%2F%2Fwww.ciudadreal.es%2Fdocumentos%2Ftransparencia%2Feconomica%2F47_informe_n_1529.pdf&usg=AOvVaw1-uOqpUPt77lDawEJ4fZz7&opi=89978449

Velasco Caballero, F. (2020). Municipios urbanos versus municipios rurales: Homogeneidad y diversidad en el régimen local. *Anuario de Derecho Municipal, 2019*(13), 21–53.

Vilalta Reixach, M. (2019). De nuevo sobre los negocios jurídicos excluidos de la Ley de contratos del sector público: Encargos a medios propios personificados y transferencias de competencias entre entidades públicas. *Revista Galega de Administración Pública, 56*, 261–295.

Villar Rojas, F. (2016). El monopolio en el servicio público de suministro de agua en España: Conflictos y tutela. *Revista de la Facultad de Derecho PUCP, 76*, 207–228. https://doi.org/10.18800/derechopucp.201601.008

Villar Rojas, F. (2018). El impacto de la nueva Ley de Contratos del Sector Público en la gestión de los servicios públicos locales. *Anuario de Derecho Municipal, 2017*(11), 75–101.

# Part III
# Ways of Public Service Provision by Urban and Rural Local Governments

# Chapter 10
# Equalization of Financing between Urban and Rural Local Governments: The case of Albania

**Elton Stafa and Anthony Levitas**

**Abstract** This chapter discusses the Albanian model for the equalization of financial disparities between urban and rural municipalities, especially after the 2014 Territorial and Administrative Reform (TAR). This reform reduced the number of local governments, merging 373 rural and urban entities into 61 larger municipalities. It aimed to streamline and harmonize service provision across regions and municipalities, but challenges persist due to the limited financial resources of local governments. The chapter explores the country's intergovernmental financial framework, including recent reforms, which enhanced municipal responsibilities and financing. Despite reforms Albanian municipalities are heavily reliant on intergovernmental transfers, with unconditional grants playing a crucial role in equalizing financial resources. While the stability and allocation of the unconditional grants has improved since 2017, rural municipalities still struggle due to higher service costs and lower fiscal capacity compared to urban centers. There are also major differences between larger urban areas and the capital, Tirana. The chapter concludes that while Albania has made strides in decentralization, further reforms are necessary to address the ongoing fiscal inequalities between urban and rural local governments, underscoring the need for more robust equalization and financing mechanisms to bridge the gap between urban and rural municipalities.

**Keywords** Fiscal equalization · Vertical transfers · Horizontal transfers · Urban financing · Rural financing · Albanian municipalities

---

E. Stafa (✉)
Network of Associations of Local Authorities of South-East Europe (NALAS), Strasbourg, France
e-mail: stafa@nalas.eu

A. Levitas
Watson School for International and Public Affairs, Brown University, Providence, RI, USA
e-mail: anthony_levitas@brown.edu



F. Velasco Caballero et al. (eds.), *Municipal Tasks and Financing*, Local and Urban Governance, https://doi.org/10.1007/978-3-031-99812-6_10

## 10.1 Introduction

Local government in Albania is organized into two levels: municipalities and regional councils. However, municipalities alone play an important role in delivering public services. Municipalities are responsible for both basic municipal services and decentralized social services such as preschool education and social care centers. All municipalities (are supposed to) perform similar functions and deliver similar services to their constituents, regardless of their size and capacity.

Over the past decade, Albania has made substantial progress in enhancing the policy and institutional framework for more effective local governance. The 2014 Territorial and Administrative Reform (TAR) consolidated the very fragmented 308 rural communes and 63 urban municipalities into just 61 larger municipalities.[1] In practical terms, the reform eliminated the previous urban-rural separation of local authorities, as rural communes were amalgamated to an urban center and are now called administrative units. It has also transformed the urban-rural jurisdiction divide into an intra-municipal problem. As a result of the TAR, the average size of the first tier of local government units in terms of population increased by 5.4 times, from 8700 inhabitants to over 47,000 inhabitants, giving Albania among the most populous first-tier local governments in Europe. In addition, in terms of territory, on average, the size of the first-tier local government units increased by 69 times. The reform was enacted through a top-down approach in less than 9 months, and without consensus across the political spectrum.

The 2015 National Strategy on Decentralization and Local Governance provided a roadmap towards a more decentralized public sector where local governments would play a stronger role. A new Law on Local Self-Government, approved in the same year, further consolidated and expanded municipal responsibilities by decentralizing some functions to municipalities, such as pre-school education, social care services, fire protection, and drainage and irrigation. These new functions were financed through earmarked specific grants for a transitory period of three years, after which they were transformed into loosely defined sectoral grants, over which local governments (should) exercise full discretion. Nevertheless, these responsibilities were transferred to municipalities with insufficient financial resources: The local governments in which the institutions associated with these services were located received some of the operational costs that the state had previously spent on maintaining them; while local governments in which these institutions did not already exist received some of their presumed operational costs, but no money to build them. Indeed, investment funding remains mostly with the central government to this day (Levitas & Stafa, 2018).

The territorial and administrative reforms consolidating the number of local governments and their functions were accompanied by changes in the intergovernmental finance system. The allocation of the unconditional (general-purpose) grant, that

[1] Law number 115/2014 on the Administrative-Territorial Division of Local Government Units in the Republic of Albania.

historically has constituted the major source of financing for local governments, was reformed in 2016. The new allocation formula reflected the changes in the territorial organization of local government and made the grant distribution mechanism more transparent, equitable, and predictable. Even with the territorial consolidation, the unconditional grant constitutes more than 50% of revenues for more than 70% of the newly established municipalities. The unconditional grant is also Albania's main instrument to equalize the financing of urban and rural local governments (Levitas & Stafa, 2016).

Albania's first ever Law on Local Self-Government Finance was approved in 2017, marking a major milestone in Albania's progress toward decentralization. The law provides a more logical and efficient framework for local taxation powers, intergovernmental transfers, public finance management, and intergovernmental dialogue. This law consolidated local government financial autonomy by introducing new rules that anchored the size of the unconditional grant at no less than 1% of the gross domestic product (GDP) and no less than the previous year's allocation. This put an end to the grant's historic—and typically—downward instability. Since the approval of this law, local government revenues from the unconditional grant have steadily increased, almost doubling between 2015 and 2024 (without adjustment for inflation) (World Bank, 2021. The law also enhanced local fiscal discipline by unifying the financial management rules and procedures of the local level with those of the central government and, for the first-time, introduced regulations for the prevention and management of local government fiscal distress. The law also requires regular dialogue between municipalities and the ministry responsible for public finances and was accompanied by plans to reform Albania's property taxation system. Indeed, since 2018, the Government of Albania has taken legal, technical, and organizational steps designed to move property taxation from an area-based system of valuation to a market value-based one.[2] Nevertheless, in general, municipalities continue to charge lump sum payments for the property tax through the water utility bill. The reform efforts are ongoing, facing continuous challenges in implementation and commitment at central and local levels (World Bank, 2022).

In 2023, the Government of Albania adopted the new Decentralization and Local Government Strategy 2023–2030, providing a new roadmap - guided by the country's European Union (EU) integration agenda and the global sustainable development goals—to consolidate the decentralization process and strengthen local self-government. The strategy has six main political goals:

1. strengthen local sustainable development;
2. improve local service provision;
3. expansion of digital governance at the local level;
4. increase local financial autonomy;
5. strengthen local democracy and advance the European integration agenda; and
6. capacity development at central and local levels, and improved coordination.

[2] The tax rate is set at 0.05% of the assessed value for household taxpayers and 0.2% of the assessed value for business taxpayers.

However, the ambitious political goals of the new strategy are not entirely complemented by concrete actions to facilitate their achievement. In the area of local financial autonomy, for example, the new strategy mentions that over the medium term it aims at bringing the size of Albania's local government finances closer to the average of South-East Europe, while over the long term it aims at achieving the EU countries average. In both cases, this goal implies almost doubling and quadrupling the current size of local government revenues, without specifying how this might be achieved.

As of 2024, there is increased discussions over another territorial consolidation reform to further reduce the number of local government units. This reform is expected to further align local governments' size and services to the demographic development of the past decade. A new housing and population census was completed in late 2023, but the publication of the results have been postponed until the summer of 2024. The census results are expected to play an important role in informing the debate over both the size and financing of local governments and the system of equalization financing between the more urban and more rural municipalities in Albania.

Overall, since the first democratic local elections in 1992, Albania has adopted several decentralization reforms that have increased the role of local government within the public sector. There is a (relatively clear) division of the responsibilities between levels of government, although recently there has been a partial recentralization of certain local government responsibilities (i.e., the water supply sector). From the political perspective of decentralization, as a transition country with a background of strong political polarization, achievements in the areas of local democracy and accountability remain fragile, as indicated by the lack of resistance from municipalities on the centralization of municipal tasks. The fiscal dimension of decentralization, despite some major achievements, remains weak with local governments suffering from systemic underfunding. The challenges of small and more rural municipalities are exacerbated by their lower fiscal capacities vis-à-vis the more urban local governments, and information on how well consolidated municipalities are servicing the rural populations within them is poor (Bartlett et al., 2018, UNDP, 2020). Nonetheless, the GoA is attempting to address the disparities between municipalities with respect to their fiscal capacities and the higher service costs associated with low population densities through two equalization components within the unconditional grant. At the same time, the central government has used the Regional Development Fund, and initiatives such as the "100 villages program" to equalize the infrastructure endowments of municipalities and to stimulate local economic development and cohesion through capital investment.

## 10.2 The Intergovernmental Finance System: An Urban-Rural Perspective on the Allocation of Grants

Albania has a relatively small public sector, with total public revenues averaging 27% of GDP over the past decade. As a result, the scope of local government remains modest compared to neighbouring countries in South-East Europe (SEE) and the Western Balkans (WB6). In fact, as shown in Fig. 10.1, Albania has the lowest levels of fiscal decentralization indicators compared to South-East Europe. In 2021, local government revenues in Albania constituted 3.8% of the GDP and 14.2% of total public revenues (general government revenues), whereas the average in South-East Europe is 6.1% of the GDP and 17.4% of total public revenues. In per capita terms, local government revenues in Albania in 2021 were at 201 EUR, or only 37% of the SEE average (558 EUR) and only 6% of the EU average (3718 EUR) (NALAS, 2023).

There was significant growth after the territorial reform due to the increase in own source revenues and intergovernmental transfers. However, local government revenues have stagnated since the 2019 earthquake and 2020 pandemic. In 2022, local government revenues in Albania, including earmarked grants from line ministries, were 12.8% of total public revenues and 3.4% of the GDP, which was similar to the 2016 levels. On the other hand, the share of own revenues to the GDP have stagnated over the past five years. The decline in local government revenue has primarily been driven by the decline in earmarked funding from the Regional Development Fund. (NALAS, 2024).

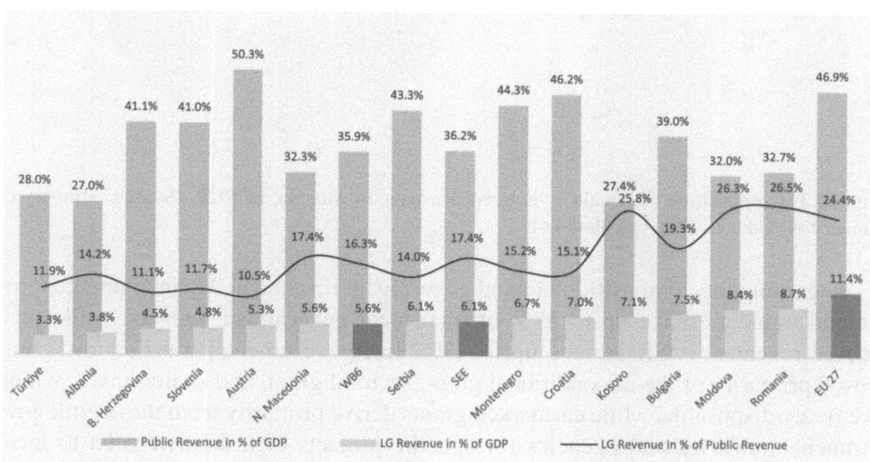


**Fig. 10.1** Public Revenue and Local Government Revenue in South-East Europe in 2021**Source:* Network of Associations of Local Authorities of South-East Europe (2023)* *The data for 2021 and 2022 in* Fig. 10.2 *does not include grants from higher levels of government for the post-earthquake reconstruction process*

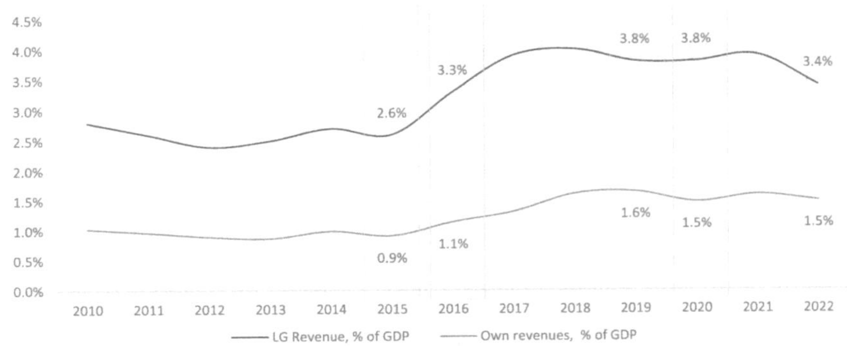


**Fig. 10.2** Local Government Revenue in Albania, percent of GDPSource: Ministry of Finance and Economy of Albania. Own calculations*Note: 2015 refers to the first year of implementation of the TAR after its approval in 2014 and 2016 is the first year that the new functions were decentralized to the local level, per the 2015 Law on Local Self-Government*

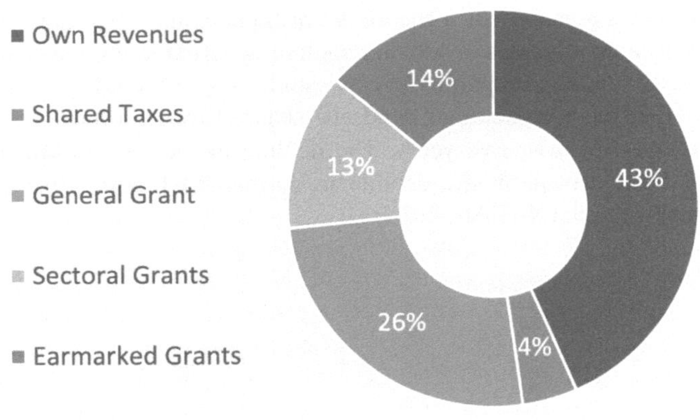


**Fig. 10.3** Composition of Local Government Revenue in Albania, in 2022. (Source: Ministry of Finance of Albania. Own calculations)

Regarding the composition of local government revenue in Albania, intergovernmental transfers make up to 57% of total local government budgets, while own source revenues (OSRs) make up to 43%. Intergovernmental transfers are composed primarily of the unconditional grant, sectoral grant, and shared taxes, which are freely disposable, while earmarked grants derive primarily from the central government ministries and agencies for specific projects or tasks delegated to local governments (Ministry of Finance, 2022).

Own source revenues are composed primarily of property taxes, taxes on new construction, and service delivery fees. However, a more analytical view shows that such figures are significantly skewed because of the predominance of the capital Tirana's own source revenues. Figure 10.3 shows the composition of the local

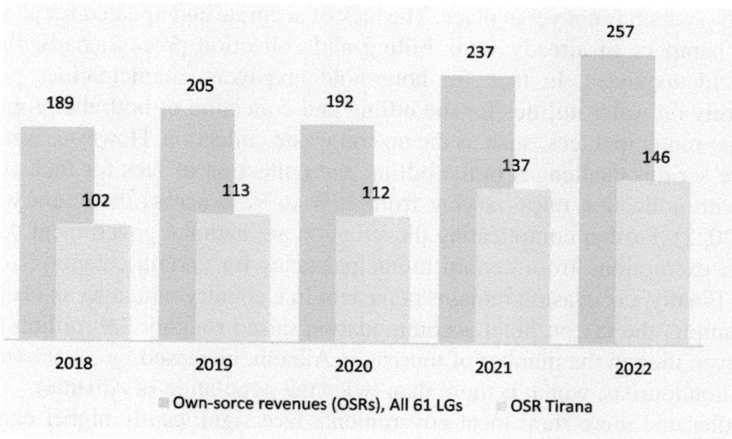


**Fig. 10.4** Own Source Revenues, in million EUR. (Source: Ministry of Finance of Albania. Own calculations)

government revenue system in Albania, while Fig. 10.4 shows the evolution of own source revenues (OSR) from 2018 to 2022, in million EUR for all 61 municipalities and Tirana. As can be seen from Fig. 10.4, Tirana collected 57% of all OSR in 2022.

OSRs have increased on average 9% yearly from 2018 to 2022 and have almost doubled since the TAR. But, over 70% of the increase has been generated by the capital city Tirana. Indeed, OSRs have increased almost exclusively in large urban areas, and is limited to a small group of taxes, despite improvements in property tax and service fee collections. In fact, Tirana and the seven largest municipalities have collected 78% of total own source revenues in 2022, while 44 smaller (and more rural) municipalities have altogether collected only 13% of own revenues. Additionally, 43% of Tirana's own source revenues derive from the Infrastructure Impact Tax, which is imposed on new construction. Indeed, Tirana accounts for 73% of the total national tax yield, demonstrating both the skewed nature of the country's economic development and the weakness of local finances outside the capital city.

Leaving Tirana aside, there are also significant disparities in the performance of local governments concerning the levying and collection of local taxes and fees. Own revenues are insufficiently diversified, and property tax rates are particularly low. The yield of the property tax amounts to only about 15 EUR per inhabitant in Albania which is about three times lower than the average for the Western Balkans and South-East Europe (NALAS 2023). Tirana raises about 43 EUR per inhabitant from the property tax—closer to the regional averages, but probably much lower than in the regional capital cities. In addition, and more problematically, fiscal registers in Albania are incomplete and the tax burden is predominantly charged on businesses for which municipal tax authorities have better information coming from central government agencies in charge of business registration. In 2018, the property tax reform initiative promised to create a functioning centralized fiscal cadastre—which is not yet in place. The lack of accurate and updated fiscal registers further hampers an already weak billing and collection process, particularly for household taxpayers. In fact, for household taxpayers, municipalities predominantly rely on water utilities for the billing and collection of both the property tax and other municipal fees, such as the one on waste collection. However, water utilities face serious challenges in the billing and collection of fees for their own services with collection rates varying from 17% to 92% across the country (World Bank, 2022). Further complicating the situation are national government decisions to grant exemptions from certain municipal taxes for certain categories of businesses. Finally, tax evasion remains persistent in a country with a weak tax culture. For example, the tax on hotel accommodation raised roughly 2.9 million EUR in 2022, even though the number of tourists in Albania increased by 32.6% (reaching 7.5 million tourists, which is more than twice the population of Albania).

Smaller and more rural local governments face significantly higher challenges than urban local governments in raising revenues through local taxes and fees. Figure 10.5 below shows the correlation between the share of own revenues to municipal revenues versus the size of municipalities, excluding Tirana. Except for some smaller coastal municipalities, own source revenues make up to 20% of municipal budgets for half of Albania's municipalities and up to 30% for 40 of the 61 municipalities. In short, the smaller the municipality, the lower the share of own revenues is to their total budgets, and the greater is their dependence on transfers.

Figure 10.6 shows the size of OSRs, as well as unconditional and sectoral grants in ALL, in 2022. As can be noted, there are considerable disparities across municipalities in their ability to raise revenues on their own from local taxes and fees. Per capita revenues from OSRs vary from about 873 ALL (approx. 8 EUR) to 27,663 in Tirana (approx. 251 EUR) and 44.968 ALL (approx. 408 EUR) in Himare, a very small coastal town. Per capita revenues from unconditional and the sectoral grants also vary significantly across the country. They are higher in the case of rural

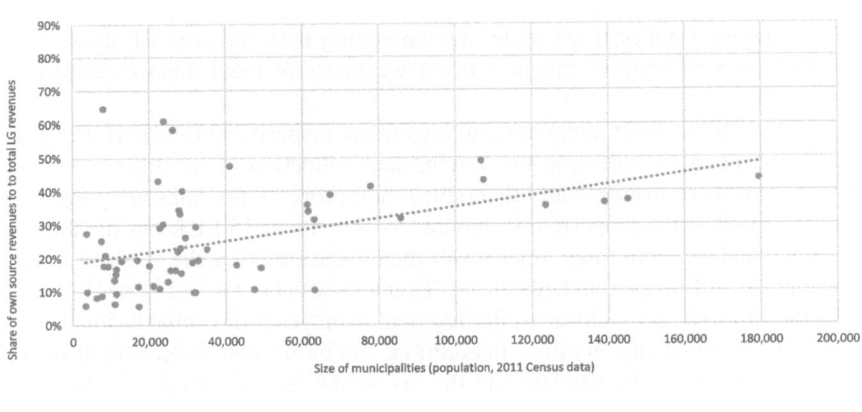


**Fig. 10.5** Share of own source revenues to total municipal revenues versus the size of municipalities (Average 2018–2022, excluding Tirana). (Source: Ministry of Finance of Albania. Own calculations)

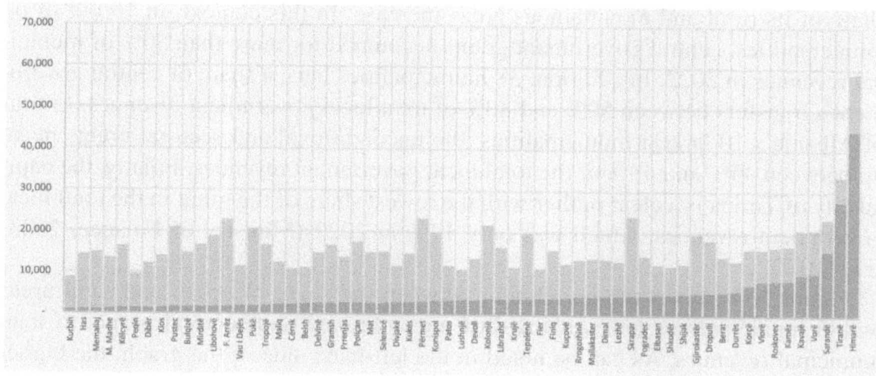


**Fig. 10.6** Per Capita Revenues from Own Source Revenues and Intergovernmental Grants, in ALL. (Source: Ministry of Finance of Albania. 2022. Own calculations)

municipalities and smaller in the case of urban municipalities. The figure shows that the grants complement OSRs and help municipalities achieve average per capita revenues of about 16,238 ALL (approx. 147 EUR).

Local governments in Albania are heavily dependent on the central government's transfers, which are the main source of municipal financing. Intergovernmental transfers are the core of local budgets in Albania. In 2022, the unconditional and sectoral transfers constituted between 50% and 90% of municipal budgets for 87% of local governments. The unconditional grant is described in more detail in the subsequent sections focusing on the vertical and horizontal equalization. Sectoral grants are provided to local governments for the functions they were entrusted with per the reform of 2016. The grant pool is determined annually by the Ministry of Finance, based on reform plans and feedback from municipalities. The allocation to individual municipalities is predominantly performed based on (reported) historical costs—except for the funding for paying preschool teachers, which is allocated on a mixed formula allocating 60% of the funding on a per pupil basis, while the remaining 40% on a per teacher basis (Levitas & Stafa, 2018). The size of the sectoral grants has increased by 96% (unadjusted for inflation) compared to 2016—reflecting a significant commitment from the central government to support the provision of service delivery on a more equal basis across the different jurisdictions (Ministry of Finance, 2023).

Dependance on intergovernmental transfers from the state budget varies dramatically across municipalities and their share is relatively higher in smaller and more rural municipalities. In 2022, on average, the unconditional and sectoral grants accounted for 66% of municipal budgets. Figure 10.6 shows the composition of municipal revenues in Albania, excluding earmarked transfers over which municipalities do not exercise any discretion. Of note, the median shares for own source revenues are 25%, for the unconditional grant 42%, for the unconditional sectoral grants 24%, and shared taxes 5%. Dependence on central government grants increases as the size of a municipality gets smaller (in terms of population) and the share of its rural and mountainous areas increase. In this context, in 15 out of 61 municipalities, central government grants accounted for more than 80% of municipal revenues in 2022. In addition, 38 municipalities have a share of central government's transfers between 50% and 80% of total local government revenues. In four of Albania's 10 largest municipalities, the unconditional and sectoral grants make up between 45% and 49% of the total local government revenues. Finally, the capital city of Tirana is a clear outlier with the lowest share of the grant in the total local government revenues, which was only 17% in 2022 (Ministry of Finance, 2023) (Fig. 10.7).

Figure 10.8 shows the correlation between the share of urban and rural areas within municipalities and the share of unconditional and sectoral grants to total municipal revenues. As can be noted in the left-hand side of the graph, the higher the share of "rurality" (share of rural areas within municipalities), the higher the share of intergovernmental grants to total municipal revenues will be. Likewise, the right-hand side of the graph shows the inverse relationship between "urbanity" (share of urban area of municipalities) and the share of intergovernmental grants to total municipal revenues. To be sure, there are some coastal and industrial municipalities with "higher rural areas" that have a lower dependency on

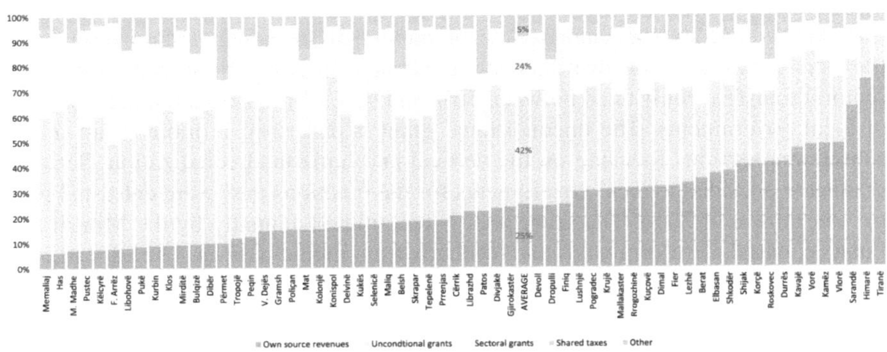


**Fig. 10.7** The structure of municipal revenues, per municipality, 2022. (Source: Ministry of Finance of Albania. Own calculations)

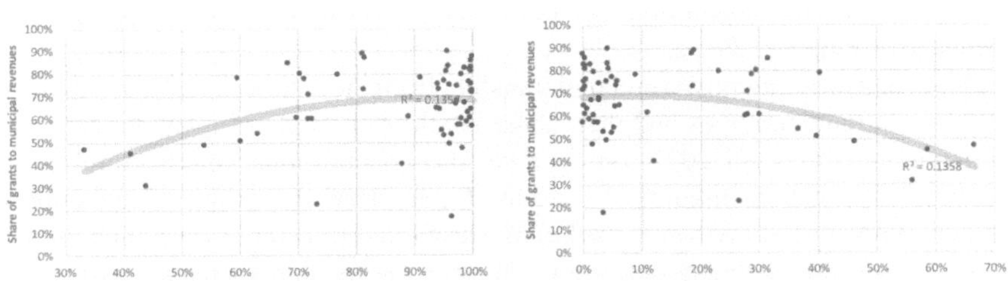


**Fig. 10.8** The share of unconditional and sectoral grants across municipalities (rural and urban areas in 2022). (Source: Ministry of Finance of Albania. Own calculations)

intergovernmental grants due to higher own source revenues, such as Saranda, Himara in the south, or Vora in the middle of Albania's economic corridor Tirana-Durrës.

With few exceptions, Albanian municipalities also remain entirely dependent on earmarked central government funding for capital investments. Initially, the government piloted capital infrastructure development at the local level through the Regional Development Fund (RDF), a national fund pooling investment funding from the state budget and line ministries whose scope intersects with local governments. The funds used to be allocated by the Regional Development Committee, chaired by the prime minister or the deputy prime minister and composed of key line ministers and one representative of the local government associations. The overall aim of the RDF has been to reduce territorial development disparities. Up until 2017, the size of the RDF grew at the same rate as that of the unconditional grant. This raised concerns that it was de-facto crowding out (investment) funding from the unconditional grant and instead placing it in an instrument entirely controlled by the central government. Formally, funding for municipalities was allocated on a competitive basis, nevertheless, over time, the allocation has been criticized as politically biased by all sides of the political spectrum (World Bank, 2021).

The 2015 National Strategy on Decentralization and Local Governance recognized the political bias in the allocation of the RDF, but not much changed until a new Law on Regional Development and Cohesion was approved in 2021, reforming the policy and institutional design of the RDF and anchoring its management to the Albanian Development Fund (ADF). The ADF is responsible for the programming, contracting, and implementation of state funds for the development of municipal and regional infrastructure. The rules and procedures for the allocation of funding across municipalities are adopted by the ADF's executive board. Nevertheless, while the allocation of the RDF to municipalities has been reformed, the size of the RDF has shrunk to extremely low levels, particularly because of limited fiscal space. Compared to its peak in 2017, the fund has decreased by 72% and currently constitutes about 6% of total local government revenues. The decline of the earmarked funding for the development of municipal infrastructure has not been compensated by an increase in the size of the unconditional grant -whose increase is fuelled by the country's economic growth. This has created a major gap in financing the much-needed capital investments at the local level). In short, while an important instrument in the past, the central government funding for regional and municipal development has lost most of its importance to local government finances. Currently, a major part of investment funding is controlled by line ministries, such as for education, water and waste management, municipal transport infrastructure, renovation of public squares, and agricultural development. In most cases, funding to individual municipalities is allocated on a case-by-case basis.

Figure 10.9 shows the correlation of earmarked investment grants with the size of municipalities. The left-hand side of the graph shows the distribution of per capita earmarked grants without the capital city Tirana. Of note, there are significant disparities in the treatment of smaller municipalities with earmarked investment

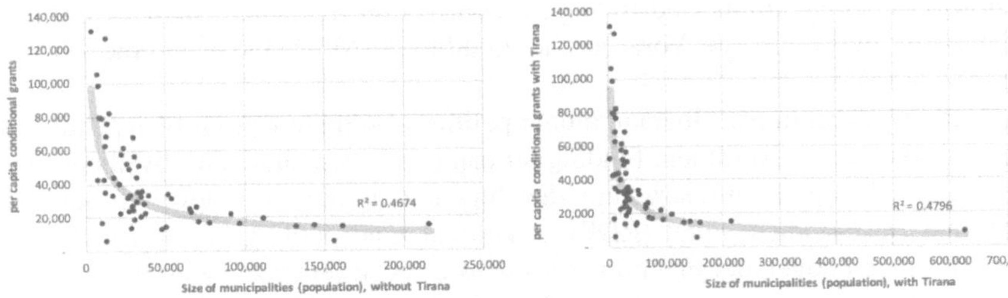


**Fig. 10.9** Per capita earmarked investment grants vis-à-vis the size of municipalities (2013–2022 average). (Source: Ministry of Finance of Albania. 2022. Own calculations)

grants—earmarked investments can vary from 5000 ALL to 130,000 ALL across municipalities with less than 50,000 inhabitants. The differences in the per capita distribution of earmarked investments persist for municipalities with a population higher than 50,000, although the differences are smaller. The right-hand side of the graph shows the per capita distribution of earmarked investment grants, including the City of Tirana. The data shows that Albania's 12 major urban and economic centers (19% of municipalities) have received about one-third of the earmarked funding for capital investments, while about 50% of Albania's municipalities (the smaller ones with less than 30,000 inhabitants) have received about one-third of the earmarked investment funding. However, it is important to note that the Municipality of Shkoder, the fourth largest municipality in Albania hosting up to 5% of the country's population, and the only municipality led by the opposition between the 2015 and 2023 local elections, received only 1.1% of the earmarked investment for the reference period (World Bank, 2022).

## 10.3 Vertical Equalization: Addressing Disparities across Municipalities in Service Delivery Costs and Revenue Raising Abilities

Officially, there is no distinction between urban and rural local governments. All municipalities have an urban center (town) and administrative units (former rural communes). The unconditional grant is the government's main instrument providing local governments with the freely disposable financial support they need to deliver the public services that they have been assigned by law, and which they cannot adequately finance from other sources. As elsewhere, the key objective of the unconditional grant in Albania is to: provide local governments with the difference between the costs of their own responsibilities (expenditure needs) and the revenues they can raise from own sources (fiscal capacity); and provide local governments with lower than average fiscal capacity, additional funds so they can provide public services of a reasonably equal standard (Blöchliger, 2014).

Measuring municipal expenditure "needs" and fiscal "capacity" is a rather challenging task because basic urban and rural services are hard to price due to the numerous factors that determine costs, such as income levels, taxpayers' preferences, geography, social and demographic developments settlement patterns etc. (Kim & Lotz, 2007). For these reasons, in particular in developing contexts, countries make reasonable political judgments and use proxies to estimate the concepts of expenditure needs and fiscal capacity that aim at ensuring that municipal services are equally provided across the different jurisdictions at reasonable levels of quality and access. The government of Albania estimates expenditure needs primarily through the number of inhabitants that benefit from the municipal services in each jurisdiction, while municipalities with a population density lower than a nationally set threshold receive vertical transfers to compensate them for their presumed higher than average costs and lower than average fiscal capacity. Municipalities also receive horizontal transfers—equalizing fiscal capacity, which is estimated based on the national and individual municipal revenues from a relatively small pool of shared national taxes (discussed below).

The Law on Local Self-Government Finance prescribes the key principles and criteria for determining and allocating of the unconditional grant to the individual municipalities, including the criteria for vertical and horizontal equalization. Municipalities are entitled to 97% of the unconditional grant, while second-tier local governments (regional councils) are entitled to only 3% of the unconditional grant pool.

The criteria for allocating the unconditional grant to municipalities are population, population density and the number of pupils in primary and secondary schools. The general unconditional grant is allocated as follows:

1. Up to *80% according to population*—based on the concept of *effective resident citizens*—which in practice is an estimated level of population for every municipality, taking into account primarily the national census data, which are then adjusted by 30% of the difference between the population number recorded in the civil register and the census.

This adjustment to the population data is necessary because there is a significant difference in the population data of the civil registry—which records about 4.5 million citizens holding an Albanian passport living in Albania or abroad—and the 2011 Census which accounts for about 2.9 million citizens living in the country at that moment. Up until 2016, when the new formula for the allocation of the unconditional grant was introduced, Albania used civil register data to allocate funding for municipalities—which was both inequitable and inefficient because scarce public resources were being directed towards local government units to support services for citizens who did not reside in the country (or resided in another local government unit) at the expense of those who did. A new population and settlements census was completed at the end of 2023, and it is expected that its results will have a major impact on the allocation of grants for individual municipalities and will probably require an adjustment of the current allocation formula.

2. Up to *15% based on the population density* - to reflect the differences in service delivery costs across municipalities by positively differentiating municipalities with a population density lower than 110% of the national average—as they are supposed to have "higher than average costs" due to fewer opportunities for economies of scale, larger territories to serve and finally weaker fiscal capacity to raise revenue on their own through local taxes, fees, and charges. Overall, 60% of the funding of the density component of the unconditional grants is allocated to more than one-third of Albania's municipalities that have a population density less than half of the country's average.

As mentioned earlier, it is extremely difficult to measure service costs across municipalities. However, the literature indicates that the diseconomies of scale play an important role in determining the level of local public expenditure and that population dispersion, as well as density, affect the unit cost of service delivery (Kim & Lotz, 2007; Blöchliger & Charbit, 2008). The literature indicates that per capita expenditures are U-shaped, meaning that very small and very large municipalities have higher per capita expenditure needs/costs than average sized municipalities. Table 10.1 below describes the vertical equalization component of the unconditional grant.

In practice, in 2024, municipalities are divided in five main categories of population density:

- Municipalities with a population density of less than 22% of the national average density. In total, 12 out of 61 municipalities fall in this category and they account for about 4% of the country's population. The population adjustment factor is 2.27—which means that every citizen in these municipalities is multiplied by a factor of 2.27. The municipalities in this category receive about 25% of the total pool of funding dedicated to the density component.
- Municipalities with a population density between 22% and 43% of the national average. In total, 11 municipalities fall in this category, and they host about 8% of Albania's population. The adjustment factor is 1.69, which means that every citizen in these municipalities is multiplied by a factor of 1.69. They receive about 35% of the density component of the unconditional grant.
- Municipalities with a population density between 43% and 75% of the national average. In total, 10 municipalities fall in the category, and they host about 10% of the country's population. The adjustment factor is 0.9, which means that every citizen is multiplied by a factor of 0.9. About 26% of the density funding is allocated to this category.
- Municipalities with a population density between 75% and 110% of the national average. In total, six municipalities fall in the category, and they host 9% of Albania's population. The adjustment factor is 0.34 and altogether, these municipalities benefit from 8% of the density funding pool.
- Municipalities with a population density above the national average of 110%. In total, 36% of Albania's municipalities (22 out of 61) fall in this category, and they host about 69% of the country's population. The adjustment factor is 0.033. These municipalities benefit from a very modest part of the population density component of the unconditional grant.

**Table 10.1** Description of the Density Component of the Unconditional Grant for 2024

| Component II: Density Component of the Unconditional Grant | | | | | | | **15%** |
|---|---|---|---|---|---|---|---|
| **Size of the unconditional grant to be allocated through population density** | | | | | | | **3,301,017,090 ALL** |
| National population density average | | | | | | | 118 inhabitants /km$^2$ |
| Per capita density component | | | | | | | 2698 ALL/ inhabitant |
| Population density thresholds with respect to the national average | | **Adjustment coefficient (factor)** | Number of benefiting municipalities | Corresponding population density | Population per group | Adjusted population as per adjustment coefficient | Additional funding for each group |
| Threshold 1 | **22%** | **2.270** | 12 | 25.3 | 132,759 | 301,363 | 813,116,552 |
| Threshold 2 | **43%** | **1.669** | 11 | 50.5 | 259,546 | 433,181 | 1,168,780,990 |
| Threshold 3 | **75%** | **0.900** | 10 | 88.2 | 347,063 | 312,357 | 842,780,786 |
| Threshold 4 | **110%** | **0.350** | 6 | 129.3 | 286,615 | 100,315 | 270,663,947 |
| Threshold 5 | **>110%** | **0.033** | 22 | >130.1 | 2,309,957 | 76,229 | 205,674,815 |
| **Total** | | | 61 | | 3,335,940 | 1,223,445 | 3,301,017,090 |

*Ministry of Finance of Albania. Law no. 97/2023, on the Budget of 2024*

It is important to highlight that all 61 municipalities receive funding from the density component of the unconditional grant. Overall, the density component of the unconditional grant constitutes up to 5% of the total projected municipal revenues for 2024. About 60% of the funding from this component is allocated to 23 municipalities that have on average a population density of up to 43% of the national density average. These are municipalities that have more rural and mountainous areas. On the other hand, municipalities with population densities closer to the national average receive less funding from the density component. Albania's 22 urban municipalities, with a density above 110% of the national average, also receive funding, although a very modest amount (Ministry of Finance, 2023).

Although the 2014 Territorial Reform made municipalities more homogenous in terms of population and surface area, there were significant variations in terms of population density. Most of the low-density municipalities have surface areas that are 50%–100% mountainous. Given the scarcity of the overall pool of resources for the unconditional grant, the Government of Albania decided to support primarily smaller and sparsely populated municipalities through the unconditional grant (Levitas & Stafa, 2016). The threshold of 110% of the national population density average was based on simulations that allowed the minimum number/scale of loss in revenues across municipalities (because of the introduction of the new allocative criteria) and the budget constraints in place.

With the introduction of the unconditional grant in 2001, the government introduced a special coefficient for the urban services of the capital city Tirana, which was terminated in 2005 when the opposition won the general elections. Over time, the capital city has pushed for a special law for the City of Tirana, and for asymmetric decentralization.

3. Up to 5% based on the pupils in public primary and secondary schools.

This criterion was introduced as the number of pupils (that need municipal services) enrolled in public schools (that need to be maintained by municipalities) is a reliable measure of expenditure need. Second and more importantly, a significant share of local government expenditure goes to maintaining primary and secondary schools, and it was considered reasonable to associate the composition of the unconditional grant with these measurable costs. Thirdly, the measure was introduced to further compensate for inefficiencies of the population data series utilized for the allocation of the first two components of the unconditional grant, considering that the no. of pupils, reflect the actual no. of pupils that are enrolled in the system, and therefore is not biased by the differences in population number between the Census and the Civil Register data, explained earlier (Levitas & Stafa, 2020).

## 10.4 Horizontal Equalization: Addressing Fiscal Capacity Disparities across Municipalities

An important aim of the unconditional grant is also addressing the horizontal disparities across municipalities in their ability to raise revenues on their own through local taxes, fees, and charges. However, it is important to understand that this component of the unconditional grant does not provide for additional funds into the intergovernmental finance system as a whole. Instead, it horizontally redistributes revenues from "richer" jurisdictions to "poorer" ones by subtracting a sum from the initial calculation of the "richer" jurisdictions' unconditional grant and then redistributing this sum to "poorer" jurisdictions by adding it to the initial calculation of their unconditional grants. As such, the horizontal equalization system does not cost the central government any additional money and is fully funded by shifting money from "richer" to "poorer" jurisdictions.

The foundation of the system lies in the redistribution of a relatively small pool of shared taxes whose yields should reflect the relative wealth of individual municipalities, but which cannot be influenced by municipal behavior (like not enforcing tax collection). As a result, the system does not create disincentives for own revenue collection (World Bank, 2021).

Table 10.2 describes the horizontal equalization component of the unconditional grant. The shared taxes utilized to calculate the national per capita average against which municipalities are equalized are the personal income tax, the vehicle circulation tax, and the property transfer tax on juridical persons. Taken together, these make up to about 5% of the projected municipal revenues in 2024. The system is based on the comparison of the individual and total municipal per capita revenues from this pool of shared taxes.

Municipalities with per capita revenues from shared taxes below 90% of the national average are entitled to benefit from the equalization fund. In 2024, they are entitled to compensation up to 120% of the difference between the individual municipal yield and the national average. Municipalities that have per capita

**Table 10.2** *The horizontal equalization component of the unconditional grant in Albania*

| Component IV: Revenue equalization component | | | | | | |
|---|---|---|---|---|---|---|
| Size of the pool of shared taxes to be used for horizontal equalization | | | | | | **3,469,288,083 ALL** |
| National per capita income from shared taxes (NPCI) | | | | | | **1040 ALL** |
| If municipal per capita income (PCI) is lower than | **90%** | Of the NPCI, then they are compensated with | **120%** | Of the difference | Funds needed for the equalization | **374,691,441 ALL** |
| By taking funds from municipalities with PCI above | **120%** | Of the national per capita income (NPCI) | **64%** | Of the difference | Funds taken from "richer jurisdictions" | **376,410,473 ALL** |

*Ministry of Finance of Albania. Law no. 97/2023, on the Budget of 2024*

revenues from shared taxes that are above 120% of the national average contribute to the equalization fund by giving up 64% of the revenues from the shared taxes in excess to the 120% revenue.

While the calculations may be considered rather complicated, in practice, only three municipalities usually have revenues above the chosen threshold and contribute to the fiscal equalization pool. In 2019, Tirana contributed about 75% of the total equalization fund, Durres (second largest municipality and economic hub in the country) contributed 22% of the total, while Saranda (small coastal municipality in the South) contributed 3% of the equalization. In 2019, these three municipalities financed the equalization grants of 48 municipalities benefiting from the horizontal equalization component. Unfortunately, detailed data on the specific calculation of the different phases of the unconditional grant formula are not published.

More important to note is the fact that the equalization pool for the horizontal component of the unconditional grant is very small (approximately 3.7 million EUR and is distributed across many municipalities (40 to 50). Overall, the horizontal equalization fund amounts to approximately 1.5% of the total size of the unconditional transfer and 0.5% of the total projected municipal revenues for 2024. To conclude, horizontal equalizing transfers in Albania are extremely low, incapable of addressing the fundamental disparities in fiscal capacity across municipalities, and more importantly, they do not bring additional funding for municipalities, but simply reshuffle the funding of the unconditional grants from richer to poorer municipalities.

## 10.5 Conclusions

Municipalities in Albania benefit from both vertical and horizontal equalizing transfers within the unconditional grant. Vertical equalization transfers aim at providing local governments with the difference between the costs of their own responsibilities (expenditure needs) and the revenues they can raise from own sources (fiscal capacity), while horizontal equalization aims at providing local governments with lower-than-average fiscal capacity, additional funds so they can provide public services of a reasonably equal standard.

The unconditional grant is the government's key instrument to equalize financing vertically and horizontally across municipalities. The unconditional grant for municipalities is the single most important revenue source for Albanian municipalities—making up on average 42% of total municipal revenues. The annual size of the unconditional grant is anchored to no less than 1% of the projected GDP for the fiscal year and cannot be lower than the amount allocated for the previous fiscal year. The unconditional grant has four main components: the population (per capita) component; the population density component—the key vehicle for vertical equalization of expenditure needs and fiscal capacity; the per pupil component; and the horizontal equalization component. Municipalities have full autonomy in utilizing the funding coming from the different components of the unconditional grant allocation.

Vertical equalization is performed by providing additional funds to municipalities with population densities below the nationally set threshold on the grounds that they have higher than average costs due to fewer opportunities for economies of scale, larger territories to serve, and weaker fiscal "capacity" to raise revenue on their own through local taxes, fees, and charges. Up to 15% of the unconditional grant is allocated based on population density. In general, the more sparsely populated a municipality is (hence the more rural it is), the more it benefits from the density component of the unconditional grant. The denser a municipality is (hence the more urban it is), the less it benefits from this component of the unconditional grant. Given Albania's territorial division, the vertical equalization component of the unconditional grant provides a reasonable base for the equalization of relative expenditure "needs". It is important to highlight that all 61 municipalities receive funding from the density component of the unconditional grant. However, about 60% of its funding is allocated to the 23 municipalities that have, on average, a population density of up to 43% of the national density average. In 2024, the vertical equalization fund corresponds to about 5% of the total forecasted municipal revenues.

The unconditional grant also has a specific component that provides for the horizontal equalization of fiscal capacity across municipalities. The system has a sound foundation as it is performed against shared taxes whose yields reflect the relative wealth of individual municipalities. However, it has two main downsides. The first is that it does not provide additional funds into the intergovernmental finance system as a whole. In other words, the government does not provide additional funding for horizontal equalization; instead, "wealthier" municipalities pay for it. The system horizontally redistributes revenues from "richer" jurisdictions to "poorer" ones by subtracting a sum from the initial calculation of the "richer" jurisdictions' unconditional grant and then redistributing this sum to "poorer" jurisdictions by adding it to the initial calculation of their unconditional grants. The second is that the scale of horizontal equalization is dramatically low, amounting to just about 1.5% of the total size of the unconditional transfer and 0.5% of the total projected municipal revenues for 2024.

The distribution of the unconditional grant is determined at the national level by the Ministry of Finance and is approved in parliament. The grant allocation for individual municipalities is based on verifiable indicators of population, population density, number of pupils in primary and secondary schools, and the revenues from shared taxes. As a result, municipalities themselves do not play any role regarding the different transfers.

## References

Bartlett, W., Kmezić, S., & Đulić, K. (2018). *Fiscal decentralization, local government and policy reversals in Southeastern Europe*. Palgrave Macmillan.

Blöchliger, H. (2014). Fiscal equalization—A cross country perspective. *OECD Network on fiscal relations across government levels*. Retrieved February 21, 2024, from https://www.shareweb.ch/site/DDLGN/Documents/OECD_Bloechliger%20Fiscal%20Equalization.pdf

Blöchliger, H., & Charbit, C. (2008). Fiscal equalization. *OECD Journal: Economic Studies, 2008*(1), 1–22. https://doi.org/10.1787/eco_studies-v2008-art8-en

Kim, J., & Lotz, J. (2007). *Measuring local government expenditure needs*. The Korea Institute of Public Finance and the Danish Ministry of Social Welfare.

Levitas, A., & Stafa, E. (2016). *Creating an equitable, transparent, and predictable unconditional grant formula in Albania*. USAID Planning and Local Governance Project in Albania (PLGP). Retrieved February 21, 2024, from https://www.academia.edu/38174924/Policy_Paper_Creating_an_Equitable_Transparent_and_Predictable_Unconditional_Grant_Allocation_Formula. Accessed 21 Feb 2024

Levitas, A., & Stafa, E. (2018). *Financing the new own functions of local governments in Albania*. USAID Planning and Local Governance Project in Albania (PLGP). Retrieved February 21, 2024, from https://pdf.usaid.gov/pdf_docs/PA00X27J.pdf

Levitas, A., & Stafa, E. (2020). *Early childhood education in Albania at the intersection of municipal finance and governance*. USAID Planning and Local Governance Project in Albania (PLGP).

Ministry of Finance and Economy. (2022). *Annual Report on local public finances*. Retrieved February 16, 2024, from https://financa.gov.al/viti-2022-2/

Ministry of Finance and Economy. (2023). *Annual Report on local public finances*. Retrieved February 15, 2024, from https://financa.gov.al/buxheti-i-pushtetit-vendor-3/

Network of Associations of Local Authorities of South-East Europe. (2023). *Local government finance indicators in South-East Europe* (3rd ed.). NALAS Statistical Brief. Retrieved February 7, 2024, from http://www.nalas.eu/category/publications/

Network of Associations of Local Authorities of South-East Europe. (2024). *Fiscal decentralization indicators in South-East Europe in the aftermath of the COVID-19 pandemic* (9th ed.). NALAS Fiscal Decentralization Report. Retrieved February 10, 2024, from http://www.nalas.eu/category/publications/

United Nations Development Program (UNDP) Office in Albania. (2020). *Governance perception in a reforming Albania: Nationwide local governance mapping in Albania.*

World Bank. (2021). *Albania—Local government strengthening: Background paper on Intergovernmental Fiscal Relations* (English). Retrieved February 21, 2024, from http://documents.worldbank.org/curated/en/255471624598584770/Albania-Local-Government-Strengthening-Background-Paper-on-Intergovernmental-Fiscal-Relations

World Bank. (2022). *Decentralization in Albania—Case study of governance and financing of solid waste management services.*

# Chapter 11
# Equalization of Financing Between Urban and Rural Local Governments: Canada

**Enid Slack**

**Abstract** Federal and provincial/territorial transfers to municipalities in Canada account for about one fifth of municipal revenues, on average. The majority of these transfers come from the provincial/territorial governments, and most of them are earmarked for specific purposes. Nevertheless, many provinces/territories provide an equalization transfer to municipalities that is usually based on a measure of fiscal capacity. Two provinces share provincial sales tax revenues with municipalities and most provide unconditional transfers based on population, road kilometres, or other variables. Many provinces provide separate transfers to rural municipalities to reflect the challenges these communities face because they may be more sparsely developed, more remote, and experience colder weather. These challenges result in higher costs for heating, housing, and transportation, and the inability to achieve economies of scale in the provision of services. These municipalities are also likely to have smaller tax bases (and less ability to raise revenue). An implicit form of equalization also exists where urban and rural municipalities in Canada have been amalgamated into one municipality. Equalization transfers, transfers to rural municipalities, and municipal amalgamation all help smaller and rural municipalities provide a reasonable level of service by levying reasonable tax rates, although they do not fully achieve that goal.

**Keywords** Intergovernmental transfers · Equalization · Earmarked transfers · Canada · Municipal amalgamation

The author would like to thank Kass Forman, Almos Tassonyi, and Dina Graser for comments on an earlier draft of this chapter.

E. Slack (✉)
Institute on Municipal Finance and Governance, School of Cities, University of Toronto, Toronto, ON, Canada
e-mail: enid.slack@utoronto.ca



F. Velasco Caballero et al. (eds.), *Municipal Tasks and Financing*, Local and Urban Governance, https://doi.org/10.1007/978-3-031-99812-6_11

## 11.1 Introduction

Canada is a federal country with ten provinces, three territories, and approximately 3500 municipalities (see Table 11.1 for the population of each of the provinces and territories).[1] It is a highly urbanized nation with over 70% of the population living in municipalities inhabited by more than 100,000 people. Although rural areas account for the majority of Canada's land mass, they account for less than 18% of the population (Statistics Canada, 2022). Municipalities function in a variety of contexts—some are enjoying rapid growth, mainly in metropolitan areas, while others are facing relative or absolute decline, largely on the periphery.

The Constitution Act sets out the division of powers between the federal and provincial governments. Municipalities are not granted specific powers in the Constitution but are listed as one of the responsibilities of provincial governments. In essence, this means that the provinces can create or dissolve municipalities, determine their geographic boundaries, set out their expenditure responsibilities and sources of revenue, and much more. The federal government, on the other hand, has no constitutional authority over local government. It can, however, influence local governments through federal transfers, which it has done to some extent at various times (Slack & Taylor, 2024).

Municipalities in Canada make expenditures on a wide range of services, including fire and police protection, water supply and distribution, sewage collection and treatment, solid waste collection and disposal, transportation (including roads and transit), parks, libraries, recreation, and planning and development. In some provinces, they are also responsible for paying part of the costs of housing, social services, and public health. The main sources of local government revenue on average across local governments in Canada, are property taxes (over 46% of total municipal revenues), user fees (21%), federal and provincial transfers (21%), and other revenues (12%) (calculated from Statistics Canada, 2023). Included in other revenues are development charges and other taxes (for example, hotel occupancy taxes, vehicle registration taxes, land transfer taxes, etc.) that municipalities in some provinces are permitted to levy. By far, the largest revenue source for local governments is the property tax, but intergovernmental transfers are also a significant revenue source.[2]

---

[1] No official count of municipalities is kept because the federal government does not collect information about local government institutions. Each province has evolved its own local government system tailored to its local conditions, resulting in considerable variation in institutional forms across the country (Taylor & Slack, 2024 forthcoming). Municipalities include, for example, cities, towns, villages, hamlets, resort municipalities, regional municipalities, counties, and more.

[2] As will be noted later in this chapter, these transfers are vertical (from the federal and provincial governments) and not horizontal (between municipalities).

**Table 11.1** Population, provinces and territories, 2023

| | Population |
|---|---|
| **Provinces:** | |
| Newfoundland and Labrador | 538,605 |
| Prince Edward Island | 173,787 |
| Nova Scotia | 1,058,694 |
| New Brunswick | 834,691 |
| Quebec | 8,874,683 |
| Ontario | 15,608,369 |
| Manitoba | 1,454,902 |
| Saskatchewan | 1,209,107 |
| Alberta | 4,695,290 |
| British Columbia | 5,519,013 |
| **Territories:** | |
| Yukon | 44,975 |
| Northwest Territories | 44,972 |
| Nunavut | 40,673 |
| Canada | 40,097,761 |

Source: Statistics Canada Table: 17-10-0009-01

## 11.2 Do Municipalities Receive Vertical Financial Transfers?

Municipalities receive vertical transfers from both the federal and provincial/territorial governments. Both the level and the structure of transfers differ across provinces/territories and have changed over time in different ways in different jurisdictions. Transfers are allocated in a variety of ways for different reasons. In most provinces and territories, the transfer system is complex, confusing, and in a word, 'messy' (Bird & Slack, 2021). Few transfers seem to be based on careful analysis or have a clear rationale, and their impact is rarely evaluated.

### *11.2.1 From Whom Do These Come: From The Central Government, from Regional Governments, or from the Second Level of Local Government?*

Unfortunately, there are no recent, comparable data by province indicating the exact shares of municipal income attributable to the provincial/territorial and federal governments. However, information from individual jurisdictions suggests that the majority of transfers comes from provincial/territorial governments. In the largest province, Ontario, for example, 84% of transfers were received from the provincial government and 16% from the federal government in 2021. The breakdown between federal and provincial transfers in 2021 in Nova Scotia was similar– 84% of the total were provincial transfers and 16% were federal. In Alberta, provincial transfers accounted for 72% of total transfers in 2022 compared to 28% federal. In British Columbia in 2021, provincial transfers were 71% compared to 29% federal transfers. These results are what one would expect given the nature of Canadian fiscal federalism, where provinces are responsible for local government.

### *11.2.2 What Proportion of Municipal Income Comes from Transfers?*

As noted earlier, and as Table 11.2 shows, federal and provincial transfers combined accounted for over 21% of total municipal revenues in 2021 (the latest year for which data are available). Two other major findings can be derived from Table 11.2—there has been relatively little change in the portion of municipal revenues made up of grants over the last 15 years (with the exception of 2020), and there is considerable variation in the reliance on transfers in different provinces and territories. This variation is partially explained by differences in the responsibilities devolved to municipalities across provinces.

Provincial grants for much of the later twentieth century provided more of total local revenue than currently (Kitchen, 1984, 2002), but the picture shown in Table 11.2 has not changed much over the last decade and a half.[3] Over the last 15 years, federal and provincial transfers combined have generally provided around 20% of municipal revenues. The exception is 2020, which saw higher transfers (almost 26% of municipal revenues) during the COVID-19 pandemic. Both the federal and provincial governments provided assistance to municipalities to cover their unexpected operating deficits arising from higher expenditures on health and social services and lower transit fare revenues.[4] In 2021, transfers fell back into the 20% range.

In terms of provincial/territorial variation, municipalities in the three territories (Nunavut, Northwest Territories, and Yukon) receive a much larger portion of their revenues in the form of transfers. The territories are considerably smaller, more rural, and more remote than Canadian provinces. Transfers are also relatively high in Prince Edward Island, which is the smallest province. At the other end of the spectrum, transfers to municipalities in British Columbia account for only 7% of municipal revenues. The relatively low transfers partially reflects that public transit, typically a large cost pressure for Canadian municipalities, is delivered by provincial agencies in British Columbia. Transfers to municipalities in Ontario are much higher,

[3] Hobson et al. (2005) show that transfers fell from 25.7% of total municipal revenues in 1995 to 16% in 2003. Unconditional transfers stayed at around 3% of municipal revenues but conditional transfers fell from over 22% to 13%.

[4] Municipalities in Canada are not permitted to budget for an operating deficit. Although they did not budget for operating deficits during the pandemic, many found that they were unable to balance their budgets at the end of the fiscal year.

**Table 11.2** Federal and provincial transfers as a proportion of municipal revenues, by province and territory, 2008–21 (%)

| | 2008 | 2009 | 2010 | 2011 | 2012 | 2013 | 2014 | 2015 | 2016 | 2017 | 2018 | 2019 | 2020 | 2021 |
|---|---|---|---|---|---|---|---|---|---|---|---|---|---|---|
| British Columbia | 7.8 | 6.0 | 10.1 | 8.2 | 5.7 | 3.9 | 4.4 | 4.5 | 8.3 | 6.0 | 7.4 | 8.4 | 13.5 | 7.0 |
| Alberta | 24.8 | 23.8 | 22.3 | 21.7 | 18.9 | 23.7 | 18.5 | 14.9 | 21.1 | 26.6 | 19.1 | 17.4 | 25.0 | 22.2 |
| Saskatchewan | 29.2 | 27.2 | 27.2 | 28.9 | 23.2 | 19.6 | 20.6 | 17.8 | 18.2 | 19.0 | 18.5 | 18.8 | 25.9 | 23.1 |
| Manitoba | 21.8 | 21.5 | 22.7 | 23.1 | 23.2 | 23.7 | 20.0 | 19.7 | 18.3 | 17.9 | 14.9 | 16.0 | 21.1 | 19.0 |
| Ontario | 20.9 | 25.5 | 27.5 | 22.5 | 22.8 | 23.3 | 22.3 | 22.6 | 23.2 | 23.1 | 25.0 | 22.3 | 29.5 | 24.0 |
| Québec | 13.4 | 16.3 | 14.8 | 14.0 | 13.8 | 12.5 | 11.0 | 12.4 | 11.2 | 17.5 | 15.6 | 14.2 | 24.9 | 22.4 |
| New Brunswick | 23.2 | 23.2 | 22.9 | 22.8 | 18.6 | 19.9 | 18.5 | 19.7 | 20.5 | 24.2 | 22.2 | 24.5 | 20.7 | 17.9 |
| Nova Scotia | 15.1 | 16.4 | 17.4 | 13.5 | 13.2 | 9.9 | 9.3 | 8.3 | 8.1 | 17.1 | 12.5 | 17.5 | 19.4 | 20.7 |
| Prince Edward Island | 21.8 | 17.6 | 41.1 | 41.6 | 37.1 | 36.6 | 34.4 | 32.0 | 35.4 | 43.0 | 42.5 | 46.9 | 51.2 | 54.1 |
| Newfoundland and Labrador | 35.9 | 40.6 | 40.7 | 35.8 | 24.3 | 25.6 | 25.0 | 24.6 | 19.2 | 21.4 | 21.8 | 21.1 | 20.2 | 19.9 |
| Nunavut | 53.4 | 54.7 | 56.0 | 53.9 | 50.5 | 54.6 | 53.2 | 50.7 | 47.5 | 45.9 | 48.4 | 45.5 | 45.5 | 45.5 |
| Northwest Territories | 66.1 | 67.9 | 62.4 | 60.4 | 56.3 | 59.9 | 58.3 | 54.1 | 47.3 | 59.2 | 61.8 | 61.7 | 63.3 | 64.2 |
| Yukon | 29.2 | 47.4 | 27.5 | 28.6 | 38.0 | 24.1 | 59.5 | 24.5 | 23.4 | 24.7 | 25.9 | 40.9 | 59.6 | 61.9 |
| Canada Total | 18.9 | 21.4 | 22.3 | 19.4 | 18.5 | 18.9 | 17.4 | 17.0 | 18.4 | 20.4 | 19.7 | 18.3 | 25.6 | 21.4 |

Source: Statistics Canada, Table 10-10-0020-01

accounting for almost one quarter of total municipal revenues, in part because social services are cost-shared with the provincial government. In other provinces, social services are delivered by the provincial government.

Grants have consistently accounted for the lowest percentage of municipal revenues in BC, Quebec, and Nova Scotia. Municipal reliance on transfers has changed in some provinces over the last decade or so. For example, transfers as a percentage of total municipal revenues in Newfoundland and Labrador are now much less than they were in 2008 and their importance has also declined in Saskatchewan. In contrast, in PEI, grants as a percentage of municipal revenues have more than doubled over this period.[5]

### *11.2.3 Are Transfers to a Greater Extent Earmarked or Unconditional?*

Transfers to municipalities in Canada are largely earmarked (conditional) in the sense that funds have to be spent on specific services designated by the provincial or federal government and they are often subject to many conditions and reporting requirements. There is no comparable data country-wide on the division between unconditional and conditional grants. However, there is some data for individual provinces such as Ontario where conditional transfers (federal and provincial combined) accounted for almost 80% of municipal transfers and unconditional transfers were just over 20% in 2021. In Nova Scotia in 2021, conditional transfers accounted for almost 97% of total transfers and unconditional transfers just over 3%. In Alberta, conditional transfers were 94% of total transfers in 2022, with unconditional transfers at 6%. The remainder of this section describes the various types of federal and provincial transfers.

For the most part, transfer from the federal government are conditional and largely dedicated to capital purposes. These transfers have been earmarked largely for transit, housing, economic development, and climate adaptation.[6] In some cases, the transfers go directly to municipalities but, in others, they go through the provincial government or municipal associations (Slack & Taylor, 2024). Some examples of federal transfers are described below.

The "Investing in Canada" plan, for example, is designed to distribute funding over a 10-year period for infrastructure. The federal government also has a 10-year National Housing Strategy which invests in affordable housing. "Local immigration partnerships" bring the federal, provincial, local governments, and local service agencies together to assist in immigrant integration (Slack & Taylor, 2024).

---

[5] In 2017, the province changed the grant program to municipalities and increased the amount. It also made a commitment to increase the grant annually for the next 5 years.

[6] For a description of these programs, see Bradford (2018).

The federal government implements programs for economic and community development. For example, the Department of Innovation, Science and Economic Development (created in 2015) is implementing two policy frameworks directed to different types of city-region growth—globally engaged urban centres and smaller cities and rural communities (Bradford, 2018).

Block transfers to municipalities are provided by the federal government for municipal infrastructure.[7] The Canada Community-Building Fund provides permanent funding for local infrastructure (Adams & Maslove, 2014). These funds are distributed to provinces/territories, municipal associations and the City of Toronto on the basis of population. The federal government requires that the transfers be used for municipal infrastructure, that the provinces do not cut their own funding in response to the transfer, and that municipalities show that they are making progress towards federal objectives around sustainability (Slack & Taylor, 2024).

The Housing Accelerator Fund is an application-based program introduced in 2022 with funding from 2023 to 2026–27. Funding is designed to encourage local governments to increase the supply of housing and supports the development of complete, low-carbon and climate-resilient, affordable, equitable, and inclusive communities. There are two streams: large/urban and small/rural/north/Indigenous.[8] There has been some controversy over the distribution of these funds because the federal government has been attaching conditions around zoning regulations and municipal charges on development for infrastructure. Some provinces and municipalities have objected to the federal government imposing such conditions on the receipt of funds.

During the pandemic, the federal government introduced the Safe Restart Agreement, which provided funding to help provinces/territories restart their economies and make the country more resilient to possible future waves of COVID-19. Part of the funding from this agreement, matched by provincial and territorial governments, was to support municipalities with their operating costs over a 6-to-9-month period. Moreover, the federal government cost-matched additional funding to support additional provincial/territorial contributions to public transit.

A number of points can be highlighted from this brief summary of federal transfers for infrastructure and housing (Slack & Taylor, 2024). First, federal transfers are generally implemented through bilateral agreements with provinces. Provincial governments then delegate operational decision-making authority to the municipalities that are eligible for the transfers. Second, in addition to provincial and local governments, local non-governmental actors have been included in decision-making about how to use these funds and deliver services. Third, federal transfers increased following the pandemic. Fourth, although there has been an increase in the number of federal transfer programs and the amount of funding attached to them, federal

[7] For a description of programs, see www.infrastructure.gc.ca/prog/programs-infc-summary-eng.html. Accessed 6 October 2023.

[8] The federal government has recently been criticized by provincial governments for providing housing funding directly to municipalities and bypassing the provinces.

transfers government do not provide as much funding to municipalities as provincial transfers .

Provincial/territorial transfers account for the majority of transfers to local governments in Canada, and they are largely earmarked for specific purposes. However, since this chapter is about equalization, the discussion focuses on unconditional grants by province/territory, of which equalization is one type. Unconditional grants can also take the form of revenue sharing or grants based on population, remoteness, or other municipal characteristics. Table 11.3 summarizes provincial-municipal unconditional grants in Canada.

Six provinces and one territory provide some form of equalization transfer to municipalities. The rationale for providing equalization transfers is to ensure that all local governments can provide reasonably comparable levels of service at reasonably comparable tax rates. The inability to provide a comparable level of service compared to other municipalities can arise for several reasons — the costs of services are higher, the need for services is greater, the tax base is smaller, or some combination of these factors.

Needs and/or costs may be greater than average because of geographic location, population density, or other factors. For example, wages and rents are usually higher in cities with high population density and the cost per unit to provide services increases with increasing population because of congestion (Fenge & Meier, 2001). Per unit costs may also be higher than average in sparsely-populated areas because of the inability to achieve economies of scale or the higher costs associated with transportation to remote areas (Kitchen & Slack, 2006). Needs may be higher for municipalities with a high proportion of low-income households who require affordable housing and social services. Taxing capacity is also unevenly distributed across municipalities, resulting in disparities in the ability to finance the provision of local public services. In rural communities, for example, the property tax base may be relatively small, compounded by lower tax rates on farm properties that may be required by provincial governments.[9]

Equalization grants, based on expenditure needs and fiscal capacity, are designed so that those municipalities with a small tax base and greater costs or needs are able to levy tax rates that are comparable to those of other jurisdictions. Explicit provincial-municipal equalization grants in Canada are limited. Many transfers include some element of equalization in their distribution formulas, but with the exception of Nova Scotia, none is based to any significant extent on "expenditure need" (the costs that arise due to circumstances beyond a jurisdiction's direct control, such as demographic and geographic factors, etc.) although some are based on "fiscal capacity" (the potential to raise revenues given the size of the tax base).[10]

The provinces of British Columbia, Ontario, Quebec, and Prince Edward Island provide small equalization grants to municipalities based on fiscal capacity. New

[9] In Ontario, for example, the tax rate on the farm class has to be no more than 25% of the residential tax rate.

[10] Until recently, New Brunswick also provided an equalization grant to municipalities based on fiscal need and fiscal capacity.

**Table 11.3** Provincial/territorial unconditional transfers by province/territory, 2023

| Province | Equalization | Revenue sharing | Other |
|---|---|---|---|
| British Columbia | Small community grant partially based on population and property assessment values | Traffic fines are shared based on a municipality's policing cost relative to total policing costs of all municipalities<br>Provincial gaming revenue is shared with local governments that host casinos and community gambling centres. Local governments receive 10% of net revenues from these establishments in their jurisdiction. | Regional district grants based on population. |
| Alberta | | | Capital grants for the two major cities (Calgary and Edmonton) are based on population (48%), education tax requisitions (48%), and kilometres of roads (4%). For other local governments, the formula is based on population (65%), tangible capital assets (15%), amortization of tangible capital assets (10%), and kilometres of roads (10%). Local governments also receive operating grants. |
| Saskatchewan | | Provincial sales tax sharing, distributed on a per-capita basis<br>Funds are split among the urban pool (cities, towns, villages, and resort villages); the rural pool (rural municipalities and organized hamlets); and the northern pool (northern municipalities)<br>For rural municipalities, the grant has three components: unconditional grant (based on population and roads data), organized hamlet grants (per capita), and conditional rural revenue sharing grants | |

(continued)

**Table 11.3** (continued)

| Province | Equalization | Revenue sharing | Other |
|---|---|---|---|
| Manitoba | | | Strategic Municipal Investment Fund to support operating expenses and infrastructure investments. |
| Ontario | Ontario Municipal Partnership Fund (OMPF): assessment equalization grant. The grant for each municipality is based on the total assessment differential, which is calculated as the total municipal assessment below the median per household amount.<br><br>OMPF northern and rural fiscal circumstances grant: The grant takes account of the fiscal circumstances of municipalities, using indicators for weighted assessment, median household income, change in assessment, employment, dependency ratio, and low-income population. | | Other OMPF components:<br>• per capita Northern communities grant<br>• per-household amount for small and rural communities based on percentage of population in rural and small communities plus additional grant for communities with large percent of farmland<br>• transitional assistance to guarantee support based on previous year's allocation. |
| Quebec | Equalization determined by a formula that provides funds to a municipality whose tax base is lower than a standard tax base. Additional funding is also provided for devitalized municipalities; 20 regional county municipalities are guaranteed a minimum amount based on fiscal circumstances. | Natural resources royalty revenue sharing with municipalities that have mining, oil, and gas production sites.<br><br>Share of the growth on one percentage point on Québec sales tax, starting in 2021, distributed on the basis of population and an index of economic vitality | Québec government reimburses 50% of the provincial sales tax paid by municipalities. |

(continued)

**Table 11.3** (continued)

| Province | Equalization | Revenue sharing | Other |
|---|---|---|---|
| New Brunswick | Equalization grant is 1 plus the difference in growth rate of the municipal tax base from the provincial tax base multiplied by the equalization grant from the previous year. Other community funding (core funding) to be phased out by 2027. | | |
| Nova Scotia | Equalization grant calculated as the difference between municipal operating per capacity cost (expenditure need) and the property assessment base (fiscal capacity). | | Towns receive a flat amount under the town foundation grant. |
| Prince Edward Island | Equalization grant based on taxable non-farm property assessment. | | |
| Newfoundland and Labrador | | | Grant based on population and remoteness index (based on proximity to services and daytime population during working hours). |
| Nunavut | Tax-based municipal corporations are eligible for equalization funds under the Municipal Funding Program to help with operating revenue. Amount is based on the municipality's ability to raise revenue through property taxes (based on factors such as number of dwelling units and property assessment), modified by the differential costs of providing services. | | Municipal Funding Program to non-tax-based communities to assist with delivering programs and services. The grant includes a basic grant based on population plus a community uniqueness factor (which includes road length), a municipal cost index and settlement allowance distinctive to each municipality, plus any approved forced growth funding. |

(continued)

**Table 11.3** (continued)

| Province | Equalization | Revenue sharing | Other |
|---|---|---|---|
| Northwest Territories | | | Under the Operations and Maintenance Funding, community costs are calculated by subtracting standard revenue from the total cost of delivery of community government services (excluding water and waste services). A community's proportionate share of funding is identified by comparing those costs to the sum of costs for all community governments. |
| Yukon | | | Funding under Comprehensive Municipal Grant uses a formula that includes factors such as population, properties, infrastructure, and the tax base of each incorporated municipalities. The grant is increased annually by the rate of inflation. |

Source: Bird and Slack (2021), Provincial and territorial government websites

Brunswick provides a grant based on an earlier equalization grant that is adjusted by the growth rate of the municipal tax base relative to the provincial tax base, and Nova Scotia, as noted above, is the only province that has an equalization grant based on fiscal capacity and expenditure need.[11] Nunavut provides equalization to tax-based municipal corporations based on fiscal capacity that is modified by the differential cost of providing services, in effect taking expenditure need into account.

The second type of unconditional transfer is provincial-local revenue sharing whereby provincial governments share their revenues with municipalities. Revenue sharing provides more reliable and predictable funding for municipalities than other unconditional transfers because the overall amount distributed increases annually with the increase in provincial revenues.

Revenue sharing occurs in two Canadian provinces—Saskatchewan and Quebec. In both provinces, the provincial government shares provincial sales tax revenues with municipalities. In Quebec, starting in 2021, the province shares the growth on

[11] As part of a major municipal restructuring in New Brunswick, the provincial government changed the equalization grant so that it is now calculated as 1 plus the difference in the growth rate of the municipal tax base from the provincial tax base multiplied by the equalization grant in the previous year.

one percentage point of the Quebec sales tax with municipalities. For 2023–24, the Government of Saskatchewan is sharing the equivalent of 0.75% of the provincial sales tax with municipalities.

Finally, there are unconditional transfers to municipalities that are based on the size of their population or other characteristics. For example, British Columbia provides grants to regional districts based on population. In Ontario, the Rural Communities Grant recognizes the unique challenges of rural municipalities and particularly those of rural farming communities; the Northern Communities Grant is also dedicated to northern communities. In Quebec, the province reimburses municipalities for 50% of the provincial sales tax that they pay. In Nova Scotia, towns receive a flat amount under a foundation grant and in Newfoundland and Labrador, municipalities receive a grant based on population and remoteness. In Alberta, municipalities receive grants based on population, kilometres of roads, and other factors.

### *11.2.4 Are There Different Vertical Fiscal Transfers for Urban and Rural Municipalities? If So, What Criteria Are Considered for Differentiation?*

Some provinces differentiate transfers for urban and rural municipalities. In Nova Scotia, for example, the equalization transfer (known as the municipal financial capacity grant) is determined by a formula that reflects the community's expenditure need and fiscal capacity.[12] The formula is applied separately to two classes of communities—Class I comprises regional municipalities and towns (the larger municipalities in the province) and Class II comprises county and district municipalities (smaller municipalities).[13] Municipalities are grouped into two classes to reflect differences in expenditures and revenue-raising capacities of municipalities of different size. Without these groupings, expenditure levels and revenue-raising capacity would exaggerate both fiscal needs and fiscal capacity in the formula because the average would be increased by the significantly higher expenditure levels and tax bases in the largest cities. As such, grouping municipalities controls for structural differences in fiscal need and fiscal capacity between smaller municipalities and large cities. Where capacity and need vary greatly, this approach avoids the imposition of an implicit common standard across all municipalities based on average fiscal capacity or standardized expenditure need.

[12] This description is based on the Nova Scotia Municipal Grants Act, Chapter 302 of the Revised Statutes, 1989, as amended and Municipal Grants Regulation made under Section 37 of the Municipal Grants Act, R.S.N.S. 1989, c. 302, O.I.C. 2024-111 (effective April 1, 2024), N.S. Reg. 72/2024.

[13] Prior to 2002, there were four classes: regional governments, large towns, small towns, and rural communities and districts.

Under section 10 (1) of the regulations under the Municipal Grants Act, the amount of grant to an individual municipality in Nova Scotia is calculated as the difference between the "derived standardized expenditure for the municipality" and the revenue calculated by a standard residential tax rate for the residential class multiplied by the residential uniform assessment for the municipality added to a standard commercial tax rate multiplied by the commercial uniform assessment for the municipality. Standard expenditures are calculated from estimates of operating expenditures as follows: "(a) 50% of general government services, not including valuation allowances; (b) protective services; (c) transportation services; (d) environmental health services; (c) 50% of recreation and cultural services; (f) environmental development services."

Standardized tax rates, as indicated above, include one for residential and one for commercial properties. Under 9 (1) of the regulations, the standard residential tax rate is calculated by multiplying "the total derived standardized expenditure for all municipalities in the class for which the standard residential rate is being calculated" by "the average proportion of residential uniform assessment in the class" all divided by "the total residential uniform assessment for all municipalities in the class for which the standard residential rate is being calculated." A similar calculation is used for the determination of the standard commercial rate. Under section 8 (1) of the regulations, uniform assessment (after adjusting for some exemptions) is equal to "the taxable assessment of the municipality minus 25% of the taxable assessment of commercial properties identified on the assessment roll as being occupied by a seasonal tourist business plus the capitalized value of payments made to the municipality in lieu of taxes and tax payments made to the municipality by a utility."[14] One criticism of this formula is that it does not include other own-source revenues, such as user fees.

As noted in the regulations,[15] "under the transitional support program, if the amount obtained for a municipality under subsection 11(2) is less than the amount received by the municipality for its financial capacity grant for the 2014–15 fiscal year, then the difference between those amounts will be provided to that municipality each year for the period specified in subsection (1)." This provision means that municipalities that no longer need equalization according to the formula are receiving funds at the expense of those that do need it (Bird & Slack, 2021).

Revenue sharing in Saskatchewan splits funds between different categories of municipalities—urban (cities, towns, villages and resort villages); rural (rural municipalities and organized hamlets); and Northern municipalities. There are three parts to the rural municipalities and organized hamlets grant: an unconditional grant based on a combination of transportation/road needs and population; an organized hamlet grant, which is a percentage of the grant received by towns, villages and

[14] In Canada, the federal and provincial governments are not required to pay property taxes to municipalities or school boards. The federal government makes payments in lieu of property taxes on its properties. Payments in lieu of property taxes by provincial governments varies across the country.

[15] See footnote 12 above for the reference.

resort villages; and a grant for communities in transition from a village to a rural municipality.

In Newfoundland and Labrador, the unconditional grant is based on population and remoteness, using a remoteness index to measure how accessible (or remote) a community is. The index is calculated as a weighted average of the community's proximity to a number of general services and the estimated daytime population during normal working hours.

In Alberta, a new capital grant introduced in 2024 under the Local Government Fiscal Framework has a different formula for the two largest cities (Edmonton and Calgary) compared to the rest of the province. For the two largest cities, the formula is based on population (48%), education tax requisitions (48%), and road kilometres (4%). For the rest of the province, the formula is based on population (60%), tangible capital assets (15%), amortization of tangible capital assets (10%), and road kilometres (10%).

Tax-based municipal corporations are differentiated from non-tax-based communities in Nunavut. Tax-based corporations receive equalization based on their ability to raise revenue through property taxes (based on factors such as number of dwelling units and property assessment), modified by the differential costs of providing services. In non-tax-based communities, there is a basic grant based on population plus a uniqueness factor (which includes a variable for road length), a municipal cost index, and settlement allowance in each municipality.

In some provinces, there is no differentiation between urban and rural municipalities. Quebec has a fairly small equalization program for municipalities. The equalization grant is based on fiscal capacity and has two parts. A municipality is eligible for the first part of the grant if its standardized property value per capita is less than 80% of the median value for all municipalities. The second part of the grant, which targets fewer municipalities, provides funds to a municipality if the average value of the dwellings situated in its territory is less than 70% of the median value of all municipalities. There is no measure of need in the formula except to the extent that population reflects the need to make expenditures.

Prince Edward Island makes an annual Municipal Support Grant payment, which includes a Municipal Services Grant and equalization funding. The formula for equalization multiplies the municipality's population by the difference between the average PEI municipal property assessment per capita and the municipality's property assessment per capita, multiplied by the municipality's non-commercial property tax rate. Farm property is excluded from the calculation. Since 2017, the annual increase in the grant reflects the average increase in municipal property assessments.

### *11.2.5 Are There Specific Funds for Rural Municipalities?*

Many provincial governments allocate specific grants for small and/or rural municipalities. These grants are designed to reflect the challenges faced by these communities that may be more sparsely developed, more remote, and experiencing colder weather. These challenges result in higher costs for heating, housing, and transportation, and the inability to achieve economies of scale in the provision of services. These municipalities are also likely to have smaller tax bases (less fiscal capacity).

Unconditional transfers are provided by the provincial government of Ontario under the Ontario Municipal Partnership Fund (OMPF). These transfers only go to small, rural, and remote communities in Ontario, although large and urban municipalities do receive conditional transfers (mainly for social services and transportation). OMPF provides funding to 389 of the 444 municipalities in the province.[16] OMPF comprises four grants, two of which are equalization grants, plus a transition grant to guarantee a level of support based on the previous year's allocation. The four grants are:

- The Assessment Equalization Grant provides funding to municipalities with a limited property tax base because overall property values are low or because there is limited non-residential assessment.[17] The grant to each eligible municipality is determined by its total property assessment differential (i.e., the total municipal assessment below the median per-household threshold). Increments in a municipality's assessment differential result in an additional amount of funding. This grant is a fairly straightforward fiscal capacity equalization grant; there is no component to reflect expenditure needs.
- The Northern and Rural Fiscal Circumstances Grant provides additional funding to those northern and rural municipalities that face relatively more challenging fiscal circumstances than others in this category as measured by the Northern and Rural Municipal Fiscal Circumstances Index (MFCI). The MFCI is determined on the basis of two primary indicators, which account for 50% of the index (25% on the basis of weighted assessment per household and 25% on the basis of median household income) and four secondary indicators, each accounting for 12.5% of the index (average annual change in assessment, employment rate, ratio of working age to dependent population, and percent of population above low-income threshold). An indicator value that is above the median will have a positive score, which is reflective of relatively positive fiscal circumstances. An indicator value below the median will have a negative score, suggesting relatively negative fiscal circumstances. The MFCI is determined based on the average indicator score for a municipality and is measured on a scale from 0 to 10.

  The Northern and Rural Fiscal Circumstances Grant formula is based on a small number of variables over which municipalities have no direct control, so they cannot influence the size of the grant. These variables attempt to capture the abil-

[16] For more details, see https://www.ontario.ca/document/2023-ontario-municipal-partnership-fund/technical-guide. Accessed 6 November 2023.

[17] Because non-residential properties are levied a higher tax rate than residential properties, a municipality with a large proportion of non-residential property is considered to have greater fiscal capacity.

ity of municipalities to make expenditures through both "capacity" variables such as weighted assessment, changes in assessment, and median income and also to some extent "need" variables such as the percentage of the population above the low-income threshold, dependency ratios, and the employment rate. Although the formula is based on only six variables, the calculation of the overall index is very complex and hard to follow.

- The Rural Communities Grant provides a grant to rural communities and especially rural farm communities, based on the proportion of the population that resides in rural areas and/or small communities, as measured by the Rural and Small Community Measure (RSCM). Municipalities with an RSCM of 75% or more receive a per household amount; municipalities with an RSCM between 25% and 75% receive a portion of this funding on a sliding scale.
- The Northern Communities Grant is a per-household grant to all northern municipalities in recognition of the unique challenges they face.

British Columbia provides a Small Community Protection Grant, which is a formula-based grant that goes to small municipalities with a population up to 19,000. The grant includes a base amount plus an equalization component (calculated by multiplying a dollar amount by a property assessment weighting factor), and an amount based on population.

Table 11.3 summarizes the provincial-municipal unconditional grant programs by province and territory.

## 11.3 Is There Any Form of Direct Horizontal Transfers Between Municipalities?

Fiscal disparities exist among jurisdictions within regional or metropolitan areas, especially those that are characterized by a large number of small local government units. The reason is that some local government jurisdictions in a metropolitan area will have high-income communities and some will have low-income communities. High-income communities will be able to provide better services at lower tax rate because they have a larger tax base and may face lower demands for services. Low-income communities may face the opposite situation where they have a smaller tax base and greater demand for services (Slack, 2017).

Direct horizontal transfers between municipalities in Canada are not common, but there are examples of implicit equalization or redistribution in metropolitan and regional districts through the creation of a regional or metropolitan government. To address inequities within metropolitan areas, one option has been to consolidate rich and poor municipalities and, in effect, tax the richer municipalities to help subsidize poorer municipalities. Metropolitan governments could be large enough in scale to raise and redistribute revenue within their own region (Slack, 2017). To the extent that a regional or metropolitan government levies taxes that are collected across the area and makes expenditures in different parts of the area, there will be implicit redistribution in the sense that there is not necessarily a direct correspondence between where the taxes are paid and where benefits are received from local services.

Canada has experience with three different governance models to address the fiscal disparities among local jurisdictions in a metropolitan region—a one-tier consolidated government model (through annexation, consolidation, or amalgamation), a two-tier government model, and a shared service delivery model.[18] In a one-tier consolidated government there is one local government with a geographic boundary that covers the entire metropolitan area and provides all of the local services.

The advantage of a consolidated model is the larger metropolitan tax base for sharing the costs of services. The result is that the availability of services does not depend on the wealth of each of the jurisdictions that make up the consolidated local government (Slack, 2019). Amalgamation means that all the municipalities in the region, rich or poor, can enjoy an adequate level of services at a reasonable tax rate. In other words, consolidation leads to a redistribution of resources across the region.

The amalgamation of Toronto, the largest city in Canada, in 1998 provides one example. The history of municipal amalgamation in Toronto goes back to 1954 with the creation of a two-tier metropolitan government (a metropolitan tier and 13 lower-tier municipalities). In 1967, the 13 municipalities were merged into six and, in 1998, the metropolitan tier and six lower tiers were amalgamated to create a single-tier City of Toronto. Although there have been many criticisms of the amalgamation, it did result in some redistribution within the metropolitan area, increasing equity among residents in terms of service levels and tax burden (Slack & Bird, 2013).

Another example of an amalgamation is the Halifax Regional Municipality (HRM) in 1996, which merged urban, suburban, and rural areas. The Halifax case is particularly interesting because the regional municipality levies different residential property tax rates for urban areas, suburban areas, and rural areas, with the highest rate in urban areas where there are more services. Similarly, commercial property tax rates differ according to whether they are in urban or rural parts of the municipality (and also by the size of the property assessment).

Fiscal disparities are also addressed in a metropolitan region by implementing a two-tier government model where there is an upper-tier governing body (usually a region, district, or metropolitan area) that encompasses a fairly large geographic area and two or more lower-tier or area municipalities (such as cities, towns, or villages). Under this model, redistribution happens at the upper-tier level which is responsible for services that provide region-wide benefits, generate externalities,

---

[18] For a more detailed discussion of metropolitan governance models, see Slack (2019) and Slack and Côté (2014).

and display economies of scale. Services that provide local benefits are the responsibility of the lower tier.

Redistribution is achieved at the upper-tier level through a combination of tax and spending policies. Taxes are generally levied at uniform rates across the region, with the contribution of each lower-tier municipality to the upper-tier municipality dependent on the size of its tax base. The upper-tier government makes expenditures on services that benefit the entire city-region and those benefits are not necessarily distributed among the lower-tier municipalities in the same way as revenues are collected. A uniform tax at the upper-tier level combined with region-wide expenditures serves to redistribute resources from municipalities with larger tax bases to those with smaller tax bases. Nevertheless, there may still be differentiation in service levels and tax rates with respect to services provided by lower-tier municipalities.

Many of the regions in Ontario outside of Toronto are two-tier, such as York, Halton, Durham, Peel, Waterloo, and Niagara. There are also two-tier regional districts in British Columbia. For example, Metro Vancouver comprises 21 municipalities, one electoral area, and one treaty First Nation. It is governed by a board of directors of elected officials from each of the member jurisdictions. Metro Vancouver plans and delivers regional utility services (water, sewers, wastewater treatment), solid waste management, planning, regional parks, and affordable housing. Unlike the Ontario model, however, participation in regional functions by the lower-tier municipalities is voluntary (Spicer, 2022).

Finally, shared service models are sometimes used to deliver specific services that cross municipal boundaries. For example, Consolidated Municipal Service Managers (CMSMs) in Ontario are an integrated system of services for welfare, childcare, social housing, land ambulance (and sometimes public health). There are 47 CMSMs (including District Social Service Administration Boards in the northern part of the province) in the province that has 444 municipalities. The costs of these services are shared on the basis of population, size of the tax base, or some other factor that they choose. As with the other models, shared service models may result in some redistribution.

## 11.4 Conclusions

In Canada, the bulk of transfers to municipalities come from provincial/territorial governments and most of these grants are conditional. These transfers may be appropriate where the benefits of services spill over municipal boundaries and municipalities are unable to cover all of the costs from their own revenues, or where the province wants to ensure that its priorities are met. They are not well suited for general support, however. Although provincial/territorial governments generally provide some unconditional support, none really delivers sufficient equalization grants to ensure that all local governments can provide a level of services of at least minimal acceptable quality, provided they exploit their own tax bases sufficiently.

Equalization also exists in Canada through implicit redistribution that occurs with the amalgamation of urban and rural municipalities or the creation of service delivery agents. Although the fiscal capacity of rural municipalities is not generally equal to that of urban municipalities, equalization transfers and municipal consolidations are designed to help smaller and rural municipalities provide a reasonable level of service by levying reasonable tax rates.

## References

Adams, E., & Maslove, A. (2014). The federal gas tax cession: From advocacy efforts to thirteen signed agreements. In C. Andrew & K. Graham (Eds.), *Canada in cities: The politics and policy of federal-local governance* (pp. 102–130). McGill-Queen's University Press.

Bird, R., & Slack, E. (2021). Provincial-local equalization in Canada: Time for a change? *IMFG Papers on Municipal Finance and Governance, 57*, 1–35. https://tspace.library.utoronto.ca/bitstream/1807/108373/1/imfgpaper_no57_provincialmunicipalequalization_richardmbird_enidslack_nov_24_2021.pdf

Bradford, N. (2018). A national urban policy for Canada? The implicit federal agenda. *IRPP Insight* (24).

Fenge, R., & Meier, V. (2001). Why cities should not be subsidized. *CESifo Working Paper* (546).

Hobson, P., Cameron, D., & Locke, W. (2005). *A question of balance—An assessment of the state of local government in Nova Scotia*. A discussion paper prepared for The Union of Nova Scotia Municipalities as part of their Fair and Equitable Funding Project.

Kitchen, H. (1984). *Local government finance in Canada*. Canadian Tax Foundation.

Kitchen, H. (2002). *Municipal revenue and expenditure issues in Canada*. Canadian Tax Foundation.

Kitchen, H., & Slack, E. (2006). Providing public services in remote areas. In R. Bird & F. Vaillancourt (Eds.), *Perspectives in fiscal federalism* (pp. 123–139). World Bank Institute.

Slack, E. (2017). The geography of local public finance. In R. Martin & J. Pollard (Eds.), *Handbook on the geographies of money and finance* (pp. 253–278). Edward Elgar Publishing Limited.

Slack, E. (2019). *Metropolitan governance: Principles and practice*. Institutions for Development Sector, Fiscal Management Division, Inter-Amercian Development Bank Discussion Paper (IDB-DP-659).

Slack, E., & Bird, R. (2013). Merging municipalities: Is bigger better? *IMFG Papers on Municipal Finance and Governance* (14).

Slack, E., & Côté, A. (2014). *Comparative urban governance*. Foresight, UK Department for Business Innovation and Skills.

Slack, E., & Taylor, Z. (2024). Canada. In N. Steytler (Ed.), *The Forum of Federations handbook on local government in federal systems* (pp. 149–176). Palgrave Macmillan.

Spicer, Z. (2022). Organizing Canadian local government. *Future of Municipal Government Series, 1*, 1–22.

Statistics Canada. (2022). *Population growth in Canada's rural areas, 2016 to 2021*. Retrieved November 6, 2023, from https://www12.statcan.gc.ca/census-recensement/2021/as-sa/98-200-x/2021002/98-200-x2021002-eng.cfm

Statistics Canada. (2023). *Canadian government finance statistics for municipalities and other local public administrations*. Table 10-10-0020-01. Retrieved January 25, 2024, from https://www150.statcan.gc.ca/t1/tbl1/en/tv.action?pid=1010002001

Taylor, Z., & Slack, E. (2024, forthcoming). Canada. In N. Steytler (Ed.), *Handbook on local government in federal systems*. Palgrave Macmillan.

# Chapter 12
# The Italian Way of Inter-municipal Equalization

**Alice Valdesalici and Francisco Javier Romero Caro**

**Abstract** This chapter deals with the equalization mechanisms established in Italy to address horizontal imbalances among local entities, paying particular attention to inter-municipal redistribution schemes, emphasizing differences between urban and rural local governments. The strong constitutional asymmetry characterizing the regional scenario and the overall system of territorial organization is, among other things, also reflected in the system of local finance and, as such, in the related equalization schemes. Thus, this chapter first explores the local financing system in the ordinary regions, which is characterized by a high degree of centralization, paying special attention to the Municipal Solidarity Fund. It then deals with the special regions, that have their own systems of inter-municipal equalization. Finally, it also covers equalization in provinces and metropolitan cities.

**Keywords** Equalization · Italy · Local government · Solidarity · Local finances

The chapter has been conceived in common by the two authors, nevertheless Sects. 12.1 and 12.2 can be ascribed to Alice Valdesalici, Sect. 12.4 to Francisco Javier Romero Caro, whereas Sects. 12.3 and 12.5 have been jointly drafted. The authors would like to thank Chiara Serioli for her assistance in the elaboration of this chapter.

A. Valdesalici (✉) · F. J. Romero Caro
Institute for Comparative Federalism, Eurac Research, Bolzano/Bozen, Italy
e-mail: alice.valdesalici@eurac.edu; franciscojavier.romerocaro@eurac.edu



F. Velasco Caballero et al. (eds.), *Municipal Tasks and Financing*, Local and Urban Governance, https://doi.org/10.1007/978-3-031-99812-6_12

## 12.1 Introduction

In Italy, local finance in ordinary regions, Sicily and Sardinia included,[1] is under the legislative responsibility of the national level of government: local revenues depend on decisions adopted by the central authority as both the power over taxation and equalization concentrate mainly at the center, with little—if any—involvement of local and subnational governments in the decision-making process thereof (Alber & Valdesalici, 2023, 283–286). In fact, the level of participation of local and regional authorities in the decision-making process over finance continues to be rather weak despite efforts towards increasing their involvement via the State-Cities and Local Authorities Conference (*Conferenza Stato-città ed autonomie locali*).[2] On top of that, the condition of fiscal dependency of the regions from the national government emphasizes this trajectory further (Ambrosanio & Bordignon, 2020). The fact that the regional power to tax is also very limited boosts the supremacy of the national over the subnational authorities in determining the scope and functioning of local finance.

According to Article 119 of the Constitution,[3] local entities of ordinary Regions–which also means Municipalities–are financed through own tax sources, shared taxes, not-earmarked equalization transfers, plus additional (specific-purpose) grants provided for extra-ordinary circumstances. Beyond equalization transfers, municipalities largely should lack additional transfers with few exceptions. For instance, measures have been enacted to support municipalities with fewer than 5000 inhabitants, which are mostly of an eminently rural nature. In 2017, the Fund for Structural, Economic and Social Development was established and distributed based on criteria that safeguarded the environment, cultural heritage, and the economic and social development of small municipalities.[4] Other funds for economically disadvantaged municipalities (those at risk of depopulation, that suffer from social deprivation or that have low-income levels) have been implemented, particularly benefitting the undeveloped South of Italy.[5] In the same vein, to address the challenge of population

[1] Although Sicily and Sardinia are special regions under Article 116 of the Italian Constitution, local finance in these regions follow a model analogous to that of the ordinary regions.

[2] The State-Regions Conference meets in Unified Conference with the State-Cities Conference "for matters and tasks of common interest of the regions, provinces, municipalities and mountain communities, with the State-regions Conference" (Article 8(1) Legislative Decree 281/97).

[3] In the text approved by the 2001 constitutional reform and progressively entering into force.

[4] This fund, established by Law 158/2017, was later developed in 2022 with the establishment of a national plan for the development of small municipalities (*Piano nazionale per la riqualificazione dei piccoli comuni*) by the Decree of the President of the Council of Ministers May 16, 2022.

[5] The Support Fund for Marginal Municipalities (*Fondo di sostegno ai comuni marginali*) was established in 2020 in order to promote social cohesion and economic development in municipalities particularly affected by the phenomenon of depopulation and that are affected by the lack of attractiveness due to the reduced offer of tangible and intangible services to people and economic activity, in compliance complementarity with the national strategy for inland areas.

decline in small municipalities, reduced taxation schemes have been introduced for foreign residents moving to the southern regions.

This special attention toward small municipalities is due to the marked cleavage between urban and rural areas in Italy. About 70% of Italian municipalities have less than 5000 inhabitants (5534 out of 7901) (Istat, 2023), and mountainous municipalities account for half of the municipalities in Italy, with 3524 being "totally mountainous" and 652 "partially mountainous", for an overall total of 4176 mountainous municipalities. Furthermore, a substantially higher per capita income is confirmed in large urban centers compared to municipalities with fewer than 5000 inhabitants. For instance, in 2021, the average per capita income in municipalities with fewer than 5000 inhabitants was €18,371, while it amounted to €25,528 for municipalities with over 250,000 inhabitants, €22,878 for those between 100,000 and 250,000, and €20,341 for those between 50,000 and 100,000 inhabitants.[6]

Concerning financing for provinces and metropolitan cities, the system is built upon the same sources, i.e. devolved and shared taxes, complemented by transfers from the experimental fund for provincial financial consolidation. However, the legal framework is intricate and uncertain. Austerity measures have led to diminishing transfers for provinces, compounded by ongoing territorial reorganization efforts that alter the functions assigned to the provincial level. For metropolitan cities, despite their establishment by Law 56/2014, their financing systems remains undefined, maintaining a provincial structure with insufficient resources and resulting in underfunded mandates.[7]

Despite demographic, territorial and socio-economic differences, all local entities of a specific type are endowed with the same responsibilities and operate under the same financing system. (Palermo, 2021, 143–147).

At the same time, the system as it is described above refers only to local entities located in ordinary regions. In special regions a different set of rules applies.[8] On the one hand, their system of financing is the result of bilateral negotiations with the national government, while respecting the fundamental principles set by the national law. Overall, the financial autonomy of special regions is greater in scope but the systems thereof vary significantly from one another. On the other hand, not all special regions are responsible for local finance. In certain cases, (Sicily and Sardinia), this is a central state competence. Despite these differences, it is a responsibility of all regions (special and ordinary) to ensure adherence to the balanced budget principle, considering all entities within their respective regional territories.

Against this overall framework, this chapter deals with the equalization mechanisms established in Italy to address horizontal imbalances among local entities, paying particular attention to inter-municipal redistribution schemes, emphasizing

---

[6] Source: MEF—Ministero dell'Economia e delle Finanza. More info at: https://www.intwig.it/reddito-degli-italiani-2021-torna-a-crescere-classifica-comuni-regioni/ (accessed on 5 March 2024).

[7] *Commissione Parlamentare per l'Attuazione del Federalismo Fiscale, 'Resoconto Stenografico'* (Audizione 99, 23 February 2017).

[8] On the genesis of the special regions in Italy and its distinctive status, see Palermo (2008, 33–45).

differences between urban and rural local governments. The ordinary system will be analyzed in Sect. 12.2, whereas Sect. 12.3 deals with local finance in special regions, with the exception of Sardinia and Sicily, which in this field behave as if they were ordinary regions. The strong constitutional asymmetry characterizing the regional scenario and the overall system of territorial organization is, among other things, also reflected in the system of local finance and, as such, in the related equalization schemes. Finally, Sect. 12.4 examines equalization in provinces and metropolitan cities.

## 12.2 The Legal Framework and the Foundation of Local Finance

Starting in 2009, transfers to local entities have been progressively reduced and replaced with own revenue sources (Valdesalici, 2021a, 84–85). At this point, the only type of transfers local entities should be receiving are the ones coming from equalization funds, with minor exceptions. Pursuant to the Constitution, local authorities in Italy—i.e. municipalities, provinces, and metropolitan cities—shall be financed by means of own tax sources, shared taxes, not-earmarked equalization transfers, plus additional transfers provided for exceptional cases (Article 119 of the Constitution). In addition, this provision prescribes that the national law sets up an equalization fund with no strings attached to foster territories with a lower per capita fiscal capacity. (Article 119(3) of the Constitution). The national authority has the exclusive legislative power over it, as equalization is a competence of the center (Article 117(2) of the Constitution). According to the Constitution, no other vertical transfers are permitted, but in extraordinary circumstances specific-purpose grants can be allocated to singled-out entities (Article 119(5) of the Constitution).

This constitutional framework is the result of a constitutional amendment approved in 2001 and only later implemented partly by Law 42/2009, partly by a series of governmental decrees.[9] Law 42/2009 prescribes the gradual dismantling of the preexisting funding scheme, which grounds the transfers on the resources spent in the previous financial exercise (so-called historic spending). The latter should be replaced by a set of criteria linked to pre-defined benchmarks and generally applied indicators (so-called standard costs and needs), which should be introduced to standardize territorial financing and foster efficiency and accountability (Antonini, 2009).

As outlined in Article 11 of Law 42/2009, inter-municipal equalization is based on two distinct mechanisms, which rely on a dual classification of local functions. A first mechanism pursue the funding of fundamental functions (approximately 80% of local spending), whereas a second mechanism is designed for other

[9] On the evolution of the Italian Constitution and its (successful and failed) reforms, see Cartabia and Lupo (2022).

(non-fundamental) functions (20% of local spending).[10] The scope of equalization is variable: full equalization is provided for fundamental functions, while partial equalization is realized for non-fundamental functions. The financing parameters also differ: transfers for fundamental functions are calculated using the 'standard costs and needs' criteria, whereas the per-capita fiscal capacity is applied as funding parameter for non-fundamental functions.

In Italy, the equalization of financial resources and the determination of fundamental functions of local entities are listed under the exclusive legislative competences of the national level. However, the Parliament has delegated to the Executive the detailed regulation of equalization mechanisms, including methodology and parameter definitions (e.g., Law Decree 216/2010 as later amended). Additionally, a public-private company (SOSE) is tasked with the calculation of the standard costs and needs for each fundamental function, taking into account the specificities of each function and the various categories of entities (e.g., the size of municipalities).

Over 20 years later, the transformations promoted by the constitutional reform are still a work in progress. Indeed, a clear path towards effective implementation has finally been embarked upon, specifically in relation to local governments and, more precisely, municipalities. It is not by chance that municipal finance has experienced a far-reaching structural metamorphosis during the decade from 2010 to 2019. This is marked by a robust increase in local taxes, a decrease in state transfers, tight budgetary constraints, and uncertainty in the regulatory framework of reference (IFEL, 2021, 41). In 2010, own municipal taxes accounted for 29.9% of total revenue, whereas transfers amounted to 45.5% (34.8% if merely current transfers are considered). In comparison, in 2019, local revenues consisted of 44.9% of tax-revenue and 32.5% of transfers (21.7% if limited to current transfers) (IFEL, 2021, 43). This is the result of changes introduced by the national authority to cope with austerity obligations set forth at the European level, with particular strength from 2012 onwards.

Despite this overall change, local finance is still based for the largest part on the so-called devolved taxes, that is tax-revenue sources set and regulated in their foundations by the central government. Local authorities are vested with a limited tax-varying power, which is mostly determined and constrained in its scope by the national government. Their margin of maneuver can typically affect either the tax rate or the tax benefits, within the limits fixed by the national legislation. Own taxes under the exclusive (or better extended) authority of local governments are the exception, with the tourist tax being one example (Tables 12.1 and 12.2).

The data reported in the tables below provide evidence of two prominent features of local finance in Italy, namely the economic gap between the north and the south of the country, and the differences, also in economic terms, between urban and rural municipalities. Regarding the North/South cleavage, given 262.8 EUR as the

[10] The determination of the fundamental functions of local entities to be guaranteed in a uniform manner across the country is listed under the exclusive legislative competence of the national authority pursuant to Article 117(2) of the Constitution.

**Table 12.1** Municipal per capita revenues in ordinary regions, including Sicily and Sardinia (in EUR per capita)

| Ordinary region (including Sicily and Sardinia) | Tax receipts | Current transfers | Of which: Municipal solidarity fund (MSF)[a] | Total[b] |
|---|---|---|---|---|
| Piedmont | 576.5 | 202.3 | 118.3 | 1202.7 |
| Lombardy | 551.3 | 180.5 | 82.9 | 1265.7 |
| Liguria | 836.7 | 218.2 | 119.5 | 1593.9 |
| Veneto | 473.5 | 190.2 | 94.4 | 1045.5 |
| Emilia-Romagna | 604.9 | 217.1 | 119.5 | 1245.87 |
| Toscana | 675.9 | 185.4 | 108.9 | 1364.8 |
| Umbria | 590 | 264.2 | 135.3 | 1242.3 |
| Marche | 529.4 | 328.1 | 116.5 | 1320.9 |
| Lazio | 771.1 | 315.9 | 79.7 | 1568 |
| Abruzzo | 548.5 | 279.8 | 114.7 | 1626.9 |
| Molise | 468.6 | 303.7 | 150.4 | 1332.4 |
| Campania | 506.5 | 284 | 175.1 | 1292.9 |
| Puglia | 520.9 | 245.1 | 114.1 | 1036.9 |
| Basilicata | 375.9 | 381.5 | 192.7 | 1304.2 |
| Calabria | 460.8 | 335.2 | 175.8 | 1365.4 |
| Sicily | 547.2 | 380.7 | 128.6 | 1280.5 |
| Sardinia | 520.3 | 715.4 | 80.4 | 1631.3 |
| **TOTAL ordinary regions (including Sicily and Sardinia)** | **575** | **262.8** | **113.8** | **1298** |

Source: own elaboration from data taken from IFEL (2021, 20–21)

[a] The Municipal Solidarity Fund forms part of the current transfers together with other transfer payments from central and local administration

[b] The total is defined as the sum of current transfers + capital revenue + revenue from reduction of financial assets + borrowing

**Table 12.2** Municipal per capita revenues in ordinary regions (including Sicily and Sardinia) per population band (in EUR)

| Population bands | Tax receipts | Current transfers | Of which: Municipal solidarity fund (MSF)[a] | Total[b] |
|---|---|---|---|---|
| 0–1000 | 552.6 | 518.5 | 216.6 | 2179.9 |
| 1001–5000 | 465.2 | 301.7 | 139.3 | 1306.5 |
| 5001–10,000 | 480.6 | 191.2 | 85.6 | 1032.9 |
| 10,001–20,000 | 495.1 | 178.9 | 88.6 | 1015.3 |
| 20,001–60,000 | 535.4 | 209.4 | 94.4 | 1062.1 |
| 60,001–100,000 | 574.1 | 248.3 | 125.6 | 1215.8 |
| 100,001–250,000 | 633.8 | 311.1 | 146.3 | 1353.1 |
| >250,000 | 866.7 | 409.9 | 137.3 | 2059.7 |

Source: own elaboration from data taken from IFEL (2021, 20–21)

[a] The Municipal Solidarity Fund forms part of the current transfers together with other transfer payments from central and local administration

[b] The total is defined as the sum of current transfers + capital revenue + revenue from reduction of financial assets + borrowing

average value of current per capita transfers to municipalities calculated on a regional base, all regions in the North and Center receive an amount below the average, whereas those in the South (with the exception of Puglia) are assigned an amount exceeding the average, with peaks reaching up to EUR 715 in the case of Sardinia. A similar trend is confirmed with specific reference to transfers from the municipal solidarity fund. With an average value per capita of 113.8, on a regional basis, values below or slightly above the average are found in the North and Center, whereas, the gap widens moving South, with values well above the average, with the interesting exception of Lazio. Regarding the urban/rural divide, instead, a decreasing of transfers is showcased as the population increases and this occurs up to the maximum threshold of 20,000 inhabitants. After that, the trend reverses, and the per capita values start increasing along with the increase in population. This applies to both current transfers and solidarity fund resources and might probably have to do with the economies of scale, considered the fact that all municipalities in ordinary regions (incl. Sicily and Sardinaia) are vested with the same competences, disregarding their even huge differences in terms of demographic size. The fact that the above illustrated trend regarding the urban/rural divide is validated observing data from 2015 to 2021, contributes to confirming the hypothesis above formulated about the determinants of such trajectory.

### *12.2.1 The Municipal Solidarity Fund*

Inter-municipal equalization in ordinary regions takes place through the Municipal Solidarity Fund (*Fondo di Solidarietà Comunale*), which was set up by the Stability Law 2013 (Law 228/2012), and later modified by the Stability Law 2014 (Law 147/2013, paragraph 729). However, the transition towards the new system only started in 2015 when equalization criteria were introduced in the distribution of resources by taking standard needs as a parameter. From 2015 onwards, increasing shares of the fund have been allocated on the basis of the difference between fiscal capacities and standard needs, with the ultimate aim to allocate 100% of the resources applying the new equalizing parameters by 2030. In 2023, the share was 65%.

The Municipal Solidarity Fund is composed of two parts. The compensatory component consists of a transfer from the national government, which is meant to compensate municipalities for the loss of revenue that occurred because of changes in municipal taxation (e.g. exemptions and concessions) introduced by the central legislator. This first part is complemented by the, so to speak, "traditional component", which is designed to rebalance historical resources (i.e. the resources that municipalities obtained under the previous system) and includes resources which are distributed partly on the basis of historical spending criteria and partly (from 2015 onwards) on the basis of equalization criteria.

The financial endowment of the fund is composed of a share of the revenues generated from the local tax on properties (IMU), accounting in 2013 for 38.23% of the revenue thereof (4.7 billion EUR), and of a state transfer of 1.9 billion EUR. This financial arrangement was later revised to adapt to the changes made by the 2016 Stability Law (Law 208/2015) on property taxation. The new regime of tax benefits entailed a redefinition of the solidarity fund, providing for both an increase of the restorative share (approximately up to 3.8 billion EUR) to compensate municipalities for the lower revenues allocated to them, and a reduction in the IMU share intended for the fund (reduced to 2.8 billion EUR, i.e. the 22.43% of the revenue thereof). As of 2017, the overall annual endowment of the fund has been set at 6.19 billion EUR, then brought to 6.2 billion EUR as of 2018. As of 2020, the restorative share has been further reduced (14.2 million EUR), following the cancellation by the national legislature of some tax benefits on local taxes. At the same time, the overall resources of the fund have gradually increased from 2020 onwards to a total of 7.1 billion EUR in 2023 as a restoration of the resources withdrawn from the fund from 2014 to 2018. These additional resources (380 million EUR in 2023 and 560 million EUR for 2024) flow into the traditional component of the fund, thus replenishing the vertical component of equalization, that is, the one financed by the national level of government. In comparison, the IMU share is to be understood as a horizontal component of the equalization mechanism.

The financial composition of the fund is subject to frequent changes. In fact, it is determined on an annual basis by law. Also, by law or by ministerial decree, increases or decreases in the fund's allocation may be adopted to take account of actual municipal tax revenues. Changes to the fund's financial endowment and, in particular, to the prime minister's decree for the distribution of the fund are adopted following an agreement reached within the State-Cities and Local Authorities Conference, which represents local authorities on a national base. Despite this procedure, the involvement of local authorities in decision-making remains weak. Not only can the decree be issued even if no agreement is reached within 15 days after submission of the proposal to the Conference, but conference-based consultation mechanisms raise several problems. The decision-making procedure tends to be too cumbersome and slow, and there is a general lack of transparency with regard to the agenda and the related decisions. Moreover, decisions have mere consultative value, and the national government is not legally bound by them; finally, being based within the national cabinet, this raises problems of autonomy and independence of this intergovernmental institution. The Conference is the only institutionalized mechanism through which the executives of the local governments meet regularly with the members of the national and regional governments, yet although of paramount importance to the political process, it is—as a mechanism—not well-oiled (Alber et al., 2024). Discussions entail primarily technical issues rather than political trajectories, and in most cases, decisions have de facto already been made elsewhere, i.e. at other levels of government (Carpani, 2009).

From 2020, specific-purpose resources have also been added. For instance, an increase of 5.5 million EUR has been foreseen to introduce a correction to the fund allocation mechanism in favor of small and mostly rural municipalities with a population of less than 5000 inhabitants, in the event that they have a negative value when distributing the resources in application of the equalization criteria. An annual increase of 2 million EUR was also introduced for 2020–2022 to be allocated to mountain municipalities with a population of less than 5000 inhabitants as compensation for the IMU share that they are required to allocate to the fund itself. Although these measures do not make explicit the distinction between large cities and the surrounding rural municipalities, they actually end up as a measure benefiting rural municipalities, or rather mountain municipalities. In Italy, mountain municipalities make up 43.7% of the total number of municipal authorities. Of these, more than 96% are mountain municipalities with less than 10,000 inhabitants, and 64.5% of the smaller municipalities (with 0–2000 inhabitants) are mountainous. As the demographic size increases, mountain municipalities decrease in number. Contrariwise, there is a directly proportional relationship between the percentage of non-mountainous municipalities with respect to the total number of municipalities belonging to each demographic size: for instance, the 12 largest cities are classified as non-mountainous municipalities, while only 35.2% of very small municipalities are not mountainous.

A significant increase in the annual budget for local finance was also introduced in 2021, with resources specifically earmarked to a list of fundamental functions in the social sphere, i.e. social services, kindergarten, and the transport of students with disabilities, thereby raising doubts in terms of constitutional legitimacy, given that Article 119 of the Constitution only allows for not earmarked equalization transfers. Following a challenge brought by the region of Liguria, the Constitutional Court, in judgment 71/2023, has acknowledged this apparent contradiction. The Court recognized that within the Municipal Solidarity Fund, in addition to the traditional ordinary not earmarked equalization—structured according to the canons of Article 119(3) of the Constitution—there is also a special equalization component, no longer aimed at bridging differences in fiscal capacity, but tied to achieving certain essential levels and service objectives that have been progressively introduced since 2021 in accordance with the enhancement of financial autonomy. This action, in the Court's eyes, has "features typically traceable to Article 119(5) of the Constitution," which provides for the possibility for the state to carry out "special interventions," directed only to certain territorial entities, allocating additional resources with a destination constraint, when required, as far as it is aimed at "cohesion and social solidarity," the removal of "economic and social imbalances," or finally, "the effective exercise of personal rights" (*ex multis*, on the characteristics of the equalization referred to in Article 119(5) of the Constitution).[11] The Court has defined this coexistence as a "hybridization extraneous to the constitutional design of financial autonomy", which, to protect the autonomy of territorial authorities, necessarily keeps the two forms of equalization distinct. Thus, the Court called on the legislator to intervene promptly to overcome this "hybrid equalization solution that is inconsistent with the constitutional design of financial autonomy under Article 119 of the Constitution" urging it to find separate, appropriate, and transparent placement in other funds of earmarked equalization.

[11] In this respect, see judgment 123/2022 of the Italian Constitutional Court.

In order to comply with the ruling of the Constitutional Court, the budget bill for 2024 created a special state fund for the removal of economic and social imbalances and to promote the effective exercise of people's rights, called the Special Fund for Equity Level of Services (*Fondo Speciale Equità Livello dei Servizi*).[12] This fund is intended to incorporate the portions of the municipal solidarity fund tied to service objectives for social welfare, kindergartens and transportation of disabled students that were censured by the Constitutional Court.

The endowment of the new fund for the years 2025 to 2029 is equivalent to the size of the planned reductions on the Municipal Solidarity Fund. The allocation of the new Fund for 2030, on the other hand, absorbs the bulk of the reduction in the Municipal Solidarity Fund planned for the same year (amounting to 835,905,000 EUR). The fund shall be exhausted as of the year 2031, which is the target date for achieving the essential levels of benefits for all three functions related to its establishment.

The only real novelty lies in the redefinition of the tools to ensure that the sums are actually used in compliance with the relevant constraints. Indeed, the budget law also regulates the procedure for monitoring compliance, i.e. the achievement of service objectives and essential performance levels by municipalities receiving resources from the fund, as well as the consequences of non-compliance or failure to achieve the assigned objectives, consisting of the national government intervention (*commissariamento*) of the entities found to be in default.

### *12.2.2 Sharing Criteria and Benchmarks: Compensation Vs. Equalization*

To understand the different functions pursued by the two components of the solidarity fund, an analysis of the sharing criteria is determinant. The resources of the restorative/compensatory component are distributed among the municipalities based on the effective revenues collected in 2015 from a selection of local taxes (IMU and TASI[13]), and as such are not equalizing. In comparison, the sharing criteria for the traditional component of the fund (1.9 billion EUR) is based partly on historical spending and partly on an equalization criterion linked to the difference between fiscal capacities and standard needs.[14] Accordingly, municipalities whose standard needs are higher than fiscal capacities receive an increase of the resources from the fund, whereas there is a reduction of resources from the fund if standard needs are lower than fiscal capacities, thereby achieving a redistribution of resources.

---

[12] Article 1 (496–501) of Law 231/2023—Bilancio di previsione dello Stato per l'anno finanziario 2024 e bilancio pluriennale per il triennio 2024–2026.

[13] Tax for indivisibile services (*Tributo per i servizi indivisibili*).

[14] This applies to municipalities in ordinary regions, whereas 464.1 million EUR are shared among municipalities located in Sardinia and Sicily, exclusively according to the criteria of compensation of historical spending.

The law furthermore mandates for the gradual increase of the share of resources distributed according to the equalization criterion. This passed from 20% in 2015 to 65% in 2023, and it is expected to be 100% in 2030.

The so-called standard needs shall reflect the needs of a certain entity in financial terms, taking into account the territorial features and socio-demographic characteristics of its populations. These are used only for financing fundamental functions. The methodology is the result of a technical decision vested in the SOSE, an in-house company of the Ministry of Economy and Finance, which is also in charge of monitoring the results and recalculating the needs at least every 3 years. The Technical Commission for Standard Needs, a technical body, is in charge of validating the methodology and updating the database used for calculation.

Fiscal capacities instead represent the potential revenue of a territory from (a selection of) own revenues, taking into account the tax base and the tax-rate fixed by law. The selection includes taxes and fees (i.e. IMU, TASI, Municipal Surcharge on IRPEF, and minor municipal taxes and fees such as advertising tax, tax on occupation of public spaces and areas, and various fees other than waste collection and disposal services), altogether accounting for 19.1 billion EUR out of a total fiscal capacity of Italian municipalities of 25.9 billion EUR.

The Budget Law for 2021 (Article 1 (791–792) of Law 178/2020) increased the endowment of the Municipal Solidarity Fund with certain sums earmarked specifically for the financing of the fundamental functions of municipalities in the social sphere. These are aimed at strengthening the development of municipal social services, with a special focus on municipal kindergartens and school transportation of pupils with disabilities, carried out in individual or associated form by the municipalities of the regions with ordinary statutes and the municipalities of the Sicilian Region and Sardinia. These resources are distributed according to the standard needs of social services, kindergartens and education.[15] To ensure that the additional resources are effectively allocated by municipalities to the strengthening of the aforementioned services, the law provides for the determination of specific service objectives and the activation of a system for monitoring and reporting on the use of resources and verifying the achievement of certain levels of services offered. In this way, for the first time since the introduction of standard requirements, the constraint of overall historical spending in the social function has been overcome by allocating additional resources tied to the achievement of service objectives and taking a step forward on the path toward guarantee of the essential levels of services. Service targets are the benchmark that the legislature has chosen to pursue a gradual approach to essential levels of performance, as provided for in Article 117 of the Constitution.

The distribution of the Solidarity Fund is defined annually by Decree of the President of the Council of Ministers (DPCM), at the latest by October 31 of the year preceding the year of reference, at the proposal of the Minister of Economy and Finance, in consultation with the Minister of the Interior, subject to an agreement to

[15] These take into account indicators such as the number of disabled students attending kindergarten, primary and secondary schools of the first grade, who are provided with transportation to reach the school premises.

be sanctioned at the State-Cities and Local Authorities Conference by October 15. For the adoption of the aforementioned "allocation decree", the prior technical opinion of the Technical Commission for Standard Requirements (provided for in Article 57-quinquies (2) of Decree-Law 124/2019) is also required from 2020. After the adoption of the DPCM, the Ministry of the Interior must distribute the shares allocated to each municipality in two installments to be paid by May and October, respectively. The first installment corresponds to 66% of the due resources. However, it must be noted that if an agreement is not reached at the Conference of State-Cities and Local Authorities Conference—as was the case in 2023 as the Conference called for an increase of 36 million EUR—the Council of Ministers can in any case proceed and approve the distribution. In 2023, 5458 municipalities benefited from the fund, receiving a total of 5.5 billion EUR, with those in the South of Italy appearing to benefit more than municipalities in any other area of the Country (Brugnano et al., 2017).

## 12.3 Inter-municipal Equalization in Special Regions

While municipal funding in ordinary regions (Sicily and Sardinia included) is mainly center-driven, this is not the case with (the Northern) special regions, i.e. Aosta Valley, Trentino-Alto Adige/Südtirol and Friuli Venezia Julia.[16] The above-described equalization mechanism applies only to local entities within ordinary regions, whereas rules are different in special regions. This is due to a two-fold reason.

In the first place, special regions have been requested to overhaul their financial legal framework to align with the fundamental principles of the national reform, as well as to define their contribution to national solidarity and the consolidation of public finances (i.e., balanced budget and reduction of public debt). As explained above, the regulations of their financing systems shall in fact be negotiated bilaterally between each special region and the central authority (Valdesalici, 2020, 207–208).

In the second place, not all special regions manage local finance. Only the ones in the north make use of their exclusive legislative competence on that, with a rather broad authority which includes also local taxes, fees, and surtaxes on national taxes. Therefore, in these cases local funding is charged to the regional budget (it is indeed the provincial budget for the Autonomous Provinces of Trento and Bolzano) (D'Orlando & Grisostolo, 2018, 140). As previously noted, in Sicily and Sardinia, these arrangements are more theoretical than practical. Although their special statutes designate local finance as a regional responsibility, in reality, this remains predominantly under the control of the national authority, with financial rules mirroring

[16] The region of Trentino-Alto Adige/Südtirol is peculiar in this sense, as financial matters are the responsibility of the two autonomous provinces that are the Autonomous Province of Bolzano/Bozen and the Autonomous Province of Trento.

those of local entities in ordinary regions. Nevertheless, both islands partially fund local entities from their own budgets (Barone Ricciardelli, 2007, 332).

Third, in the wake of the financial crisis, the three special regions of the north have further extended their responsibilities in local finance, again by signing bilateral agreements with the state. As of today, they are responsible for ensuring that the regionally agreed contribution to the consolidation of national public finance is respected by all territorial and non-territorial entities located in their jurisdiction and are therefore responsible for the financial coordination thereof.

This structure clearly affects the scope and functioning of equalization mechanisms within these (three) regional systems, which are therefore not directly included in the equalization scheme provided on a national scale (i.e. they cannot benefit from that). However, they do contribute to national solidarity, as well as to the consolidation of public finance through a number of mechanisms and resources bilaterally negotiated with the state.

Consequently, each special region, by virtue of their exclusive legislative competence over local finance as attributed by their respective Statute of Autonomy, has enacted its own system of inter-municipal equalization. For instance, the Province of Trento has developed a comprehensive system that aims at (i) rebalancing the level of services offered with respect to average provincial standards; and (ii) guaranteeing the efficiency in the use of the transferred resources.[17] As stated in Article 6 of the Provincial Law 36/1993, the system is subject to an annual agreement that shall take into account several variables. These are: "(a) the differentials in the costs to deliver services in relation to the different environmental and demographic context; (b) the imbalances in the territorial distribution of the taxable bases and of the revenues from municipal assets; (c) the weight of actual revenues deriving from taxes, duties and tariffs with respect to the standard values; (d) the exercise of functions connected with the provision of specific services characterized by a non-homogeneous distribution throughout the provincial territory and pertaining to singular municipal socio-economic situations; (e) the financial effects on the expenditures of the municipalities resulting from policies of interest to the province in matters of municipal competence" (Valdesalici, 2021b, 32). Also in this case the equalization mechanism features a vertical and a horizontal dimension, with both the provincial government and the richest municipalities contributing to it.

The above mentioned variables are the framework criteria used for determining the annual distribution within the agreement for local finance. For instance, with the 2020 Agreement, distribution criteria were applied to strengthen the position of small municipalities with less than 15,000 inhabitants, these being *de facto* mostly rural and mountainous municipalities. The general distribution criteria were in fact adjusted to include, on the one hand, a standard level of expenditure, estimated per each municipality, taking into account demographic, socioeconomic and geographical characteristics; on the other hand, the level of own revenues, so as to also take

---

[17] See Article 81 of the Autonomy Statute of Trentino-South Tyrol, Decree of the President of the Republic 670/1972 and Articles 3 and 6 of the Provincial Law on Local Finance, Provincial Law 36/1993.

into account the ability of each municipality to independently finance the standardized level of expenditure (Valdesalici, 2021b, 34–35).[18]

In the Autonomous Province of Bolzano, Provincial Law 6 of February 14, 1992 initially outlined the provisions on local finance and the equalization fund in Article 7, which was later replaced by Article 9(5) of the Provincial Law 15 of December 21, 2011, and by Article 31(3) of the Provincial Law 18 of December 23, 2015. As a result, the equalization fund is allocated to municipalities to support the preservation of balanced budgets. The allocation of funds and their distribution among individual municipalities are agreed upon annually between the president of the provincial council, the competent provincial councilor and a representation of the municipalities (coordination committee for local finance—*Comitato di coordinamento per la finanza locale*). For this purpose, the overall resources and tax policy of the municipalities are considered and computed at the minimum rate set or to the extent set by law.

In Friuli Venezia Giulia, following Article 11(b) of the Regional Law 18 of July 17, 2015, the region supports territorially and economically disadvantaged local authorities, with reference to needs and revenue. Thus, according to Article 14(2–3), the ordinary and equalization fund for municipalities and inter-municipal territorial unions contributes to the operational and management expenses of public services. More specifically, this fund is divided into two parts: one for ordinary assistance in financing budgets and equalization of resources, and the other for consolidated expenditure. Concerning the first portion, the ordinary and equalization fund, municipalities and inter-municipal territorial unions benefit from the distribution of an ordinary share and of an equalization one. The latter is based on a regional regulation which considers the demographic, territorial and socioeconomic characteristics of the entity, and, where already determined, standard spending and fiscal capacity, as specified in Article 45(2b).

Differently, the region of Valle d'Aosta does not resort to a Municipal Solidarity Fund. Regional interventions in local finance are regulated by Regional Law 48 of November 20, 1995. The basic principles of this law can be summarized through four main objectives: ensuring certainty of resources for local authorities to carry out their functions; allocating almost the entirety of the IRPEF (personal income tax—*imposta sul reddito delle persone fisiche)* to local finance to redistribute the wealth produced by citizens over the territory; establishing objective criteria for allocation among municipalities and among the *Unités des Communes valdôtaines*[19]; allocating upstream the available sums in three types of transfers:

[18] This standardized level of expenditure is estimated through an econometric model that considers the following variables: number of inhabitants; growth rate (or decrease) of the resident population; share of the population from 1 to 5 years; share of the population over 65 years; altitude; area (territorial dimension/size of the municipality); population density; number of tourist presences; number of local units (enterprises).

[19] In Aosta Valley, the *Unités des Communes Valdotâines* are administrative units placed between the region and the municipalities, similar to associations of communes, active since 2015. These are regulated in Regional Law of August 5, 2014, 6 *Nuova disciplina dell'esercizio associato di*

unrestricted sectoral allocation, interventions for investment programs, and with sectoral allocation constraint (e.g. services to the elderly, management of kindergartens, etc.). Concerning this last point, some clarifications must be made for the three types of transfers. First, the allocation of unrestricted sectoral transfers takes place for the *Communes*, based on objective parameters that consider the expenditure needs of the *Communes* themselves, as deduced from their characteristics (e.g. population, territorial size or presence of tourist facilities). At the same time, the value of their own revenues (especially the IMU) negatively intervenes as an equalizing element in favor of the poorer municipalities.[20] The *Unités des Communes valdôtaines* constitute another possible recipient of this type of transfer, based on percentages determined by parameters linked to their exercised functions.[21] Second, interventions for investment programs, which provided a mechanism for financing major works, have been reduced to zero over the years. On the other hand, funding with sectoral destination constraints, which can be defined as instruments useful for financing sectors considered as priorities, are distributed either through a "call for proposals" system (e.g. prevention interventions for hydrogeological risks) or through parameters that consider the actual expenses borne by the entities (e.g. services to the elderly). However, it must be mentioned that in recent years, due to financial constraints and restrictions, the total amount allocated to local finance has been determined, as an exception to Regional Law 48/1995, based on the availability of the regional budget. Finally, it is interesting to notice that, although the region of Valle d'Aosta does not have a Municipal Solidarity Fund, the criterion used for unrestricted sectoral transfers benefits territorially and economically less favored municipalities through two mechanisms owning an equalization nature. Namely, this type of transfer assumes an equal fixed share for all municipalities (equal to 22.5%) to carry out the institutional functions of the entity. Moreover, it contemplates a deduction from the "reference expenditure" (i.e. from the amount of the transfer due to each municipality, as determined by the parameters set by the regional council) of each municipality's self-financing capacity, especially the amount of IMU revenue as established by the resolution of the regional council.

*funzioni e servizi comunali e soppressione delle Comunità montane*, which replaced the pre-existing Mountain Communities. The capital, Aosta, is not included in any of these units.

[20] For the year 2023, the Regional Council Resolution No. 300 dated April 3, 2023, allocates the unrestricted transfers to municipalities, available at https://www.regione.vda.it/enti_locali/cartella_i.asp?pk_cartelle=536. Annex 3 to the same resolution contains the objective parameters and their weights to determine the amount of the transfer due to each municipality.

[21] Regional Council Resolution No. 299 dated April 3, 2023, apportions the unrestricted transfers to the *Unités des Communes valdôtaines*, available at https://www.region.vda.it/enti_locali/cartella_i.asp?pk_cartelle=537. Annex 1 to the same resolution contains parameters and related weights for defining the percentages to be used to apportion the amount available.

## 12.4 Equalization for Provinces and Metropolitan Cities

The financing schemes for provinces and metropolitan cities replicate in their foundations the structure of municipal finance, though they depend mainly on devolved and/or shared taxes, plus equalization transfers from the fund for the financial consolidation of provinces. The legal framework and its effective implementation are, however, more complex.

With regard to the provinces, this complexity is the result of austerity measures that have reduced finances progressively and of an ongoing process of territorial reorganization, to the extent that the cuts affecting the fund from 2012 onwards have effectively wiped out its financial endowment, nullifying the redistributive purpose assigned to it by law. Since 2016, extraordinary measures have then been introduced in their favor (also for metropolitan cities) that have provided, among other things, specific-purpose transfers to offset the reduction of resources caused by the need to contribute to the consolidation of national public finance.

Law 42/2009 (Article 15) grants significant tax autonomy to metropolitan cities but requires a further legislative act for its implementation, to the extent that the financing system of metropolitan cities is still largely undefined. Similarly, Law 56/2014 does not provide specific rules for their funding. As a result, despite the expanded functions of metropolitan cities, the provincial funding regime still largely applies with overall limited resources. Cities are thus heavily reliant on transfers both from the national and regional governments. Moreover, their budgets have been severely impacted by national austerity measures introduced to address the economic and financial crisis, leading to significant problems of underfunded mandates (Kössler & Kress, 2020, 292).

Finally, the Budget Laws for 2021 and 2022 have introduced new rules following a model similar to that applied to municipalities. As of 2022, two different funds (one per each type of local authority) have been set up, which envisage a new financing scheme for both provinces and metropolitan cities. The national government has committed to supplement the fund with the allocation of a new state contribution of 80 million EUR in the year 2022, gradually increased up to the amount of 600 million EUR on a structural basis as of 2031. This is intended to finance the basic functions of provinces and metropolitan cities.

The revenue distribution takes place by application of equalization criteria so as to take into account the difference between standard needs and fiscal capacities. This is defined based on the instructions of the Technical Commission for Standard Needs and after the enactment of a decree, assuming an agreement is reached within the State-Cities and Local Authorities Conference. In addition, the procedure and mechanism must resemble the one applied to municipalities and have the aim of progressively overcoming the previous criterion based on historical expenditure. However, this criterion keeps being dominant, with the horizontal component that takes into account the difference between standard needs and fiscal capacities being limited to 10% in 2023, a percentage that should rise progressively until 60% in 2031.

Finally, it should be noted that the idea of horizontal solidarity has also been adopted within the metropolitan cities, some of which, such as Bologna and Milan, have internal equalization mechanisms aimed at supporting municipalities or union of municipalities within areas characterized by greater social, demographic, and economic fragility. For instance, the Metropolitan Territorial Plan (*Piano Territoriale Metropolitano*; PTM) of the metropolitan city of Bologna provides for the use of territorial equalization to build a metropolitan-wide redistribution mechanism of the financial resources generated by territorial transformations. This important decision was taken in continuity with Article 15(3) of Regional Law 20 of 2000, according to which territorial agreements may provide for forms of territorial equalization. Specifically, according to Article 5(3) of the PTM, territorial equalization aims to support the municipalities (or unions of municipalities) characterized by a lower overall building capacity and suffering from significant negative impacts from new urbanization processes. At the same time, an equalization fund is established for the creation of territorial facilities, infrastructures and public services, which can promote a sustainable and balanced development of the territory at a metropolitan or inter-municipal level. Last, the equalization fund aims to support areas characterized by greater social, demographic and economic fragility.

Similarly, the PTM of the metropolitan city of Milan has the objective of fostering the principle of territorial equity by promoting coordination actions and forms of equalization. These actions aim to fairly distribute among the municipalities the advantages and disadvantages deriving from the construction of settlements and infrastructures that present externalities and supra-municipal effects. As detailed in Article 11, the PTM specifically considers the promotion of territorial regenerative schemes, environmental sustainability, the efficiency of mobility networks and services, and the formation of platforms providing pro-cohesive services under the responsibility of the metropolitan city.

## 12.5 Conclusions

Although 23 years have passed since the 2001 constitutional reform, the implementation of the so-called fiscal federalism reform is far from being concluded. The reform package of 2009 and the implementing decrees have set the trajectories of the new systems (i.e. regional and local), but their effective implementation was delayed and, in part, is still lacking. In this regard, it is worth noting that, although 15 years have passed since the 2009 reform on fiscal federalism, in 2023, only 65% of the resources from the municipal solidarity fund have been distributed according to the new model. Additionally, there is the ongoing issue of the still incipient inter-municipal equalization models in certain special regions, or the limited development of such models in metropolitan cities.

The methodological choices made by the legislature in 2009 and in the implementing decrees of 2011 appear decisive in contributing to the sluggishness of progress compared to the ambitious objectives set with the reform. In fact, the "standard costs and needs" criteria chosen to overcome the inefficiencies associated with a funding scheme based on historical spending, whereby transfers were calculated on the last year's expenditure, must be called into question. From a theoretical perspective, the new model can certainly approach an ideal of equalization. In this scenario, all entities receive exactly the amount of resources necessary to finance the functions assigned to them. This is meant to provide that this amount does not exceed the cost that functions should have in each territory, net of inefficiencies and shortcomings related to concrete management.

However, the actual implementation of such a system is so complex and sophisticated that, to date, this mechanism has not yet been fully operational. Although the implementation of this reform is at a more advanced stage for local authorities, compared to the new regional financing system, it is also true that after more than two decades it is still a (never-ending) work in progress and, if there are no hiccups, the new system will only become fully operational in 2030.

Beyond the merit, i.e. the effectiveness of the standard criteria in pursuing a fair redistribution, it should be pointed out in this regard that this system is ultimately destined to be a victim of its own complexity. There is in fact the high risk of achieving its full operational capacity through a system that may already be obsolete. Furthermore, given the difficulties in its enforcement, it is likely that this will be associated with heavy maintenance costs that the volatility of contemporary economies and public finance systems cannot sustain. Contrary to what the political debate may suggest, there is no equalization mechanism that can be considered permanent, as its constant maintenance is essential for its effectiveness. Therefore, the Italian equalization system, including the inter-municipal one, is destined to be born (if and when it ever happens) with a genetic flaw that will jeopardize not only the concrete possibilities of achieving the redistributive objectives set but also its own sustainability over time. How can one think that a system, that required 29 years to be set up, may perform the buffer function that equalization mechanisms are naturally called to carry out?

Also, the choice to provide for two different redistributive schemes depending on the fundamental or non-fundamental nature of the function at stake does not help in this regard. As shown by the same constitutional enumeration of competences, such listings suffer from intrinsic weaknesses inherent in the nature of public action. While moving to the level closest to citizens, functions become more concrete and tangible (services are more easily categorized than competences). However, it remains an approximation, by nature non-exhaustive, if only due to the impact of global transformative dynamics (e.g. the digital and climate transitions) that all countries are currently called upon to face.

The comparative perspective reveals the prevalence of equalization systems where the predominant criteria are constituted by differences in fiscal capacity, with, at most, corrective measures which consider spending needs. Overall, equalization mechanisms are the result of a balance between the best possible outcome in terms of redistributive capacity and the best technically and politically feasible compromise. Without doubts, this is not the case for the equalization system in Italy, nor for the inter-municipal one.

Furthermore, looking at the data from 2023, the gap between the north/center and the south of the country is confirmed, with the Italian municipalities located in southern regions receiving a much higher amount per capita in terms of both current state transfers and—specifically—equalization transfers compared to the amount paid to municipalities in the northern and central regions. The well-known gap between the north and south of Italy has therefore not yet been erased, even after 9 years of operation of the (only partially) new equalization system. Such a conclusion is confirmed looking back to 2015, i.e. the first year of operation of the Inter-municipal Solidarity Fund. Per capita current transfers, including solidarity transfers, were (and still are) below the average for northern and central regions, and well above the average for southern regions.[22]

Finally, from a comparative perspective, when pursuing equalization, solutions must be both transparent and flexible. These characteristics are evidently lacking in the Italian system of (subnational and) local financing, as the choice was made to resort to particularly complex criteria, which hinder the overall understanding of the system. If this may have the merit of keeping the debate on equalization substantially out of the political arena, thus being relegated to the technical level of the public administrations in charge, even in this way the desired results have not been achieved. Such a framework has rather favored the increase in the current state transfers, apart from equalization, which have risen from 52.7 (2015) to an average of 56.6 (2021). While this is not a significant increase in absolute terms, it becomes so in relative terms, considering that with the 2001 reform it was entrenched in the constitution that all territorial entities should not receive any other transfers from the state outside of non-earmarked equalization transfers (with limited of transfers to cope with extraordinary circumstances).

To conclude, while from a theoretical and economic viewpoint, the new system of inter-municipal equalization has the merit of faithfully representing the diversity among the territories and of attempting to correct existing inefficiencies, in practice, this mechanism requires an enormous outlay of time and human (and therefore also economic) resources. And this is just to get the new system up and running, not to think about its necessary maintenance over time. It seems that in some cases, and especially when dealing with territorial equalization, the best is the enemy of the good.

## References

Alber, E., & Valdesalici, A. (2023). Italy. In J.-F. Tremblay (Ed.), *The Forum of Federations handbook of fiscal federalism* (pp. 257–296). Palgrave Macmillan.

Alber, E., Valdesalici, A., & Klotz, G. (2024). Italy. In N. Steytler (Ed.), *The Forum of Federations' handbook on local government in federal systems* (pp. 281–311). Palgrave Macmillan.

Ambrosanio, M. F., & Bordignon, M. (2020). Il nodo (irrisolto?) della perequazione regionale in Italia. In F. Palermo, S. Parolari, & A. Valdesalici (Eds.), *Costituzioni finanziarie e riforme: Italia e Spagna a confronto* (pp. 151–176). ESI.

Antonini, L. (2009). La rivincita della responsabilità. A proposito della nuova legge sul federalismo fiscale. *I quaderni della sussidiarietà* (7).

[22] IFEL, *La finanza comunale in sintesi. Rapporto 2016,* https://www.fondazioneifel.it/documenti-e-pubblicazioni/item/download/1656_27edb001e4f2b74b77244cd82cc67701 (accessed on 6 March 2024).

Barone Ricciardelli, E. (2007). Le novità in materia di finanza delle Regioni Sicilia e Sardegna. *Tributi Locali e Regionali, 12*(3), 331–344.

Brugnano, C., Ferraina, G., Ferri, A., Minzyuk, L., & Russo, F. (2017). Federalismo municipale e nuovo sistema perequativo: Il Fondo di solidarietà comunale 2016. *Economia Pubblica, 2017*(2), 93–133.

Carpani, G. (2009). La collaborazione strutturata tra Regioni e tra queste e lo Stato: Nuovi equilibri e linee evolutive dei raccordi "verticali" ed "orizzontali". *federalismi.it* (19).

Cartabia, M., & Lupo, N. (2022). *The Constitution of Italy. A contextual analysis*. Bloomsbury Publishing.

D'Orlando, E., & Grisostolo, F. E. (2018). La disciplina degli enti locali tra uniformità e differenziazione. In F. Palermo & S. Parolari (Eds.), *Le variabili della specialità. Evidenze e riscontri tra soluzioni istituzionali e politiche settoriali* (pp. 99–161). Edizioni Scientifiche Italiane (Ius publicum europaeum, Nuova serie, 4).

IFEL. (2021). *La finanza comunale in sintetesi. Rapporto 2021* (Andrea Ferri, Ed.). www.fondazioneifel.it

Istat. (2023). *Codici statistici delle unità amministrative territoriali: Comuni, città metropolitane, province e regioni*. https://www.istat.it/it/archivio/6789

Kössler, K., & Kress, A. (2020). European cities between self-government and subordination: Their role as policy-takers and policy-makers. In E. H. Ballin, G. Van der Schyff, & M. De Visser (Eds.), *European Yearbook of Constitutional Law 2020* (pp. 271–300). T.M.C. Asser Press.

Palermo, F. (2008). South Tyrol's special status within the Italian Constitution. In J. Woelk, F. Palermo, & J. Marko (Eds.), *Tolerance through law. Self governance and group rights in South Tyrol* (pp. 33–49). Brill-Nijhoff.

Palermo, F. (2021). Asymmetries in the Italian regional system and their role model. In E. Arban, G. Martinico, & F. Palermo (Eds.), *Federalism and constitutional law. The Italian contribution to comparative regionalism* (pp. 136–151). Routledge.

Région Autonome Vallée d'Aoste. (2023a). *Regional Council Resolution 299*. Retrieved February 5, 2024, from https://www.region.vda.it/enti_locali/cartella_i.asp?pk_cartelle=537

Région Autonome Vallée d'Aoste. (2023b). *Regional Council Resolution 300*. Retrieved February 5, 2024, from https://www.regione.vda.it/enti_locali/cartella_i.asp?pk_cartelle=536

Valdesalici, A. (2020). Riforma del federalismo fiscale e Regioni speciali: Gli opposti a volte si attraggono. In F. Palermo, S. Parolari, & A. Valdesalici (Eds.), *Costituzioni finanziarie e riforme: Italia e Spagna a confronto* (pp. 205–222). ESI.

Valdesalici, A. (2021a). Financial relations in the Italian regional system. In E. Arban, G. Martinico, & F. Palermo (Eds.), *Federalism and constitutional law. The Italian contribution to comparative regionalism* (pp. 82–99). Routledge.

Valdesalici, A. (2021b). The revision of the inter-municipal equalization mechanism in Trentino. In K. Kössler & T. Morandell (Eds.), *Local government in Italy. Responses to urban-rural challenges* (pp. 31–55). Zenodo. https://doi.org/10.5281/zenodo.5733368

# Part IV
# Special Fees and User Charges as Alternative Sources of Local Revenue

# Chapter 13
# The Role of Municipal Fees in Croatian Local Service Provision: Balancing Benefits and Challenges

**Dario Runtić**

**Abstract** This chapter explores the role of municipal fees as an alternative funding source for local service provision in Croatia. Through a review of relevant legislation, the analysis examines both the benefits and challenges associated with utilizing municipal fees, as well as the delicate balance between national regulation and local autonomy in setting specific fees and exemptions. The research explores the diverse types of municipal fees and critically evaluates their potential impact on equity, efficiency, and sustainability of local services. It further examines the challenges associated with fee implementation, including administrative complexity, transparency concerns and potential burdens on vulnerable populations, and it offers mitigation strategies for addressing the identified challenges. By analyzing the legal framework and its practical implications, this chapter aims to contribute to a more informed discussion on the effectiveness of municipal fees in supporting local service delivery and promoting balanced territorial development in Croatia.

**Keywords** Croatian local governance · Municipal fees · Local tax autonomy · Urban-rural fiscal disparities · Territorial development · Equity and efficiency in municipal services

## 13.1 Introduction

The system of subnational governance of the Republic of Croatia is comprised of regional and local government units. At the regional level, Croatia is divided into 21 units of self-government, namely 20 counties (županija) and the City of Zagreb, functioning as both a city and a county. Each county possesses its own legislative and executive bodies, elected through democratic means for a 4-year term

D. Runtić (✉)
Association of Cities of the Republic of Croatia, Zagreb, Croatia
e-mail: dario@udruga-gradova.hr



F. Velasco Caballero et al. (eds.), *Municipal Tasks and Financing*, Local and Urban Governance, https://doi.org/10.1007/978-3-031-99812-6_13

(Government of Croatia, 2020a). The City of Zagreb, with its unique dual status, operates under a separate legislative framework. This framework grants Zagreb the authority to execute responsibilities at both the local and regional levels, including certain functions of state administration delegated by the central government (Government of Croatia, 2020b).

Local self-governance in Croatia is exercised through 556 units classified as municipalities, towns, and large towns. There are 428 municipalities (općina) and a total of 128 towns and large towns (grad, veliki grad).

Towns are generally characterized by their urban nature and a population exceeding 10,000 inhabitants, although exceptions exist based on historical, economic, or geographical considerations. Municipalities, conversely, are typically rural with populations below 10,000. Both towns and municipalities have elected representative and executive bodies serving 4-year terms.

Further subdivision exists within these local government units, with each encompassing one or more settlements. These settlements, whether urban or rural, may be represented by neighborhood councils. These councils consist of elected representatives who serve in a non-professional capacity, providing a hyperlocal level of citizen participation in governance.

Large towns are units of local self-government that are also economic, financial, cultural, health, transport and scientific centers of development of the wider environment and have more than 35,000 inhabitants (Government of Croatia, 2020a). In accordance with the Article 19 of the Local Government Law: "Municipalities and cities, within their self-governing sphere of activity, perform tasks of local importance that directly meet the needs of citizens, and which are not assigned to state bodies by the Constitution or law, in particular tasks related to: settlement development and housing, spatial and urban planning, communal economy, childcare, social welfare, primary health care, upbringing and primary education, culture, physical culture and sports, consumer protection, protection and improvement of the natural environment, fire and civil protection, traffic in their area and other tasks in accordance with special laws" (Government of Croatia, 2020a).

"The county, within its self-governing sphere of activity, performs tasks of regional importance, and in particular tasks related to: education, health, spatial and urban planning, economic development, traffic and traffic infrastructure, maintenance of public roads, planning and development of a network of educational, health, social and cultural institutions, issuing construction and location permits, other acts related to the construction and implementation of spatial planning documents for the area of the county outside the area of a large city, and other tasks in accordance with special laws" (Government of Croatia, 2020a). Large towns can perform tasks of cities and municipalities, as well as tasks of the counties.

Local governments can provide services directly, through institutions established by local governments, local government-owned enterprises, or by entrusting public services to private operators through public procurement contracts or concessions.

Local governments typically provide general services related to all responsibilities within the nationally imposed legal framework—organization of services, contracting, funding, planning and taxation. They also organize settlement and housing, spatial planning services, construction permits, business permits, and the provision of social welfare benefits. Institutions established by local governments provide childcare, health protection, social welfare services, elementary education, culture, and fire protection. Local government-owned enterprises mostly perform utility services, environmental protection, and maintenance of roads and infrastructure. Public procurement contracts and concessions are mostly used for infrastructure construction and maintenance, waste management, public lighting, public transport, parking, and green market management. Few public-private contracts for public service provision have been implemented in areas of sport and education. However, this form of public service provision is not widespread due to downfalls of early public-private partnership (PPP) contracts. (Runtic, 2021)

Croatian municipalities exhibit a degree of fiscal autonomy, with the authority to engage in inter-municipal collaborations to enhance service delivery efficiency. This cooperation, enabled by the Article 54 of the Local Government Law,[1] allows for the joint establishment of administrative departments, companies, or institutions. While such collaborations are voluntary, the legislation provides incentives for joint service provision and municipal amalgamation, promoting economies of scale and resource optimization.

Subnational government revenue in Croatia, encompassing both local government units (LGUs) and budgetary users, constitutes 12.5% of the national GDP in 2022 (Eurostat, 2023).

Within this framework, the Personal Income Tax (PIT) holds significant importance, generating 41% of consolidated local and regional government revenue. Although LGUs possess the authority to determine PIT rates, the central government retains control over brackets, exemptions, and credits. This arrangement can introduce volatility into local budgets, as frequent central government adjustments to the PIT parameters impact revenue predictability. Consequently, LGUs may face challenges in ensuring uninterrupted service provision and engaging in long-term fiscal planning.

Significant disparities in fiscal capacities are present among Croatian LGUs, despite their largely uniform service delivery responsibilities. While rural LGUs focus on providing essential public services, their urban counterparts often offer a broader scope of services through specialized public institutions such as libraries and museums. This discrepancy underscores the need for effective fiscal equalization mechanisms to ensure equitable service provision across all municipalities.

Own-source revenues (OSR) are one of the most important sources of funding for local governments, accounting for an average of 33% of their total revenue in South-East Europe (SEE) and 29% in Croatia (Network of Associations of Local Authorities of South-East Europe (NALAS), 2023). Own-source revenues are crucial for local governments because they provide them with the flexibility to respond to the needs of their constituents and finance essential services. Without adequate OSR, local governments would be heavily reliant on intergovernmental transfers from the federal and state governments, which may not be responsive to their

[1] Official Gazette 19/13.—consolidated text, 137/15.—correction, 123/17., 98/19. and 144/20.

specific needs or priorities. OSR consist of taxes, fees, and other charges levied by local governments on individuals, businesses, and property owners.

Own-source revenues can be broadly classified into two categories:

1. Taxes: These are compulsory levies on individuals or businesses based on their income, property ownership, or consumption of goods and services. Property taxes are the most common type of tax for local governments.
2. Non-taxes (fees): These are charges and fees for specific services or activities provided by local governments. Examples include construction and infrastructure fees, sewer and water charges, and business permits.

Croatian municipalities derive own-source revenues from a diverse range of levies listed below.

Among these, communal fees represent the largest component, contributing 39.5% of own-source revenues. Asset rentals account for 19.5%, while the PIT surtax (prior to 2024 decentralization of PIT rate setting powers) constituted 14.7%.

This revenue structure is characterized by varying degrees of regulatory control. Taxes on vehicles, boats, and inheritance are subject to stringent regulations. Conversely, the communal fee, while regulated, is not subject to a cap. Taxes on public space usage have the least regulatory constraints. This diversified approach allows municipalities some flexibility in revenue generation while operating within a framework of central government oversight (Table 13.1).

Local taxes in Croatia are non-earmarked revenues which can be used freely to fund local public policies and community priorities. Local taxes are predictable and a stable source of funding. In contrast, shared taxes and governments grants can be subject to annual appropriations and political agendas. Furthermore, communities can leverage local taxes to advance or improve various locally provided services as demanded by the residents. Due to their non-earmarked status, local governments in Croatia often use revenue from local taxes to complement insufficient services fees for service provision or maintenance costs, or to cover the costs of exemptions or subsidize service costs for vulnerable populations.

Selection of the most relevant fees in Croatia

1. *Communal fee*: Mandatory payment for property owners/users to maintain public infrastructure (e.g., roads, lighting, cleaning). Funded by base fee multiplied by size, location, and type of property (set by local governments).
2. *Communal contribution*: One-time fee for new construction to fund supporting infrastructure. Capped at 10% of average construction cost.
3. *Concession fee for maritime property*: Payment for commercial use of sea areas (e.g., ports, aquaculture). Granted through public tenders or requests.
4. *Permit fees for public area use*: Similar to maritime concession fees, but with broader local government discretion. Used for kiosks, mobile devices, events, etc.
5. *Memorial fee*: Paid by businesses operating in cultural/historical areas. Based on usable area, set at €0.13–€0.53 per square meter monthly.
6. *Indirect memorial fee*: 0.05% of income from specific commercial activities (e.g., tobacco, cosmetics) for cultural preservation.

**Table 13.1** Subnational tax autonomy in Croatia

| **Regional taxes** | **Rate** | **Rate determined by** | **Base determined by** | **Exceptions determined by** |
|---|---|---|---|---|
| Gifts and inheritance tax | 4% | CG | CG | CG |
| Vehicle tax[a] | | CG | CG | CG |
| Vessel tax[b] | | CG | CG | CG |
| Tax on games of chance | 13.30 € per device | CG | CG | CG |
| **Local taxes** | **Rate** | **Rate determined by** | **Base determined by** | **Exceptions determined by** |
| Beverage tax | 0–3% | LGU | CG | – |
| Second home tax | 0/0.6–1.99 € per square meter | LGU | CG | CG |
| Public area tax[c] | | LGU | LGU | LGU |
| Real-estate tax | 3% | CG | CG | CG |
| Personal income tax (2024) | 15–23.6%/25–35.4% | LGU | CG | CG |

Source: Compiled by the author from the Law on Local Taxes (Official Gazette 115/16, 101/17, 114/22 and 114/23) and the Personal Income Tax Law (Official Gazette 115/16, 106/18, 121/19, 32/20, 138/20, 151/22 and 114/23)

[a] Rate is determined from the tax table that differentiates vehicles by engine power and age

[b] Rate is determined from the tax table that differentiates vessels by engine power and length of vessel

[c] There is no upper limit for this tax

7. *Tourist fee*: Fixed amount per overnight stay in tourist accommodation, used for tourism promotion and improvement. Exemptions for children and vulnerable groups.
8. *Forest fee*: 5–10% of wood sale price, used for communal infrastructure in local units.
9. *Kindergarten fee* (parental fee): Paid for voluntary nursery/kindergarten programs, heavily subsidized to encourage enrollment. Varies depending on program length and local government subsidies.
10. *Water and wastewater fees*: Strictly regulated, full cost recovery required. No discrimination based on consumer factors or location. Affordability limits set (2.5–4% of average income).

## 13.2 Importance of Fees as Alternative Source of Revenues

Municipal fees are a valuable tool for funding essential services, but they require thoughtful implementation and consideration of potential drawbacks to ensure fairness, efficiency, and sustainability. The specific importance of fees varies depending on the municipality, its size, and the services it provides. The design and structure of fees are crucial for maximizing their benefits and mitigating potential downsides, while effective communication and public engagement are essential for building understanding and support for municipal fees.

Municipal fees play a crucial role in funding the services that are essential for the day-to-day lives of residents. In terms of revenue generation, fees act as a significant source of income for municipalities, supplementing local taxes, government grants and other traditional revenue streams. This allows them to fund services beyond what taxes alone can cover and serves as a means of revenue diversification. By diversifying revenue sources, local governments make sure that economic downturns or changes in tax base or rates does not affect the stability of revenue streams that are essential for funding local public services or maintaining service level standards as expected by the constituency (Farvacque-Vitkovic & Kopanyi, 2014). Having a diversified revenue base makes municipalities less reliant on any single source, which can improve overall municipal financial stability and resilience. Moreover, increased reliance on non-tax revenue sources, such as charges and fees, improves budgetary solvency (Jimenez & Whitney, 2022).

Unlike taxes with rigid structures, fees can be adjusted according to service costs or policy goals. This allows for greater flexibility in resource allocation and responding to changing needs. For specific services that benefit identifiable user groups, fees can directly recover the cost of providing that service. Examples include garbage collection fees, and water and sewer charges. This promotes fairness and incentivizes responsible use. User fees can also incentivize the efficient use of natural or scarce resources. For example, higher water fees might encourage conservation efforts, and user fees for waste collection might encourage people to reduce waste generation.

By directly linking fees to specific services, they enhance transparency and accountability in how public funds are spent. When properly implemented, local fees make citizens more aware of how their money is being used. Fees tied to specific services or benefits can create a direct link between the cost and the value received and/or what it takes to continue their upkeep. This awareness can motivate citizens to hold officials accountable for the efficient use of funds and quality of service delivery. Charging fees can help recover the costs associated with providing certain services or maintaining public infrastructure. This can make officials more accountable for justifying the need for the fee and ensuring its efficient use.

Another beneficial effect of fees on transparency is that implementing or changing fees often requires clear communication of what the fee covers and how it is used. This can lead to increased transparency in government budgeting and spending, allowing citizens to track where their money goes. When information about fees is readily available, it opens the possibility for public scrutiny and analysis. This can help identify potential inefficiencies or misuse of funds, leading to pressure for improvement.

The impact of public fees on accountability and transparency depends on how they are designed and implemented. While they can offer potential benefits, careful consideration is needed to address equity concerns, minimize administrative burdens, and ensure the responsible use of collected funds. Transparency and clear communication about the purpose and use of fees are crucial for maximizing their positive impact.

If not carefully designed, fees can disproportionately burden low-income individuals (More & Stevens, 2000). Public fees are often fixed amounts, regardless of income. This means they represent a larger proportion of income for low-income individuals and households than for wealthier ones and can have a cumulative effect as low-income individuals often rely on various public services, each with associated fees. These fees can accumulate, creating a substantial financial burden resulting in reduced access to services such as participation in important programs like community centers, after-school activities, or recreational facilities. These programs can provide crucial support and opportunities for children and families, especially those with limited resources. Programs like fee waivers or subsidies can mitigate this challenge, but applying for fee waivers or subsidies can involve complex procedures and documentation, adding an additional burden to accessing services.

Local governments could review options for fee exemptions for low-income individuals or households and use sliding scales based on income to help mitigate the burden. Also, providing targeted assistance programs specifically for low-income individuals can help offset the cost of fees and ensure access to essential services. Going back to transparency, clearly communicating the purpose and use of fees, along with available assistance programs, can foster understanding and trust.

Fees may impose a burden on municipal administration as collecting and managing fees can be administratively complex and costly, potentially outweighing the benefits in the case of low-yielding fees. Depending on the fee's complexity and volume, collecting fees can increase staff workload and/or require dedicated staff for tasks like processing payments, issuing permits, responding to inquiries, and managing exemptions. In terms of data management and tracking, such as recording, storing, and managing fee-related data, it can be complex, requiring robust systems and procedures to ensure accuracy and prevent errors. Ensuring compliance with fee requirements can involve enforcement measures and audits, adding further administrative work. All of the above requires additional capital and operational costs for the collection of fees, so municipalities should carefully weight the costs and benefits of introducing fees.

Noteworthy mitigation strategies for the above issues include:

1. Fee Design and Structure: Ensure fees are fair, equitable, and aligned with service costs and benefits.
2. Public Engagement: Involve the community in discussions about fees and service delivery to address concerns and gather feedback.
3. Streamlining processes: Simplifying application, payment, and reporting processes can save time and effort for both government and citizens.
4. Online options: Providing user-friendly online platforms for applying, paying, and managing fees can improve accessibility and efficiency.
5. Clear communication: Regularly communicating about fees, including eligibility for exemptions and assistance programs, can reduce confusion and frustration.

6. Investment in technology: Prioritizing investments in efficient and secure technology infrastructure can streamline fee collection and reduce administrative burdens.

While not without challenges, municipal fees play a vital role in financing essential services and ensuring their sustainability. By implementing them thoughtfully, ethically, and transparently, local governments can leverage this valuable revenue source to meet the needs of their communities and enhance their overall well-being (Farvacque-Vitkovic & Kopanyi, 2014).

## 13.3 Balancing Autonomy and Regulation

Municipalities have the power to decide the funding of their services with varying autonomy in setting taxes, fees, and charges. The balance between local autonomy and national control over user fees is a complex issue that is often debated in Croatia. On the one hand, municipalities argue that they need the flexibility to set fees that are fair to their residents and that reflect the costs of providing services. On the other hand, the national government argues that it is important to set a uniform framework for user fees to ensure that all municipalities are treated fairly and that consumers are not unfairly burdened. In general, municipalities have more discretion in setting fees for services that are considered optional or non-essential. For example, municipalities have more flexibility in setting fees for parking or kindergarten services than they do for essential services such as waste collection or water supply.

There are several factors that influence municipal decisions when setting fees for particular services:

1. The cost of providing the service
2. The demand for the service
3. The ability of residents to pay the fees
4. The impact of the fees on policy goals
5. The impact of the fees on affordability and equity
6. The need to raise revenue to fund other services

For example, when setting fees for kindergarten services, municipal decisions are affected by multiple factors. The kindergarten services are optional but in high demand. The full recovery fee for costs of the provision of the service would exceed the ability of residents to pay the fee, leaving a number of lower-to-mid-wage earners without a daycare service, thus exacerbating the workforce shortage and negatively impacting national strategic goals for kindergarten enrollment set to 97% by 2030, currently ranging between 30 and 75% in various municipalities (Government of Croatia, 2021a, 2021b). Due to those reasons, costs are primarily borne by the municipalities and topped with parental fees that account for 14% of the total cost of the service (Network of Associations of Local Authorities of South-East Europe (NALAS), 2021). Municipalities predominantly set a fixed monthly parental fee, irrespective of users' personal circumstances. Some municipalities offer discounts or exemptions depending on household income levels or the number of siblings attending the kindergarten, while few wealthy municipalities offer kindergarten services for free.

On the other hand, wastewater and water supply service fees are strictly regulated (Government of Croatia, 2023).[2] Operators are required to fully recover operational and capital costs of service provision from fees, but are not allowed to form fees based on the economic powers of consumers or the distance of consumers. Revenue and expenditure limitations apply. Tariffs for socially vulnerable consumers may not exceed 60% of the regular tariff and the municipality will bear the remainder of the water tariff (Government of Croatia, 2019).[3] Furthermore, operators are expected to maintain tariffs within the affordability range of 2.5–4% of average annual household income (Ministry of Economy of Croatia, 2022).

Overall, own source revenues play an important role in funding local service provision, keeping in mind that 29% of Croatian municipal revenues come from own source revenues and even more so in the SEE. Specific fees and charges represent the cornerstone of funding arrangements for individual services these fees are earmarked for. For example:

1. 87.2% of revenues of municipal waste companies come from user fees[4]
2. 72.4% of revenues of municipal water supply companies come from user fees[5]
3. 51% of annual municipal capital investments is funded by communal fees and charges[6]
4. 14% of the total cost of kindergarten services is funded through parental fees

## 13.4 Croatia's Diverse Landscape of Local Fees

Croatia boasts a blend of cultural richness, diverse landscapes, and historical significance. From the Adriatic Sea at the south with over 1777 km of coastline dotted with over 1200 islands to the inland filled with rolling plains, rugged mountains, and valleys, it paints a diverse picture. Local governments, with their individual specificities, have a diverse selection of fees at their disposal. Some, reflecting aforesaid diversity, are listed below.

*A communal fee* is a mandatory payment levied on property owners or property users to cover the costs of maintaining public infrastructure and services within their local community. These fees are typically used to finance the upkeep of public

---

[2] Article 4 of the Decree.

[3] Article 44 of the Water Services Act.

[4] Author's calculation from select utility financial reports.

[5] Author's calculation from select utility financial reports.

[6] Author's calculation from municipal financial reports.

areas, unclassified roads, public lighting, cleaning of public areas, drainage of atmospheric water, cemeteries and crematoriums, and other communal activities of local importance. The primary purpose of communal fees is to ensure that the costs of maintaining public infrastructure and services are shared equitably among property owners and users. This helps to ensure that all residents benefit from these essential services, regardless of their income level or property value. By paying communal fees, property owners and users contribute to the well-being of their community and ensure that their neighborhoods remain attractive and livable for all residents.

Municipal councils may approve the financing of the construction and maintenance of pre-school, school, health and social facilities, public buildings for sports and cultural purposes, and energy efficiency improvements of buildings owned by the local government unit from the communal fee.

All property owners or users of residential, business, and garage premises, construction land used for business activities, and undeveloped construction land are obliged to pay communal fees in Croatia. This includes both Croatian citizens and foreign nationals. The amount of the fee is calculated by multiplying the (uncapped) base fee with the size, location, and the type of the property. All of the elements of the formula are set at the discretion of local governments.

The *communal contribution* is a one-time fee that is paid to the municipality when new construction is completed. The purpose of the communal contribution is to fund the infrastructure and public services that are necessary to support new development. The amount of the communal contribution is determined by the municipality based on the volume of the new construction project and its location. The maximum amount of the contribution is capped by national legislation at no more than 10% of the average cost of construction of 1 m cubed of a building in Croatia.

Municipalities offer exemptions, fully or partially, to owners and users who are subject to communal fees or contributions. Exemptions are usually extended to socially vulnerable residents, elderly households, or low-income households at the discretion of the municipality.

*A concession fee for maritime property* is paid for a time-limited right to commercial use of a maritime property, with or without the right to build. It is granted on the basis of a public tender (in specific cases, it can be awarded at request) for purposes planned in the spatial plan, namely:

1. for a special purpose port
2. for nautical anchorage
3. for mooring
4. for capturing the sea (e.g. filling pools with seawater, the exploitation of the sea for medical products, desalinizers, for breeding fish and other marine organisms, etc.)
5. for the use of sea power for heating and/or cooling, installation and use of a solar/photovoltaic system and for other innovative solutions related to energy efficiency

6. for the performance of production and service activities (e.g. sea saltworks, catering facility, facility for fishery and aquaculture products, including live shellfish, etc.)
7. for the object of transport infrastructure and superstructure (airport on water, helipad, etc.)
8. for the economic use of the beach
9. for maritime service, built beach or swimming pool facility
10. for the cultivation of fish and other marine organisms, with the necessary accompanying infrastructure, which includes floating facilities that are placed at the location of the concession and are used for aquaculture activities

The concession can be granted for already built and/or constructed buildings and/or interventions in the area which, according to the special regulations governing construction, are not considered construction and may include the construction and economic use of buildings on the maritime property.

*Permit fees for commercial use of maritime property* may be granted in a public tender process for commercial activities and the use of maritime property of minor importance that does not limit the general use of the property (rental, lending, sale of food and beverage). Public tenders are generally published by February 1 and awarded to the highest bidder. Permits on maritime property are issued for a period of 2–5 years. A permit on maritime property may also be granted upon request for a period of up to 20 days for the performance of temporary or special activities, only once in a calendar year (cultural, commercial, sports events, recording of commercial programs, etc.), with the possibility of general use restrictions in terms of fencing and entrance fees. By decree, the Government of the Republic of Croatia prescribes the types of activities and the amount of the minimum fee for granting licenses on maritime property.

*Fees for the use of a public area* is similar to the permit fee for maritime property. However, local governments have broad jurisdiction over this fee and can set every aspect of it. Therefore, one can find several variations of this fee within a single municipality depending on the service performed at a selected public surface/area. Generally, a *rent* is paid for using the public area to set up kiosks and mobile devices for retail trade (sale of goods and/or services) and hospitality. The use of the public area for the installation of mobile devices for non-retail use, temporary buildings, communal facilities, organizing events, filming advertisements, films, series, shows, distribution of promotional material and commercial photography is subject to *a fee*.

Generally, the amount of the rent or fee for the use of the public area is determined according to the zone in which the surface of public use is located, type of facility, activity performed (purpose), the size of the lot and the period for which the surface is used, multiplied by the base fee. Fees can be one-time or recurring. For larger surface areas, advance payment discounts may apply. Some local examples include:

1. For the installation of kiosks and temporary devices for the sale of goods, services, and food and beverage, the rent for the use of public areas is calculated by

multiplying the area on which the kiosk or temporary device is installed, the period for which it is installed and the base amount of the rent.
2. For the use of advertising lockers, the fee is calculated by multiplying each meter square of the display area of the locker and the base amount.
3. For setting up a stage for holding concerts and/or entertainment content, the fee is calculated by multiplying the area (in meter squared) on which the stage is set, the period (number of days) for which it is set up, and the base amount.
4. For exhibiting a vehicle, the fee is calculated by multiplying the period (number of days) for which the vehicle is exhibited and the base amount.
5. For the use of the stage set up for the purpose of a political activity, the fee is calculated by multiplying the time period (number of hours) of use and the base amount.

Commercial entities operating in immovable cultural property or in a cultural-historical preservation area, are liable for a *memorial fee*. The basis of the memorial fee is the usable area of the business premises located in immovable cultural property or in the area of a cultural-historical preservation. The municipality can set the fee from 0.13 to 0.53 euros monthly per square meter of usable area of business premises. The municipality collects and enforces collection of the memorial fee.

Specific commercial activities are subject to an *indirect memorial fee* at the rate of 0.05% of the total income generated by the performance of the commercial activities such as:

1. Wholesale of tobacco products,
2. Wholesale of perfumes and cosmetics,
3. Retail sale of tobacco products in specialized stores,
4. Telecommunications (except maintenance of the communication network and transmission of radio and television programs),
5. Monetary intermediation,
6. Ancillary activities in financial services, except for insurance and pension funds,
7. Gambling and betting activities.

Collection and enforcement of the indirect memorial annuity is performed by the tax administration. Income from the memorial fees is used exclusively to protect and preserve cultural assets. The respective local government receives 60% of the fee and 40% is paid to the state budget for the costs of the national program of historic-cultural preservation.

The *tourist fee* is paid by persons who reside in tourist accommodation, persons who reside on a nautical tourism vessel, ships on a round trip in international maritime transport and international traffic on inland waters when the ship is at a berth in a port or anchorage port, etc. The tourist fee is paid for each overnight stay, in a fixed amount, and used for funding tourist promotion, tourist programs and improvement of conditions for tourists. Exemptions apply to children up to the age of 12, pupils, students, and vulnerable groups. The fee is a shared revenue of national, regional, and local tourist associations, as well as local government. Part of the fee is distributed in a fund for underdeveloped tourist destinations.

Persons, except for small forest owners, who sell products of forest exploitation (wood assortments) are subject to a *forest fee* in relation to the selling price of the product per stump. The forest fee, which is 10% of the selling price, is paid to underdeveloped local government units and to local government units in hilly and mountainous areas. In other local units, the fee is 5% of the selling price. Proceeds from the forest fee are used exclusively for financing the construction and maintenance of communal infrastructure.

The kindergarten fee or *parental fee* is a fee paid per child for attending voluntary nursery or kindergarten programs, while pre-school programs are generally mandatory and free of charge. Programs can vary from several hours to full-day programs. Parental fees are heavily subsidized to foster enrollment and affordability. Current enrollment levels are below the national target set for 2030 (Matković et al., 2020), so local units and the national government are undertaking several measures to achieve this goal. Full price for full-day programs may discourage lower-income families from enrolling and so local governments are heavily subsidizing parental fees. Some local governments have set fixed subsidy levels irrespective of individuals' circumstances, while others have a set sliding scale based on household income levels. Kindergarten operators in Croatia can be public or private, and some municipalities are extending subsidies to private service providers. There are notable examples of municipalities that carry out joint enrollment processes for public and private kindergartens, those who offer discounts or exemptions depending on number of siblings attending the kindergarten, while a few wealthy municipalities offer kindergarten services for free.

Recently, in order to boost enrollment rates and reduce parental fees, the expansion of kindergarten facilities has been financed from the Recovery and Resilience Fund (Government of Croatia, 2021a, 2021b) and employers can finance parental fees for children of their employees free of taxes and social contributions.

On the other hand, *wastewater and water supply service fees* are strictly regulated and subsidy options are restricted. Operators are required to fully recover operational and capital costs of service provision from fees but are not allowed to form fees based on the economic powers of consumers or the distance of consumers. Revenue and expenditure limitations apply. Tariffs for socially vulnerable consumers may not exceed 60% of regular tariff and the municipality will bear the remainder of the water tariff. Furthermore, operators are expected to maintain tariffs within the affordability range of 2.5–4% of average annual household income.

## 13.5 Bridging Urban: Rural Fiscal Disparities

Croatia, along with numerous other nations, grapples with the challenge of balancing local governance and finance between its urban and rural areas. This ongoing effort is particularly influenced by demographic shifts, with a trend of population migration from rural to urban centers. This phenomenon results in shrinking populations and tax bases in rural municipalities, consequently hindering their ability to deliver essential services to residents.

The lack of proper transportation networks, high-speed internet access, and waste management facilities in rural areas compared to urban counterparts further impedes economic development and restricts access to opportunities for residents. Additionally, urban areas tend to attract more funding and investment due to their larger populations and economic clout. This disparity is compounded by the demographic makeup, with urban centers typically boasting a larger and wealthier population base compared to rural areas. This translates into a larger personal income tax base in cities, generating significantly higher tax revenue for the government.

The most significant locally collected fee in Croatia, the communal fee, is levied primarily on constructed buildings. It is a fixed-rate payment for a number of services such as maintenance of basic infrastructure, maintenance of green areas and public lighting. Rural areas, with their characteristically lower building density and limited commercial or industrial development, have fewer properties contributing substantially to this revenue stream. However, an exception exists for rural coastal and island municipalities. These regions experience a higher concentration of vacation homes compared to continental areas, which are subject to both the Second Home Tax and the communal fee.

Furthermore, agricultural land, which dominates the landscape of many rural areas in Croatia, enjoys full exemption from property-related taxes and fees. This significantly restricts the ability of rural local governments to raise much-needed funds.

In recognition of these urban-rural fiscal disparities, the Croatian Government implemented an improved fiscal equalization mechanism in 2018 (Bajo & Primorac, 2017). This mechanism provides general grant funding to local governments with a below-average fiscal capacity, aiming to bridge the financial gap. Additionally, as of September 2023, a fiscal sustainability grant system was introduced specifically for kindergartens, primarily benefiting underdeveloped local governments. These initiatives aim to mitigate the challenges faced by rural municipalities and promote a more balanced local governance system.

## 13.6 Funding Territorial Development in Croatia: A Mix of Sources

The financing of territorial development actions, like land transformation or public works, comes from a mix of sources, varying depending on the specific project, location, and scale. In general, as listed above, local governments in Croatia rely heavily on communal contribution, communal fees, and local taxes for land transformation from rural or undeveloped to urban development land. Additional parts of the funding mix are dependent on specific characteristics of local government. Predominantly tourist areas of historic significance may opt for higher tourist and memorial fees to contribute to community development projects, while labor intensive areas may utilize income taxes more intensively on top of basic fees earmarked for development.

Croatian local governments are increasingly using available European Union (EU) funding for territorial development and capital investments in service provision facilities. In 2016, EU capital grants accounted for 11% of total local government capital expenditures, and in 2023 the share of EU capital grants increased to 51% of total local government capital expenditures.[7]

Large development projects often require funding levels which are beyond the available capacities of local governments. Therefore, local governments frequently *borrow at domestic and international markets* and use development fees to secure funding for debt servicing. Less often, municipalities and communal companies issue *municipal or commercial bonds* for financing of such projects.

A long-standing and underutilized source of funding for territorial development actions is a *voluntary contribution*, a vehicle through which residents can contribute with non-refundable fixed or incremental payments for specific community projects.

Recently, smaller local governments in Croatia have been using innovative tools to fund small-scale development projects, such as *crowdfunding* (The International Center for Crowdfunding, 2016). Crowdfunding has emerged as a promising alternative way for local governments to finance specific projects and directly engage communities. It attracts smaller contributions from a wider range of individuals, businesses, or foundations interested in specific projects and boosts community engagement because citizens feel empowered to participate in shaping their community by supporting projects they care about. In addition, project goals and funding progress are publicly displayed, fostering trust and understanding.

However, crowdfunding is typically not suitable for large-scale infrastructure projects due to funding limitations, platform fees and administrative burdens, as well as regulations and legal compliance. Municipal crowdfunding might involve specific regulations or legal requirements to adhere to.

Despite these challenges, crowdfunding can be a valuable tool for local governments when approached strategically. By understanding the limitations, planning effectively, and addressing equity concerns, municipalities can leverage this innovative approach to engage communities, pilot projects, and diversify their funding streams.

## 13.7 Conclusions

This chapter examined the role of municipal fees in financing local service provision in Croatia. It analyzed the existing regulatory framework, highlighting the balance between national legislation and local autonomy in fee setting. The chapter

---

[7] Author calculation from local government financial reports.

further explored the diverse types of fees, their applications, and their potential impact on equity, efficiency, and sustainability. Finally, it discussed challenges associated with fee implementation and strategies for navigating them effectively.

OSR play an important role in funding local service provision in Croatia. They consist of taxes, fees, and other charges levied by local governments on individuals, businesses, and property owners. Municipal fees constitute a critical source of revenue for local governments, enabling them to finance essential services and infrastructure. Croatia implements a mixed system, where national regulations establish parameters for fee application, while municipalities possess some autonomy in defining specific fees and exemptions.

Regulation and Autonomy: Essential services, characterized by high-cost recovery requirements, often have strictly regulated fees. Conversely, services deemed optional or non-essential experience greater local discretion in fee setting. This balance enables municipalities to adapt fees to local needs and resource availability.

Fee Flexibility and Equity Concerns: Municipalities possess the flexibility to modify fees based on service type, usage, and individual circumstances. This allows for differentiated charging, potentially fostering fairness by requiring higher contributions from more privileged users. However, concerns regarding potential inequities, particularly for vulnerable populations, must be addressed through targeted exemptions and subsidies.

Challenges and Strategies: While municipal fees offer significant financial benefits, implementation challenges cannot be ignored. Administrative complexity, lack of transparency, and potential burdens on low-income residents require careful consideration. To mitigate these challenges, transparency measures, clear communication strategies, and targeted social support programs are crucial.

Municipal fees in Croatia play a significant role in local service provision. Navigating the inherent benefits and challenges demands thoughtful implementation, equitable design, and a commitment to transparency and community engagement. By addressing these crucial aspects, municipalities can leverage this valuable revenue source to enhance sustainability and promote the well-being of their communities.

## References

Bajo, A., & Primorac, M. (2017). Improvement of fiscal equalization system in Croatia. *Aktualni osvrti, 10*(96), 1–2.

Eurostat. (2023). *Government revenue, expenditures and main aggregates*. Eurostat. https://doi.org/10.2908/GOV_10A_MAIN

Farvacque-Vitkovic, C., & Kopanyi, M. (2014). *Municipal finances: A handbook for local governments*. World Bank. https://doi.org/10.1596/978-0-8213-9830-2

Government of Croatia. (2019). *Water Services Act*. Official Gazette. Retrieved December 15, 2023, from https://narodne-novine.nn.hr/clanci/sluzbeni/2019_07_66_1286.html

Government of Croatia. (2020a). *Law on local and regional self-government*. Official Gazette. Retrieved December 9, 2023, from https://narodne-novine.nn.hr/clanci/sluzbeni/2020_12_144_2762.html

Government of Croatia. (2020b). *Law on the City of Zagreb*. Official Gazette. Retrieved December 9, 2023, from https://narodne-novine.nn.hr/clanci/sluzbeni/2020_12_144_2764.html

Government of Croatia. (2021a). *Amendments to the Preschool Education Act*. Official Gazette. Retrieved December 9, 2023, from https://edoc.sabor.hr/Views/AktView.aspx?type=HTML&id=2026597

Government of Croatia. (2021b). *National Recovery and Resilience Plan*. s.n.

Government of Croatia. (2023). *Decree on methodology for water service tariff setting*. Official Gazette. Retrieved December 15, 2023, from https://narodne-novine.nn.hr/clanci/sluzbeni/2023_06_70_1163.html

Jimenez, B. S., & Whitney, A. B. (2022). Revisiting the theory of revenue diversification: Insights from an empirical analysis of municipal budgetary solvency. *Public Budgeting and Finance, 42*, 196–220. https://doi.org/10.1111/pbaf.12309

Matković, T., Visser, M., Stropnik, N., & Williams, C. (2020). *A study on financing and governance of pre-primary education*. Oxford Policy Management.

Ministry of Economy of Croatia. (2022). *Water tariff affordability in joint service areas*. Ministry of Economy of Croatia.

More, T., & Stevens, T. (2000). Do user fees exclude low-income people from resource-based recreation? *Journal of Leisure Research, 32*(3), 341–357. https://doi.org/10.1080/00222216.2000.11949920

Network of Associations of Local Authorities of South-East Europe (NALAS). (2021). *Social welfare at the intersection of municipal finance and governance in South-East Europe*. NALAS.

Network of Associations of Local Authorities of South-East Europe (NALAS). (2023). *Local government finance indicators in South-East Europe, Statistical Brief*. NALAS.

Runtic, D. (2021). *Local government in Croatia: Responses to urban-rural challenges*. Eurac Research.

The International Center for Crowdfunding. (2016). *Successful campaign "You and me for kindergarten in Pregrada"*. Retrieved December 15, 2023, from https://crowdfundingvision.com/uspjesno-zavrsila-crowdfunding-kampanja-ti-i-ja-zajedno-za-vrtic-u-pregradi/

# Chapter 14
# Fees as Alternative Sources of Local Revenue in South Africa

**Thabile Chonco-Spambo**

**Abstract** The general statement that local government has extensive revenue-raising powers often hides the huge disparities in revenue generation among municipalities in South Africa and creates the perception that all municipalities are self-sufficient. The chapter looks at fees as an alternative source of revenue for local governments in South Africa. The chapter explores three primary ways of financing municipalities. It then discusses the financing of municipal services, with a focus on the importance of fees. Comparators of rural municipalities versus urban municipalities are used throughout the chapter to show how varied these two types of municipalities perform when raising their own revenue, are allocated their share of nationally raised revenue (the local government equitable share) and in how they receive financing for territorial actions. The comparators show that poor, rural municipalities get the shorter end of the stick across the fiscal framework. A descriptive research approach was used for this chapter, coupled with an evaluative conclusion. The latter argues in support of a bigger focus being given to assisting municipalities to leverage their revenue-raising powers, specifically that of collecting fees, as opposed to dependence on the equitable share as an equalization mechanism.

**Keywords** Local revenue · Equitable share · Municipal services · Indigent policy

## 14.1 Introduction

South Africa has three spheres of government: national, provincial, and local. All three spheres are financed through the national fiscus through what is referred to as an equitable share of nationally raised revenue (Section 214(1) of the 1996

T. Chonco-Spambo (✉)
Dullah Omar Institute, University of the Western Cape, Bellville, South Africa
e-mail: tchonco-spambo@uwc.ac.za



F. Velasco Caballero et al. (eds.), *Municipal Tasks and Financing*, Local and Urban Governance, https://doi.org/10.1007/978-3-031-99812-6_14

Constitution of South Africa[1] and Section 3 of the Division of Revenue Act 5 of 2023[2]).[3] Local government also finances itself through revenue generated from providing municipal services. Municipalities are responsible for providing roads, social development, water, electricity, and municipal infrastructure services. They can apportion resources to meet needs and respond to local concerns, while fulfilling national objectives (National Treasury, 2023a, 3). In light of the aforementioned, a discussion on municipal finance thus becomes important. Municipal finance is about the revenue and expenditure decisions of municipalities. These decisions can only be taken based on how much money a municipality expects to receive and how much money is needed to meet the municipality's needs.

The White Paper on Local Government 1998[4] provides that municipalities must have access to adequate sources of revenue—either own resources or intergovernmental transfers—to empower them to perform the functions assigned to them (Section G(1) of the White Paper 1998). Furthermore, municipalities are encouraged to fully exploit these sources of income to meet their developmental objectives. There are various sources of local revenue, which include an equitable share from the nationally raised revenue; conditional grants from national and/or provincial government; transfers from district municipalities to the local municipalities within their jurisdiction; and own revenue generated from property rates, other taxes, surcharges and fees, borrowings and investments (Section 214(1) of the Constitution). About one-third of local government revenue is transferred from the National Revenue Fund and the remaining two-thirds are derived from property rates and user fees (National Treasury, 2023b, 2).

Overall, this chapter is focused on fees as alternative sources of local revenue for municipalities in South Africa. The chapter begins with an overview of local government finances. This is followed by a discussion on how municipal services are financed, as well as the relevant authority that decides on the financing of municipal services. Thereafter, the chapter considers the importance of financing municipal services through fees, as well as the types of activities and/or services usually financed through fees. This is followed by a section on the financing of territorial development actions. The chapter then discusses the management formula for municipal services and its impact on the nature and characteristics of user fees. Lastly, the chapter considers the principles applied by municipalities to determine the amount of user fees to charge for services. Differences between urban and rural municipalities are provided in all the abovementioned sections.

---

[1] Hereafter referred to as the Constitution.

[2] Hereafter referred to as DORA.

[3] The division of funds between the three spheres takes into account government's spending priorities, each sphere's revenue-raising capacity and responsibilities, input from intergovernmental forums, and the Financial and Fiscal Commission.

[4] Hereafter referred to as the White Paper 1998.

## 14.2 Financing Municipalities

The national government transfers more than half of nationally raised revenue to the 257 municipalities (and 9 provinces) so they can perform their mandated functions. Local government's equitable share is decided through DORA, which allocates revenue between national, provincial, and local governments annually (National Treasury, 2023b, 72). Municipalities provide basic services such as electricity reticulation, water, sanitation, roads and community services. The division of revenue considers the differences between urban and rural municipalities and redistributes considerable resources from urban areas to fund rural services, which are generally provided at higher costs. The division of revenue also subsidizes services to poor households in cities and towns through allocations to urban municipalities (National Treasury, 2023b, 72).[5]

### *14.2.1 The Equitable Share*

The equitable share consists of unconditional transfers made to municipalities. Section 227(1)(a) of the Constitution sets out each municipality's right to its equitable share to enable it to provide basic services and perform the functions allocated to it. This provision is reinforced by Section 5 of the DORA, which provides for the equitable division of the local government share among municipalities for every financial year. The allocation of the equitable share indicates how much each metropolitan, local, and district municipality will receive from local government's allocation. Local government as a sphere receives the smallest share of the allocation because it has the power to raise its own revenue. For example, Table 14.1 shows that for the 2023/24 financial year local government's allocation totalled R96.5 billion (about 4.8 billion EUR) accounting for 9.7% of the national fiscus (Schedule 1 of the DORA 2003; National Treasury, 2023b, 71).

The equitable share fund provides for municipalities' operational needs, such as the financing of basic services [for poor households]; institutional costs such as councillor salaries; and community services such as municipal health and other district services (National Treasury, 2023a, 36). Consequently, municipalities' equitable share may not be affected if they raise additional revenue or if they fail to raise their own revenue (Section 227(2) of the Constitution). The formula used to allocate the equitable share is intended to be re-distributive and considers demographic information like population size and age, as well as developmental factors (National Treasury, 2012, 5–6; Section 214(2) of the Constitution). This is referred to as the

[5] Metropolitan municipalities contribute 70.1% of personal income tax revenue but receive only 32.6% of local government tax, whilst the 61 mostly rural local municipalities contribute only 5.7% of personal income tax revenue and receive 27.3% of transfers to local government (National Treasury 2023b, 72).

**Table 14.1** Division of nationally raised revenue

| R billion | Outcome | | | Revised estimate | Medium-term estimates | | | Average annual |
|---|---|---|---|---|---|---|---|---|
| Division of available funds | 2019/20 | 2020/21 | 2021/22 | 2022/23 | 2023/24 | 2024/25 | 2025/26 | MTEF growth (%) |
| **National departments**: | **749.8** | **790.5** | **823.0** | **854.4** | **828.6** | **835.7** | **877.9** | **0.9** |
| – Indirect transfers to provinces | 2.9 | 2.9 | 3.7 | 4.6 | 4.2 | 4.4 | 4.8 | 1.1 |
| – Indirect transfers to local government | 5.6 | 4.1 | 5.7 | 7.2 | 8.5 | 8.9 | 9.3 | 8.9 |
| **Provinces:** | **613.4** | **628.8** | **660.8** | **694.6** | **695.1** | **720.5** | **754.7** | **2.8** |
| – Equitable share | 505.6 | 520.7 | 544.8 | 570.9 | 567.5 | 587.5 | 614.3 | 2.5 |
| – Conditional grants | 107.9 | 108.1 | 116.0 | 123.7 | 127.5 | 133.0 | 140.4 | 4.3 |
| **Local government:** | **123.0** | **137.1** | **135.6** | **147.8** | **164.0** | **174.4** | **183.3** | **7.4** |
| – Equitable share | 65.6 | 83.1 | 76.2 | 83.7 | 96.5 | 103.8 | 109.4 | 9.3 |
| – Conditional grants | 44.2 | 40.0 | 44.8 | 48.7 | 52.0 | 54.5 | 57.1 | 5.4 |
| – General fuel levy sharing with metros | 13.2 | 14.0 | 14.6 | 15.3 | 15.4 | 16.1 | 16.8 | 3.2 |

Source: Author's creation from data provided by the National Treasury (2023b)

**Table 14.2** Per household allocations to municipalities, 2023/24

| Types and numbers of municipalities | Allocations per Household (HH) in R thousand | |
|---|---|---|
| | Average equitable share per HH | Average conditional grant per HH |
| Metro (8) | 3200 | 2400 |
| Secondary cities (19) | 4100 | 2500 |
| Large towns (26) | 5300 | 2800 |
| Small towns (99) | 6900 | 3900 |
| Rural municipalities (61) | 8500 | 5000 |

Source: Author's creation from data provided by the National Treasury (2023a)

"vertical division" of revenue, which is the total share of revenue allocated to local government. In addition, each municipality's share is said to take into account local conditions such as the number of poor households and the cost of providing free services (National Treasury, 2012, 9–10, 2023a, 37–42). This is referred to as the "horizontal division" of revenue, which is the total amount that is divided between the municipalities. Municipalities vary dramatically, with poor rural municipalities receiving most of their income from transfers, while urban municipalities raise most of their income themselves. The horizontal division of the equitable share necessitates for differences between rural and urban municipalities to be considered in the formula, which is done through a revenue adjustment factor (National Treasury, 2023a, 41–42)[6] that considers the taxing capacity of each recipient municipality (Section G(2)(2)(3) of the White Paper 1998).[7] As shown in Table 14.2, differences in the way municipalities are funded result in transfers per household to rural municipalities being more than double those per household in metropolitan municipalities.

### 14.2.2 *Conditional Grants*

Intergovernmental transfers are important to the fiscal relationship between national and local government as they assist municipalities in fulfilling national development programs and realizing the developmental duties of municipalities. Conditional grants, such as the Municipal Infrastructure Grant, the Infrastructure Skills Development Grant, the Program and Project Preparation Support Grant, and the

[6]The LGES formula has three parts, made up of five components: the basic services component, the institutional component, the community services component, the revenue adjustment factor, and the correction and stabilization factor.

[7]The dominant principle of the LGES formula is equity—the formula should enable all municipalities to provide a basic level of services to low-income households in their jurisdiction at an affordable cost. The second dominant principle is effective administrative infrastructure—the formula should ensure that even the most financially incapacitated municipality is able to have a basic level of administrative infrastructure to enable it to govern effectively.

**Table 14.3** Transfers to local government

| R million | Outcome | | | Adjusted budget | Medium-term estimates | | |
|---|---|---|---|---|---|---|---|
| | 2019/20 | 2020/21 | 2021/22 | 2022/23 | 2023/24 | 2024/25 | 2025/26 |
| Direct transfers | 122,986 | 138,098 | 135,625 | 154,188 | 163,972 | 174,382 | 183,330 |
| Equitable share and related | 66,627 | 83,102 | 76,169 | 87,311 | 96,546 | 103,772 | 109,368 |
| General fuel levy sharing with metros | 13,167 | 14,027 | 14,617 | 15,335 | 15,433 | 16,127 | 16,849 |
| Conditional grants | 44,191 | 39,969 | 44,839 | 51,542 | 51,992 | 54,484 | 57,113 |
| Indirect transfers | 5591 | 4194 | 7727 | 8171 | 8481 | 8862 | 9259 |
| **Total** | **128,576** | **141,292** | **143,352** | **162,359** | **172,453** | **183,244** | **192,589** |

Source: Author's creation from data provided by the National Treasury (2023a)

Local Government Financial Management Grant are allocated to municipalities to achieve specific objectives based on an accepted business plan for the grant's use (Schedules 4–6 of DORA).[8] Conditional grants enable municipalities to improve and increase services, therefore municipalities must meet certain criteria to receive these grants and must fulfil conditions when spending these grants (Part 3(194) of DORA). Intergovernmental transfers to municipalities are entrenched in a national Medium Term Expenditure Framework (MTEF), which is a three-year rolling budget containing the government's entire income and expenditure plans over three-year projections. This ensures predictability and transparency of grant revenue for municipalities (de Visser, 2009, 282). Table 14.3 shows the equitable share and conditional grant allocations made to local government over six financial years. In the 2023/24 financial year, local government received a total of R60.4 billion (about 3 billion EUR) in conditional grants and indirect transfers, with a minimal increase projected for the 2024/25 financial year.

[8] There are four types of local government conditional grants provided for in the DORA: Schedule 4 Part B provides the general grants that supplement various programs partly funded by municipalities. Schedule 5 Part B are grants that fund specific responsibilities and programs implemented by municipalities. Schedule 6 Part B grants provide allocations-in-kind through which a national department implements projects in municipalities. And, Schedule 7 Part B grants provide for the quick allocation and transfer of fund to a municipality in times of disaster. In addition, the above grants are divided into two: infrastructure grants and capacity-building grants. The latter three grants listed here are capacity-building grants (National Treasury 2023a, 55–56).

### 14.2.3 Own Revenue

National transfers account for a fairly small percentage of local government's finances because municipalities have extensive revenue-raising powers (National Treasury, 2023b, 72).[9] The White Paper 1998 provides that the power to tax is crucial to sustainable and accountable municipalities. The four important areas of local decision-making regarding taxation are:

1. The choice of tax to be imposed.
2. The definition of the tax base.
3. The choice of the tax rate.
4. The tax administration (Section G(2.1) of the White Paper 1998).

According to the White Paper 1998, the most vital factor out of the four to promote municipal fiscal autonomy is the choice of tax rate because the choice to vary the tax rate strengthens local accountability and empowers communities to challenge municipalities about the value-for-money of the services provided. Where communities receive good value for money, they are more inclined to pay for the services at the rate set by municipalities. However, if there is no value for money, communities may boycott rate payments and challenge rate increases set by municipalities (Ngcamu, 2019; Section G of the White Paper 1998).

Per Section 229(1)(a) of the Constitution, municipalities have original powers to raise revenue through the imposition of rates on property, as well as surcharges on fees for services provided by municipalities or on their behalf. Municipalities may also impose other taxes, levies and duties, excluding income tax, value-added tax, customs duty and general sales tax, if authorized by the Municipal Fiscal Powers and Functions Act 2007[10] (Section 229(1)(b) of the Constitution; MFPFA 2007). The income raised provides for basic services such as electricity, water, sanitation, and waste management. The cost of the aforementioned can be recovered through tariffs set by municipalities, together with the National Electricity Regulator of South Africa, which exercises regulatory powers over the imposition of electricity tariffs. In essence, a majority of municipalities fund most of their expenditure through property rates, fees and user charges/fees. The operating municipal income budgets for the 2023/24 financial year of R535.9 billion (about 26.6 billion EUR) were based on fees (mainly water and electricity); property rates; operational transfers from the national government, investment revenue, and other own revenue in the form of fines, tariffs, and subsidies as income sources (National Treasury, 2023c).

[9] In comparison to national and provincial government who have large spending responsibilities and limited revenue raising powers (National Treasury 2023b, 72), most municipalities would appear to be self-supporting, which gives them discretion to pursue local priorities. However, there are several factors that limit this independence, such as unfunded mandates from national government; increased socio-economic needs from society without the requisite tax base for municipalities to exploit their taxing capacity; effects of corruption, etc.

[10] Hereafter referred to as the MFPFA.

The ability of municipalities to raise income differs between rural and urban municipalities. Rural municipalities raise less income than large urban and metropolitan municipalities, who raise a majority of their own revenue. One of the major sources of local taxation is the property rates, currently levied by metropolitan and local municipalities in urban and semi-urban areas. Property owners (houses and businesses) in municipalities have to pay a tax based on a valuation of their property to finance municipal services. This is an important source of revenue for municipalities and enables them to function effectively. Another major source of local revenue are user fees which are directly related to the provision of municipal services.

## 14.3 Financing Municipal Services

Among the objects of local government is the object to "ensure the provision of services to communities in a sustainable manner" (Section 152(1)(b) and 153 of the Constitution; Section 73 of the Local Government: Municipal Systems Act 32 of 2000[11]). The duty to provide municipal services is accompanied by the right to levy a surcharge on fees for services provided. A municipal service is defined as "a service that a municipality in terms of its powers and functions provides for the benefit of the local community irrespective of whether –

1. such a service is provided, or to be provided, by the municipality through an internal mechanism contemplated in Section 76 of the Systems Act or by engaging an external mechanism contemplated in Section 76; and
2. fees, charges or tariffs are levied in respect of such a service or not (Section 1(1) of the Systems Act)."

The term "powers and functions" refers to the functional competencies provided in Schedule 4 Part B and Schedule 5 Part B of the Constitution. As such, surcharges may be levied on fees for services provided in the exercise of Schedule 4(b) and 5(b) powers and functions of municipalities, where such functions are tied to trading services such as electricity, water, sanitation, refuse removal, and public transport (Steytler & de Visser, 2021, 9–15).

To give effect to the objects of local government, per Section 153(a) of the Constitution, municipalities must provide "basic municipal services" for all. This is also provided for in the White Paper 1998, which lists water, sanitation, electricity, storm water drainage, roads, and refuse collection as "good basic services" (Section B of the White Paper 1998). Basic municipal services are municipal services that are "necessary to ensure an acceptable and reasonable quality of life and, if not provided, would endanger public health or safety or the environment" (Section 1(1) of the Systems Act 2000).

[11] Hereafter referred to as the Systems Act.

Generally, municipalities have enough revenue-raising powers to finance the bulk of the spending and finance the majority of their recurring expenditure out of their own proceeds. Their constitutional power to levy surcharges on fees for services is also entrenched in the Systems Act, which states that a municipal council has the right to finance the affairs of the municipality by charging fees for services and imposing surcharges on fees. Furthermore, Section 75(a) of the Systems Act grants municipalities the power to impose and recover fees, charges or tariffs in respect of any function or service they provide; and recover collection charges and interest on any outstanding amount. The constitutional power to levy a surcharge on fees for services provided implies the constitutional power to charge fees for the same services (*Rate Action Group v City of Cape Town* 2004, (12) BCLR 1328 (C), para 71). As such, a distinction has to be provided between "fees" and "surcharges on fees".

The imposition of a "fee" or "service charge" is calculated based on consumption. The imposition of a surcharge results in a compulsory flat rate paid in addition to the fee or service charge, irrespective of the level of consumption (MFPFA 2007). A "municipal base tariff" is the "fee necessary to cover the actual cost associated with rendering a municipal service" (Section 1(1) of the MFPFA 2007). A surcharge is thus an indirect tax, as it is a payment in addition to the normal fee and not in exchange for the service provided (Section 3 of the MFPFA 2007). Surcharges from trading services, such as electricity, are usually used by municipalities to fund or subsidize other important activities where limited or no charges are imposed (Fanoe, 2007, 732–755). The power to impose a surcharge is an original constitutional power given to municipalities. However, it may be regulated by national legislation. For example, Section 8 of the MFPFA 2007 empowers the Minister of Finance to prescribe compulsory national norms and standards for imposing municipal surcharges. To date, the minister has not prescribed such norms and standards. However, this has not prevented municipalities from imposing surcharges as per Section 229(1)(a) of the Constitution (read together with Section 75(a) of the Systems Act). There is, however, uncertainty about the process that municipalities need to follow to impose surcharges, which heightens the need for regulation to ensure "the reasonableness of the overall tax burden on consumers"; that surcharges on fees for services do not prejudice economic activities across municipal boundaries; and that they are set through a transparent process involving all affected customers or users (Fanoe, 2007).

### 14.3.1 Municipal Tariff Policy

Before a municipality imposes fees and tariffs for municipal services, the municipal council must adopt a general tariff policy that sets out the framework for determining fees, tariffs, and charges. This policy must comply with the provisions of the Systems Act, the MFMA, and any other applicable legislation (Section 74(1) of the

Systems Act 2000). Nine principles should guide a tariff policy, which include proportionality between actual consumption and payment; the equitable treatment of consumers in the application of tariffs; and the actual cost of a service being reflected in a tariff, to name a few (Section 74(2) of the Systems Act 2000). The application of these principles will vary when applied in reality due to differences between users. To address this, a tariff policy may differentiate between categories of customers, debtors, services, service standards and geographical areas, provided the differentiation does not unfairly discriminate (*White v City of Cape Town* 2010, ZAWCHC 79).

The tariff policy must be followed by passing a by-law to give effect to the implementation and enforcement of the policy. Lastly, the municipal council must pass a resolution to determine the actual amounts of the tariffs, fees, or charges for a specific year or whenever the council is required. Fees, tariffs or charges can only be imposed after a council passes a resolution with the supporting vote of a majority of its members (Sections 75(1), 75(2), and 75(a)(2) of the Systems Act 2000). It is important that a municipality's tariff enforcement be linked to improved credit control mechanisms (Section G (2)(1)(4)–(2)(1)(5) of the White Paper 1998).

### 14.3.2 Municipal Credit Control and Debt Collection Policy

For fees to be a lucrative source of local revenue, it must be a guaranteed source of revenue. The right of members of the local community "to have access to municipal services, is accompanied by the corresponding duty to pay for service received" (Section 5(1)(g) of the Systems Act 2000). The duty of municipalities to deliver services and levy fees, charges, or tariffs is often hampered by customers' unwillingness to pay. The unwillingness to pay can be divided into three parts: (1) affordability issues where users genuinely cannot pay for services; (2) the unwillingness of customers to pay resulting in "a culture of non-payment"[12] (Masungini et al., 2023; Enwereji & Potgieter, 2018; *City Council of Pretoria v Walker* 1998, (3) BCLR 257 (CC) at para 92); and (3) the unwillingness of municipalities to enforce payment due to capacity constraints or inconsistently applied debt collection policies and by-laws (that sometimes perpetuates (2) above). Whilst those falling into (1) may be provided for through free basic services programs (DPLG, 2006, 1)[13] or

[12] This culture of non-payment for municipal services has a long history in South Africa. Initially adopted to resist Apartheid injustice and inequality, before the ANC came into power it encouraged residents in townships not to pay municipal levies in order to make the country ungovernable. ANC succeeded and the culture of non-payment was born. Once in power, the ANC encouraged everyone to start paying for municipal levies, however, this was unsuccessful and remains so to date. The culture of non-payment has remained a constant feature in democratic South Africa.

[13] The term "free basic services" is used loosely as legislation extends basic rights to indigents to have basic services at no cost within a system of subsidization, which does not indicate that services are actually "free". All services have a cost attached to them, it is only a matter of who is paying for them and not whether they are paid for or not.

the municipal indigent program, those in (2) may not be paying due to poor and inconsistent services. This can be attributed to municipalities not having an effective billing system and not billing according to actual services consumed. Some customers choose not to pay as a way to avoid being exploited and targeted with higher bills from their municipality, knowing that the municipality will not enforce payment from customers in debt. The South African Cities Network (SACN) submits that "the willingness to pay responds to the willingness to enforce. The debate is more about what happens at a municipal level that causes municipalities not to enforce payment rather than what the community problem is" (SACN, 2015, 10). This means the focus should be on strengthening municipalities' payment enforcement mechanisms, instead of people's inability to pay, as well as their unwillingness to pay. That way if the willingness to enforce changes, that should change the dynamic of the willingness to pay. If people cannot get away with not paying, they will have to pay. An effective and efficient credit control and debt collection system goes a long way in ensuring this.

Municipalities must collect the fees due to them for services provided (Section 96(a) of the Systems Act 2000). This is essential to the long-term financial viability of any municipality. Therefore, municipalities must have suitable credit control mechanisms in place, as provided for in Chapter 9 of the Systems Act. These are provided through municipal credit control and debt collection policies. Municipalities must be able to measure the amount of services that households in their jurisdiction consume—which requires the efficient metering of services (Section 95(d) of the Systems Act). This further entails maintenance of infrastructure to reduce water leakages, for example, so that customers are not incorrectly charged (Gladwin-Wood & Pereira, 2015; Cokayne, 2023; and Sections 95(f)-(h) of the Systems Act). Secondly, municipalities must have accessible mechanisms to aid poor households in applying for discounts on fees. Where targeted relief is available for those households who cannot afford to pay for municipal services, a municipality's credit measures can be stabilized to reflect the gaps in revenue collected. Such gaps should be accounted for through municipal indigent programs. Thirdly, households need to receive accurate bills for the services they use, in an understandable format and on a regular basis (Section 95(e) of the Systems Act). Fourthly, municipalities must take robust measures to deal with those households that can afford to pay for municipal services but do not do so. Municipalities must keep a proper record of outstanding debts and act against debtors after a specified notice period (Chauke, 2016).

A municipality's credit control mechanisms must be provided in a credit control and debt collection policy that is given effect to by a credit control and debt collection by-law. The credit control and debt collection policy must be consistent with a municipality's tariff policy (Section 96(b) of the Systems Act 2000). The policy must provide for the following: it must require the municipality to set realistic targets for the income estimated from a particular source of income; provide for credit control procedures and mechanisms to regulate the extension of time for payment of accounts when money is due for payment of a service; provide debt collection procedures and mechanisms, such as notice requirements; provision for indigent debtors; set out consequences for payments in arrears, such as interest charges or termination of services; and set out measures to deal with theft and unauthorized usage of service (Section 97(1)(a), (b), (d), (e), (g), and (h) of the Systems Act). Once the credit control and debt collection policy is adopted, a by-law must be adopted to give effect to the policy's implementation and enforcement (Section 98 of the Systems Act 2000).

## 14.4 The Importance of Financing Through Fees

Local government's autonomy is solidified by its ability to raise its own revenue. Revenue raised through exchange or trading services such as electricity, water, wastewater management or sewage, and refuse removal flows into a municipality's budget and funds various municipal expenditure, including funding municipal services, which the municipality generates an income from. It is a cycle, requiring all parts to work to ensure continuity. To determine the importance of financing through fees, and the degree to which it takes place, one needs to look at municipal budgets. These provide the information needed to determine a municipality's operating revenue and sources funding it, as well as its operating expenditure and how it is funded by the municipality.

This section uses data from the 2022/23 financial year because the reporting is complete, and the data is readily available. The section will begin with consolidated information for all 257 municipalities to show the general importance of financing through fees. This will be followed by a look at the importance of fees in the operating and expenditure budgets of an urban municipality against the operating and expenditure budgets of a rural municipality. This contrast seeks to show the variations between urban and rural municipalities. It also aids the submission that the importance of fees as a financing tool is more prevalent for urban municipalities, as they raise much of their own revenue through fees. For rural municipalities, financing through fees is not as important as these municipalities are dependent on the equitable share and conditional grants from national and provincial governments, which often are used to fund the institutional needs of municipalities instead of service delivery.

### *14.4.1 Consolidated Municipal Budget*

Table 14.4 sets out local government's financial performance for the financial year 2022/23 and shows that much of the revenue (YTD Budget column) came from fees, followed by operational transfers and subsidies, property rates, other own revenue, and investment venue, which brings the total revenue, excluding capital transfers and contributions, to R470.3 billion (about 23.4 billion EUR) (National

**Table 14.4** (a) Local government consolidated operating budget FY 2022/23. (b) Local government consolidated expenditure budget FY 2022/23

(a)

| Description | Financial performance | | | | | |
|---|---|---|---|---|---|---|
| R thousands | Property rates | Service charges (fees) | Investment revenue | Transfer and subsidies - operational | Other own revenue | Total revenue (excluding capital transfers and contributions |
| 2021/22 Audited outcome | 70,781,321 | 189,533,585 | 3,280,099 | 98,482,651 | 36,021,694 | **398,099,350** |
| Original budget | 85,409,250 | 243,512,260 | 3,528,688 | 100,134,021 | 54,727,851 | **487,312,069** |
| Adjusted budget | 86,552,452 | 242,022,684 | 4,290,515 | 100,809,058 | 57,729,859 | **491,404,568** |
| Q1 Sept actual | 26,700,700 | 59,624,787 | 873,270 | 37,741,185 | 19,033,620 | **143,973,563** |
| Q2 Dec actual | 18,448,386 | 52,616,350 | 1,108,570 | 28,539,571 | 3,766,731 | **104,479,608** |
| Q3 Mar actual | 19,354,739 | 63,332,742 | 1,350,459 | 28,371,428 | 15,246,107 | **127,655,474** |
| Q4 June actual | 19,711,068 | 53,790,242 | 1,750,122 | 5,634,310 | 13,344,105 | **94,229,847** |
| YTD actual | 84,214,892 | 229,364,122 | 5,082,422 | 100,286,494 | 51,390,563 | **470,338,492** |
| YTD budget | 86,552,452 | 242,022,684 | 4,290,515 | 100,809,058 | 57,729,859 | **491,404,568** |
| YTD variance | (2,337,560) | (12,658,562) | 791,906 | (522,564) | (6,339,297) | **(21,066,076)** |
| YTD variance % | (2.70) | (5.23) | 18.46 | (0.52) | (10.98) | **(4.29)** |
| Full year forecast | 86,552,452 | 242,022,684 | 4,290,515 | 100,809,058 | 57,729,859 | **491,404,568** |

(b)

| Description | Financial performance | | | | | | | |
|---|---|---|---|---|---|---|---|---|
| R thousands | Employee costs | Councillor remuneration | Depreciation and amortisation | Finance charges | Inventory consumed and bulk purchases | Transfers and subsidies | Other expenditure | Total expenditure |
| 2021/22 Audited outcome | 115,513,196 | 4,085,863 | 34,842,087 | 10,238,265 | 133,558,845 | 3,711,372 | 126,843,449 | **428,793,076** |

(continued)

**Table 14.4** (continued)

| (b) | | | | | | | | |
|---|---|---|---|---|---|---|---|---|
| Description | Financial performance | | | | | | | |
| R thousands | Employee costs | Councillor remuneration | Depreciation and amortisation | Finance charges | Inventory consumed and bulk purchases | Transfers and subsidies | Other expenditure | Total expenditure |
| Original budget | 141,737,054 | 4,859,559 | 35,942,203 | 10,625,204 | 156,004,099 | 3,809,501 | 134,983,050 | **487,960,670** |
| Adjusted budget | 140,106,009 | 4,911,432 | 36,801,099 | 11,145,266 | 157,346,698 | 4,031,630 | 141,049,354 | **495,391,489** |
| Q1 Sept actual | 32,396,900 | 1,126,766 | 6,348,835 | 2,055,756 | 40,666,630 | 1,938,671 | 24,892,542 | **109,426,100** |
| Q2 Dec actual | 33,109,711 | 1,152,596 | 7,362,942 | 2,844,414 | 30,691,425 | 2,319,696 | 28,894,346 | **106,375,405** |
| Q3 Mar actual | 30,972,821 | 1,117,093 | 7,446,028 | 3,048,716 | 32,446,203 | 2,037,586 | 26,823,349 | **103,891,496** |
| Q4 June actual | 32,648,968 | 1,088,100 | 8,254,155 | 6,320,967 | 38,077,081 | 2,064,422 | 36,011,727 | **124,465,419** |
| YTD actual | 129,128,400 | 4,484,555 | 29,411,961 | 14,269,853 | 141,881,339 | 8,360,349 | 116,621,964 | **444,158,421** |
| YTD budget | 140,106,012 | 4,911,432 | 36,801,100 | 11,145,266 | 157,346,699 | 4,031,630 | 141,049,355 | **495,391,495** |
| YTD variance | (10,977,612) | (426,877) | (7,389,139) | 3,124,587 | (15,465,360) | 4,328,718 | (24,427,391) | **(51,233,074)** |
| YTD variance % | (7.784) | (8.69) | (20.08) | 28.04 | (9.83) | 107.37 | (17.32) | **(10.34)** |
| Full year forecast | 140,106,009 | 4,911,432 | 36,801,099 | 11,145,266 | 157,346,698 | 4,031,630 | 141,049,354 | **495,391,489** |

Source: Author's creation from data provided by the National Treasury (2023d), Annexure A

Treasury, 2023d). When the figure for operational transfers and subsidies is deducted from local government's total revenue, own revenue amounts to R370 billion (about 18.4 billion EUR). Fees accounted for most of local government's revenue, supporting the generalization that local government has extensive revenue-generating powers that it can leverage, hence its minimal allocation of the equitable share.

Out of the consolidated R229.3 billion (about 11.4 billion EUR) for fees, eight metropolitan municipalities were responsible for R146.5 billion (about 7.2 billion EUR) of the figure (Table 14.5), and secondary cities for R35.8 billion (about 1.7 billion EUR) (National Treasury, 2023d, 4–6). The data also shows that much of the revenue collected was spent on bulk purchases for municipal basic services and inventory consumed in the amount of R141.8 billion (about 7 billion EUR) (Table 14.4 consolidated).

### 14.4.2 Municipal Budget of a Rural Municipality

The municipal budget of Thulamela Local Municipality in rural Limpopo province is considered next. The municipality's financial performance for the financial year 2022/23 shows that from total operating revenue of R823.8 million (about 41 million EUR), much of it came from operational transfers and subsidies from the national government, followed by property rates and refuse removal fees (Table 14.6). The municipality is highly dependent on the equitable share, which makes up R577.5 million (about 28.7 million EUR) of its total operating revenue. The municipality does not receive many fees from trading services as there is no revenue for electricity, water, and wastewater management. The electricity function is performed by ESKOM, while the water and wastewater management functions are performed by Vhembe district municipality, under whose jurisdiction Thulamela is located. From the data, fees do not appear to be an important funding source for the municipality.

### 14.4.3 Municipal Budget of an Urban Municipality

The municipal budget of Tshwane Metropolitan Municipality in the urban Gauteng province is considered next. The municipality's financial performance for the financial year 2022/23 shows that from total operating revenue of R29.5 billion (about 1.4 billion EUR), much of it came from fees, followed by property rates, and transfers and subsidies for operational needs. Fees account for a majority of the revenue, at a sum of R16.8 billion (about 836.5 million EUR), while total operational expenditure amounted to R33.4 billion (about 1.6 billion EUR), representing a deficit for the municipality. Table 14.7 shows that Tshwane had budgeted R42.2 billion (about 2.1 billion EUR), yet collected R29.5 billion (about 1.4 billion EUR) at the end of 2022/23 financial year. Financing through fees is an important factor for the City of

**Table 14.5** Metropolitan municipalities' operating budget FY 2022/23

| Description | Financial performance | | | | | |
|---|---|---|---|---|---|---|
| R thousands | Property rates | Service charges (fees) | Investment revenue | Transfer and subsidies—operational | Other own revenue | Total revenue (excluding capital transfers and contributions |
| Original budget | 59,301,323 | 161,281,265 | 1,942,015 | 33,561,885 | 36,366,050 | **292,452,538** |
| Adjusted budget | 59,950,884 | 160,954,188 | 2,211,383 | 34,009,595 | 37,757,661 | **294,883,711** |
| Q1 Sept actual | 18,062,130 | 41,846,367 | 471,218 | 14,624,577 | 17,585,389 | **92,589,680** |
| Q2 Dec actual | 12,682,764 | 34,676,787 | 625,289 | 9,576,678 | 10,475 | **57,571,992** |
| Q3 Mar actual | 13,677,351 | 33,533,827 | 741,420 | 9,860,394 | 11,375,192 | **69,188,184** |
| Q4 June actual | 14,253,788 | 36,467,065 | 842,157 | 2,369,558 | 8,702,581 | **62,635,150** |
| YTD actual | 58,676,033 | 146,524,045 | 2,680,084 | 36,431,207 | 37,673,638 | **281,985,006** |
| YTD budget | 59,950,884 | 160,954,188 | 2,211,383 | 34,009,595 | 37,757,662 | **294,883,711** |
| YTD variance | (1,274,851) | (14,430,143) | 468,701 | 2,421,612 | (84,024) | **(12,898,705)** |
| YTD variance % | (2.13) | (8.97) | 21.19 | 7.12 | (0.22) | **(4.37)** |

Source: Author's creation from data provided by the National Treasury (2023d), Annexure A

**Table 14.6** Thulamela Local Municipality's operating revenue FY 2022/23 (preliminary results)

| R thousands | Budget | | First quarter | | Second quarter | | Third quarter | | Fourth quarter | | Year to date | |
|---|---|---|---|---|---|---|---|---|---|---|---|---|
| | Main appropriation | Applied budget | Actual expenditure | Q1 as % | Actual expenditure | Q2 as % | Actual expenditure | Q3 as % | Actual expenditure | Q4 as % | Actual expenditure | Total expenditure as % of adjusted budget |
| **Operating revenue** | 842,804 | 829,298 | 274,328 | 32.5 | 253,425 | 30.1 | 225,165 | 27.2 | 70,900 | 8.5 | 823,818 | 99.3 |
| **Exchange revenue** | | | | | | | | | | | | |
| Service charges—electricity | 0 | 0 | 0 | 0 | 0 | 0 | 0 | 0 | 0 | 0 | 0 | 0 |
| Service charge—water | 0 | 0 | 0 | 0 | 0 | 0 | 0 | 0 | 0 | 0 | 0 | 0 |
| Service charge—waste water management | 0 | 0 | 0 | 0 | 0 | 0 | 0 | 0 | 0 | 0 | 0 | 0 |
| Service charge—waste management | 40,993 | 29,167 | 7353 | 17.9 | 6366 | 15.5 | 7093 | 24.3 | 7649 | 26.2 | 28,461 | 97.6 |
| Goods and services | 20,100 | 14,365 | 2926 | 14.6 | 911 | 4.5 | 1016 | 7.1 | 1233 | 8.6 | 6085 | 42.4 |
| Agency services | 0 | 0 | 0 | 0 | 0 | 0 | 0 | 0 | 0 | 0 | 0 | 0 |
| Dividends | 0 | 0 | 0 | 0 | 0 | 0 | 0 | 0 | 0 | 0 | 0 | 0 |
| Interest | 0 | 0 | 0 | 0 | 0 | 0 | 0 | 0 | 0 | 0 | 0 | 0 |
| Interest from receivables | 22,088 | 10,160 | 2543 | 11.5 | 2571 | 11.6 | 2559 | 25.2 | 2627 | 25.9 | 10,301 | 101.4 |
| Interest from current and non-current assets | 22,000 | 50,000 | 10,531 | 47.9 | 15,429 | 70.1 | 15,432 | 30.9 | 19,145 | 38.3 | 60,538 | 121.1 |
| Rent on land | 0 | 0 | 0 | 0 | 0 | 0 | 0 | 0 | 0 | 0 | 0 | 0 |
| License and permits | 4538 | 1 | (96) | (2.1) | 0 | 0 | (23) | (2275.2) | 119 | 11,916.0 | 0 | 0 |
| Rental from fixed assets | 4858 | 4000 | 1530 | 31.5 | 512 | 10.5 | 33 | 0.8 | 510 | 12.7 | 2585 | 64.6 |

(continued)

**Table 14.6** (continued)

| R thousands | Budget | | First quarter | | Second quarter | | Third quarter | | Fourth quarter | | Year to date | |
|---|---|---|---|---|---|---|---|---|---|---|---|---|
| | Main appropriation | Applied budget | Actual expenditure | Q1 as % | Actual expenditure | Q2 as % | Actual expenditure | Q3 as % | Actual expenditure | Q4 as % | Actual expenditure | Total expenditure as % of adjusted budget |
| Operational revenue | 9760 | 4241 | 1087 | 11.1 | 1403 | 11.4 | 3732 | 88.0 | 1095 | 25.8 | 7318 | 172.6 |
| **Non-Exchange revenue** | | | | | | | | | | | | |
| Property rates | 99,633 | 93,243 | 23,090 | 23.2 | 22,927 | 23.0 | 23,240 | 24.9 | 25,198 | 27.0 | 94,455 | 101.3 |
| Surcharges and taxes | 1000 | 0 | 343 | 34.3 | 0 | 0 | (343) | 0 | 0 | 0 | 0 | 0 |
| Licences or permits | 11,638 | 12,277 | 2940 | 25.3 | 3137 | 27.0 | 2773 | 22.6 | 4745 | 38.6 | 13,594 | 110.7 |
| Fines, penalties and forfeits | 5352 | 9396 | 965 | 18.0 | 1499 | 28.0 | 2224 | 23.7 | 1767 | 18.8 | 6455 | 68.7 |
| Transfer and subsidies—operational | 586,173 | 586,449 | 217,095 | 37.0 | 194,580 | 33.2 | 163,318 | 27.8 | 2535 | 0.4 | 577,528 | 98.5 |
| Fuel levy | 0 | 0 | 0 | 0 | 0 | 0 | 0 | 0 | 0 | 0 | 0 | 0 |
| Interest | 0 | 0 | 0 | 0 | 0 | 0 | 0 | 0 | 0 | 0 | 0 | 0 |
| Gains on disposal of assets | 0 | 0 | 0 | 0 | 0 | 0 | 0 | 0 | 0 | 0 | 0 | 0 |
| Other gains | 0 | 0 | 0 | 0 | 0 | 0 | 0 | 0 | 0 | 0 | 0 | 0 |
| Operational revenue | 0 | 0 | 0 | 0 | 0 | 0 | 0 | 0 | 0 | 0 | 0 | 0 |
| Discontinued operations | 0 | 0 | 0 | 0 | 0 | 0 | 0 | 0 | 0 | 0 | 0 | 0 |

Source: Author's creation from data provided by the National Treasury (2023e), Consolidated section 71 Q4

**Table 14.7** City of Tshwane Metropolitan municipality's operating revenue FY 2022/23 (preliminary results)

| R thousands | Budget | | First quarter | | Second quarter | | Third quarter | | Fourth quarter | | Year to date | |
|---|---|---|---|---|---|---|---|---|---|---|---|---|
| | Main appropriation (MA) | Applied budget | Actual expenditure | Q1 as % of MA | Actual expenditure | Q2 as % of MA | Actual expenditure | Q3 as % of MA | Actual expenditure | Q4 as % of MA | Actual expenditure | Total expenditure as % of adjusted budget |
| **Operating revenue** | 42,151,840 | 42,294,940 | 12,345,354 | 29.3 | 2,852,933 | 6.8 | 5,660,098 | 13.4 | 8,702,287 | 20.6 | 29,560,671 | 69.9 |
| **Exchange revenue** | | | | | | | | | | | | |
| Service charges—electricity | 15,697,113 | 15,677,660 | 4,068,675 | 25.9 | 1,075,300 | 6.9 | 2,097,550 | 13.4 | 3,095,883 | 19.7 | 10,337,407 | 65.9 |
| Service charge—water | 5,554,721 | 5,445,662 | 1,232,510 | 22.2 | 494,403 | 8.9 | 931,876 | 17.1 | 1,290,757 | 23.7 | 3,949,545 | 72.5 |
| Service charge—waste water management | 1,502,943 | 1,612,221 | 365,949 | 24.3 | 193,388 | 12.9 | 266,326 | 16.5 | 370,394 | 23.0 | 1,196,057 | 74.2 |
| Service charge—waste management | 41,727,398 | 1,775,382 | 521,874 | 30.2 | 26,350 | 1.5 | 288,477 | 16.2 | 489,892 | 27.6 | 1,326,593 | 74.7 |
| Goods and services | 0 | 0 | 0 | 0 | 0 | 0 | 0 | 0 | 0 | 0 | 0 | 0 |
| Agency services | 0 | 0 | 0 | 0 | 0 | 0 | 0 | 0 | 0 | 0 | 0 | 0 |
| Dividends | 0 | 0 | 0 | 0 | 0 | 0 | 0 | 0 | 0 | 0 | 0 | 0 |
| Interest | 0 | 0 | 0 | 0 | 0 | 0 | 0 | 0 | 0 | 0 | 0 | 0 |
| Interest from receivables | 839,462 | 539,414 | 351,528 | 41.9 | 49,125 | 5.9 | 119,346 | 22.1 | 205,148 | 38.0 | 725,148 | 134.4 |
| Interest from current and non-current assets | 52,870 | 66,085 | 19,279 | 36.5 | 4810 | 9.1 | 18,181 | 27.5 | 48,946 | 74.1 | 91,216 | 138.0 |
| Rent on land | 0 | 0 | 0 | 0 | 0 | 0 | 0 | 0 | 0 | 0 | 0 | 0 |

(continued)

**Table 14.7** (continued)

| R thousands | Budget | | First quarter | | Second quarter | | Third quarter | | Fourth quarter | | Year to date | |
|---|---|---|---|---|---|---|---|---|---|---|---|---|
| | Main appropriation (MA) | Applied budget | Actual expenditure | Q1 as % of MA | Actual expenditure | Q2 as % of MA | Actual expenditure | Q3 as % of MA | Actual expenditure | Q4 as % of MA | Actual expenditure | Total expenditure as % of adjusted budget |
| License and permits | 0 | 0 | 0 | 0 | 0 | 0 | 0 | 0 | 0 | 0 | 0 | 0 |
| Rental from fixed assets | 185,329 | 167,563 | 12,007 | 6.5 | 8702 | 4.7 | 26,845 | 16.0 | 61,175 | 36.5 | 108,729 | 64.9 |
| Operational revenue | 468,969 | 560,796 | 129,939 | 27.1 | 59,823 | 12.8 | 80,860 | 14.4 | 198,746 | 35.4 | 469,368 | 83.7 |
| **Non-Exchange revenue** | | | | | | | | | | | | |
| Property rates | 9,102,662 | 9,101,842 | 2,163,426 | 23.8 | 741,674 | 81.1 | 1,485,675 | 16.3 | 2,289,121 | 25.2 | 6,679,897 | 73.4 |
| Surcharges and taxes | 0 | 0 | 0 | 0 | 0 | 0 | (29,071) | 0 | 29,071 | 0 | 0 | 0 |
| Licences or permits | 54,534 | 44,728 | 7086 | 13.0 | 3967 | 7.3 | 6698 | 15.0 | 15,153 | 33.9 | 32,903 | 73.6 |
| Fines, penalties and forfeits | 274,803 | 228,836 | 38,708 | 14.1 | 12,587 | 4.6 | 12,912 | 5.6 | 51,452 | 22.5 | 115,659 | 50.5 |
| Transfer and subsidies—operational | 4,496,044 | 4,619,121 | 2,826,201 | 62.9 | 113,455 | 2.5 | 182,940 | 4.0 | 254,186 | 5.5 | 3,376,781 | 73.1 |
| Fuel levy | 0 | 1,653,094 | 0 | 0 | 0 | 0 | 0 | 0 | 0 | 0 | 0 | 0 |
| Interest | 0 | 351,394 | 0 | 0 | 31,756 | 0 | 88,647 | 25.2 | 150,695 | 42.9 | 270,099 | 77.1 |
| Gains on disposal of assets | 0 | 0 | 0 | 0 | 0 | 0 | 0 | 0 | 718 | 0 | 718 | 0 |
| Other gains | 0 | 0 | 0 | 0 | 0 | 0 | 0 | 0 | 813 | 0 | 813 | 0 |
| Operational revenue | 0 | 0 | 0 | 0 | 0 | 0 | 0 | 0 | 0 | 0 | 0 | 0 |
| Discontinued operations | 0 | 0 | 0 | 0 | 0 | 0 | 0 | 0 | 0 | 0 | 0 | 0 |

Source: Author's creation from data provided by the National Treasury (2023e), Consolidated section 71 Q4

Tshwane and the under-collection from service fees appears to have impacted the municipality's budget.

The differences between the consolidated municipal budgets of Thulamela and the City of Tshwane are clear. The City of Tshwane's budget is a closer reflection of the consolidated municipal budgets, as it is one of the metropolitan municipalities that contribute massively to local government's budget. This supports the assertion that the degree of importance of funding through fees varies from municipality to municipality, especially between rural and urban municipalities. Urban municipalities generate more own revenue through fees, whilst rural municipalities lack the industry, businesses, and economies of scale to be able to do so (Harper, 2022; *Ingonyama Trust v eThekwini Municipality* 2012), hence they are highly dependent on the equitable share.

## 14.5 Financing Territorial Development Actions

It was envisaged that the capital expenditure budgets of municipalities would be mostly funded through national and provincial transfers. This, however, has not materialized as transfers are largely between the national government and municipalities (de Visser 2009, 283). Provinces have found it difficult to transfer grants to municipalities as a bulk of their income comes from transfers, which are spent on predetermined national norms on the payment of social grants, pensions, and salaries for provincial administration (Steytler 2005, 183–211).

Capital projects are investments in new infrastructure that are required to improve and increase services in a municipality. Capital projects are usually financed through grants from the national government that are targeted specifically at developmental needs. The infrastructure grant allocations to local government as of 2023 are outlined in Table 14.8. Various infrastructure grants (and the capital budgets of municipalities) have an objective to boost social and economic development.

One of the biggest infrastructure grants that channels funds to municipalities is the Municipal Infrastructure Grant (MIG). "Municipal infrastructure" is broadly defined as "the capital works required to provide municipal services". The phrase "works" includes "all the activities necessary to ensure that the works are delivered effectively, such as feasibility studies, project planning and capacity building to establish sound operational arrangements for the works" (DPLG 2004, 4). The MIG was established as a consolidated grant mechanism in 2003/04 by DPLG (now known as the Department of Cooperative Governance and Traditional Affairs, COGTA), to remove the backlog regarding access to basic municipal services, expand service delivery and alleviate poverty (DPLG 2004). Through the MIG, the national government provides grant finance to cover the capital cost of basic municipal infrastructure for basic services, roads and social infrastructure for poor households in various non-metropolitan municipalities. However, this grant is not provided to municipalities unconditionally. The key principles of the MIG are:

**Table 14.8** Infrastructure grants to local government

| R million | Revised budget 2022/23 | Medium-term estimates 2023/24 | 2024/25 | 2025/26 |
|---|---|---|---|---|
| **Direct transfers** | **48,857** | **49,733** | **52,123** | **54,646** |
| Municipal disaster recovery | 3319 | 321 | 0 | 0 |
| Informal settlements upgrading partnership | 4273 | 4365 | 4561 | 4765 |
| Energy efficiency and demand-side management | 223 | 224 | 243 | 253 |
| Neighbourhood development partnership | 1293 | 1475 | 647 | 676 |
| Rural roads asset management system | 115 | 115 | 121 | 126 |
| Water services infrastructure | 3701 | 3864 | 4038 | 4219 |
| Integrated urban development | 1085 | 1172 | 1227 | 1284 |
| Municipal infrastructure | 16,842 | 17,545 | 18,311 | 19,150 |
| Urban settlements development | 7352 | 8149 | 8793 | 9343 |
| Integrated national electrification programme | 2120 | 2212 | 2311 | 2415 |
| Public transport network | 6013 | 6794 | 7752 | 8369 |
| Regional bulk infrastructure | 2521 | 3496 | 4099 | 4045 |
| **Indirect transfers** | **8030** | **8335** | **8709** | **9099** |
| Neighbourhood development partnership | 201 | 101 | 105 | 110 |
| Water services infrastructure | 771 | 805 | 841 | 879 |
| Integrated national electrification programme | 3588 | 3821 | 3993 | 4172 |
| Regional bulk infrastructure | 3470 | 3607 | 3769 | 3938 |
| **Total** | **56,888** | **58,068** | **60,832** | **63,745** |

Source: Author's creation from data provided by the National Treasury (2023a)

1. focus on infrastructure that is required for a basic level of service
2. providing services to the poor and as such, funds must be targeted to reach the poor;
3. the provision of infrastructure must be managed to ensure local economic spin-offs through employment and development of local enterprise;
4. there must be equity in the allocation and use of the funds to make progress in closing the infrastructure gaps experienced mostly by the poor;
5. spending authority must be decentralized to the municipal level, within national norms, standards, and spending conditions;
6. there must be an efficient use of funds to ensure access to basic services;
7. the MIG must reinforce local, provincial and national development objectives to promote spatial integration and select appropriate service levels; and
8. there must be predictability and transparency in the allocation of capital grants, as it is important for municipalities and other stakeholders to understand how and when the grants are distributed (DPLG 2004, 3).

Transfers are distributed annually to municipalities per a formula. The formula comprises of five components:

Municipal infrastructure grant = C + B + P + E + N.

C—Constant to ensure a minimum allocation for small municipalities (this allocation is made to all non-metropolitan municipalities and provides a R5 million (about 248,973 EUR) base to all municipalities receiving the MIG).

B—Basic residential infrastructure (proportional allocations for water supply and sanitation, road and other services such as street lighting and solid waste removal).

P—Public municipal service infrastructure.

E—Allocation for social institutions and micro-enterprise infrastructure.

N—Allocation to the 27 priority districts identified by government (National Treasury 2023a, 46–47).

Municipalities play a key function in increasing economic growth by providing functioning and maintained infrastructure services. Municipalities are, however, finding it hard to build the infrastructure needed for growth, as well as balancing the increased demands of urbanization and closing the infrastructure backlog in rural municipalities. Although the MIG comes with close oversight and support from national departments, many municipalities struggle to use the grant appropriately and within the timeframes set by COGTA. In a study undertaken by the Financial and Fiscal Commission, the non-performance of municipalities and the underspending of MIG funds were credited to capacity constraints, especially institutional capacity. The absence of chief financial officers, project managers and other critical skills affects project implementation and service delivery (Financial and Fiscal Commission 2012, 2; Maake 2017, 25). The result is that the MIG allocation is at times underspent by receiving municipalities (Kruuse 2023; Ellis 2023; Parliament of South Africa 2018). For example, between the years 2012/13 to 2017/18, MIG transfers in the region of R3.4 billion (about 169 million EUR) were stopped and reallocated from underspending municipalities to better-spending municipalities. This had the effect of penalizing municipalities with lower capacity and consequently punishing poor communities (COGTA 2018). During the 2023 Medium-Term Budget Policy Statement, the Minister of Finance announced a reduction of R1.2 billion (about 59.7 million EUR) to the MIG allocation over the 2023/24, 2024/25 and 2025/26 MTEF due to municipalities underspending R4.2 billion (about 209.1 million EUR) of their allocation in the 2022/23 financial year. In a briefing to Parliament's Finance Standing Committee, the National Treasury criticized municipalities for using MIG funds to pay salaries for municipal staff, when the funds are meant for infrastructure development and maintenance (Parliamentary Monitoring Group 2023). The above case shows that some municipalities prioritize operational requirements, especially the wage bill, and lack an appreciation for the importance of the MIG in driving capital development to further service delivery, create a conducive environment to attract investment, and in turn boost job creation efforts.

## 14.6 Principles Applied to Determine the Amount of User Fees

Cost recovery is an important part of sustainable service delivery. The duty to pay for municipal services is not always fulfilled by customers due to many reasons, such as an inability to pay or other personal or family circumstances. The aforementioned circumstances can impact a municipality's ability to generate revenue from water and electricity provided to such households. With great foresight, the White Paper provides the following set of principles to guide municipalities in setting their tariff policies:

1. full payment of service costs: all households, except for the indigent, should pay the full costs of the services consumed;
2. payment in proportion to the amount consumed;
3. ability to pay: municipalities should develop a system of targeted subsidies to make sure that poor households have access to at least a minimum level of basic services;
4. fairness: tariff policies should be fair, meaning all people should be treated equitably;
5. transparency: tariff policies should be transparent to all consumers and any subsidies granted to a municipality must be visible and understood by all customers;
6. local determination of tariff levels: municipalities must be flexible in developing their own tariffs that align with these principles;
7. consistent tariff enforcement: municipalities must develop a consistent/reliable policy to deal with non-payment of tariffs, which must be targeted and applied with sensitivity to local conditions; and
8. ensure local economies are competitive: municipalities are discouraged from burdening local businesses unjustifiably through higher tariffs (Section (G)(2)(1)(4) of the White Paper 1998).

The White Paper 1998 further states that "municipalities must treat citizens equitably with regard to the provision of services". This must be done through the redistribution of resources, particularly with respect to subsidizing the provision of basic services (Section (G)(1) of the White Paper 1998). Because municipalities are at the coalface of the realization of most basic human rights, and thus at the coalface of service delivery, they are required to implement national policies and programs that impact their financial standing (Steytler 2005, 201). Municipalities are thus empowered to cross-subsidize between high- and low-income consumers, both between services and within particular services (Robert 2008). The extent of such cross-subsidization is at a municipality's discretion; however, discretion must be exercised within the framework of the municipal integrated development plan (Section 25 of the Systems Act 2000). One such approach that municipalities have adopted is through targeted subsidies to poor households or the free basic services program in the form of municipal indigent policies (White Paper 1998, Section (G)(2(2)(4); Fuo 2020, 290–296). This policy/program is subsidized by an increase in local government's equitable share to support municipalities in providing free basic services (National Treasury 2023a, 35). The National Framework on Municipal Indigent Policies 2006 (NIP) is the national policy driving municipal indigent policies and aims to ensure that indigents and indigent households are provided a package of free basic services (DPLG 2006, 3, 9–10, and 13). The NIP provides a framework which municipalities should use to develop and implement their own locally based indigent policies. Municipalities with necessary resources may provide higher levels of free basic services or more than those set out in the NIP (the four trading services) (DPLG 2006, 6 and 15). The NIP proposes three means of financing free basic services: revenue from property rates and other tariffs levied by municipalities; cross-subsidization where high-income customers subsidize the consumption of poor households; and from a municipality's local government equitable share (LGES) allocation (DPLG 2006, 6, 10–11, and 26). The LGES received more support and provisions for the basic services component in its formula, making it the ideal means to finance municipal indigent policies (DPLG 2006, 10).

The central message from the White Paper and the NIP is that the indigent must be accounted for in a municipality's tariff policy, and revenue-raising measures. It is submitted that a municipality's tariff policy, its indigent policy, its LGES allocation, and its annual financial statement or Section 71 quarterly reports must be aligned to show that indigent households are provided for and the effect this has on a municipality's own revenue. In testing this submission, the author examined the tariff policy, municipal indigent policy, LGES allocations, and annual financial statements of seven randomly selected municipalities[14] to determine whether principles such as the ability to pay or the personal and family circumstances of the user were taken into account when determining the amount of user fees for the 2022/23 financial year.

The following questions were used in the examination:

1. Does the municipality have a tariff policy? If YES, does it consider a user's ability to pay or family/personal circumstances?
2. Does the municipality have an indigent policy? If YES, does it align with the NIP? Does it align with the tariff policy?
3. Does the municipality provide basic municipal services? If YES, what is the revenue budgeted from each service for FY 2022/23?[15]
4. Does the LGES allocation include a basic services component? If YES, for which service/s and how much is the total allocation?[16]

[14] These seven randomly selected municipalities comprise of category A (City of Tshwane Metropolitan Municipality), B (Msunduzi LM, uMvoti LM, Makana LM and Thulamela LM) and C (Namakwa DM and Ngaka Modiri Molema DM) municipalities, and category B1, B2, B3, B4, C1 and C2 municipalities, from all nine provinces.

[15] Data on the operating revenue budgets is available at National Treasury n.d.b.

[16] "Total allocation" means the total basic services component figure, not the total LGES allocation. The Total LGES allocation may differ where revenue adjustment of the institutional component and community services component is applied (National Treasury n.d.a.).

5. Does the revenue from municipal services cross-subsidize the provision of free basic services?

From the seven municipalities sampled, some municipalities do not have up-to-date tariff policies (2022 going forward). However, where an older tariff policy makes mention of the indigent or refers to its indigent policy or program, a reasonable conclusion can be drawn that an updated tariff policy would have the same wording. With reference to question (1), most of the sampled municipalities have tariff policies or tariff by-laws to guide them in setting tariffs. Two out of the seven (Namakwa DM and City of Tshwane) did not have tariff policies or by-laws. However, the City of Tshwane had enough information in its credit control and debt collection policy that linked to the principles guiding tariff setting. The remaining municipalities' tariff policies considered a users' ability to pay or family/personal circumstances in as far as the policies make provision for the indigent (Msunduzi LM, Makana LM, uMvoti LM, Thulamela LM and Ngaka Modiri DM).

Regarding question (2), five out of the seven have indigent policies or programs that align with the principles in the NIP (six kilolitres of water, 50kWh of electricity, free sewage and free refuse removal for indigent households). The indigent policies have different eligibility criteria, levels of free basic services provided, and range of free basic services provided. Two of these municipalities go beyond the NIP benchmark (Tshwane and Msunduzi LM). However, two out of the seven did not have indigent policies (Namakwa DM and Ngaka Modiri Molema DM) (Ngaka Modiri Molema District Municipality 2019, 17–18). This is understandable considering that both municipalities are district municipalities with several local municipalities within their areas. They would have to subscribed to the indigent policies of all the local municipalities within their jurisdiction, especially if exercising the water service function on their behalf, as is the case with Ngaka Modiri Molema DM. Ngaka Modiri, together with the five local municipalities within its jurisdiction, must ensure that indigent households receive their six kilolitres of free water every month, per each local municipality's indigent policy.

Concerning questions (3) and (4), only three of the seven municipalities (Tshwane, Msunduzi and Makana) provide the full complement of basic services, as such their LGES allocations include a basic services component for water, electricity, sanitation and refuse removal. Two municipalities (uMvoti and Thulamela) only provide electricity and refuse removal service and as such, receive an allocation for electricity and refuse, as water and sanitation costs were allocated to the DMs that they fall under. The remaining two municipalities' (Namakwa and Ngaka Modiri) do not provide any basic services.

Regarding question (5), except for Tshwane, Namakwa and Ngaka Modiri, the remaining four municipalities' indigent policies indicate that they use either their ES or a combination of the ES and own revenue to cross-subsidize the provision of free basic services (Msunduzi Local Municipality 2023, 7; uMvoti Local Municipality 2022, 5; Makana Local Municipality 2023, 17 and 21; Thulamela Local Municipality 2022, 8). One would expect the municipalities with large amounts of budgeted revenue to propose using own revenue to fund free basic services, however, that is not the case. The municipalities with lower budgeted revenue (uMvoti and Makana) are proponents of using both own revenue and the ES, vocalizing this proposition in their tariff and/or indigent policies. Take uMvoti local municipality, for example, which does not generate much revenue from fees as it only renders electricity and refuse removal services. It generates little revenue from these two sources, yet its indigent policy strongly supports using own revenue to fund free basic services for the indigent, with a portion of the equitable share. On one hand, the boldness of this proposition may be driven by the municipality's need to fulfil its objectives, especially being a rural municipality. On the other hand, however, it is a strange proposition as the municipality is highly dependent on the equitable share and struggles to make own revenue. This makes one wonder: where would uMvoti Local Municipality derive the revenue to truly drive what they have set out in their policies and could such a proposition be setting it up for failure.

## 14.7 Conclusions

The viability of municipalities has been and continues to be a big problem for the South African government. National transfers make up a small portion of local government's revenue, with the majority of the revenue having to be raised by municipalities through their revenue-raising powers. Although these powers are said to be extensive, the number of municipalities exercising them and attaining self-sufficiency from them are few. The solution to this gap was to seek an equalization mechanism through the LGES, however, this mechanism has its own issues. The focus appears to be on providing for, rather than enabling all municipalities to exhaust their powers to provide for themselves.

The LGES, lauded as an equalizing system, is meant to place municipalities on the same financial footing. National Treasury reported that "transfers per household to the most rural municipalities are more than twice as large as those to metropolitan municipalities" (National Treasury 2023a). This, however, has not resulted in actual equalization in practice. An observation of the LGES formula shows that the formula does not cater for the higher costs associated with delivering municipal services in rural areas compared to urban areas as the allocations per component are standardized. Historic underfunding, and infrastructural, and geographic characteristics add to higher costs that more rural municipalities experience when compared to the more urban ones. Perhaps the formula could be modified by adjusting the "basic services" component by a geographical factor that explicitly represents rurality to cover the costs of service delivery. Adjusting the "basic services" component for rurality may send a strong message about the need for rural-urban equity in basic municipal service delivery.

The quest for equalization through the LGES comes at a big cost and creates overreliance on national transfers. This in turn hampers local autonomy. Should we continue seeking to equalize through the LGES? The submission is no. The differences between municipalities are too wide and varied to try and equalize using the ES. How the LGES formula differentiates or acknowledges differentiation (through the revenue adjustment component) has not resulted in big changes. Since the LGES formula comprises of the "basic services"; "institutional"; "community services"; and "revenue adjustment" components, the latter component is used to rank municipalities according to their revenue-raising potential. Where a municipality cannot raise a significant amount of own revenue, it receives a revenue adjustment score that enables it to receive the full allocation or a large portion of its institutional capacity and community services allocations of the LGES. Those municipalities that can raise their own revenue receive a score of zero and as such, do not receive an allocation from the "institutional" and "community services" components. This creates an incentive for municipalities to under-collect revenue to receive a higher allocation of their ES, which contradicts the notion of self-sufficient local government envisaged in the Constitution and government's fiscal framework. The LGES in its current form emphasises the financial disparities between municipalities, especially rural and urban municipalities. Even the proposition made above to adjust the "basic services" component would not guarantee equality. Instead of throwing money at the financial viability problem, through transfers and increases in transfers, there needs to be a bigger focus on assisting municipalities to leverage their revenue-raising powers to achieve viability. One way may be to lessen the high level of regulation of revenue generation at municipal level.

## References

Chauke, K. (2016). *Municipal revenue collection: A comparative study on the efficiency and effectiveness of Tshwane Metropolitan Municipality and the South African Revenue Service*. Phd thesis, University of Limpopo. Retrieved December 26, 2023, from http://ulspace.ul.ac.za/bitstream/handle/10386/1528/chauke_kr_2016.pdf?sequence=1&isAllowed=y

Cokayne, R. (2023). More COJ billing issues raised by high court order. *Moneyweb*. Retrieved January 30, 2024, from https://www.moneyweb.co.za/news/south-africa/more-coj-billing-issues-raised-by-high-court-order/#:~:text=The%20City%20of%20Johannesburg%20(CoJ,meter%20and%20other%20billing%20issues

CoGTA (Department of Cooperative Governance and Traditional Affairs). (2018). *Statement by the Minister of CoGTA, Dr Zweli Mkhize on interventions to support municipalities in distress*. Retrieved December 24, 2023, from https://www.gov.za/news/speeches/minister-zweli-mkhizeinterventions-support-municipalities-distress-20-mar-2018

DPLG (Department of Provincial and Local Government). (2004). *Policy framework for the introduction of the Municipal Infrastructure Grant (MIG)*. Retrieved December 17, 2023, from https://www.cogta.gov.za/mig/docs/2.pdf

DPLG (Department of Provincial and Local Government). (2006). *National Framework for Municipal Indigent Policies*. Retrieved December 17, 2023, from https://www.westerncape.gov.za/text/2012/11/national_framework_for_municipal_indigent_policies.pdf

de Visser, J. (2009). Republic of South Africa. In N. Steytler & J. Kincaid (Eds.), *Local government and metropolitan regions in federal systems* (pp. 268–297). McGill-Queen's University Press.

Ellis, E. (2023). Treasury orders Makana Municipality to pay back R60.7 million in unspent infrastructure grants. *The Daily Maverick*. Retrieved December 24, 2023, from https://www.dailymaverick.co.za/article/2023-11-27-treasury-orders-makana-municipality-to-pay-back-r60-7m-in-unspent-infrastructure-grants/

Enwereji, P., & Potgieter, M. (2018). Establishing a payment culture for municipal services in the North West province: A conceptual framework. *International Journal of Economics and Financial Issues, 8*(3), 227–234. http://www.econjournals.com

Fanoe, W. (2007). The Municipal Fiscal Powers and Functions Act: Towards the coordination of macro-economic tax policy. *Local Government Bulletin, 9*(5), 732–755.

Fuo, O. (2020). Nativism in South African municipal indigent policies through a human rights lens. *Law, Democracy and Development, 24*, 271–317. https://orcid.org/0000-0002-1442-8599

Gladwin-Wood, C., & Pereira, R. (2015). Unusually high water bill? *Schindlers*. Retrieved December 26, 2023, from https://www.schindlers.co.za/2015/unusually-high-water-bill/

Harper, P. (2022). Lights are back on at the Ingonyama Trust, but further municipal conflict looms. *Mail and Guardian*. Retrieved December 17, 2023, from https://mg.co.za/news/2022-09-12-light-are-back-on-at-ingonyama-trust-but-further-municipal-conflict-looms/

Kruuse, J. (2023). Makana municipality unspent conditional grant funds to be returned, shameful underspending by 83% of infrastructure grant. *Public Service Accountability Monitor*. Retrieved December 24, 2023, from https://psam.org.za/news/makana-municipality-unspent-conditional-grant-funds-to-be-returned-shameful-underspending-by-83-of-infrastructure-grant/

Maake, K. (2017). *Causes of unspent Municipal Infrastructure Grant in the Capricorn District Municipality: A case of two selected local municipalities*. Master's thesis, University of Limpopo.

Makana Local Municipality. (2023). *Tariff Policy 2023*. Retrieved December 23, 2023, from http://www.makana.gov.za/statutory-documents/policies/

Masungini, A., Maseko, G., & Robbetze, N. (2023). Evaluating the implementation of a municipal credit management policy. *Journal of Local Government Research and Innovation, 4*. https://doi.org/10.4102/jolgri.v4i0.101

Msunduzi Local Municipality. (2023). *2023–2024 Approved Indigent Policy*. Retrieved December 23, 2023, from http://www.msunduzi.gov.za/site/policies/index.html

National Treasury. (2012). *LGES Discussion Paper 1—Principle and objectives*. Retrieved December 1, 2023, from http://mfma.treasury.gov.za/Media_Releases/LGESDiscussions/Pages/default.aspx

National Treasury. (2023a). *Budget Review: Budget 2023, Annexure W1. Explanatory memorandum to the Division of Revenue*. Retrieved December 1, 2023, from https://www.treasury.gov.za/documents/National%20Budget/2023/review/Annexure%20W1.pdf

National Treasury. (2023b). *Budget Review: Budget 2023*. Retrieved December 1, 2023, from https://www.treasury.gov.za/documents/National%20Budget/2023/review/FullBR.pdf

National Treasury. (2023c). *Local government revenue and expenditure: First quarterly local government section 71 report for the period: 1 July 2022–30 September 2023, Annexure—Summary of total monthly operating revenue*. Retrieved December 1, 2023, from http://mfma.treasury.gov.za/Media_Releases/s71/2324/1st_2324/Pages/default.aspx

National Treasury. (2023d). *Local government revenue and expenditure: Fourth quarterly local government section 71 report for the period: 1 July 2022–30 June 2023, Annexure A*. Retrieved December 1, 2023, from http://mfma.treasury.gov.za/Media_Releases/s71/2223/4th_2223/Pages/default.aspx

National Treasury. (2023e). *Local government revenue and expenditure: Fourth quarterly local government section 71 report for the period: 1 July 2022–30 June 2023, Consolidated section 71 Q4*. Retrieved December 1, 2023, from http://mfma.treasury.gov.za/Media_Releases/s71/2223/4th_2223/Pages/pdf.aspx

National Treasury. (n.d.a). *Local government Equitable Share formula review discussion documents*. Retrieved December 17, 2023, from http://mfma.treasury.gov.za/Media_Releases/LGESDiscussions/Pages/default.aspx

National Treasury. (n.d.b). *Section 71 information (In-year management, monitoring and reporting)*. Retrieved December 17, 2023, from http://mfma.treasury.gov.za/Media_Releases/s71/2223/4th_2223/Pages/pdf.aspx

Ngaka Modiri Molema District Municipality. (2019). *Tariff Policy 2019*. Retrieved December 23, 2023, from https://www.nmmdm.gov.za/policies/
Ngcamu, B. (2019). Exploring service delivery protests in post-apartheid South African municipalities: A literature review. *Journal for Transdisciplinary Research in Southern Africa, 15*(1). https://doi.org/10.4102/td.v15i1.643
Parliament of South Africa. (2018). *Spending of Municipal Infrastructure Grant (MIG) remains a concern*. Retrieved December 24, 2023, from https://www.parliament.gov.za/press-releases/spending-municipal-infrastructure-grant-mig-remains-concern
Parliamentary Monitoring Group. (2023). *2023 MTBPS: National Treasury briefing with Ministry*. Retrieved December 24, 2023, from https://pmg.org.za/committeemeeting/37876/
Robert, V. (2008). Municipal service charges as a Masakhane tax. *FA News*. Retrieved December 24, 2023, from https://www.fanews.co.za/article/magazine-archives-fanews-fanuus/60/tax/1319
SACN (South African Cities Network). (2015). *Pricing and paying for municipal rates and charges*. Retrieved December 17, 2023, from https://www.sacities.net/wp-content/uploads/2020/03/pricing_and_paying_for_municipal_rates_and_charges_final.pdf
Steytler, N. (2005). Local government in South Africa: Entrenching decentralized government. In N. Steytler (Ed.), *The place and role of local government in federal systems* (pp. 183–211). Konrad-Adenauer-Stiftung.
Steytler, N., & de Visser., J. (2021). *Local government law of South Africa*. Lexis-Nexis.
Thulamela Local Municipality. (2022). *Indigent subsidy 2022–25*. Retrieved December 23, 2023, from https://www.thulamela.gov.za/docs/cpolicies/Indigent%20subsidy-08132022085808.pdf
uMvoti Local Municipality. (2022). *Indigent and pensioners rebate policy*. Retrieved December 23, 2023, from https://umvoti.gov.za/download/indigent-and-pensioners-rebate-policy-3/?wpdmdl=9414&refresh=6590d4e69178b1703990502
White Paper on Local Government 1998.

# Chapter 15
# Financing Municipal Services in Spain Through User Fees

**Ester Marco Peñas**

**Abstract** The financing of municipal services through user fees has been particularly controversial in Spain. This controversy has primarily arisen due to determining the appropriate legal form for the intended pricing. The issue has been addressed by the establishment of three distinct categories of user fees, each governed by a significantly different legal framework. Municipalities have the freedom to decide whether to charge for the provision of their services. The only service where the power to charge or not to charge a fee does not exist is the waste collection service. As of April 2025, all Spanish municipalities must require a fee to ensure that this service is not in deficit. The chapter also delves into other topics, such as the suitability of fees for financing urban development and whether user fees should be linked to an individual's ability to pay.

**Keywords** User fee · Garbage fee · Property tax · Development charges · Ability-to-pay

## 15.1 Introduction: The Power of Spanish Municipalities to Decide on the Financing of Its Services Through a Direct Payment by the Citizens/Users (Fees)

Spain's territorial organization comprises the central government, 17 autonomous communities, and two autonomous cities, Ceuta and Melilla, which hold a distinct legal status due to their geographic location in North Africa. The autonomous communities operate independently, overseeing sectors such as education and healthcare. Additionally, there are 50 provinces varying in significance across regions, alongside over 8000 municipalities that manage local affairs. According to data from the Spanish Statistical Institute, as of January 1, 2023, the number of municipalities stands at 8131.

E. M. Peñas (✉)
Institute of Local Government Law, Autonomous University of Madrid, Madrid, Spain
e-mail: ester.marco@uam.es



F. Velasco Caballero et al. (eds.), *Municipal Tasks and Financing*, Local and Urban Governance, https://doi.org/10.1007/978-3-031-99812-6_15

The services provided by municipalities encompass a wide range of activities, contingent upon factors such as population and geographical configuration. Spanish regulations establish a list of essential services that municipalities must provide. This list varies based on the number of inhabitants in the municipality (less than 5000, more than 20,000 and more than 50,000).[1] In municipalities with less than 20,000 inhabitants, some of the mandatory services may be carried out in coordination with or provided by a local government entity with territorial jurisdiction above that of the municipality, usually the provincial councils (*Diputaciones Provinciales*).

The design of the financing system for Spanish municipalities is the exclusive competence of the state (see Ruling 233/1999 of the Spanish Constitutional Court, ECLI:ES:TC:1999:233). Its regulation, currently provided for in the 2004 Local Finance Regulatory Act (LHL),[2] is intended to conform to the two principles established in Articles 140 and 142 of the Spanish Constitution: a system that provides them with sufficient means to carry out their functions (the principle of financial sufficiency) but which, at the same time, recognizes a margin of autonomy over their income (the principle of financial autonomy). As we will see, one manifestation of the principle of financial autonomy is that, in general, the decision as to whether a fee is established for services rendered is the competence of the municipality itself (Martínez Sánchez, 2017, 54).

The municipalities' financing system is not directly based on the specific services they are required to provide, which are dependent on their population. The primary funding sources consist of five taxes outlined in the LHL, with particular emphasis on the real estate tax (*Impuesto sobre Bienes Inmuebles—IBI*). Besides these taxes, public services can be financed through user fees, which can assume various legal forms depending on their characteristics.[3]

The considerable revenue potential from the *IBI* in some municipalities makes it unnecessary to resort to other sources of income to fund municipal services (Miranda Hita, 2004, 24). For example, one of the arguments put forward to justify the establishment of the *IBI* in 1988, the configuration of which substantially increased its revenue potential compared to its predecessor, was that from that moment on, the solid waste collection fee would be eliminated (Ayuntamiento de Madrid, 2009). Despite their legal compatibility and independence, many current political decisions in this field continue to be justified in this manner (for example, an increase in

[1] See Article 26 of Law 7/1985 regulating the Basis of the Local System (LBRL). All municipalities are required to provide the following services: street lighting, cemetery services, waste collection, street cleaning, water supply, sewers, access to populated areas, and paving of public roads. Here are the services that are added to this list based on population size: more than 5000 inhabitants (public park, public library, and waste treatment); more than 20,000 inhabitants (civil protection, certain social services, fire prevention and extinction, and sports facilities); and more than 50,000 inhabitants (urban collective passenger transport and urban environmental services).

[2] Royal Legislative Decree 2/2004 approving the consolidated text of the Local Finance Regulatory Act (LHL).

[3] See Sect. 15.4 below.

the waste collection fee has been justified by approving a reduction in the property tax, and vice versa).

The financing of municipal services through user fees has been particularly controversial in Spain. This controversy has arisen primarily due to the determination of the appropriate legal form for the intended pricing, considering the existing three distinct modalities, each governed by a significantly different legal framework: fees (*tasas*), public rates (*precios públicos*), and non-tax property contributions for public purposes (*prestaciones patrimoniales de carácter público no tributarias).* This topic will be addressed in Sect. 15.4 below. Here, we will focus exclusively on whether there are any limitations when deciding on funding public services through the establishment of direct user payments.

Generally, municipalities have the freedom to decide whether to charge for the provision of their services. Therefore, the decision to require payment is equally valid as the decision to offer the service for free. This explains, for example, why in some larger municipalities such as Madrid, there is no waste collection fee, at least for residential properties (Castells Rey et al., 2023, 18).

However, there are some limitations in this area. On the one hand, there are provisions that preclude a fee from being established. On the other hand, there may be cases where the municipality is obliged to charge a fee for the provision of a service, therefore preventing it from providing it free of charge. As will be discussed later in this section, these cases are exceptional.

Article 21 of the LHL sets forth a list of services for which municipalities may not levy a fee:

1. Water supply from public fountains.
2. Street lighting.
3. Public security in general.
4. Civil protection.
5. Street cleaning.
6. Compulsory levels of education.

Most of the cases in this list do not represent a real prohibition, since they concern services that are not divisible (Martínez Sánchez, 2017, 58–62). Therefore, it is the lack of divisibility of the service that prevents requiring the payment of a fee. In short, the divisibility of the service is a condition for the possibility of charging a fee. In fact, it is the divisibility of the service that makes it possible to establish a justified correlation between the cost of the service and the amount that the user has to pay.

Street lighting is a clear example of an indivisible public service. It is a service intended for the citizens as a whole, with no special consideration for any individual. The same principle extends to public security. However, it is possible to impose a fee in cases where the municipality is requested to carry out special surveillance of certain properties (Article 20(4)(f) of the LHL). Under such circumstances, the local authority is entitled to levy a fee for this specialized surveillance. Indeed, some municipalities implement charges for surveillance services rendered during large-scale events where the beneficiary of the service is identifiable. Lastly, civil protection and street cleaning are within this group of indivisible services.

However, we can find a real prohibition to levy a fee in 'water supply' and 'compulsory education', where services are easily divisible. The prohibition on charging a fee for providing a water supply from public fountains has historical roots. It relates to a time when most households lacked access to drinking water, so access to this basic need required the use of public fountains. The prohibition aimed at ensuring equitable access to this essential need. The current reality is quite different, so there is nothing to prevent eliminating the legal prohibition, although it is true that its practical application could be counter-economic. 'Compulsory education' is somewhat outdated as public education is no longer under local jurisdiction but falls under the purview of autonomous communities. The prohibition was initially based on the fundamental nature of compulsory education, which aligns with the current provision in the 1978 Constitution (Article 27(4)), stipulating it as a free service.

Finally, the reverse situation will be analyzed, i.e., services for which the municipality is obliged to levy a fee on the user, thus preventing the services from being provided for free. The only case where such an obligation exists concerns the waste collection service. This obligation stems from Law 7/2022 on waste and contaminated soils, which aims at fostering a circular economy. This law is based on Directive 1055/2022/EU, designed to harmonize regulations on managing packaging waste across the member states.

Article 11(3) of Law 7/2022 stipulates an obligation for municipalities, effective from April 10, 2025. Starting from this date, municipalities are mandated to impose a fee for waste collection, transportation, and treatment services (Ruiz Garijo, 2023, 35). Consequently, after this deadline, the provision of these services free of charge, as is currently the practice in some major municipalities such as Madrid, particularly for residential properties, will no longer be feasible.

Law 7/2022 does not directly determine the fee, but it does establish two criteria shaping how municipalities calculate it. Firstly, it requires that the waste collection service must not operate at a deficit. Thus, when calculating the fees, municipalities must ensure that the overall amount covers the total costs of providing this service. Secondly, the regulation specifies that user payments should correspond to the amount of waste they generate ("pay as you throw"). This requirement prevents the use of methods that do not accurately quantify the waste generated by users.

This obligation established by state legislation gives rise to the following reflection. Drafting and approving municipal regulations to establish user fees are inherently intricate (Martín Fernández, 2013, 72–76). Primarily, the complexity stems from the legal obligation contained in the LHL requiring municipalities to substantiate fee quantification by means of an economic and financial study (*memoria económico-financiera,* Articles 25 and 44 of the LHL). However, many municipalities lack the necessary resources, both material and human, to adequately conduct such a study. This poses a significant problem because an inadequately substantiated study might result in the courts withdrawing the regulation that establishes the fee (Gomar, 2023, 166).

This situation is not uncommon, especially concerning the establishment or amendment of fees related to waste collection services, leading to extensive legal disputes in various local councils. A notable case is the city of Madrid, which faced numerous appeals in 2009 when it decided to implement a waste collection fee[4] that was finally withdrawn for residential properties. Prior to that decision, dating back to 1985, no fee had been put in place for waste collection.

Considering this perspective, we believe that the states' role should extend beyond simply requiring the imposition of a fee. There should have been more of an effort to better coordinate regulations by establishing the fundamental components of this fee through legislation. In our view, this approach would yield several benefits.

Primarily, it would facilitate a degree of consistency nationwide, aligning with the trend observed in the regulation of local taxes. This harmonization initiative is justified since this fee stands as the sole compulsory user fee outlined in the LHL.

Secondly, it would simplify the justification for quantifying a fee for a service as complex as waste collection. This action would not be unprecedented. For example, the LHL extensively regulates the quantification aspects of another controversial fee, i.e., that applicable to companies operating services of general interest (such as electricity and gas) utilizing municipal public roads' ground, subsoil, or surface (Acín Ferrer, 2005).

Thirdly, if the quantification of the fee, including its essential components, were clearly defined in legislation, it would significantly reduce conflicts in this area. By anchoring the quantification to provisions in legislation, challenges from users regarding fee justification, based solely on shortcomings in the economic-financial study, would be mitigated.

Lastly, to preserve local autonomy, state regulation of the fee could be optional. Meaning, when establishing the fee, municipalities could choose whether to adopt their own regulations or adhere to those mandated by the central government.

## 15.2 Relevance of Financing Services Through User Fees

This table shows the aggregate revenues for Spanish municipalities in the year 2021 (Ministerio de Hacienda, 2023, 42):

[4] In 2010, a total of 62,691 administrative appeals were lodged against this fee, constituting 80.19% of the appeals filed that year, which amounted to 78,176 in total (TEAMM, 2010, 19).

| Revenue of Spanish municipalities in 2021 | | | |
|---|---|---|---|
| Type of revenue | | Amount | % |
| Own revenue 36,818,878,000 EUR 61.54% | Taxes (property tax: *IBI*) | 14,593,802,000 EUR | 24.39% |
| | Taxes (other: business tax, vehicle tax, construction tax and land value increase tax) | 9,278,812,000 EUR | 15.51% |
| | Fees (*tasas*) | 5,507,249,000 EUR | 9.21% |
| | Fees (public rates, *precios públicos*) | 563,523,000 EUR | 0.94% |
| | Other revenue | 2,255,005,000 EUR | 3.77% |
| | Equity revenue | 1,295,443,000 EUR | 2.17% |
| | Financial revenue | 3,325,044,000 EUR | 5.56% |
| Transfers 23,006,127,000 EUR 38.46% | Transfers for running costs TRC(State) | 12,607,686,000 EUR | 21.07% |
| | TRC (Autonomous Communities) | 4,910,565,000 EUR | 8.21% |
| | TRC (Provincial Councils) | 2,657,366,000 EUR | 4.44% |
| | TRC (Other bodies) | 317,830,000 EUR | 0.53% |
| | Transfers for capital expenditure | 2,512,680,000 EUR | 4.20% |
| | **Total** | **59,825,005,000 EUR** | **100.00%** |

Most of the municipalities' revenue derives from their own sources (61.54%) and not from transfers (38.46%). Although it is true that many of these transfers are unconditional and arise from the financing system provided for in the LHL.

Within own revenue, *IBI* outweighs any other revenue (24.39%). Revenue from the provision of services (including fees and public rates) represents a smaller but not insignificant fig. (10.15%). However, this figure does not fully represent the reality of public services financed by users for two reasons.

The first scenario occurs when the service is provided by a company (public or private). The payment made by the user does not contribute to the municipality's revenue. This applies to crucial services like water supply. For instance, in the autonomous community of Madrid, this service is provided to all municipalities by a public company (Canal de Isabel II), while in Catalonia and other parts of Spain, it is managed by a private company (Agbar).

The second scenario arises when a municipal service is provided by another public entity, such as the provincial council. In these cases, the revenue is not accounted for in the municipality's budget but rather in the budget of the respective public body.

Identifying the service with the greatest financial impact is challenging due to the way revenue information is presented in published data, often grouping various service types together (Ministerio de Hacienda, 2023, 52):

| Revenue from municipal fees in 2021 | | |
|---|---|---|
| Fees | Amount | % |
| Essential public services (water, sewerage, waste collection, sanitation) | 3,027,856,000 EUR | 54.98% |
| Social services (hospital, care, education and sports) | 405,342,000 EUR | 7.36% |
| Local services (licences, urban planning, tow services, etc.) | 593,639,000 EUR | 10.78% |
| Use of public domain (parking, supply companies, etc.) | 1,480,412,000 EUR | 26.88% |
| Total | 5,507,249,000 EUR | 100.00% |

Based on this data, services categorized as essential account for 54.98% of total fee revenue. However, due to the aggregated nature of the information, it proves challenging to determine which specific service generates the highest revenue. Additionally, as we have pointed out, certain services, such as the water supply, when managed by private entities, may not generate revenue for municipalities. Nonetheless, alternative sources suggest that waste collection and treatment services generally yield the highest revenue (Castells Rey et al., 2023, 30). There's a growing trend in waste-related revenue, especially considering the obligation, as discussed in Sect. 15.1, for all municipalities to enforce waste collection and treatment fees for users starting from April 10, 2025.

## 15.3 Financing Territorial Development Projects

Transforming rural land into urban areas through urban development requires the provision of essential basic services—such as water, sewerage, road access, and electricity—that must be adequately linked to municipal utility services (Ramón Fernández, 2023, section 3(2)(2). The costs arising from these urban development projects are borne by the owners of the land in the form of development charges (*cuotas de urbanización*). Therefore, municipalities do not assume these costs, unless they are the owners of the land to be developed. However, municipalities do collaborate in the collection of "urbanization charges", as they can use their enforcement powers to collect unpaid fees from the owner, so that they can be assigned to cover the costs derived from the urban development process (Velasco Caballero, 2021, 224).

Conversely, urban planning laws grant municipalities the authority to expropriate land earmarked for development. This enables the municipality, or a concessionaire appointed by the administration to directly undertake the development. In such cases, although the administration bears the development costs, municipalities will ultimately hold the resulting urban land as part of their assets.

Article 47 of the Spanish Constitution stipulates that the community should participate in the benefits generated by urban development. Currently, this benefit sharing is enacted through a requirement mandating landowners to transfer two specific types of land to the municipality, free of charge during land development: firstly, the allocation of land designated by urban planning for public facilities such as streets, parks, schools, health centres, administrative buildings, sports facilities, etc. (Article 18(1)(a) of the Royal Legislative Decree 7/2015, approving the revised text of the Law on Land and Urban Rehabilitation (LLUR). Secondly, it involves a proportion, often around 10%, of the developed urban area—specifically, a segment of the resulting land intended for construction purposes (Article 18(1)(b) LLUR).[5]

The second category of land designated for compulsory transfer offers municipalities the potential to generate revenue in two ways. Firstly, owners may have the option to monetize the land by providing its cash value to the municipality instead of physically transferring the property. Secondly, once this land becomes municipal property, it can subsequently be sold; however, any income generated from such sales is legally earmarked to finance investments and cannot be allocated for current expenditure (Article 51(1) of the LLUR). The municipalities' ability to generate revenue through these channels is contingent upon the level of urban development within their jurisdiction. For instance, municipalities like Barcelona, fully developed in urban terms (without any remaining rural land), face challenges in generating revenue via these means. In 2021, across Spanish municipalities collectively, monetizing urban development yielded 111,635,000.00 EUR (0.19% of total income), while the sale of these plots generated 313,860,000.00 EUR (0.52% of total income) (Ministerio de Hacienda, 2023, 61). Though these figures might not seem substantial on a national scale, they can significantly impact a municipality based on the extent of urban development activities within its boundaries.

Furthermore, municipalities have the authority to impose special contributions (*contribuciones especiales*) for executing specific public projects or extending municipal services, e.g., consider a scenario where residents in a specific neighbourhood are required to contribute to the installation of a new sewer system that directly benefits their area. These contributions can coexist with the fees charged for these services. Their aim is to have beneficiaries of these public works or services share a part of the associated costs (García Rubio, 2007, 251–253). Currently, this mechanism is underutilized due to the complexities involved in identifying beneficiaries and fairly distributing the contributions among them. In addition, there is a

[5] The tax on the increase in value of urban land (*Impuesto sobre el Incremento de Valor de los Terrenos de Naturaleza Urbana -IVTNU-*) is one of the five taxes that municipalities can levy (Sections 1 and 2). The *IVTNU* has traditionally been justified in Article 47 of the Constitution. This tax is levied when urban property is transferred. It has been a very controversial tax from the point of view of the ability-to-pay principle, which explains why its calculation system was deemed unconstitutional in 2021. The tax was modified at the end of 2021 to align its regulation to the Constitutional Court ruling 182/2021, ECLI:ES:TC:2021:182. In 2021 it collected 2,449,107,000.00 EUR (which represented 4.09% of the municipality's total revenue). However, this figure may be unrealistic, as a portion of this revenue could have been reimbursed to taxpayers in later years following its declaration of unconstitutionality in 2021 (Marín-Barnuevo Fabo, 2022).

significant political cost for any municipal government trying to implement this measure, as well as a substantial increase in litigation that has arisen in the limited cases where it has been employed (Martínez Sánchez, 2014, 317–318). It remains difficult to accurately pinpoint the exact amount of revenue that has been generated by special contributions in 2021 as they are grouped together with "other revenue" in statistical reports.[6]

Lastly, some autonomous communities have introduced compensatory contributions (*prestaciones compensatorias)* regarding the extraordinary utilization of rural land (e.g., for constructing desalination plants or solar power facilities). These contributions require the project owner to pay the municipality an amount equivalent to a percentage (usually 10%) of the investment value (Martínez Olmos, 2023, 121–122).

In practice, these contributions generate very important revenues for the municipality, albeit of an extraordinary nature, since they are only required when the investment is made. Additionally, they indirectly increase current revenues by elevating the land's taxable value for property tax (*IBI*) purposes. However, it is important to highlight that constructions capable of generating substantial revenue for municipalities often have a significant environmental impact. This explains why citizens may mobilize against these projects, despite their revenue-generating potential. It is not possible to determine the income generated by these contributions nationwide because aggregated data provided by the Ministry of Finance lacks a specific section to identify them (Ministerio de Hacienda, 2023).

## 15.4 Relationship Between a Service's Management Formula (Directly Managed by the Local Government or Through a Public-Private Partnership) and the Legal Nature of User Fees

One of the most controversial aspects regarding user fees in Spain has been the determination of their legal nature and, consequently, their regulation. This issue has given rise to successive legal changes, together with a long list of case law. Throughout this section, we will only refer to the legal and case-law evolution when it is necessary for a better understanding of the configuration and scope of the different legal concepts currently included in the broad category of "user fees".

There is no legal concept that subsumes the multiple formulas through which user payments can be instrumentalized. The broadest legal concept is that of "property contributions for public purposes" (PCPP), which encompasses all obligations of a pecuniary character (in most cases to give money) regardless of their legal nature (Menéndez Moreno, 2018, 3). There are two general types of PCPP: PCPPs that constitute the user's payment for public services received; and PCPPs that are

[6] See Sect. 15.2 above.

imposed without any service being provided (Arrieta Martínez de Pisón, 2018; Sanz Gómez, 2021, 183–232). In this chapter we will focus on the first type. The legal problem regarding the second type arises when establishing the difference between these PCPPs and taxes, since both are imposed without contributions, but the latter is characterized as being based on the ability-to-pay principle.

Regarding the regulation of the PCPPs, Article 31(3) of the Spanish Constitution states that "personal or property contributions for public purposes may only be imposed in accordance with the law". Therefore, the only regulation that is common to the PCPPs is that their establishment and regulation are subject to law (Palao Taboada, 2023, 10).

The Spanish Constitutional Court (in its leading case on this topic, Ruling 185/1995, ECLI:ES:TC:1995:185), pointed out that PCPPs are "coercive imposed payments". This specification was made to distinguish PCPPs from public rates (*precios públicos,* introduced by Law 8/1989, on Public Fees and Prices -LPFP-), referring to payments for services provided by the administration without the presence of coercive measures. The Spanish Constitutional Court defined coercion (*coactividad*) as the absence of real and effective freedom of the individual to bear the payment, except by refraining from using the service required by the public entity.

This absence of freedom can be observed in three scenarios (third conclusion of law in Ruling 185/1995). Firstly, when the realization of the taxable event results from an obligation imposed on the individual by the public entity, for example, when it arises from the provision of services or activities whose request or reception is mandatory. Secondly, when the activity or service required is objectively essential to satisfy the basic needs of the personal or social life of the individuals. Finally, when the services or activities provided by the public entities are carried out in a *de facto* or *de jure* monopoly situation.

Thus, even if the activities are not compulsory or essential, if they are only provided by public entities, individuals are forced to choose between not receiving the service or subscribing to the obligation to pay for the service from the public entity (Lozano Serrano, 2002, 625–626). This scenario shows a purely factual form of coercion, characterized by a high degree of uncertainty, and susceptible to change across different temporal and spatial contexts (Palao Taboada, 2023, 13). Such variability poses significant challenges regarding enforcement (Martínez Sánchez, 2020, section 2(1)(1)(1)(1)(3)), particularly in defining concepts such as "essential service" (second scenario) or "*de facto* monopoly" (third scenario).

To reduce the uncertainty that this notion of coercion may generate, Article 20(4) of the LHL lists public services and activities where the existence of coercion is considered, and consequently, a fee (*tasa*) rather than a public rate (*precio público*) should be levied. This list is not exhaustive, so this regimen should be applied to the provision of any other service if coercion exists under the terms previously outlined.

In summary, the primary distinction regarding user payments depends on the presence of coercion. If a user's payment to a public entity is coercive, it falls under the scope of a PCPP. However, if there is no coercion, the user's payment to a public entity is considered a public rate (*precio público*). As it falls outside the PCPP category, the establishment of public rates does not require a law. Finally, if the non-coercive service is provided by a private entity, it will be a private rate.

After the Constitutional Court's Ruling 185/1995, some doubts that already existed (Agulló Agüero, 1993, 559) were brought to the forefront, namely, whether the notion of PCPP was equivalent to the notion of tax (Ramallo Massanet, 1996; Lozano Serrano, 1998; Martín Jiménez, 2000). The ruling dismissed this equivalence to avoid the redundancy of considering the expressions "taxes", in Article 133(1) of the Spanish Constitution, and the more generic PCPPs, in Article 31(3) to be synonymous. It should be clarified that the Spanish legal concept of "tax" (*tributo*) is broader as it includes not only taxes (*impuesto*) but also fees for service provision when coercion is present (*tasa*).

The matter was clarified by the Constitutional Court's Ruling 182/1997 (ECLI:ES:TC:1997:182), which upheld that while all taxes are PCPPs, not all PCPPs have a "tax nature". Finally, the Constitutional Court's Ruling 233/1999 (ECLI:ES:TC:1999:233) confirmed the distinction between both concepts, stating that while taxes are paid to a public entity to fund public expenditure, PCPPs can be collected by both public and private entities. Moreover, they serve a "public interest" purpose, although this is not always directed towards financing public spending in every case.

This distinction is essential for two reasons: firstly, although both figures are subject to the rule of law, the principle of legality is more flexible with respect to PCPPs ("in accordance with the law", Article 31(3) of the Spanish Constitution) than to taxes ("by law", Article 133(1) of the Spanish Constitution). Secondly, non-tax PCPPs avoid the criteria of tax justice outlined in Article 31(1) of the Spanish Constitution, particularly the ability-to-pay principle. This aspect has not been without criticism (Martín Jiménez, 2000, 184; Lozano Serrano, 2002, 645).

Despite articulating the distinction between both concepts, the interpretation established in the 185/1995 ruling, based on coercion, resulted in an extensive understanding of fees/*tasas* (with a tax nature, at least according to Spanish law) that almost became blurred with the notion of PCPPs. Within this legal framework, it was not feasible to finance essential public services provided by private entities using fees (private rates). Typically, these services were provided through concessions where users paid the private entities directly.

This issue caused a large number of legal disputes, particularly in sectors such as household water supply. Firstly, if the payment made by the user qualified as a fee/*tasa* (of a tax nature), the service's charge had to adhere to the quantitative limitations inherent in fees, tied to the service's cost. In particular, at the state level, the cost of the service is set as an objective to be achieved (Article 7 of LPFP "Fees shall aim to cover the cost of the service or activity that constitutes the taxable event"), while at the local level, it functions as a limit not to be exceeded (Article 24 of LHL specifies that "the amount of fees for a service or activity provision must not, as a whole, surpass the actual or foreseeable cost of the service or activity concerned, or alternatively, the value of the service received").

Therefore, neither of these provisions set limitations preventing the service cost from being covered by fees. In addition, the doubts surrounding the inclusion of industrial profit in the calculation of the costs covered by the fees was positively overcome (Falcón y Tella, 2016, 5). Despite the above, it was understood that the legal framework of the fees (*tasas*) under Spanish domestic law implied limitations to the concessionaire's profit, potentially leading to undesired effects such as crowding out private investment or negatively impacting the quality of the service.

Secondly, if the payment qualifies as a fee (*tasa*), the concessionaire no longer collects any payments directly from the users. Instead, their remuneration will depend on the administration's payment through the revenue budget (Tornos Mas, 2011, 28).

Lastly, it was considered that if the concessionaire was financed through tariffs (private rates), the private operator assumed a greater share of the contract's operational risk (Tornos Mas, 2018, 1475; Martín Rodríguez, 2019, 303). The transfer of this operational risk to the private sector is required by Article 5 of Directive 2014/23/EU for the existence of a concession contract. In turn, it reduced the impact of the contract on the municipality's public deficit and debt levels.

The situation described prompted regulatory changes to allow the use of tariffs, primarily by modifying the concept of fees (*tasa*) outlined in Article 2(2) of the General Taxation Law. Legal scholars attributed various effects to this legislative reform (Villar Rojas, 2005, 9; Tornos Mas, 2011, 25–26; Falcón y Tella, 2011, 7–8; Martínez Sánchez, 2019, 242), contributing to fluctuating case law with evolving criteria (among others, SSTS of September 28th, 2015, ECLI:ES:TS:2015:3990, and November 23rd, 2015, ECLI:ES:TS:2015:5037).

Finally, the issue has been solved with the introduction of a new legal concept: the non-tax PCPP. In particular, the 43rd additional provision of the Spanish Public Procurement Law 9/2017 establishes that the coercive payments perceived for the exploitation of public works or the provision of public services directly by the administration, through a public company, or via indirect management (primarily concessions), will fall under the category of non-tax PCPPs.

This essentially means that the legal nature of the payment will be determined by the service management formula. Thus, even if the payment is coercive (according to the terms outlined in Ruling 185/1995), if it is made to a private operator or to the public administration (via a public company or public business entity), it will not be deemed to be a fee (*tasa*). It will be considered as a non-tax PCPP.

The establishment of the non-tax PCPPs was not free from debate; however, the Constitutional Court (Ruling 63/2019, ES:TC:2019:63) upheld the constitutionality of the PCPPs without a tax nature. The Court ruled that, under the Constitution, the legislator has considerable flexibility to devise the framework for providing and managing public services, extending this flexibility to its method of financing. Therefore, the Constitution does not mandate a singular model for the management of public services, nor does it stipulate that funding the provision of public services must exclusively derive from coercive fees (*tasas*).

Regarding the quantification of non-tax PCPPs, two critical aspects merit attention. Firstly, although these charges are not formally subject to the ability-to-pay principle contained in Article 31(1) of the Spanish Constitution, due to their non-tax nature, the legislator remains constrained by the broader constitutional framework when introducing such payments. Consequently, they must align with the requisites and constraints outlined therein (Villar Rojas, 2000, 114; particularly in the context of a non-tax PCPP, Gómez-Ferrer Rincón, 2015, 54–55).

Given the coercive nature of a non-tax PCPPs, which operates independently of market logic, doubts arise about completely disregarding the principle of equivalence when establishing it. The concept of benefits deriving from service provision is fundamentally associated with the principle of equivalence and the overarching notion of commutative justice (Ortiz Calle, 2018, 24).

Moreover, this interpretation of non-tax PCPPs quantification serves to prevent potential infringements of the principle of equality. It prevents situations where citizens from different municipalities pay considerably different amounts for equivalent services—a possibility contemplated by some authors (Aneiros Pereira, 2018, 33).

Secondly, regarding the non-tax PCPP quantification method, Article 20(6) of LHL does not specify how they should be quantified, as it only refers to Article 103 of the Spanish Public Procurement Law 9/2017, which establishes the regime for the revision of prices in contracts in the public sector. Some authors argue that the complete absence of regulations on the quantification of non-tax PCPP should have led to them being declared unconstitutional (Martínez, 2020, 57–83). In contrast, other authors consider that it cannot be stated that fees *(tasa)* have, by definition, greater guarantees than the tariff (*tarifa*) with a non-tax nature, and it is necessary to analyze how the latter is determined (Fernández, 2012, 256–258).

The establishment of non-tax PCPPs by the municipality, like municipal taxes and fees, must be carried out with the approval of a regulatory provision by the body representing the citizens (the plenary, *pleno).* These regulatory provisions or bylaws, when referring to a tax (*impuesto*) or a coercive fee (*tasa*) are called tax ordinances (*ordenanzas fiscales*), which are regulated in detail in the LHL.[7] When they do not affect a tax, they are simply referred to as ordinances (*ordenanzas),* the regulations are different, although they are also approved by the municipal plenary. Non-tax PCPPs will be approved through a non-tax ordinance.

Despite non-tax PCPPs being approved through a non-tax ordinance, the content of the latter should closely resemble that of tax ordinances, at least in their essential elements (Acín Ferrer, 2018, 3 and 9). In particular, there must be an economic-financial study (*memoria económico-financiera*) for the approval and quantification of the non-tax PCPP, as with the case of fees (*tasas*). The justification behind this need is the same as that pointed out by the Supreme Court for requiring such a study not only for fees (*tasas*) but also for public rates "because it is in the nature of things. If it is a matter of financing the cost of certain municipal activities and services, it is essential to know what the cost is" (Ruling September 29, 2015,

[7] The special contributions (*contribuciones especiales*) also fall within the broad concept of tax in the Spanish legal system. Therefore, their establishment is also carried out through approval by the municipal plenary of a tax ordinance.

ECLI:ES:TS:2015:4011). Therefore, the economic-financial study serves as a tool to prevent arbitrariness. Without such a study, it would be challenging to determine the service cost, even if the administrative and technical conditions are provided (Aneiros Pereira, 2018, 33).

## 15.5 The Role of the Ability to Pay and Individual/Family Circumstances of the User in Establishing Public Service Fees

The ability-to-pay principle holds a secondary position in the design of user fees, since, unlike taxes, the obligation to pay is not based on a specific event reflecting higher or lower economic capacity. Instead, the payment obligation for user fees arises from receiving a service from the administration, hereby emphasizing the prevalent application of the benefit principle (Martínez Sánchez, 2022, section 2(1)(2)(1)(4); Tassonyi & Kitchen, 2021, 2).

The Spanish Supreme Court has acknowledged the modulation of fee amounts according to criteria related to economic capacity. This approach, however, may result in certain individuals being compelled to contribute an amount surpassing the individual cost of the service (Martínez Sánchez 2022, section 2(1)(2)(1)(4)). However, as explained in Sect. 15.4, the user fees under the ability-to-pay principle have a clear limit established by law, i.e., that the overall amount should not exceed the cost of the service (Article 24(2) of LHL, this limitation does not apply to public rates (*precios públicos*)). A paradigmatic example of the quantification of the fee according to economic capacity is the waste collection fee in municipalities where it is established based on the value of the property for real estate tax purposes (IBI) (see the Spanish Supreme Court Ruling of January 4, 2013, ECLI:ES:TS:2013:1).

In summary, establishing fees based on the ability-to-pay principle is possible but not mandatory. The integration of the ability-to-pay principle together with the rest of the user's personal and family circumstances has been addressed, in general, through the introduction of exemptions and reductions in the fee, rather than in the drafting of a system for quantifying the fee. In fact, the LHL restricts municipalities from granting tax benefits based on factors other than the economic capacity of the user, unless these are officially recognized in a regulation that has the status of law (Martín Fernández, 2013, 90 and Articles 9(1), 24(4) and 44(2) of LHL). For instance, the Supreme Court has ruled that a municipality cannot establish fees for different amounts for the use of sports facilities based on whether the users reside in the municipality (see Ruling of the Supreme Court of July 20, 2023, ECLI:ES:TS:2023:3567).

It is challenging to systematize the implementation of these tax benefits in practice since achieving this would require analyzing the regulations of each fee across over eight thousand municipalities in Spain. In general, tax benefits have been established for three specific groups: unemployed individuals, large families,[8] and individuals or families with limited income. Additionally, the advanced age of users is also considered, albeit to a lesser extent.

In this regard, the allocation of tax benefits to both large families and elderly users may face challenges, particularly if their income surpasses specific thresholds. Hence, it becomes appropriate to consider modulating these tax benefits by factoring in the economic capacity of users, as is the case at a national level, in relation to the percentage of the price that users of the public health system have to pay when purchasing medicines (Article 102 of Royal Legislative Decree 1/2015, which approves the Law on guarantees and rational use of medicines and health products). Given that there is already a monitoring system in the health sector for determining the contribution rate (for the purchase of medication) based on economic capacity, it should not be too complex to use the same system for regulating and managing fees for public services.

Finally, it is important to note the absence of data regarding the revenue impact resulting from the application of these benefits. The Ministry of Finance's aggregate data fails to address this matter. It is striking that the annual report released by the ministry omits this information, especially considering that municipalities are mandated, per Article 168(1)(d) of the LHL, to include in their budgets an annex detailing how the implementation of these, and other tax benefits, influence their revenues.

## 15.6 Conclusions

Spanish municipalities hold a high degree of autonomy in deciding whether to establish fees for the provision of services. Generally, they can freely choose whether or not to charge for their services.

However, this freedom has recently been limited. As of April 10, 2025, a new obligation will take effect, which requires all municipalities to impose a fee for such a crucial local service as waste collection. Until this date, not all municipalities charged for this service, and those that did often excluded residential properties. The widespread implementation of a waste collection user fee across Spain will make this charge one of the primary revenue sources for municipalities, alongside the property tax.

[8] In general, large families are defined as those with three or more children under the age of 25 who are economically dependent on their parents (stipulated in Article 2 of Law 40/2003, concerning the Protection of Large Families). Article 12 of Law 40/2003 requires all Spanish public administrations to establish exemptions and reductions for large families in relation to the fees for the provision of the following public services: transport; access to social, cultural, sporting and entertainment services; and access to recruitment tests for entry into the civil service. It is worth noting that the economic capacity of these large families is not considered when implementing these tax benefits.

The establishment of user fees for the provision of public services at the municipal level has traditionally been a complex issue in Spain. This complexity arises from the existence of up to three different categories, each governed by a very different legal framework: fees (*tasas*), public rates (*precios públicos*), and non-tax property contributions for public purposes (*prestaciones patrimoniales de carácter público no tributarias)*. The application of one category or another is closely linked to the quantification of the fee, a quantification that municipalities must justify during the establishment or modification process. Regardless of the applicable category, this justification must be supported by an economic and financial study. The absence or lack of motivation in this study can result in the fee being declared illegal.

Finally, when quantifying user fees, the ability-to-pay principle holds a secondary position because the cost of the service takes precedence. However, municipalities generally establish certain tax benefits to address the economic capacity of citizens with low income.

## References


Agulló Agüero, A. (1993). Los precios públicos: Prestación patrimonial de carácter público no tributaria. *Civitas: Revista Española de Derecho Financiero, 80*, 547–570.

Acín Ferrer, A. (2005). Tasas y precios públicos: Más sobre la tasa del 1.5% de los ingresos brutos y sus ordenanzas. *Tributos Locales, 54*, 55–62.

Acín Ferrer, A. (2018). Ordenanzas no fiscales. *Las prestaciones de carácter público no tributario. La Administración práctica: Enciclopedia de administración municipal, 12*.

Aneiros Pereira, J. (2018). La incorporación al Derecho positivo tributario del concepto de prestación patrimonial de carácter público por la Ley de Contratos del Sector Público de 2017 y sus pretendidas consecuencias. *Quincena Fiscal, 7*.

Arrieta Martínez de Pisón, J. (2018). Nuevas figuras y su encaje en las categorías tributarias tradicionales. Las "nuevas" contraprestaciones por servicios públicos tras la Ley de Contratos de 2017. *VI Encuentro de Derecho Financiero y Tributario, IEF*.

Ayuntamiento de Madrid. (2009). *La supresión de la Tasa de Basuras de 1985*. Retrieved February 7, 2024, from https://www.madrid.es/

Castells Rey, I., García, P. P., & Ventosa, I. P. (2023). *Las tasas de residuos en España*. https://www.fiscalidadresiduos.org/

Falcón y Tella, R. (2011). El concepto de tributo "desde la perspectiva constitucional" y la supresión del párrafo segundo del art. 2.2.a) LGT. *Quincena Fiscal* (11).

Falcón y Tella, R. (2016). La contraprestación del servicio público de abastecimiento domiciliario de agua: SSTS de 23 y 24 de noviembre de 2015. *Quincena Fiscal, 7*, 13–20.

Fernández Farreras, G. (2012). Sobre la naturaleza jurídica de la tarifa por la prestación del servicio de abastecimiento de agua, El precio del agua. In *Aspectos jurídicos y financieros en la gestión urbana del agua en España*. Fundación Agbar.

García Rubio, F. (2007). *Problemas actuales del derecho urbanístico*. Dykinson.

Gomar Sánchez, J. I. (2023). La tasa de reciclaje de residuos urbanos: Ajuste al Derecho local español y a la realidad tributaria municipal. *Documento de Trabajo del Instituto de Estudios Fiscales, 3*, 160–170.

Gómez-Ferrer Rincón, R. (2015). Las prestaciones patrimoniales de carácter público y naturaleza no tributaria. In López-Ramón (Dir), *Las prestaciones patrimoniales públicas no tributarias*

*y la resolución extrajudicial de conflictos.* (pp. 31–67). Spanish Association of Administrative Law Professors, INA.
Lozano Serrano, C. (1998). Las prestaciones patrimoniales públicas en la financiación del gasto público. *Civitas. Revista Española de Derecho Financiero, 97*, 25–52.
Lozano Serrano, C. (2002). Calificación como tributos o como prestaciones patrimoniales públicas de los ingresos por prestación de servicios. *Civitas. Revista Española de Derecho Financiero, 116*, 611–678.
Marín-Barnuevo Fabo, D. (2022). La definitiva declaración de inconstitucionalidad de la plusvalía municipal y la nueva regulación del impuesto. *Revista de Contabilidad y Tributación. CEF, 468*, 5–58.
Martínez Olmos, R. (2023). La prestación compensatoria autonómica y su incidencia ambiental sobre las entidades locales. *Tributos Locales, 164*, 119–164.
Martín Fernández, J. (2013). *Tasas y precios en la Hacienda local: La experiencia española.* Marcial Pons.
Martín Jiménez, A. (2000). Notas sobre el concepto constitucional de tributo en la jurisprudencia reciente del TC. *Civitas. Revista Española de Derecho Financiero, 106*, 181–212.
Martín Rodríguez, J. (2019). Análisis de la STC 63/2019, de 9 de mayo de 2019, ¿Es inconstitucional la nueva regulación de las tarifas como prestaciones patrimoniales de carácter público no tributarias? *Nueva Fiscalidad, 2*, 291–306.
Martínez Sánchez, C. (2014). *El principio de equivalencia en el sistema tributario español.* Marcial Pons.
Martínez Sánchez, C. (2017). La imposibilidad de exigir tasas por determinados servicios públicos locales: un estudio del art. 21 TRLHL. *Tributos Locales, 128*, 47–64.
Martínez Sánchez, C. (2019). *Tasas, tarifas y prestaciones patrimoniales de carácter público no tributario. La fiscalidad del agua: Situación actual y perspectivas de reforma* (pp. 223–265). Tirant lo Blanch.
Martínez Sánchez, C. (2020). *Tasas locales y otras figuras afines*. Lefebvre-El Derecho.
Ministerio de Hacienda. (2023). *Haciendas Locales en Cifras. Año 2021.* Retrieved February 7, 2024, from https://www.hacienda.gob.es/
Miranda Hita, J. (2004). El Catastro y el IBI. *Catastro, 50*, 7–49.
Menéndez Moreno, A. (2018). Criterios axiológicos para delimitar la noción y régimen jurídico de los tributos y de las prestaciones patrimoniales públicas. *Quincena Fiscal, 4.*
Ortiz Calle, E. (2018). Las fronteras del derecho tributario. A propósito de las prestaciones patrimoniales de carácter público no tributario. *Quincena Fiscal, 19.*
Palao Taboada, C. (2023). Prestaciones patrimoniales de carácter público. *Revista de Contabilidad y Tributación. CEF, 481*, 5–58.
Ramallo Massanet, J. (1996). Tasas, precios públicos y precios privados (hacia un concepto constitucional de tributo). *Civitas. Revista Española de Derecho Financiero, 90*, 237–274.
Ramón Fernández, T. (2023). *Manual de Derecho Urbanístico*. Aranzadi.
Ruiz Garijo, M. (2023). Cuenta atrás para el establecimiento de gravámenes por el servicio de residuos municipales (*pay as you throw*). *Tributos Locales, 165*, 11–34.
Sanz Gómez, R. (2021). Las prestaciones patrimoniales de carácter público no tributarias a la luz de las transformaciones del modelo de Estado: Una propuesta de clarificación. *Civitas. Revista Española de Derecho Financiero, 191*, 183–232.
Tassonyi, A., & Kitchen, H. (2021). Addressing the fairness of municipal user fee policy. *IMFG Papers on Muncipal Finance and Governance, 54.*
TEAMM-Tribunal Económico-Administrativo Municipal. (2010). *Memoria 2010.* Retrieved February 7, 2024, from https://www.madrid.es/
Tornos Mas, J. (2011). La tarifa como forma de retribución de los concesionarios: Una figura constitucional y necesaria. *El Cronista del Estado Social y Democrático de Derecho, 24*, 22–29.
Tornos Mas, J. (2018). El contrato de concesión de servicios. In J. M. G. Feliú (Ed.), *Estudio sistemático de la ley de contratos del sector público* (pp. 1447–1484). Aranzadi.
Velasco Caballero, F. (2021). *Derecho urbanístico en la Comunidad de Madrid.* Marcial Pons.

Villar Rojas, F. (2000). *Tarifas, tasas, peajes y precios administrativos: Estudio de su naturaleza y régimen jurídico*. Comares.
Villar Rojas, F. (2005). Dictamen sobre el concepto de tasa de la nueva Ley General Tributaria y su eventual impacto en las tarifas por prestación del servicio municipal de abastecimiento domiciliario de agua potable. *Quincena Fiscal, 10*.

# Chapter 16
# Comparative Conclusions

**Martin Burgi, Francisco Velasco Caballero, and Philipp Sandmann**

**Abstract** In the comparative conclusions, the various facets of the urban–rural divide are examined from different perspectives. The analysis shows that this divide is not only real, but also recurs in similar ways across different countries and political systems. Building on this, potential solutions are compared and contrasted, whose relevance will remain significant in many countries in the coming years due to challenges such as climate change and demographic shifts.

**Keywords** Comparative country analysis · State of research · Perspectives and ideas on addressing the urban–rural divide

## 16.1 International Comparison of Issues and Challenges

The above chapters cover five continents, with countries that vary widely in terms of the history and legal status of local government. They include nations with long-established systems of federalization, confident local self-government, and historically centralized nations that first had to develop their approach to local administration and autonomy (Díez Sastre, chapter 9.1 in this volume; Marrara, 7.2; Mills and Blaxell, 6.1; Stafa and Levitas, 10.1; Runtić, 13.1; Chonco-Spambo, 14.1). Nevertheless, the chapters show specific patterns: there is growing imbalance between urban and rural self-governments regarding the burden of tasks and the

M. Burgi · P. Sandmann
Chair of Public Law, Business Administrative Law, Environmental and Social Security Law, Ludwig-Maximilians-Universität München, Munich, Germany
e-mail: martin.burgi@jura.uni-muenchen.de; philipp.sandmann@lmu.de

F. Velasco Caballero (✉)
Institute of Local Government Law, Autonomous University of Madrid, Madrid, Spain
e-mail: francisco.velasco@uam.es



F. Velasco Caballero et al. (eds.), *Municipal Tasks and Financing*, Local and Urban Governance, https://doi.org/10.1007/978-3-031-99812-6_16

ability to cope with them. This imbalance manifests in various forms. In detail, this inequality can be seen in the areas of allocation of tasks (1) and service provision of local government (2), as well as equalization of revenues (3) and fees and other special sources of revenue (4).

### *16.1.1 Allocation of Tasks in Local Government*

A common characteristic of many legal systems is that municipalities are categorized into a system that usually consists of multiple levels based on fixed, rigid criteria, with each level creating new tasks and legal options for the municipalities. The foundations are basic obligations for all municipalities, which are gradually extended in (often three) levels when certain population thresholds are reached (Díez Sastre, 9.2; Mähle and Wolff, 2.3.1).

The thresholds commonly used are size-related, financial or efficiency/effectiveness criteria, or a combination of these (Díez Sastre, 9.2, table 1; Wolff and Mähle 2024, 2.2.2.). In contrast, the fact that a municipality is located in an urban or rural area is only indirectly taken into account within these parameters (Mähle and Wolff, 2.2.1). Little attention is given to the fact that many countries are very heterogeneous and that there is often a sharp contrast between urban agglomerations and rural areas.

This phenomenon, for which some countries have even established their catchphrases e.g., "España vaciada" - "emptied Spain" (Castillo, 5.1) or "Brasilia is not Brazil" (Marrara, 7.8), describes a consequence of the standard 'one-size-fits-all approach', which refers to a system that applies the same rules and standards to all municipalities regardless of their unique characteristics.

However, this systematic neglection of the urban-rural divide is not inevitable. Particularly in territorial states with highly heterogeneous population distribution, legal systems take greater account of the structural character of the region, for example, in Brazil or Canada. The range of variance here extends from differences in the requirements for drawing up development plans to an internally differentiated distribution of administrative competences (Marrara, 7.5; Horak, 4.3).

While the legal frameworks studied vary widely, so too do the assessments of their functionality. The international comparison reveals a spectrum of opinions, ranging from those who believe that multi-level systems based on strict criteria are essentially valid (Castillo, 5.1) to those who argue that comprehensive reforms are needed (Mähle and Wolff, 2.4.).

However, there is agreement that the one-size-fits-all approach described above presents considerable problems: the less flexible distribution of tasks and competences almost inevitably leads to a difference in the allocation of tasks as smaller municipalities have to perform some of the same tasks as larger and significantly more capable municipalities (Mähle and Wolff, 2.2.1.). Consequently, this approach can lead to a discrepancy between the performance of rural and urban municipalities, with rural areas often being underserved and overburdened. This is called the mismatch problem (Mähle and Wolff, 2.1.).

But even in more flexible systems, there are sometimes severe problems. Differentiating between rural and urban areas requires precise parameters and more sophisticated fact-finding, as more complex values are established in contrast to the often easy-to-determine values of the one-size-fits-all approaches. In practice, this offers considerable potential for omissions or political abuse, as substantial private interests are linked to the qualification of spaces (Marrara, 7.5). In addition, a precise differentiation in allocation management can lead to a fragmentation of responsibilities, which multiplies the costs of solving problems (Horak, 4.3). This is the very advantage of the one-size-fits-all approach, which offers the possibility of devolution to the next higher and, therefore, more capable administrative authority in the usually integrated multi-level system.

### *16.1.2 Service Provision of Local Government*

With regard to the provision of services, a broad range of legal structuring tools can be identified in an international comparison. These range from the direct provision of services by the state to indirect provision through cooperation with external organizations and privatization. Trends can be recognized across some countries (Germany and Brazil, for example, but the contrary in Spain): while historically, the direct provision of services by the state and its authorities has been at the forefront, a shift is taking place. At different stages, a gradual transition towards indirect forms of provision occurs in many sectors (Krönke and Hagen, 8.1; Marrara, 7.6).

Public enterprises and private-public partnerships (private actors providing public services) are emerging, in various forms, as the means of choice for local administrations (Krönke and Hagen, 8.3 and 8.4.1).

As for issues of reform, it can be observed in direct administration that municipalities in a rigid multi-level system (see above) are confronted with a constant task load, even though the number of inhabitants is falling. This initially leads to uneconomical overcapacity, which in the long term jeopardizes the maintenance of service levels (Schantl, 3.2). This is less true for urban areas, as the trend towards urbanization is still evident, meaning that urban municipalities can expect at least moderate population growth in the future (Marrara, 7.3; Mähle and Wolff, 2.2.1; Schantl, 3.2). The opposite applies to rural areas, which often struggle with a declining population and a corresponding decrease in population density. Providing services over a large area for a small number of inhabitants is a particular burden, especially in the case of standard municipal services such as electricity, water and transport (Castillo, 5.5). In rural areas, the lack of population makes it impossible to finance municipal services through fees. Supra-municipal grants are then essential (3.5.3 below).

In this case, the multi-level system offers only partially satisfactory solutions. The obvious mechanism would be a vertical shift of the fulfillment task to the next higher authority. The latter will regularly have more resources, expertise, and the ability to utilize synergies. However, this happens at the expense of the right to self-government, an essential principle of local government (Krönke and Hagen, 8.3.1).

Problems also arise where services are provided indirectly. The provision of services by persons under private law has been identified as a frequent and effective instrument, e.g., in the context of public-private partnerships (PPPs). A comparison shows a strong imbalance in the preconditions between rural and urban areas (Krönke and Hagen, 8.4.3).

This is ultimately due to the basic idea of the indirect service provision: the free market forces should be utilized to provide services, but this also exposes the administration to said forces. Particularly in heterogeneous countries, different regions offer different attractive markets for potential providers. The natural environments in rural areas are often less attractive for investors, as the low population density results in additional costs, and the realization of profits is more challenging (Marrara, 7.7).

While in attractive (and mostly urban) market environments the administration has many providers to choose from, in less attractive (often rural) environments the opposite is true. As a result, the options for providing services depend on market conditions and, accordingly, on whether the municipality is located in an urban or rural area (Marrara, 7.7).

In practice, rural communities are disadvantaged for a second reason: they lack the legal and organizational know-how to deal with PPPs. Given the often complex legal requirements, smaller local authorities are unlikely to have suitably qualified staff or a sufficient budget to hire external experts (Krönke and Hagen, 8.4; Marrara, 7.7).

## *16.1.3 Equalization*

In general terms, the issues raised around local powers and tasks also extend to local financing. Local financing is substantially homogeneous for both rural and urban municipalities. In most countries, rural or small municipalities face serious difficulties to finance their activities with only their own taxes and fees paid by users. The shortcomings are partially compensated by supra-municipal transfers. But these are normally insufficient: they only ensure the provision of fundamental or essential services, and only moderately correct the structural financial imbalance between urban and rural municipalities (3.4.4 below). Based on article 9.5 of the European Charter of Local Autonomy, the Congress of Regional and Local Authorities of the Council of Europe repeatedly insist upon all European countries must guarantee by law not only the sufficiency of the financially weakest municipalities, but also that the financial resources of these municipalities should be comparable to those of urban municipalities. Unfortunately most of the concerned countries repeated fail to comply with the Council of Europe's recommendations and resolutions.

### 16.1.4 Financing by Fees and Other Special Sources of Revenue

Some contemporary economic trends, clearly liberal in nature, recommend that residents should pay less taxes and more fees for the specific municipal services they receive. An indirect form to expand the fees comes from the contractual provision of municipal services, especially those managed through public-private partnerships. They normally stipulate that the corresponding service is financed, partially or totally, through deferred payments on account of the users.

Certainly, fees can be a useful financing tool for local governments, but they have clear limitations, especially for rural municipalities. Fees present serious equity objections, to the extent that payment for the service received can hardly meet the economic capacity of each resident.

## 16.2 Opportunities and State of Research

The chapters in this book show that many of the phenomena described are already subjects of academic debate in the respective countries. In several respects, however, it seems particularly worthwhile to deepen current research efforts, as such the contrast between rural and urban regions continues to be highlighted. This is illustrated by the example of PPPs. While their mode of operation and role in the administrative system have long been the subject of scientific study, there is still a lack of empirical data regarding the different applications in rural and urban areas (Krönke and Hagen, 8.4.3).

Similar problems with largely comparable causes can be observed throughout the urban-rural interplay. It has also been demonstrated that solutions to these problems have been found to varying degrees in different countries. The resulting experiences could be valuable for other legal systems' implementation.

However, this gain in knowledge is, of course, not limitless. It will always be a challenge to transfer the general findings to the specific circumstances of the individual countries. There are considerable differences in the basic requirements concerning comparability (Horak, 4.7).

## 16.3 Perspectives: Local Governments in Transition

### 16.3.1 Surrounding Matters

Examining the differences between rural and urban areas is not a purely academic endeavor. Recent past and present events have placed this research topic at the center of pressing local government issues.

The Covid-19 pandemic has led to a lasting change in citizens' perceptions of local government. A good example is the common Australian derisive description of local government functions as the "three Rs" (rates, roads, rubbish). Despite its proximity to the people, local government was seen primarily as an instrument for delivering basic services to the local population, with little political significance. Important decisions were seen as coming primarily from the state level (Mills and Blaxell, 6.4).

In this respect, the Covid-19 pandemic represents a turning point where municipalities have often proven to be a key player and point of contact for citizens (Mills and Blaxell, 6.4).

Beyond this direct consequence of the pandemic, lifestyle changes are evident, such as the permanent change in the mobility of workers and the resulting need for housing, workspaces, and social services, which requires a high degree of flexibility in providing services (Mähle and Wolff, 2.3.3.).

These consequences require solutions to new problems. This applies particularly to cost-intensive infrastructure, which is now being used to a lesser extent due to lifestyle changes and is causing funding gaps in local government budgets. As a result, there is a growing need for state support in the fulfilment of some municipal tasks (Horak, 4.4). A considerable divergence between urban and rural areas is also likely to be recognizable.

Another topical issue has been climate change which affects municipalities in two ways: through natural events that are already taking place, such as droughts, floods, forest fires, etc., and in the future through long-term climate change with the associated consequences for nature and people.

With regard to the consequences of current climate phenomena, local governments are increasingly being recognized as effective actors in creating climate resilience. It is therefore logical to transfer the relevant competences and financial resources, as can already be observed in Australia (Mills and Blaxell, 6.4). Apart from that, the direct effects of climate change also force local authorities to adopt new forms of action based on cooperation with neighboring communities (Krönke and Hagen, 8.5).

Additionally, local government is becoming increasingly important in the long-term fight against climate change. Several chapters focused on transport as a key sector in this context.

However, the preferences and political objectives of administrations are also changing to varying degrees. While in urban areas, for example, the promotion of climate-friendly means of transport like local public transport services can be observed, many rural communities are still struggling to provide a minimum service without being able to take additional aspects such as climate protection into account (Castillo, 5.4). In addition, urban mobility solutions are not always appropriate in rural areas due to different natural conditions (Schantl, 3.3).

An even more serious problem is the widespread depopulation of rural areas, which is exacerbating the contrast between rural and urban areas. As mentioned above, rural depopulation creates even greater problems for rural communities, as the same number and quality of services are expected to be provided to a smaller and smaller group of users (Schantl, 3.2). There is a risk of a downward spiral, as the opportunities to provide services often become scarcer as the number of inhabitants decreases. Rural areas become even more unattractive when these services disappear, thus exacerbating the rural exodus.

The provision of municipal services has, therefore, been identified as the key to combating depopulation in rural areas across all countries (Díez Sastre, 9.1). Skillful and forward-thinking municipal planning is becoming increasingly important in the constant tension between scarce resources and decreasing population density. To maintain a stable level of service, municipal governments must conduct needs-based analyses, for example in the area of local public transport, to increase efficiency, which is particularly critical in rural areas (Castillo, 5.5).

Conversely, urban areas also need sufficient flexibility to absorb the consequences of urbanization and to be able to provide new services accordingly (Mähle and Wolff, 2.3.3).

The differences noted call for local financing schemes more adaptable to municipal diversity and with greater equalizing capacity (*infra* 3.4.4).

### *16.3.2 Allocation of Tasks in Local Government*

Two leading solutions to the existing mismatch problem have been identified across the observed countries: 1. the (forced) amalgamation of municipalities as part of a territorial reform, and 2. the adaptation of the existing multi-level system.

A logical solution would be merging several municipalities to utilize synergies and save resources. However, such endeavors have often failed due to bitter resistance from residents nationwide. The local community is still the reference point for identity and the center of local ties. Furthermore, the effectiveness of such a measure is still controversial (Mills and Blaxell, 6.2.1; Mähle and Wolff, 2.1). As has been shown, the recognizable trend, "back to the municipality," is likely to fuel this resistance further.

It is becoming clear that the functionality of the existing multi-level system per se is not the subject of criticism. Instead, it focuses on the specific legal implementation of the model (Castillo, 5.1; Wolff and Mähle, 2.3).

The foundation for effective reforms could be the decisive adjustment of allocation variables. Instead of the previously rigid and unadjusted values, the threshold values should become more flexible to distinguish between rural and urban areas (Mähle and Wolff, 2.3.1). As explained, this adjustment can lead to major political difficulties and can often only be realized in practice with great effort (Marrara, 7.5). A possible solution to this subsequent problem is the identification of easily ascertainable parameters that allow reliable categorization. In this context, it would be feasible to link the thresholds to the financial strength and qualifications of the employees of the municipality in question (Mähle and Wolff, 2.3.1).

In order to allow for an even finer differentiation that ultimately corresponds to the capabilities of the municipalities, an extension of the often existing 3-tier system to a 4-tier system should also be considered. A variant in which municipalities must fulfil the basic tasks by default but can be exempted from this if a particularly weak performance is identified, appears to be highly innovative and versatile. In this way, hard-hit and overburdened municipalities (especially in rural areas) could be relieved of some of their obligations without completely giving up their autonomy of self-government and without reducing the scope of their tasks across the board (Mähle and Wolff, 2.3.2).

### *16.3.3 Service Provision of Local Government*

Standardized solutions are also emerging in response to the challenges of direct service provision. As is already the case at the level of task allocation, the amalgamation of municipalities is rarely a viable option for the direct provision of services. This is due to the political resistance that has already been identified, as well as the controversial efficiency of such projects, which rarely justifies the effort involved.

With regards to less extensive forms of horizontal collaboration, there is a substantial body of experience in certain countries, such as Spain and Germany, where a wide range of differentiated forms can already be identified. The establishment of limited special-purpose communities comprising different municipalities to address specific issues, such as waste disposal or water supply, appears to be a particularly promising modus operandi (Díez Sastre, 9.2; Krönke and Hagen, 8.5). Consequently, there is no risk of the politically unpopular loss of municipal identity.

Nevertheless, the existing imbalance between the tasks and opportunities for service provision in rural areas requires greater flexibility for local authorities. To be able to react appropriately to the challenges, they require new instruments. A comparison reveals that the legal framework for this has not yet been created to a sufficient extent in all legal systems (Marrara, 7.8). Consequently, it can be concluded that a key outcome of the comparison of the chapters is the evaluation and, if necessary, improvement of the relevant regulations.

In particular, where there is still a lack of a sufficiently concrete legal framework, there is often a lack of sufficient coordination of operations. Otherwise, as the example of the Canadian public transport system clearly shows, there is a risk of fragmentation of service efforts, resulting in inefficient and inconsistent government structures (Horak, 4.3, 4.6).

This is especially relevant in the context of the provision of basic services by small municipalities that are underperforming. The Austrian case study has demonstrated that municipal collaboration can facilitate the achievement of economies of scale and the development of joint expertise. This is particularly pertinent in regions where communities are affected by population decline. In such cases, it is necessary to frequently ensure comprehensive coverage by pooling resources (Marrara, 7.8; Schantl, 3.2).

With regard to the indirect provision of services, the statistical analysis shows that PPPs are used particularly in areas of operation where there is a strong urban-rural divide in terms of municipal capacity, e.g. in the construction and operation of public transport infrastructure and in the construction and management of public facilities (Krönke and Hagen, 8.4.1).

There is still considerable potential here for local administrations in rural areas. The use of PPPs could create new scope for action for struggling local authorities. The problems identified here lie in the lack of know-how of the often legally very complex processes involved in (partial) privatizations. However, local authorities will only be able to overcome some of the challenges of the market economy on their own. This is most evident in sparsely populated rural municipalities, which are generally less attractive due to higher infrastructure costs and fewer customers (Marrara, 7.8).

Here too, horizontal cooperation could create synergies. On the one hand, shared know-how can be built up, and administrative costs can be reduced through joint administration. This already increases the profitability of such projects. On the other hand, cooperation with neighboring municipalities can create a common and therefore more attractive market.

### *16.3.4 Equalization*

Local financing has a very similar structure in most countries, including the six specifically analyzed in this book: Croatia, South Africa, Spain, Canada, Italy and Albania. In most countries, local financing relies on three main sources of revenue: own taxes, state or regional transfers, and fees for services. Other sources of financing, such as public and private credit, income from municipal assets, or revenue from fines, usually play a very secondary role. Some seemingly alternative sources of financing, such as shared taxes and contributions for urban development, can be traced back to one of the above-mentioned typical sources of local revenue, depending on how they are legally shaped. For example, municipal participation in state taxes (such as income tax) can be qualified as a state grant when according to the corresponding tax law, municipalities lack any regulatory power over the elements of the tax.

Therefore, the differences between countries lie more in the relative importance and specific legal configuration of each source of revenue than in the structure of the financing system. Normally, the greatest differences between countries (or between states, regions or provinces within the same country) tend to be the greater or lesser financial importance of municipal taxes and supra-municipal transfers. Fees are usually the third most important source of revenue, although they are sometimes very close to transfers.

Transfers naturally respond to the lower self-financing capacity of municipalities. This is usually because typical municipal taxes (property tax, business tax, etc.) cannot generate as much revenue as state taxes (such as income tax, VAT or corporation tax). To deal with this issue, the various national schemes of local financing supplement municipal revenues through vertical transfers (from central, regional or provincial and county governments). More infrequent, and less relevant, are horizontal grants. In this case, municipalities with more own revenues (usually large cities) transfer a part of it to municipalities with lower revenues (usually small rural or mountain municipalities). In comparative terms, transfers are very high in Albania (57% of total municipal revenues), less so in Italy (around 32%) and even lower in the various Canadian provinces, at around 21% (see, respectively Stafa and Levitas, 10.2; Slack, 11.2.2; and Valdesalici and Romero, 12.2).

Financial transfers to local governments can be analyzed from multiple perspectives, such as: their centralized or decentralized management; the position of each type of local government (municipal, metropolitan, county or provincial); the participation of the local governments themselves in the configuration of the transfer system; or the typology of the grants (conditional *vs* unconditional, capital or operational; full or partial [matching grants], vertical or horizontal). The chapters in this book have focused on the ability of each transfer's scheme to equalize the financial capacity of urban and rural municipalities. For this purpose, all transfers have been considered: both conditional and unconditional grants; and both capital transfers (for infrastructure) and operational transfers (for the financing of ordinary municipal functioning).

Although the various chapters of the book have focused on the equalizing function of financial transfers, the chapters on Canada and Italy explain that the equalizing objective can also be achieved by indirect means, as an alternative to transfers. The specific chapter on Canada highlights the existence of other indirect forms of financial equalization between rural and urban municipalities: amalgamation (whereby smaller municipalities can benefit from the better financial capacity of nearby urban municipalities); the existence of second-tier local governments (counties) that prioritize spending in the most financially weak municipalities; and the creation of metropolitan areas, where the spending of smaller municipalities is reduced (Slack, 11.3). Also for Italy, the levelling function of metropolitan areas is pointed out, especially through the *Metropolitan Territorial Plans* of Bologna and Milan (Valdesalici and Romero, 12.4).

All transfers serve to supplement revenues from municipal taxes and fees, given that these own sources of financing are normally and structurally insufficient. Nevertheless, this main objective of financial sufficiency may or may not be accompanied by a complementary objective of equalization or rebalancing between rich (usually urban) and poor (usually rural or mountain) municipalities.

The objective of financial sufficiency is generally aimed at ensuring the provision of essential municipal services (usually mandated by law). This objective is directly or indirectly present in the calculation of transfers. In the case of Italy, the state financial law itself distinguishes between transfers for essential (mandatory) or non-essential (voluntary) municipal functions (Valdesalici and Romero, 12.2). In any case, and from the perspective of financial equalization, it should be stressed that not all transfers have an equalizing purpose, as they do not necessarily benefit the poorer or financially weaker municipalities as opposed to the richer ones.

As explained in more detail below, the different financial situation of rural and urban municipalities is present in supra-municipal transfers, albeit usually only implicitly. It is generally assumed that rural municipalities have less financial capacity through own resources (because their tax bases are weaker). It is also assumed, implicitly or explicitly, that the costs of municipal services are higher in small or rural municipalities (Stafa and Levinas, 11.3). Consequently, national or regional transfer systems usually include criteria or items that aim to improve the financial position of small or rural municipalities.

While this is true, equalization is also sometimes insufficient. Large cities often benefit in parallel from other very large grants for specific purposes, such as transport infrastructure or social policies. These conditional transfers may reduce or even eliminate the equalizing effect of the general scheme of unconditional transfers.

In the various countries analyzed, supra-municipal transfers are articulated through one or more local financing funds. In Italy, the state unitary fund (*Municipal Solidarity Fund*) or a regional fund (in regions with special status) concentrates most of the transfers (Valdesalici and Romero, 12.2.1). This makes the internal structure of the corresponding unitary fund particularly complex, integrating different concepts for different purposes: to guarantee the financing of certain essential municipal functions; to equalize the financial position of the different municipalities; and to provide specific financial resources for specific functions (such as certain social services) (Valdesalici and Romero, 12.1 and 12.2.3). This hybrid structure of the Italian unitary fund has been questioned by the Italian Constitutional Court (Valdesalici and Romero: 12.2.1). In Albania, too, there is a unified fund for municipal transfers containing several financial equalization instruments (Stafa and Levinas, 10.1). In Canada, as a federal state, there is no unitary state fund, although there are some sectoral state transfers (for infrastructure). Most Canadian provinces have one or more local financing funds that serve almost exclusively for financial equalization between municipalities. For example, the province of Ontario has the *Municipal Partnership Fund* (OMPF), which, through its various programs, provides financial resources to the most isolated or remote rural municipalities, as well as the most depopulated ones or those with special financial needs (Slack, 11.2.3).

In principle, the greater economic wealth of cities means that any correct legal configuration of municipal taxes should generate sufficient revenue for the municipality concerned. This is the legislative premise in the various Canadian provinces, where municipal taxes (especially the property tax) provide sufficient funding for cities without overtaxing residents (Slack, 11.1). This explains why transfers to cities, such as those articulated in the *Community-Building Fund*, are very limited (Slack, 11.2.3) and often conditional, for transport infrastructure programs, for housing construction or to co-finance social services (Slack, 11.3).

Conversely, the lower relative wealth of rural municipalities generates lower tax bases, and thus a lower capacity for municipal self-financing through taxation (Slack, 11.2.3). This could explain why Canadian provinces—albeit with important nuances in the case of Nova Scotia and Saskatchewan—focus their unconditional transfers on rural municipalities, and why conditional-sectoral grants finance the very costly capital investments necessary for the provision of essential services, such as water supply or wastewater treatment. In these cases, vertical transfers naturally fulfil a levelling function, as far as their function is not to ensure the financial sufficiency of all municipalities, but to help the financially weaker municipalities, which are usually rural municipalities. This makes horizontal transfers between rich and poor municipalities unnecessary in principle.

In other cases, such as in Italy and Albania, vertical transfers serve a dual function: they complement the revenues of all municipalities; and they balance the financial position of richer municipalities vis-à-vis poorer ones. Vertical transfers in favor of all kinds of municipalities are calculated on the basis of the number of inhabitants (or the historical revenues of individual municipalities) improve the financial sufficiency of all municipalities. But they do not level them out. Moreover, these transfers can widen the gap between the richer (usually more populated) municipalities and the poorer ones. For a vertical transfer to also fulfil a levelling function, it must also include some other allocating criteria, such as lower population density, remoteness, greater orographic complexity, or a greater aged population.

Regarding Albania, Chap. 10 of this book explicitly refers to horizontal transfers between rich and poor municipalities (Stafa and Levinas, 10.4). Without questioning this qualification, it must be pointed out that those transfers derive from taxes shared between the state and the municipalities, including income tax, vehicle circulation tax, and property transfer tax. In this case, the equalization output consists of the state withholding part of the revenue from the shared taxes pertaining to the richer municipalities. That same amount is transferred to the poorer municipalities. Thus described, there is indeed a levelling effect. Not with revenues collected through municipal taxes, but through taxes shared between the municipalities and the state. The final outcome of this scheme, modest in its amount, is that the three urban municipalities (Tirana, Durres and Saranda) indirectly provide financial resources to the other 121 Albanian municipalities.

In parallel to vertical transfers, even when they include some levelling elements, laws may provide for purely horizontal transfers. Examples are rare, but not non-existent. Italy includes, within its *Municipal Solidarity Fund*, a horizontal equalizing element. That is, part of the fund's transfers is financed by money collected by the richer municipalities through the local tax on properties (IMU) (Valdesalici and Romero, 12.2.1).

While transfers usually include some levelling element, the criteria for such a rebalancing function are diverse and interact in multiple ways. As local financial schemes result from complex political negotiations, criteria for the allocation of transfers are sometimes incompatible with each other or reduce the potential equalizing role of another criterion.

In general, the levelling effect of transfers can be defined by paying attention to the fiscal capacity or to the financial needs of each municipality. Fiscal capacity is, in principle, easier to assess, because it results from the actual revenue collected by each municipality through its own taxes and fees. The lower wealth of a municipality normally results in a weaker tax base and, taking an average tax rate as reference, lower tax revenue. The greater simplicity of this levelling criterion may explain its use as the sole criterion in most Canadian provinces, of which Quebec is a good example (Slack, 11.2.3 and 11.2.4). Its major drawback is that it does not pay attention to the specific demographic, social and geographic circumstances of each municipality, which are not necessarily reflected in the fiscal capacity data.

In order to take into account the specific circumstances of each municipality, it is necessary to introduce criteria of financial needs into the transfer scheme. The possible indicators of or proxies for financial need are very diverse, although they normally refer to the type of population (children, elderly, immigrants), socio-economic circumstances (level of unemployment), population density (number of inhabitants per square meter), remoteness from large urban centers, and orography (degree of slope of the land). All these circumstances are indicative of special spending needs, either because they increase the costs of ordinary services—such as water supply, when there is a low population density—or because they increase the extent or intensity of certain municipal services, such as social services, when there is a large immigrant population. Obviously, not all these indicators of financial need favor rural or small municipalities. For example, larger school-age populations or larger immigrant populations tend to favor transfers to large cities. Consequently, from the perspective of financial equalization between urban and rural municipalities, not all indicators of financial need necessarily favor rural municipalities. On the other hand, as important as a specific indicator of need is, just as important is the weight or relevance given to it. In this sense, although Albania's transfer system considers the financial needs of each municipality, it does so mainly by reference to the absolute population of each municipality (a decisive indicator for 80% of transfers) and to a much lesser extent by reference to density, which only determines 15% of transfers (Stafa and Levinas, 10.1).

From a comparative perspective (between urban and rural municipalities) few transfer schemes expressly include this distinction in the corresponding legislation. Such a distinction is explicitly found in the Canadian provinces of Nova Scotia and Saskatchewan (Slack, 11.2.4), although this can be considered the exception rather than the rule. More frequently, the urban-rural distinction is implicitly present in certain indicators of fiscal need, such as population density, that directly refer to rural municipalities. Also indirectly, the various indicators of fiscal capacity tend to reflect the lower revenues of rural municipalities.

Given the fundamental distinction between financial needs and fiscal capacity, each country or region's transfer system may use each of those criteria for different purposes. Thus, the sophisticated Italian equalization system through the *Municipal Solidarity Fund* uses 'standard costs and needs' only for municipal fundamental functions (compulsory services) but not for the voluntary activities of municipalities. For the latter it only considers indicators of per-capita fiscal capacity (Valdesalici and Romero, 12.2.2).

The assessment of both financial needs and fiscal capacities is normally executed by reference to standardized values. Those standardized data are the statistical average of expenditure and/or cost for the effective provision of municipal services (for all services, or a selection of them) or the statistical average of own revenues (those derived from municipal taxes and fees). When the municipal expenditure and/or cost is higher than the standard value, it is considered that there is an unsatisfied financial need that has to be compensated or equalized. The same applies when own revenues are below the standard value, as long as the tax rates are homologous to those of other municipalities. All these values can be used independently or in combination. Thus, for example, in the province of Nova Scotia (Canada) financial equalization uses a standardized reference value that results from first calculating the standard expenditure and then subtracting the standard revenue (Slack, 11.2.3). The result of this subtraction is then compared with the corresponding expenditure and revenue figure of each municipality.

### 16.3.5 Financing by Fees and Other Special Sources of Revenue

As indicated above (16.3.4), fees are, together with supra-local transfers and taxes (local or shared), a main source of local funding, although their relative weight varies considerably in different countries. Moreover, and following the general perspective of this book, fees have a different financing scope in urban and rural municipalities. It can be observed that in South Arica fees are the main source of financing for urban municipalities, but a secondary resource for rural municipalities (Chonco-Spambo, 14.4.3). Fees are very important in Croatia (Runtić, 13.1) and only relatively important in Spain, where they account for 10.15% of total municipal revenues (Marco, 15.2). However, in the latter two countries there is no clear distinction (in terms of financial weight) between fees in urban and rural municipalities.

Strictly speaking, the very concept of a fee, as opposed to a transfer or a tax, is not homogeneous in the different countries. In general terms, the fee is linked to the financing of a specific local service. And, also in general terms, the fee is to be paid by the specific neighbor who receives or benefits from a specific municipal activity (Chonco-Spambo, 14.2 and 14.7; Marco, 15.2.). Typical fees, present in many countries, are those levied for the provision of a municipal service, such as the water supply or refuse collection, and those deriving from the special use of a public good (such as fees for advertising on public spaces). However, in addition to these typical fees, there are other more complex and doubtful fees.

Some fees are difficult to differentiate from taxes. For instance, Croatian municipalities have a so-called communal fee (Runtić, 13.1 and 13.4) which obliges all property owners to pay a contribution for the maintenance of a set of infrastructures (roads, lighting, cleaning). The contribution is determined according to the location, size and type of property. Given that this fee does not pay for a specific service or municipal action, but for a broad group of them, it is notoriously similar to taxes. This qualification may be legally relevant because in most countries taxes are subject to more limits and a greater requirement of prior legal provision than fees, where the principle of legality is more flexible and there is greater municipal autonomy. Also unique is the tourist fee, which is not linked to any specific municipal service or activity, but to a generic enjoyment of cities by tourists (Runtić, 13.4).

This could explain why in some countries the tourist levy is considered a tax (e.g. for Italy: Valdesalici and Romero, 12.2) and in others a fee. In South Africa, a distinction is made between fees and 'surcharges on fees'. While fees, in the strict sense, refer directly to the receipt of a specific municipal service, surcharges on fees are, despite their name, indirect taxes. These 'surcharges on fees' do not pass on to the user the individualized cost of the municipal service or activity they receive but add an additional burden under the implicit premise that those who receive and pay for a certain municipal service show a certain economic capacity susceptible to taxation (Chonco-Spambo: 14.3).

Among the most peculiar taxes are those for urbanization works (roads, sewers, pavements, etc.). In Croatia, developers pay the so called "communal contribution" to the municipality, which is on average 10 percent of the building budget (Runtić, 13.1). In this case, the final beneficiaries of these works are the future residents, who will benefit from the new service networks of lighting, water supply, etc. However, urbanization is not always a municipal task financed by developer fees. In other countries, such as Spain, urbanization is a compulsory activity for developers (who recover the cost of the works by passing it on to the final price of the building). In this case there is no municipal fee for the municipal activity, simply because it is not the municipality that executes the urbanization works (Marco, 15.3).

Although municipal fees differ from country to country, they all raise some common issues. Firstly, the question of local autonomy by the imposition and regulation of fees arises in all countries. In general terms, fees are foreseen and partially regulated in state or regional laws, but it is up to each municipality to establish them and determine their specific scope for each municipal activity or service. As a result, each municipality normally has a wide margin of discretion to determine whether a given service or activity is financed by a specific charge or through the common revenue of the municipality. Nevertheless, municipal autonomy is not the same for all kinds of municipal fees. In some countries, the constitution and laws require parliamentary laws to authorize and regulate municipal taxes in detail. The criteria determining this requirement for legal regulation vary from country to country.

As the example of Croatia shows, the local autonomy to impose fees is lower for essential municipal services (such as water distribution) than for complementary and social state services, such as municipal childcare (Runtić, 13.3). Also in South Africa, the highest legal demands on tariff policies refer to basic or essential services (Chonco-Spambo, 14.3.1 and 14.7). Here a clear connection can be drawn between municipal competences and their financing. Mandatory municipal activities or services—such as water supply—are often financed through fees densely regulated by laws. On the other hand, voluntary municipal services and activities are less densely regulated by law and therefore broadly open to local autonomy.

Municipal autonomy in Spain works differently. The municipal discretion to impose and regulate fees is not directly related to the type of service (essential or complementary), but to the way the service is provided (directly by the municipality or by means private entities, such as contracts and service concessions). Thus, for example, the water supply service, which is an essential and compulsory service for all municipalities, is often managed by private companies through concessions. In this case, the residents' contribution is not a fee, but a "non-tax public obligation", the legal regulation of which is considerably more flexible than that of fees (Marco, 15.4).

Charges or fees for municipal services are particularly complex when the provision is not carried out directly by the municipality, but indirectly by private companies (through a contract or a service concession). Contractual management of municipal services is common in waste collection and treatment, public lighting, public transport and parking (Runtić, 13.1). In Spain, water supply is also frequently provided through contracts with private companies (Marco, 15.4). Contractual provision of municipal services is apparently not a major reality in South Africa, where the two main management options are direct management (by a municipal department) or by municipal companies, to which the same rules apply as to the municipality itself (Chonco-Spambo, 14.6).

When contractual provision is the municipal option, the term "public-private partnership" or PPP (above 16.3.3) is often used. In these PPP contracts, the private company assumes the initial infrastructure investment for the start-up of the service. The investment is later compensated through payments by the users of these services. The providing companies assume a certain economic risk (of supply or demand) but are compensated with long periods of payment of charges by the users. Just the economic business risk has been a determining factor for a low implementation of PPP in many countries (Runtić, 13.1).

In the case of PPPs, as well as in other service contracts, the residents receive the corresponding services from a private company and, normally, also pay the private company for the service. As the Spanish case shows, very complex questions arise here as to the legal qualification of this payment. That is, whether it is similar to a common rate or comparable to a fee. In Spanish local law a triple distinction is made, in this sense, between fees in the strict sense, "non-tax public obligations" and rates. Behind this legal classification there are very important questions, such as how the charge is calculated and the need for prior legal regulation.

Fees are a very flexible financial instrument, as they can be directly linked to the actual costs of services. In addition, they are highly visible burdens for residents, as they are paid for specific activities and services. The sum of flexibility and visibility connects the fees very directly to the political preferences of the electorate and subjects them to intense public scrutiny (Runtić, 13.2). Consequently, in democratic terms, fees are a very valuable financial instrument. However, there are several compelling objections to their widespread use.

First of all, taking into account that the laws normally attribute the same competences and functions to rural and urban municipalities (Valdesalici and Romero, 12.1; Runtić, 13.1; Marco, 15.1), the fees are particularly suitable for large urban municipalities, and are very insufficient for the financing of municipal services in rural areas (Chonco-Spambo, 14.1). Many municipal services, such as water supply, waste collection and treatment or road maintenance, require high capital investment and maintenance expenditure. These costs are difficult to finance through fees alone. For this reason, other sources of financing for public services are essential in rural municipalities, even when these services have individualized beneficiaries. These financial supplements cannot come from municipal taxes either, because the tax bases are also small in rural areas. Consequently, municipal services in rural areas tend to be financed largely through operating or capital grants from central or regional governments (Chonco-Spambo, 14.4.2).

Fees also raise issues of equity and management, both of which are closely connected (Runtić, 13.2). Since the fee normally rewards the specific benefit obtained with the municipal service or activity, its amount is in principle indifferent to the economic capacity of each resident. Thus, for some citizens a municipal service may be very affordable and for others it may be very burdensome, or even inaccessible. This raises the possibility that fees, like taxes, should also be progressive or at least take into account the contributive capacity of each citizen. This can be legally articulated through differentiated rates based on individual income, or through discounts in the quota, in favor of vulnerable social groups.

Although differentiation by economic capacity is possible, laws do not usually introduce such a distinction. The fundamental reason lies in the technical and political difficulty to establish and assess, when a resident has a low economic capacity (Runtić, 13.2; Marco, 15.4). One of the advantages of the fee is precisely its easy management, because its quantification is automatic with the perception of the service or individualized benefit. And this itself makes a fee manageable even by municipalities with little technical or management capacity. For the same reason, by introducing valuation elements in the quantification of the fee (such as the income of each recipient), the municipal management of collection also becomes more complex and costly. This means that, very often, neither the laws nor the municipalities introduce elements of equity in the calculation of the fees. More frequently, the objectives of equity and social sustainability are channeled through aid or subsidies for people in need. In view of the above, the legal regulation of municipal fees in South Africa can be considered exceptional, as far as municipalities can both adapt the amount of the fee to the economic capacity of each resident and even increase the amount of the fee above the individual cost of the service received, thus taxing citizens with a greater contributive capacity (Chonco-Spambo, 14.3.2 and 14.7). As mentioned above, this raising of the fee beyond the cost of the service blurs the boundaries between fees and taxes.

## 16.4 A Plea for More Research

The urban-rural divide is real. This unsurprising conclusion is a key finding of this book. Behind this simple statement, however, a complex cause-and-effect relationship quickly becomes apparent. This book has identified some of the main reasons and factors for the widening urban-rural divide. Again, similarities between the countries analyzed quickly become apparent. As similar as the problems are, as different are the solutions. The international comparison has revealed a wide range of possible solutions, each with specific advantages and disadvantages.

However, there remains an unshakeable common ground: All the factors identified as exacerbating the urban-rural divide will not lose their impact in the foreseeable future. After the widespread adoption of remote working, a return to pre-pandemic lifestyles seems as unlikely as a rapid reversal of climate change. Ultimately, the same applies to countries undergoing demographic change, where population trends have been set for decades. In the absence of reforms, the urban-rural divide is likely to widen further.

In summation, the chapters also show that local government research has not fully recognized the urban-rural divide. In this respect, the chapters in this book should be seen as a starting point for even broader research. The urban-rural divide has been examined from a number of different perspectives, using concrete practical constellations as examples. The promising results should encourage the research to be on an even broader basis. The discovery of numerous commonalities, and the resulting potential to learn from the mistakes and successes of other systems, is the essential value of international comparative research projects. The motto should, therefore, only be: research globally, act locally.

# Index





F. Velasco Caballero et al. (eds.), *Municipal Tasks and Financing*, Local and Urban Governance, https://doi.org/10.1007/978-3-031-99812-6

MIX
Papier aus verantwortungsvollen Quellen
Paper from responsible sources
FSC® C105338

If you have any concerns about our products,
you can contact us on
**ProductSafety@springernature.com**

In case Publisher is established outside the EU,
the EU authorized representative is:
**Springer Nature Customer Service Center GmbH**
**Europaplatz 3, 69115 Heidelberg, Germany**

Printed by Libri Plureos GmbH
in Hamburg, Germany